Reforming Rape Trials

OXFORD MONOGRAPHS ON CRIMINAL LAW AND JUSTICE

This series aims to cover all aspects of criminal law and procedure including criminal evidence. The scope of this series is wide, encompassing both practical and theoretical works.

OTHER TITLES IN THIS SERIES

Sentencing Discretion and the Constitution
Due Process of Time
Donald A Dripps

Victims as Agents of State Accountability
A Comparative and Normative Analysis
Marie Manikis

How Juries Work
And How They Could Work Better
Rebecca K Helm

Civil Recovery of Criminal Property
Colin King and Jennifer Hendry

The Insanity Defence
International and Comparative Perspectives
Ronnie Mackay and Warren Brookbanks

Justice In-Between
A Study of Intermediate Criminal Verdicts
Federico Picinali

Criminal Fraud and Election Disinformation
Law and Politics
Jeremy Horder

Policing the Borders Within
Ana Aliverti

Criminalizing Sex
A Unified Liberal Theory
Stuart P Green

Reasons to Doubt
Wrongful Convictions and the Criminal Cases Review Commission
Carolyn Hoyle and Mai Sato

Fitness to Plead
International and Comparative Perspectives
Ronnie Mackay and Warren Brookbanks

Criminal Misconducts in Office
Law and Politics
Jeremy Horder

The Preventive Turn in Criminal Law
Henrique Carvalho

Criminal Justice and Taxation
Peter Alldridge

In Search of Criminal Responsibility
Ideas, Interests, and Institutions
Nicola Lacey

Preventive Justice
Andrew Ashworth and Lucia Zedner

Character in the Criminal Trial
Mike Redmayne

Homicide and the Politics of Law Reform
Jeremy Horder

The Insecurity State
Vulnerable Autonomy and the Right to Security in the Criminal Law
Peter Ramsay

Manifest Madness
Mental Incapacity in the Criminal Law
Arlie Loughnan

The Ethics of Plea Bargaining
Richard L Lippke

Prosecuting Domestic Violence
A Philosophical Analysis
Michelle Madden Dempsey

Abuse of Process and Judicial Stays of Criminal Proceedings
Second Edition
Andrew L-T Choo

Reforming Rape Trials

The Impact of Law Reform on Criminal Trials in Australia

JULIA QUILTER
Professor of Law, University of Wollongong, Australia

LUKE McNAMARA
Professor of Law, University of New South Wales, Sydney, Australia

OXFORD
UNIVERSITY PRESS

OXFORD
UNIVERSITY PRESS

Great Clarendon Street, Oxford, OX2 6DP,
United Kingdom

Oxford University Press is a department of the University of Oxford.
It furthers the University's objective of excellence in research, scholarship,
and education by publishing worldwide. Oxford is a registered trade mark of
Oxford University Press in the UK and in certain other countries.

Published in the United States of America by Oxford University Press
546 Fifth Avenue, New York, NY 10036, United States of America.

British Library Cataloguing in Publication Data
Data available

Library of Congress Control Number: 2026939753

ISBN 9780198948148

DOI: 10.1093/9780198948155.001.0001

Printed and bound by
CPI Group (UK) Ltd., Croydon, CR0 4YY

The manufacturer's authorized representative in the EU for product safety is
Oxford University Press España S.A. of Parque Empresarial San Fernando de Henares,
Avenida de Castilla, 2 – 28830 Madrid (www.oup.es/en or product.safety@oup.com).
OUP España S.A. also acts as importer into Spain of products made by the manufacturer.

MIX
Paper | Supporting responsible forestry
FSC® C013604

Artist's Note

Who controls the story of heterosexual sex, and how men and women should engage in it? This powerful book, by two leading scholars in the field, demonstrates that, despite an abundance of rape law reform, rape trials continue to draw on deep-seated beliefs about the proper sexual roles of men and women. Women who survive rape, and then have the temerity to go to court and act as the chief witness for the prosecution, may well find that their complaint is transformed into something quite alien to them. Notwithstanding the many legislative efforts to bring rape law into the modern world, the credibility of women who complain of rape can still depend on ancient lore about how good and trustworthy women do, and should, behave. Thus attention is subtly shifted away from the accused and his criminal responsibility, and the victim herself goes on trial. The deep and sustained injustice to women, which is the focus of this book, has exercised me as a legal scholar for many years and now also as an artist. The art work on the cover of this book, entitled 'The Rip', shows what should happen to the rape myths which still endure.

Ngaire Naffine
Emerita Professor of Law
Adelaide University

Acknowledgements

Big projects like this don't get done without the goodwill and contributions of multiple individuals and organizations. We acknowledge and thank, in particular:

- the Australian Research Council for providing funding in the form of a Discovery Project Grant: 'Intoxication Evidence in Rape Trials: A Double-Edged Sword?' (DP200100101); including support for the PhD candidate who worked on the project
- the then Chief Judge of the County Court of Victoria, the Hon Justice Peter Kidd, for granting permission for us to access trial transcripts
- the Victorian Law Reform Commission, especially the Hon Mr Anthony North QC, Chairperson, for commissioning us to complete a transcript analysis study for the VLRC's report on *Improving the Justice System Response to Sexual Offences* (2021)
- the Office of Public Prosecutions and Victoria Legal Aid for assistance in identifying cases for inclusion in our Victorian trial sample
- Jacinth Pathmanathan, (then) Team Leader, Victorian Law Reform Commission, for assistance with facilitating access to and delivery of court transcripts
- the County Court of Victoria for locating and making trial transcripts available to us, and the Victorian Government Reporting Service for assisting in this process
- the then Chief Judge of the District Court of NSW, the Hon Justice Derek Price AM for granting permission for us to access trial transcripts
- the Office of Director Public Prosecutions (NSW) and the Public Defenders for assistance in identifying cases for inclusion in our NSW trial sample
- the NSW Department for Communities and Justice for commissioning us to complete a transcript analysis study on the 'Experience of Complainants of Adult Sexual Offences in the District Court of NSW'
- the District Court of NSW for locating and making trial transcripts available to us, especially Judicial Registrar James Howard and Ms Lisa Freeman for their generous assistance
- Jackie Fitzgerald, Suzanne Poynting, and Alana Cook at the NSW Bureau of Crime Statistics (BOCSAR) for support at all stages of our NSW commissioned research and for facilitating access to and delivery of court transcripts
- the members of the Research Advisory Panel that was established by BOCSAR to guide our NSW commissioned research

- staff from the University of Wollongong's Information Management & Technology Services (IMTS) who assisted us with data management, security, and confidentiality
- Elisabeth McDonald (University of Canterbury) and Paulette Benton-Greig (University of Waikato) for generously sharing insights and methodological advice from their research on rape trials in Aotearoa/New Zealand

Over the span of six years, we have benefited from the various contributions of members of our research team. We thank Dr Zahra Stardust and Graces Bowles for excellent research assistance at, respectively, the beginning and the end of the project. We thank Melissa Porter for her continuous research assistance since the project commenced in 2020, especially for her meticulous work on the important and time-consuming task of de-identifying transcripts.

We thank Dr Sarah Croskery-Hewitt, who joined the project as a PhD candidate in 2021. In addition to her contributions to de-identification and coding of transcripts, Sarah completed a doctoral thesis on NSW sexual assault trials that featured intoxication evidence: Sarah Croskery-Hewitt, *Intoxication Evidence and the Rewriting of Sexual Assault: A Study of NSW Trials* (PhD Thesis, University of Wollongong 2025).

We thank Ngaire Naffine for providing the wonderful art that features on the cover. Her contribution is fitting for this book, given that its origins can be traced back to Julia Quilter's last century doctoral thesis, for which Professor Naffine served as an examiner. Julia also acknowledges the guidance of her PhD supervisor all those years ago, Professor Terry Threadgold.

We thank Fiona Briden, Mirza Rizwaan Ahmad, and Madeline Hoverkamp at Oxford University Press, and Victoriya Sherly at Newgen KnowledgeWorks, for their editorial input, patience, and professionalism. We also thank Fiona Tatham for copy-editing, and Phillipa Findlay and Puddingburn Publishing Services for indexing.

Many of the findings and arguments that come together in this book have benefited from the feedback and suggestions offered by participants and audience members when we have presented our work, including:

- Judicial College of Victoria (2025)
- Reforming Legal and Policy Responses to Investigating and Prosecuting Sexual Violence Conference, Queen's University Belfast (2025)
- 25th IUSTI World Congress Incorporating the Australasian Sexual and Reproductive Health Conference (2024)
- Reforming Rape Prosecutions Workshop, University of Glasgow (2024)
- NSW District Court Annual Conference (2024)
- ACT Office of Director of Public Prosecutions (2024)

- Enhancing Safe Practice: A National Justice Forum on Sexual Assault, Australian Institute of Judicial Administration (2024)
- Legal Aid Criminal Law Conference (2024)
- Children's Court of NSW (2024)
- Faculty of Law and Justice, UNSW (2024)
- Jury Research and Practice Conference, ACT Supreme Court (2024)
- Judicial Council on Diversity and Inclusion Conference (2023)
- Applied Research in Crime and Justice Conference (BOCSAR) (2023)
- Australian Criminal Law Workshop (2022 and 2023)
- University of Queensland, Bar Association of Queensland, and Queensland Supreme Court Library (2022)

This book has benefited from our engagement with public inquiries including those conducted by the NSW Law Reform Commission, the Queensland Law Reform Commission, the Senate Legal and Constitutional Affairs Committee, the Law Commission (UK), and the Australian Law Reform Commission.

Some chapters draw on findings and analysis previously presented in the following:

J Quilter and L McNamara, 'Experience of Complainants of Adult Sexual Offences in the District Court of NSW: A Trial Transcript Analysis', Crime and Justice Bulletin No 259 (NSW Bureau of Crimes Statistics and Research 2023)

J Quilter, L McNamara, M Porter, and S Croskery-Hewitt, 'Intoxication Evidence in Rape Trials in the County Court of Victoria: A Qualitative Study' (2023) 46(2) UNSWLJ 579

J Quilter, L McNamara, and M Porter, 'Differences in Accounts and the "Lying" Complainant: A Qualitative Study of Rape Trials from Victoria, Australia' (2023) 73 International Journal of Law, Crime and Justice 100593

J Quilter, L McNamara, and M Porter, 'The Most Persistent Rape Myth?: A Qualitative Study of "Delay" in Complaint in Victorian Rape Trials' (2023) 35(1) Current Issues in Criminal Justice 4

J Quilter, L McNamara, and M Porter, 'The Nature and Purpose of Complainant Intoxication Evidence in Rape Trials: A Study of Australian Appellate Court Decisions' (2023) 43(2) Adelaide Law Review 606

We acknowledge the feedback provided by anonymous peer reviewers which improved these publications, and as a result, this book.

Finally, we acknowledge the victim-survivors, whose experiences of sexual violence and of participation in criminal trials are the focus of this book. Although their names have been anonymized to ensure confidentiality and to protect privacy, we are acutely aware that their stories are at the heart of what we have learned about the continuing barriers to justice, and what might be needed to overcome them. Their voices are present in this book in (anonymized) quotes from transcripts.

* * *

We have co-authored a number of conference papers, articles, and chapters, but this is our first book. It has been a unique experience. When we first sat down to start reading rape trial transcripts in 2020, Australia was in pandemic lockdown. We sat side-by-side in make-shift 'working from home' arrangements in the dining room (while children participated in the COVID-19 version of 'home schooling' from other rooms).

It turned out to be a surprisingly healthy environment in which to process what we were reading. Anticipating that reading hundreds of pages of trial transcripts daily might cause some distress, we had put in place some research well-being protocols, for us and the whole research team. But the close proximity between us, borne of stay-at-home orders under the Public Health Act 2010 (NSW), meant that organic ad hoc debriefing sessions were readily available. Whenever one of us heard or detected sounds or movements indicative of the other's emotional agitation (sighs, groans, busy fidgeting, expletives)—usually prompted by reading yet another passage of complainant cross-examination that made us angry—we would pause, chat, collect ourselves, and continue.

From those early days to the final tasks of editing and proofing, and everything in between, writing this book has been a project of mutual learning and deep collaboration. We are grateful to have had the opportunity.

Julia Quilter and Luke McNamara
Sydney
July 2025

Contents

Table of Cases

Table of Statutes

NORTHERN TERRITORY

QUEENSLAND

SOUTH AUSTRALIA

TASMANIA

VICTORIA

WESTERN AUSTRALIAN

1
Introduction

1. The Promise and the Reality

When the then Premier of New South Wales (NSW), Neville Wran, introduced the Crimes (Sexual Assault) Amendment Bill to the Legislative Assembly of the NSW Parliament on 18 March 1981, he described the bill as:

> . . . an historic measure and one of the most important reforms this Government has ever presented to this Parliament. The object of the principal bill – the Crimes (Sexual Assault) Amendment Bill – is to remedy major defects in the law relating to rape and sexual assault. These reforms are designed to protect the victims of rape from victimization under the legal process; to encourage rape victims to report offences to the authorities; to facilitate the administration of justice and the conviction of guilty offenders; at the same time, to preserve the rights of the accused; and to serve an educative function in further changing community attitudes to sexual assault.[1]

The Premier continued:

> Many rape victims have been reluctant to report the crime and to seek legal justice. They have feared the shame of public exposure, they have feared, the complex double standard which appears to condemn the victims for any act of sexual aggression committed against them, and they have feared the humiliation they face in the courts. That humiliation involves their being forced to recount, not once, but at least twice in minute detail, the most humiliating and degrading experience they have ever gone through, and then to suffer under cross-examination the imputations and insinuations about the victim's own responsibility for the offence and against the victim's character and morals. The common law has also laid down different rules for sexual assault offences. Different rules of evidence relating to corroboration and prior sexual history operate against a complainant in a sexual assault case more stringently than apply in any other criminal trials. The changes to be effected by this bill are designed to ease, so far as is possible, the humiliation experienced by sexual assault victims, to remove the stigma attached

[1] New South Wales, *Parliamentary Debates*, Legislative Assembly, 18 March 1981, 4758 (Neville Wran, Premier).

Reforming Rape Trials. Julia Quilter and Luke McNamara, Oxford University Press.
 DOI: 10.1093/9780198948155.003.0001

> to the rape victim, to encourage victims to report the offences, and to bring the offenders to justice as justice demands.[2]

There is an established political narrative about this bill, and its equivalents introduced across other jurisdictions in the Australian federation, and in many parts of the common law world, since the late 1970s. The narrative is that such legislative amendments heralded the beginning of continuous and significant waves of statutory reform to *transform* rape trials—from sites of intense scrutiny, hostility, and harm for victim-survivors of sexual violence (that produce low conviction rates and deter police reports and prosecutions), to proceedings that make a fair assessment of an accused's criminal responsibility without retraumatization of the complainant. According to this account—and the self-congratulatory story into which it sometimes veers—while there is still room for further improvement, rape myths and victim-shaming are no longer welcome in criminal courtrooms.[3] The transformation is characterized as approaching completion, and this point will be brought ever closer when the current frontiers of this decades-long statutory reform project—which has played out, at different speeds, and to different degrees, but according to the same general formula, across all Australian jurisdictions—have been enacted via legislation. These final frontiers include 'perfecting' the concept of consent, including the 'affirmative consent' model, jury directions to 'educate' jurors about a wide variety of rape myths and stereotypes that might otherwise impede their inclination to believe the complainant's account, and the provision of independent legal advisers for complainants.

A more sanguine version of the narrative is that legislatures have earnestly and incrementally tried to transform rape trials, but, confoundingly, rape myths continue to circulate in rape trials, with potential implications for two dimensions of the justice-seeking endeavour: *process justice* and *outcome justice*—terminology which we explain further below. It is important to recognize that the objective of enhanced justice for victim-survivors of sexual violence has both dimensions, and to avoid a myopic focus on conviction rates as the only measure of reform 'success'.[4]

Having spent a good part of the last five years reading transcripts from Australian rape trials, and reviewing the detail of rape law reforms since the 1970s, it is clear to us that neither of these narratives is well supported by the evidence, and there is some considerable distance between the rhetoric surrounding rape law reform and the reality of how rape trials are conducted. Consider the following question

[2] ibid 4759–60.

[3] See, eg, Queensland, *Parliamentary Debates*, Legislative Assembly, 11 October 2023, 2910 (Shannon Fentiman, Minister for Women).

[4] See Wendy Larcombe, 'Falling Rape Conviction Rates: (Some) Feminist Aims and Measures for Rape Law' (2011) 19 Feminist Legal Studies 27; Wendy Larcombe, 'Rethinking Rape Law Reform: Challenges & Possibilities' in Ron Levy and others (eds), *New Directions for Law in Australia: Essays in Contemporary Law Reform* (Australian National UP 2017) 143.

sequences[5] from cross-examination of complainants in rape trials conducted in the last 10 years:

- *But you change into shorts knowing you're going to get on the bed with him next to you, is that right? I understand from your interview it was a hot night? You couldn't simply leave your leggings on? It didn't cross your mind, you've got this guy who's trying it on, on the airbed, and you're giving him perhaps easier access to legs, your upper-thighs, whatever else?*
- *Why didn't you close your mouth when he's got his penis in it? Are you slack-jawed or something, are you? Sorry, Your Honour. You have no control over your jaw, is that what you are saying? You couldn't bite down on his penis that you didn't want in your mouth?*
- *You know, don't you, that when you got home, you did not tell your mother or father what had occurred; you know that, don't you? You know that when you got home around about 3 or 4 or whenever it was that morning, you did not go and say to your mum or you dad, 'I've been raped', did you, then?*
- *You didn't suffer any injuries as a result of this incident? Physical injuries?*
- *Madam, I suggest to you, you will say whatever you think helps your story whether it's true or untrue?*

These questions are not outliers. As we will illustrate throughout this book, having read thousands of pages of complainant cross-examination transcripts, we observed many such exchanges, across every conceivable rape myth or stereotype about what 'real rape' looks like.

The fact that the sort of questioning depicted in these illustrative examples still features in contemporary rape trials suggests that Premier Wran's vision, articulated more than 40 years ago—of a time when complainants will no longer have to 'suffer under cross-examination the imputations and insinuations about [their] own responsibility for the offence and against . . . [their] character and morals'—is a long way from having been realized. The large majority of victim-survivors who appear as complainants in rape trials will be accused of being liars. Later in this book we reflect on the common defence bar retort that in a 'word on word' trial (a phrase whose accuracy we interrogate in this book), there are few other strategic options available to the defence. Here we want to emphasize that the rape trial feature to which we are drawing attention is not simply that complainants are routinely accused of lying, but that in most of these instances the assertion will be advanced in a way that relies on what we will refer to in this book as 'rape myths'—cultural understandings that purport to assist in differentiating between 'true' and 'false' allegations, but which embody attitudes and 'knowledges' that are both

[5] These examples from our transcript analyses in NSW and Victoria focus on the *questions* asked. In subsequent chapters we provide numerous examples of questions asked *and* answers given.

normatively problematic—including in deeply gendered ways—and empirically inaccurate.[6]

The starting point for the analysis presented in this book is a question: why are rape myths still everywhere in criminal trials?

If the primary objective of the statutory reform movement that began 50 years ago (and that has continued apace since) is to have the accused's criminal responsibility assessed on its merits—without denigration of the complainant's behaviour or character—why is aggressive wide-ranging scrutiny of the alleged *victim* of sexual violence still the centrepiece of most rape trials?

2. Explaining the Problem

We are by no means the first scholars to draw attention to this issue, or ponder what it means for the possibility of law reform-led change.[7] In Chapter 2, we will survey some of the complex theoretical and empirical explanations that have been offered, but here, at the outset of this book, we reflect briefly on characterizations that suggest some version of a *translation to practice* problem. This has been variously referred to as an 'implementation gap' a 'justice gap', or a case of 'reform resistance',[8] or as a reminder about the 'significant difference between enacting new laws and the effective enforcement of those laws'.[9]

In this book, we seek to make a contribution to the literature on rape law reform, building especially on what we have learned from qualitative analysis of over 100 rape trials in the Australian states of Victoria and NSW. That experience revealed a disturbing picture of how complainants are questioned and treated. The worst of the appalling courtroom practices may well be in the past,[10] and there is little doubt that there has been improvement to 'make the experience of being a complainant in a sexual offence prosecution less harrowing'.[11] However, as the examples offered above demonstrate, much that is problematic still remains, and as we illustrate below, complainants still describe the experience as traumatic and unfair.

We understand (and are sympathetic towards) those who have made similar discoveries in other jurisdictions and who have leaned towards an explanation that characterizes the problem as one of 'unfinished business'—including the need to

[6] We explain the concept of rape myths further in Chapter 2.

[7] See, eg, Vanessa E Munro, 'A Circle That Cannot Be Squared? Survivor Confidence in an Adversarial Justice System' in Miranda Horvath and Jennifer Brown (eds), *Rape: Challenging Contemporary Thinking—10 Years On* (2nd edn, Routledge 2022).

[8] A selection of the literature that advances these explanations is discussed in Chapter 2.

[9] Charnelle Van der Bijl and Phil Runmey, 'Attitudes, Rape and Law Reform in South Africa' (2009) 73 Journal of Criminal Law 414.

[10] For examples from 1970, see Lisa Featherstone, *Sexual Violence in Australia, 1970s—1980s: Rape and Child Sexual Abuse* (Palgrave Macmillan 2021) 56, 127.

[11] Virginia Bell, 'Keynote Opening Speech' (Enhancing Safe Practice: A National Justice Forum on Sexual Assault, New South Wales, 2 August 2024).

keep improving the processes by which (good) new laws are turned into better trial practices. There are strong incentives to hold onto the idea that meaningful improvement through law reform *is* possible—even as we recognize that some feminist activists and scholars have, for some time, been charting more radical courses to justice for victim-survivors,[12] including approaches that eschew criminalization altogether in favour of abolitionist alternatives.[13]

Rather than adopting an a priori position on whether the limits of intra-criminal justice system change have been reached, our inclination was always to approach the question empirically—to understand what is happening in rape trials, and only then to connect our observations with larger debates about the potential for further law reform. Our findings do provide some support for the proposition that progressive reforms have been hampered by uneven implementation. For example, we observed trials in which the judicial obligation to disallow 'improper' questions[14] could have been used more regularly, and trials in which an educative jury direction, such as the direction on 'delayed' complaint,[15] should have been given and was not. However, translation failures of these sorts did not account for the majority of the problematic trial practices we observed.

The evidence we present and the arguments we advance in this book suggest that it is time to confront the fact that much of what has been reformed to date could be said to amount to tinkering at the edge of the adversarial trial process. Our thesis is ultimately a simple one: rape myth engagement and victim-survivor character assassination remain at the heart of rape trials, because policy-makers and law-makers have never really attempted to eradicate them. To put it another way, there is a mismatch between many of the legal mechanisms of transformation (eg complex explanations of the meaning of consent and non-consent; educative jury directions) and the nature of the practices that cry out for transformation—such as rape-myth-inspired lines of cross-examination. We don't underestimate the comfort that many complainants derive from being able to give their evidence remotely via CCTV, and the benefits of more respectful and sensitive modes of address, and opportunities to take breaks while they are giving evidence. As former High Court Justice Virginia Bell observed recently, reflecting on her memory of Australian courtrooms in the 1970s: 'Over the course of my professional life I have been witness to the very considerable reforms both procedural and evidential that have served to make the experience of being a complainant in a sexual offence prosecution less harrowing.'[16]

[12] See, eg, Marie Keenan and Estelle Zinsstag, *Sexual Violence and Restorative Justice: Addressing the Justice Gap* (OUP 2022).

[13] See, eg, Rachel Loney-Howes, Marlene Longbottom, and Bianca Fileborn, 'Gender-Based Violence and Carceral Feminism in Australia: Towards Decarceral Approaches' (2024) 32 Feminist Legal Studies 163.

[14] See Evidence Act 1995 (NSW), s 41; Evidence Act 2008 (Vic), s 41.

[15] Jury Directions Act 2015 (Vic), s 52; Criminal Procedure Act 1986 (NSW), s 294.

[16] Bell (n 11).

In Chapter 5, we discuss our generally positive findings on how various special measures are working (as well as our surprise that their operation wasn't always as seamless and consistent as it should be). Here, we observe that such changes are largely (important) *procedural* improvements. The argument we advance in this book is that statutory reforms have not (yet) gone to the heart of what makes rape trials traumatic for—and unfair to—victim-survivors.

We realize that this might be regarded as a provocative claim that flies in the face of just how much *has* changed on the statute books. We do not deny the *volume* of legislative change. How could we? In our home jurisdiction of NSW alone, the Crimes Act, Criminal Procedure Act and Evidence Act have been modified so as to improve the statutory architecture of rape and sexual offence laws by no fewer than 99 amending acts since 1981.[17] The original Crimes Act 1958 (Vic) devoted three lines to the offence of rape.[18] In 2025, the series of provisions that constitute the statutory definition of rape take up eight pages of that Act.[19] In Queensland, following the passage of the Criminal Law (Coercive Control and Affirmative Consent) and Other Legislation Amendment Act 2024 (Qld), the Evidence Act 1977 (Qld) went from having zero sexual offence trial-specific jury directions to nine directions that trial judges are expected to incorporate, in an attempt to disabuse juries of any rape myths that might otherwise contaminate their processing of the evidence and deliberations.[20]

We discuss the depth and breadth of statutory reforms across Australia in greater detail in Chapter 3, but these illustrative calculations and examples attest to the fact that statutory reform has touched multiple dimensions of the law governing rape trials—from substantive offence definitions to procedural arrangements and technological innovations to rules on evidence admissibility and guidance given to juries.

Our point is not that the law hasn't changed or grown much; it has. The argument we advance in this book is that it is an error to conclude that the limited and inadequate *practical* change in the conduct of rape trials—and the associated negative experiences that complainants continue to report[21]—proves that statutory reform doesn't 'work'. Our analysis suggests that it is important to closely interrogate precisely what changes have been required by the large suite of 'progressive' rape

[17] This is the number of times that an Act has amended the Crimes Act 1900 (NSW) since 1981, and the Criminal Procedure Act 1986 (NSW) and the Evidence Act 1995 (NSW) since the year these statutes were first enacted.

[18] Section 44(1) of the Crimes Act 1958 (Vic) (since repealed) stated: 'Whosoever is convicted of rape shall be guilty of felony and except as herein provided shall be liable to imprisonment for a term of not more than twenty years.'

[19] Crimes Act 1958 (Vic), ss 35A, 36, 36AA, 36A, 36B, 38.

[20] Evidence Act 1977 (Qld), ss 103ZO–103ZZA. Victoria now has a total suite of 12 directions available for rape trials: Jury Directions Act 2015 (Vic), ss 46–54K. There are seven in NSW: Criminal Procedure Act 1986 (NSW), ss 292–294.

[21] Elena Campbell and others, '"This Is My Story. It's Your Case, But It's My Story": Interview Study' (KPMG and RMIT Centre for Innovative Justice 2023).

law reforms—and what practices have deliberately been left unimpeded. In short, we think the 'transformation' narrative has been overstated. Most of the legislative reforms were never intended to 'work' to the extent of removing rape myths from trials and shifting the trial's gaze away from intense scrutiny of complainants. Those features of rape trials are still very much in place.

Some readers will be perplexed by these claims. Surely the multiple changes that have been made to the substantive definition of rape, the concerted effort to legislate an ethical concept of consent, the remaking of fault elements (including the incorporation of expectations of *reasonable* behaviour), have *modernized* the law of rape? And what about the multiple ways in which the courts have introduced trauma-informed procedures and rules, to better protect victim-survivors when they appear in court, including the opportunity to give evidence from a remote location via CCTV, to have a support person present, to be protected from questions about their sexual 'reputation' and past sexual experiences? And don't juries now receive strong guidance from judges that educate them about the danger and unfairness of bringing rape myths and gendered stereotypes to the decision-making process? All of these things have happened, and yet . . .

The authors of a recent interview-based study of the experience of complainants in sexual offence matters in NSW summarized their findings on cross-examination as follows:

> . . . despite attempts at improvement over recent years, the research clearly indicated that this process remains distressing. Informants and complainants agreed that cross-examination is the most difficult aspect of the criminal justice system for complainants; a judicial officer described it as a 'torture chamber' for victim-survivors. Ultimately, victim-survivors fear not being believed and the line of questioning that takes place during cross-examination contributes to this. . . . Multiple interview participants . . . spoke about the confronting and humiliating nature of questions from the defence during cross-examination. Overall, interview participants suggested that the cross-examination process was designed to humiliate and discredit them and also undermine their feeling of agency in finally being able to tell their story.[22]

These reported experiences align strongly with what we saw when we read all the words spoken and recorded during 108 rape and sexual offence trials from the Australian states of NSW and Victoria. When we compared what we were reading,

[22] ibid 82. See also Australian Law Reform Commission (ALRC), *Safe, Informed, Supported: Justice Responses to Sexual Violence* (ALRC Report 143, 2025) 100, 141; Women's Safety and Justice Taskforce (Qld), 'Hear Her Voice: Women and Girls' Experiences across the Criminal Justice System' (Report No 2, Queensland Government 2022) 343–44; Clare McGlynn and Nicole Westmarland, 'Kaleidoscopic Justice: Sexual Violence and Victim-Survivor's Perceptions of Justice' (2019) 28 Social & Legal Studies 179.

again and again, with the requirements for conducting a rape trial envisaged by the multiple statutory reforms, we concluded that the 'transformation' effected by 50 years of statutory reform has been much more limited and circumscribed than is suggested by the 'five decades of progressive reform' narrative. In particular, to date, statutory measures have not been directed at significantly changing the substance of how rape trials are conducted, including how the Crown frames its case and how complainants are cross-examined by the defence. Trial features which are known to adversely impact on the experience of complainants continue to operate—largely undisturbed by the multiple 'progressive' reforms that have happened around them.

The argument advanced in this book is that this is not primarily a problem of recalcitrance (or ignorance) on the part of judges and lawyers. Where a change has been legislated, our transcript analyses suggest that, with some limited exceptions, the change has been operationalized. We expand on these findings in Chapter 5, but we are talking here about special measures, including closed courts, support persons, complainants giving evidence via CCTV, as well as limitations (and pre-trial adjudication) on the admissibility of sexual experience evidence. These are undoubtedly 'wins' for the movement towards reduced retraumatization for complainants. The problem is that such reforms barely touch the adversarial process and the substantive content of complainant examination and cross-examination. Statutory reforms have made only modest incursions into the essence of what makes sexual offence trials so traumatic for many complainants, including the adversarial nature of proceedings, the sensitivity of topics complainants might be asked to address, the length of time the complainants might be examined, the absence of substantive barriers to the evocation of rape myths and stereotypes, and the broad parameters of 'relevant' evidence over which cross-examiners are permitted to roam.

The point is illustrated by our findings on how Crown prosecutors and defence counsel both continue to invoke the presence or absence of certain culturally familiar attributes of a 'real' (or believable) sexual violence incident to frame their case. We expand on and discuss these findings in Chapters 6 and 7, but our key argument is that both ends of the bar table are engaging rape myths to advance their case. They 'help' the prosecution when the complainant's behaviour aligns with 'real rape' expectations. Conversely, they are engaged by the defence to challenge the Crown case where the complainant's behaviour is said *not* to align.

Traditionally, rape has been 'known' and recognizable by the presence of certain 'real rape'[23] attributes, including injury, resistance, immediate complaint, and observable distress on the part of the complainant. Quilter has previously argued that case presentation in rape trials has tended to rely on a pre-determined 'rape

[23] Susan Estrich, *Real Rape: How the legal system victimizes women who say no* (Harvard UP 1987).

schema' which is underpinned by centuries-old 'knowledges' (and, for a long time, *legal requirements*) about what qualifies as a 'true rape' allegation.[24] We expand on the rape schema's elements in Chapter 2, but a key insight is that even though they are no longer legal requirements, they continue to circulate and hold power—both outside and inside the courtroom.

3. Modes of Statutory Influence

In this book, we revisit Quilter's earlier work on the rape schema, aided by our analysis of contemporary rape trial transcripts, and with a sharper focus on precisely which parts of the rape trial statutory reforms law-makers have tried to change, and which parts have been largely untouched or uninterrupted. In Chapter 3, we offer an overview of the ways in which laws governing Australian rape trials have changed over the last 50 years. We consider not only the subject matter of the reform but *how* legislatures have attempted to change the conduct of trials. We distinguish between legislation that *prohibits* aspects of traditional rape trials or *mandates* new approaches, and legislation that attempts to influence by other means, such as *guidance* and *education*. Drawing loosely on regulation theory, we are talking about something like the difference between 'command' regulation, on the one hand, and 'process' or 'communication' regulation, on the other.[25] We think it is important to identify, with some precision, the *mode of statutory influence* employed in legislation that reforms rape laws.[26] This is an important step in determining whether the rape schema is ultimately 'immovable' (by statutory reform) or whether its persistence is explained by the failure of legislatures to foreclose or remove the spaces that the rape schema currently fills.

The tendency to characterize the continued circulation of rape myths in the courtroom and the continued interrogation of complainants as signs of the 'failure' of law reform in a global sense is partly explained by a lack of differentiation between discrete modes of statutory intervention and influence. The test of whether a particular reform has been successful or unsuccessful depends very much on its terms and the changes to the operation of trials it was designed to make. We argue in this book that, 'modernization' and 'progressive' reform rhetoric notwithstanding, many of the features of rape trials that, from the perspective of complainants (and reform advocates), continue to be experienced and observed as morally

[24] Julia Quilter, 'Re-Framing the Rape Trial: Insights from Critical Theory about the Limitations of Legislative Reform' (2011) 35 The Australian Feminist Law Journal 23, 31. See also Julia Quilter, 'Re-Inventing Rape: An Analysis of Legal, Medical, Feminist and Governmental Discourses' (DPhil thesis, Monash University 2000).

[25] See Bronwen Morgan and Karen Yeung, *An Introduction to Law and Regulation: Text and Materials* (Cambridge UP 2012) ch 3.

[26] See generally, Luke McNamara and others, 'Theorising Criminalisation: The Value of a Modalities Approach' (2018) 7 International Journal for Crime, Justice and Social Democracy 91.

suspect, antiquated, or improper, persist because they have never been prohibited. This is not a case of legislative oversight or poor drafting—it is deliberate.

One of the few exceptions is the statutory ban on the admissibility of evidence about a complainant's sexual 'reputation' and restrictions to evidence of past sexual experience that were first introduced in Michigan, USA in 1974,[27] and which are now commonplace in Australia,[28] and elsewhere.[29] 'Rape shield' laws, as they are widely known, are often mistakenly taken to be emblematic of the progressive rape law reform programme. Research into their operation has yielded a wide variety of findings, and we share our own in Chapter 5.[30] Here we emphasize that, to the extent that rape shield laws *prohibit* or significantly restrict certain categories of rape-myth inspired and complainant distress-inducing evidence, they are something of an outlier amongst rape law reforms. For the most part, law-makers have preferred to guide and educate rather than mandate—especially when it comes to the content of questions asked (and evidence adduced) in rape trials.

The recent enthusiasm for educative jury directions as an antidote to the influence of rape myths in trials is illustrative. We explore this dimension of rape law reform more fully in Chapter 9, but in short, even where they are mandatory (ie they *must* be given by the trial judge), jury directions prohibit nothing. A 'delay' direction (ie advice that delay in complaining does not necessarily indicate falsity) has been available in NSW and Victoria for many years,[31] but this mode of statutory influence does not prohibit questions that seek to evoke the very rape myth with which the direction is concerned. There is a material difference between statutory reforms that *prohibit* and those that seek to *educate*: complainants are routinely challenged during cross-examination (and accused of fabrication) on the basis of an asserted 'delay' in their report to the police.

In drawing attention to these details—often lost in the narrative of 50 years of progressive reform—one of our aims is to bring law-makers into the conversation about responsibility for reform 'failure'. Lawyers and judges (and perhaps juries) deserve a share of the blame for how little has changed. In the pages that follow, we will draw attention to where we think this criticism is warranted, because human actors have failed to realize the full potential of specific reforms. But law-makers should not be let off the hook, as the prevailing narrative of *progressive reform stymied by implementation gap* tends to do. Legislators are sometimes portrayed (or self-described) as brave and bold reformers who have listened to the lived experience of victim-survivors, and who moved to radically alter the parameters of

[27] Criminal Sexual Conduct Act 1974 (Michigan).

[28] See, eg, Criminal Procedure Act 1986 (NSW), s 294CB; Criminal Procedure Act 2009 (Vic), ss 341–343. See further ALRC, *Safe, Informed, Supported* (n 22) 382–87.

[29] See, eg, Criminal Code (RSC, 1985, c C-46), s 276; Criminal Procedure (Scotland) Act 1995, ss 274–275.

[30] We also refer in Chapter 5 to the findings of studies in other jurisdictions.

[31] See now Criminal Procedure Act 1986 (NSW), s 294; Jury Directions Act 2015 (Vic), s 52.

rape law and the conditions under which rape trials are conducted. The reality is often very different. Lawyers and judges (and jurors) may have been nudged in a more ethical and modern direction by all sorts of 'soft' legislative means, but the binding rules of the game have changed relatively little. Perhaps unsurprisingly, in an adversarial system, we found that lawyers play by the actual *rules* (non-compliance with which yields adverse consequences) rather than 'rules' that encourage rather than require a rape myth free trial. And their trial practice is unlikely to be influenced by the (laudable) rhetorical messaging that is expressed to the wider community whenever the latest improvements are made to the architecture of rape law.

Perhaps the high-water mark of triumphant posturing came when the NSW Government boasted in 2021 that its statutory amendments on the meaning of consent—in the form of a new gold standard of 'affirmative consent'—went even further than the 'communicative consent' model recommended by the NSW Law Reform Commission.[32] Our transcript analysis of NSW trials (finalized before these reforms came into effect on 1 June 2022) suggests that a thoroughly modernized statutory formulation of consent—even if it may have important symbolic, expressive, and communicative benefits outside the courtroom—is likely to be of little consequence in most rape trials. In a typical trial, the defence position is that the complainant was consenting (indeed, was an active participant or the *initiator* of sexual activity), and defence counsel is largely unencumbered in their ability to aggressively pursue a line that the complainant is an untrustworthy liar, and is free to rely heavily on rape myths and culturally embedded conceptions about 'real rape' to make this case to the jury.

4. Origins of this Book

One of us first began exploring the disconnect between formal changes to the face of rape law and the experiences of complainants in rape trials in doctoral work during the 1990s.[33] At the time, the other was teaching criminal law to undergraduate law students and struggling to explain why the practices of the criminal law on sexual violence aligned so poorly with its post-1980s reformist ambitions, and why attrition and complainant dissatisfaction rates remained so high.[34] This is

[32] New South Wales Government Department of Communities and Justice, 'Consent law reform' (Media Release, 25 May 2021) <https://dcj.nsw.gov.au/news-and-media/media-releases-archive/2021/consent-law-reform.html> accessed 11 July 2025; New South Wales Law Reform Commission, 'Consent in Relation to Sexual Offences' (Report 148, 2020). See now Crimes Act 1900 (NSW) Pt 3, Div 10, Subdiv 1A, as amended by the Crimes Legislation Amendment (Sexual Consent Reforms) Act 2021 (NSW).

[33] Quilter, 'Re-Inventing Rape' (n 24).

[34] For the latest figure in NSW, see Brigitte Gilbert, 'Attrition of Sexual Assaults from the New South Wales Criminal Justice System' (Report No 170, NSW Bureau of Crime Statistics and Research 2025). See also Campbell and others (n 21).

a conversation we have both engaged in now for more than a decade—with each other, with our students, with other teachers and researchers[35]—and we are aware that versions of this conversation have been happening amongst scholars, students, and activists in similarly situated jurisdictions around the word.[36]

There were two more recent catalysts for the projects that formed the basis for this book.

One was the rise of Australia's most recent wave of progressive law reform that began in the late 2010s and which is most often attributed to the victim-survivor activism of Saxon Mullins, including her appearance on the Australian Broadcasting Corporation's flagship current affairs programme, *Four Corners* in a story titled 'I am that girl' that aired on national TV on 7 May 2018.[37] As we explain in Chapter 3, this was only the most recent of a recurring pattern of periodic attempts at law reform to address identified injustice or unfairness to complainants in sexual offence trials, dating back to the 1970s. This has often occurred in different Australian states and territories at different times, but on this occasion, there was a discernible domino effect, intensified by local advocacy in other states and territories. Between 2020 and 2025 every Australian state and territory established some form of law reform inquiry directed at sexual offences.[38]

Unusually in Australia (given the constitutional division of powers), the topic attracted federal government attention. In 2023, the Australian Parliament's Senate Legal and Constitutional Affairs References Committee conducted an inquiry and released a report titled *Current and proposed sexual consent laws in Australia.*[39] Most recently, after a January 2024 referral from the Australian Attorney General, a 600-page report from the Australian Law Reform Commission (ALRC) titled *Safe, Informed, Supported: Reforming Justice Responses to Sexual Violence* was tabled in the Australian Parliament in March 2025.[40] In light of what we have learned over the years about the evidence of high attrition rates, low complainant satisfaction levels, and low conviction rates for sexual offence matters, this latest flurry of nationwide attention prompted us to reflect on the continued faith in criminal law reform and the determination of proponents for further change to get the law 'right'.

The other catalyst was a little more indirect: our collaborative work on the concept of 'intoxication' in Australian criminal law.[41] This included a study of more

[35] David Brown and others, *Criminal Laws: Materials and Commentary on Criminal Law and Process of New South Wales* (8th edn, Federation Press 2025) ch 8.

[36] See, eg, Celia Wells, Oliver Quick, and Nicola Lacey, *Reconstructing Criminal Law: Text and Materials* (4th edn, Cambridge UP 2010) ch 15.

[37] See Louise Milligan, 'I am that girl' *ABC* (7 May 2018) <https://www.abc.net.au/news/2018-05-08/i-am-that-girl/9736126> accessed 11 July 2025.

[38] For an overview, see ALRC, *Safe, Informed, Supported* (n 22) 8–9, 190, 317.

[39] The Senate Legal and Constitutional Affairs References Committee, *Current and proposed sexual consent laws in Australia* (Parliament of Australia September 2023).

[40] ALRC, *Safe, Informed, Supported* (n 22).

[41] Julia Quilter and others, '"Intoxication" and Australian Criminal Law: Implication for Addressing Alcohol and Other Drug-Related Harms and Risks' (Report to the Criminology Research Advisory

than 300 appellate decisions that examined how 'intoxication' and alcohol and other drug (AOD) use featured in criminal cases across a variety of criminal offences.[42] The rape and sexual assault cases stood out and demanded closer attention. We were struck by how evidence of a complainant's intoxication at the time of the alleged offence operated in ways that appeared at odds with the grand narrative of progressive rape law reform, both generally and in relation to undoing the historically and culturally assumed nexus between intoxication and consent. To date, our only 'window' into what was happening in rape trials was provided by the appellate decisions we had been reading. The words of appellate judges are important, but we were most interested in the words spoken by trial participants—lawyers, judges, complainants, other witnesses, experts, and defendants—and appellate judgments offer only select glimpses of these words at best.

Our immediate interest was in what was being said about intoxication—about which we wanted to learn in a more complete way—and we recognized that access to transcripts was the only way that we could rigorously and systematically access the specificity of the words spoken in questions and answers, in openings and closings, objections and *voir dire* submissions, and in rulings, summing up, and directions to juries. In time, we came to recognize how many others features of the rape trial were opened up for examination via transcript analysis, but initially our priority was to learn more about rape trials that featured intoxication evidence.

We began to conceive and design a targeted study. Knowing that a large proportion of reported rapes are associated with AOD consumption, and this relationship has traditionally worked to the disadvantage of complainants in rape trials, we proposed to assess the impact of legislative reforms that have been introduced to break the assumed nexus between complainant intoxication and consent, and limit the opportunity for an accused person to rely on their intoxication as exculpatory.[43] We proposed a mixed method approach that would combine: systematic analysis of appellate decisions in appeals from rape trials in all Australian jurisdictions; interviews with prosecutors and defence lawyers; and qualitative analysis of a sample of trial transcripts from selected Australian jurisdictions.

We secured research funding to commence the project,[44] and began the process of obtaining university ethics approval and seeking court system permission to access rape trial transcripts.

Council 2018). This research was funded by the Australian Institute of Criminology's Criminology Research Grants Programme 2014/15.

[42] Luke McNamara and others, 'Evidence of Intoxication in Australian Criminal Courts: A Complex Variable with Multiple Effects' (2017) 43 Monash University Law Review 148; Julia Quilter and Luke McNamara, 'The Meaning of "Intoxication" in Australian Criminal Cases: Origins and Operation' (2018) 21 New Criminal Law Review 170.

[43] We discuss relevant evidence, literature, and law in Chapter 8.

[44] Australian Research Council Discovery Project: 'Intoxication Evidence in Rape Trials: A Double-Edged Sword?' (DP200100101).

Serendipity played a large part in what happened next; specifically, in how the path to accessing rape trial transcripts in Victoria and NSW opened up, and in the opportunities that arose to widen our gaze—encompassing, but extending far beyond, the intoxication evidence dimension of rape trials. In consecutive years (2020 and 2021), we were commissioned by the Victorian Law Reform Commission and the NSW Department of Communities and Justice to write reports (based on transcript analysis) about a broad range of rape trial features, with an emphasis on the experiences of complainants and the impact of rape law reforms.[45]

5. The Wider Relevance of Our Analysis

The analysis presented in this book is very much anchored in what we have learned from examining the recent operational experience of two Australian jurisdictions. One of our goals is to encourage more empirical research on the operation of reformed rape laws—and this must be at the local jurisdiction-specific level. However, we are also confident that our findings and arguments will have wider relevance—certainly across Australia, but also generally in the many jurisdictions that are some way along the 'transformation' path that Australian states and territories have been on for 50 years. Although pace, priorities, and specificities are varied,[46] sexual violence prevention is undoubtedly a global concern.[47] We are grateful for the opportunity to contribute to a growing body of scholarship that promotes cross-border conversations about rape law reform and that blends theoretical and empirical approaches to understanding law's relationship to sexual violence and its prevention.[48]

[45] Julia Quilter and Luke McNamara, *Qualitative Analysis of County Court of Victoria Rape Trial Transcripts* (Report to the Victorian Law Reform Commission 2021); Julia Quilter and Luke McNamara, 'Experiences of Complainants of Adult Sexual Offences in the District Court of NSW: A Trial Transcript Analysis,' Crime and Justice Bulletin No 259 (NSW Bureau of Crime Statistics and Research 2023).

[46] Sara Uhnoo, Sofie Erixon and Moa Bladini, 'The Wave of Consent-Based Rape Laws in Europe' (2024) 77 International Journal of Law, Crime and Justice art ID no 100668.

[47] Cécile Miele and others, 'International Guidelines for the Prevention of Sexual Violence: A Systematic Review and Perspective of WHO, UN Women, UNESCO, and UNICEF's Publications' (2023) 146 Child Abuse & Neglect art ID no 106497.

[48] Kate Gleeson and Yvette Russell (eds), *New Directions in Sexual Violence Scholarship: Law, Power and Change* (Taylor & Francis 2023); Miranda A H Horvath and Jennifer M Brown (eds), *Rape: Challenging Contemporary Thinking—10 Years On* (2nd edn, Routledge 2022); Rachel Killean, Eithne Dowds, and Anne-Marie McAlinden, *Sexual Violence on Trial: Local and Comparative Perspectives* (Routledge 2021); Susan Leahy, Eithne Dowds, and Siobhan Weare (eds), *Researching Rape Trials: Methods, Ethics and Empirical Perspectives* (Routledge 2026).

6. Terminology

One of the decisions faced by authors writing on rape law and rape trials is which language to use to refer to people who have experienced sexual violence and come to the police and the courts in pursuit of justice. 'Victim-survivor' is in wide use but is often avoided where the topic under discussion is the person's participation in a criminal trial, where respect for the presumption of innocence is taken to dictate that 'complainant' be used. In this book, we generally adopt this protocol, but for the record we note that we think it can sometimes tend to blur our focus on the true subject of progressive rape law reform: people who have been raped or subjected to other forms of sexual violence. Law-makers have sought to modernize the rape trial experience, not out of sensitivity to the complainant as a witness per se, but out of concern to minimize the retraumatization of a person who has already been traumatized (by sexual violence). To treat the terminology of complainant as 'neutral' is to elide its historical relationship to gendered scepticism about rape allegations. The terminology of complainant tends to inscribe the doubt and suspicion that has traditionally surrounded the entry of the (alleged) victim-survivor into the courtroom. This, in turn, is related to the frequency with which they are (still) called a 'liar'.

The gender-neutral language of 'they' to refer generally to victim-survivors/complainants is another aspect of terminology that tends to occlude reality—this time, the fact that sexual violence is disproportionately experienced by women, and perpetrated by men. However, recognizing that sexual violence *is* experienced by people of all genders, and that contemporary laws employ gender neutral language, we generally adopt gender-neutral language except where we are discussing a specific trial where the gender identity of the person is known to us because it is revealed in the transcripts.

We have already, in this chapter, used terminology which may be regarded as opaque or loaded or in need of a definition. For example, to talk of 'progressive' rape law reform rather begs the question: what counts as progressive change in this context?[49] In the context of this book, 'progressive' refers to changes to rape law that are designed to (or said to) improve the capacity of the criminal law and its institutions to offer *justice* to victim-survivors, against a historical background of the common law's poor treatment of the complainant, disregard for her well-being, and tendency to put *her* on trial. Our analysis is attuned to detecting the continued presence of *process injustice*—by which we mean negative complainant experiences including character attacks and retraumatization—and *outcome injustice*—that is, unmeritorious acquittals that do not hold culpable persons accountable for

[49] See generally, Susan Armstrong, 'Evaluating Law Reform' (2006) 10 University of Western Sydney Law Review 157; Andrew Dyer, 'Criminal Law Reform and the Progressives—the Case of Provocation' (2023) 35 Current Issues in Criminal Justice 180.

criminal conduct.[50] We think this dual-track inquiry is necessary in order to keep in sight the fact that the objective of enhanced justice for victim-survivors of sexual violence has both of these dimensions, and in recognition of the fact that conviction rates should not be the only measure of reform 'success'.

7. Chapter Outline

In Chapter 2, we locate our contemporary empirical research on rape trials in the context of the rich and diverse feminist literature which has interrogated and theorized the enduring problems with rape law and trials. In Chapter 3, we provide an overview of the major changes to rape laws in Australia since the 1970s—encompassing changes to the laws governing offence definition, courtroom procedures, and rules of evidence. In Chapter 4, we locate the work undertaken for this book in the context of general socio-legal research and empirical work on the operation of rape trials specifically, and explain the transcript collection and analysis methodology that is the centrepiece of the book's insights.

Consistent with the thesis outlined above, the first set of results we present and discuss in Chapter 5 relates to the 'special measures' that have been introduced to reduce the traumatization associated with appearing as a complainant witness in a rape trial. Here we show that legislated changes were largely operating as intended, albeit with some inconsistencies.

In Chapter 6, we reveal a sometimes-under-appreciated aspect of the practices that occur in rape trials. We show that the *prosecution* is partly responsible for the enduring influence of rape myths. This is not because prosecutors actively set out to perpetuate them, but because the Crown case is often framed in a way that engages (the presence of) 'real rape' attributes because they are (understandably, but, we argue, problematically) regarded as strengths.

Chapter 7 focuses on cross-examination of the complainant, the part of the trial which has long been identified as the most distressing for complainants, and thus a litmus test for the veracity of the 'progressive reforms have transformed trials' narrative. We show that rape myths are everywhere in this phase of the trial.

In Chapter 8, we zoom in on the aspect of rape trials with which this project began—intoxication evidence—both as an important aspect of rape trials, deserving of attention in its own right, and as an opportunity to develop the book's argument about the need to interrogate the specificity of 'progressive' statutory

[50] We have adapted the more familiar dichotomy of procedural justice/outcome (or distributive) justice: see, eg, Klaus F Röhl, 'Procedural Justice: Introduction and Overview' in Klaus F Röhl and Stefan Machura (eds), *Procedural Justice* (Routledge 1997); Anthony Bottoms and Justice Tankebe, 'Procedural Justice, Legitimacy, and Social Contexts' in Denise Meyerson, Catriona Mackenzie, and Therese MacDermott (eds), *Procedural Justice and Relational Theory: Empirical, Philosophical, and Legal Perspectives* (Routledge 2020).

reforms as a condition of understanding their modest impact. We show that justice is even more elusive for victim-survivors who were affected by AOD consumption at the time of the alleged rape.

Chapter 9 considers the influence of judges in rape trials, including the missed opportunities to reorient the practices of lawyers away from rape myth-inspired lines of questioning, and the limitations of the statutory jury direction as a corrective mechanism.

In Chapter 10, we conclude by reflecting on what our findings mean for how we assess past efforts to reform rape law and continuing efforts to further modernize the statute books in the direction of justice for victim-survivors of sexual violence.

2
Theorizing the Problems with Rape Law and Trials

1. Introduction

During the 1960s a range of disciplines drawing upon statistical methods created 'new knowledges' about rape in what came to be known as the 'rape situation'. This body of literature uncovered significant gaps between how the law, medicine, psychology, and popular culture had constructed rape and its 'reality'. A strong tenor of this scholarship was to oust 'false' claims about rape and provide its 'truth'—more commonly referred to today as challenging rape myths. This work spurred a large volume of literature. Alongside the production of these new knowledges, the rise of the women's movement led to significant lobbying for reform to rape laws and a raft of statutory reforms (which we discuss in Chapter 3).

A large body of feminist and other literature has attempted to explain why these law reforms have been so ineffective. This literature is voluminous and diverse, and so in this chapter we attempt only to provide an overview of a number of broad categories of arguments that seek to explain the 'failure' of law reform efforts. First, feminist (often philosophical) scholarship argues that the gendered nature of law means it cannot respond effectively to the harm of rape. This body of literature recognizes the compromise involved in law reform which is likely to only make 'adjustments' but not address the gendered structures that systematically erase the feminine. Secondly, a body of feminist and governmental law reform literature argues that there is a 'translation gap' with progressive reforms being undermined in practice. Finally, a broad range of scholarship has focused on the continued reliance on rape myths in the courtroom which are said to undermine progressive law reforms.

The first body of literature tends to reject a focus on law reform as 'solution'. The second and third typically relocate the problem to one of 'uptake', calling for the education of key players (practitioners, judges, and jurors particularly through jury directions) to act in accordance with contemporary values embedded in the law. For others, questions have been raised as to whether the limits of law reform have been reached, and it is time to look elsewhere—including to forms of restorative justice. These bodies of scholarship are not necessarily distinct categories and

Reforming Rape Trials. Julia Quilter and Luke McNamara, Oxford University Press.
 DOI: 10.1093/9780198948155.003.0002

often overlap; there are also a variety of theoretical and methodological differences between them. Our aim in this chapter is less about being comprehensive and rather to overview the main theoretical arguments that try to explain the 'failure' of rape law reforms in the trial context. While our approach is sympathetic towards further exploration of solutions that reside outside the criminal law and the criminal justice system, our focus here is on the criminal trial, including to investigate more closely what our findings suggest about how law reform and practice intersect and how further reforms may be devised.

We commence with a discussion of the 'new knowledges' that can be traced from the 1960s. They advanced understanding of the crime of rape by demonstrating the gap between the law's representation of rape and the empirical reality of rape. This important work provided a foundation for articulating what we now refer to as rape myths and misconceptions.

2. New Knowledges

From the 1960s, a range of disciplines (medicine, sociology, psychology, government, gender studies, statistics) created new knowledges about rape by analysing the 'rape situation' through statistical methods. These knowledges moved away from earlier psychiatric and medical models that had focused on individual case pathologies and deviancy, and which constructed the rape complainant as 'perverse', and the rapist as a 'monster' or a 'sexual psychopath'.[1] Three broad characteristics of the rape situation emerged as the focus for analysis: the act, the offender, and the victim. These categories were broken down further by recording the victim/offender's race, age, marital status, employment, and the relationship between the victim and offender (stranger, acquaintance, family member). The 'act' was categorized by where the 'meeting' took place (house, pub, street) and, if different, where the rape took place (victim or offender's house, public area such as a park, car, etc). The time of the rape was recorded (season, month, day of the week, and time). Finally, attention was paid to whether there were 'aggravating circumstances' such as injuries or the presence of a weapon. By these means it was considered that a 'true' picture of rape could emerge.

Such an approach to constructing the offence of rape was widespread, from the paradigmatic sociological study of rape (Amir's *Patterns in Forcible Rape*[2]) to medical studies.[3] Locally, the first NSW Bureau of Crime Statistics study into rape

[1] Julia Quilter, 'Re-Inventing Rape: An analysis of Legal, Medical, Feminist and Governmental Discourses' (DPhil thesis, Monash University 2000); Julia Quilter, 'From Raptus to Rape: A History of the "Requirements" of Resistance and Injury' (2015) 2 Law & History 89; Julia Quilter, 'Rape Trials, Medical Texts and the Threat of Female Speech: The Perverse Female Rape Complainant' (2015) 19 Law Text Culture 231.

[2] Menachem Amir, *Patterns in Forcible Rape* (University of Chicago Press 1971).

[3] Eg Arthur Schiff, 'Statistical Features of Rape' (1969) 14 Journal of Forensic Sciences 102.

categorized the police reports of rape from 1973 using similar characteristics: the age of the victim and offender, the number of attackers, the presence/absence of injury, use of a weapon, relationship between the victim and attacker, location including place where the rape occurred (both city and location such as street, home, etc), length of time taken to report the offence, conviction rates, and penalties.[4] While this early study is modest (11 pages), it reflected the shift that was occurring towards statistical averaging of the particular characteristics of the rape situation.

As this statistical 'average' or profile of rape emerged, it demonstrated a deep chasm between the reality of rape and previous representations of it, including the legal frameworks for prosecuting rape. Studies began to document what are now widely referred to as 'rape myths'.[5] Second-wave feminists pursued ever-more reliable 'facts' about the crime to dispute these myths. While Clark and Lewis, in the first Canadian study,[6] explored the 'profile' of both the (un/successful) complainant and rapist through *reported rape statistics*, later feminist accounts (especially post-1980) contested the validity of using only *reported* rape statistics. Many of these feminist studies used a variety of other sources, such as surveys and interviews with women[7] (and rapists[8]) and phone-ins,[9] to demonstrate the problems of relying exclusively on reported rape statistics. For instance, Russell's analysis of rape, child sexual abuse, and workplace harassment was based upon studies with 960 randomly selected San Francisco women interviewed in the summer of 1978 regarding their experiences of the prevalence of rape and attempted rape.[10] From these interviews, Russell argued that rape was far more prominent (13 times higher) than rates given by the Uniform Crime Reports, which were based only on reported rapes.[11]

Second-wave feminists demonstrated that rather than a 'plague' of false complaints—the assumption embedded in the law including the corroboration warning, discussed in Chapter 3—rape was seriously under reported.[12] Studies

[4] D West, 'Rape Offences' (Statistical Report 21, NSW Bureau of Crime Statistics and Research 1974).

[5] See Quilter, 'From Raptus to Rape' (n 1); Quilter, 'Re-Inventing Rape' (n 1).

[6] Lorenne Clark and Debra Lewis, *Rape: The Price of Coercive Sexuality* (Women's Press 1977).

[7] See, eg, 'The Voice of the Australian Woman' *Women's Weekly Survey* (1980), discussed in Quilter, 'Re-Inventing Rape' (n 1) 239; and the *Sunday Telegraph* questionnaire regarding victims' experiences of rape: NSW Sexual Assault Committee, 'Sexual Assault Phone-In Report' (Ministry for the Status and Advancement of Women 1994). See also Diana Russell, *The Politics of Rape: The Victim's Perspective* (Stein & Day 1975).

[8] See Diana Scully, *Understanding Sexual Violence: A Study of Convicted Rapists* (Unwin Hyman 1990).

[9] See, eg, Real Rape Law Coalition, 'No Real Justice: The Findings of a Confidential Phone-In on Sexual Assault' (Victorian Health Promotion Foundation 1992); NSW Sexual Assault Committee (n 7).

[10] Diana Russell, *Sexual Exploitation: Rape, Child Sexual Abuse and Workplace Harassment* (Sage 1984).

[11] ibid 43.

[12] Clark and Lewis (n 6); Russell, *Sexual Exploitation* (n 10); Gregory D Woods, 'Sexual Assault Law Reform in NSW: A Commentary on the Crimes (Sexual Assault) Amendment Act 1981 and Cognate Act' (Department of the Attorney-General and of Justice 1981) 28. Today, estimates suggest 5% of rape complaints to police may be false: Claire Ferguson and John Malouff, 'Assessing Police Classifications

showed that the practices of rape trials made it a *difficult* accusation to make rather than one that was 'easily to be made' and 'harder to be defended by the party accused, tho never so innocent'.[13] These new discourses demonstrated that victims of rape were generally *known* to their offenders, not strangers.[14] Studies in social-psychology with undergraduate and senior high school students, demonstrated that it was regular dating situations which were characterized by the greatest levels of violence.[15] Despite the high frequency of rape found by these studies, a polarized debate continued over the believability of complainants, with medico-legal studies after 1960 repeating the belief that most rape charges were false.[16] Medical texts gave a range of asserted explanations for false complaints: to cover up pregnancy; for coming home late; and to hide consensual intercourse with men other than husbands or boyfriends. With minor modifications, these 'motives' still resonate with current cross-examination techniques discussed in Chapter 7.

In terms of the 'act', medico-legal studies revealed that rapists generally did not severely physically injure their victims. Studies from the 1960s documented the infrequency of physical genital[17] and general injuries.[18] Furthermore, as social psychologists began to study 'normal' undergraduate males, medical writings showed that micro-trauma to the vagina was also associated with consensual intercourse.[19] Increasingly it was being shown that physical injuries were rare and

of Sexual Assault Reports: A Meta-Analysis of False Reporting Rates' (2016) 45 Archives of Sexual Behavior 1185.

[13] Matthew Hale, *Historia Placitorum Coronae*, vol 1 (PR Glazebrook ed, Professional Books 1971) 635.

[14] Amir (n 2); Roseanne Bonney, 'Crimes (Sexual Assault) Amendment Act 1981 Monitoring and Evaluation: Interim Report No 1—Characteristics of the Complainant, the Defendant and the Offence' (New South Wales Bureau of Crime Statistics and Research 1985); Law Reform Commission of Victoria, 'Rape: Reform of Law and Procedure' (LRCV Report No 43, 1991).

[15] Eugene Kanin, 'Male Sex Aggression in Dating-Courtship Relations' (1957) 63 The American Journal of Sociology 197.

[16] See Quilter, 'Re-Inventing Rape' (n 1); Quilter, 'Rape Trials, Medical Texts and the Threat of Female Speech' (n 1).

[17] Joe Massey, 'Management of Sexually Assaulted Females' (1971) 38 Obstetrics and Gynecology 29, 31; Charles Hayman, Charlene Lanza, and Kathe Algor, 'Rape in the District of Columbia' (1972) 113 American Journal Obstetrics and Gynecology 91; Frederick Zuspan, 'Alleged Rape: An Invitational Symposium' (1974) 12 The Journal of Reproductive Medicine 133, 134; Royice Everett and Gordon Jimerson, 'The Rape Victim: A Review of 117 Consecutive Cases' (1977) 50 Obstetrics and Gynecology 88, 89–90; Peter Cartwright and others, 'Genital Injury and Implied Consent to Alleged Rape' (1986) 31 Journal of Reproductive Medicine 1043, 1044; TI Manser, 'Findings in Medical Examinations of Victims and Offenders in Cases of Serious Sexual Offences—A Survey' (1991) 39 The Police Surgeon 4, 16–17.

[18] See Hayman, Lanza, and Algor (n 17); Charles Hayman and Charlene Lanza, 'Sexual Assault on Women and Girls' (1971) 109 American Journal of Obstetrics and Gynecology 480; Massey (n 17); J K Mason (ed), *The Pathology of Violent Injury* (Edward Arnold 1978) 169. See further Quilter, 'Re-Inventing Rape' (n 1) ch 3.

[19] Mark Norvell, Guy Benrubi, and Robert Thompson, 'Investigation of Microtrauma after Sexual Intercourse' (1984) 29 The Journal of Reproductive Medicine 269; Alison Lauber and Micki Souma, 'Use of Toluidine Blue for Documentation of Traumatic Intercourse' (1982) 60 Obstetrics and Gynecology 644; N C Smith, H A Van Coeverden de Groot, and K D Gunston, 'Coital Injuries of the Vagina in Non-Virginal Patients' (1983) 64 South African Medical Journal 746.

medical evidence was unlikely to add to a rape investigation. Arguably, this should have mounted an evidence-based case for why it was misguided for the law to focus on resistance and 'injuries' to prove rape in trials.

Studies showed that rape was not an infrequent and arbitrary event (as previously portrayed) and it was said to be increasing at alarming levels.[20] Many of these new articles begin their discussions with a statistical reference to the high incidence of rape, suggesting it potentially affects all women and rape is at crisis levels.[21] These new studies refuted the historically held belief that rape occurs in remote locations. Study after study showed that a woman was more likely to be raped by a man she knew and in her or the assailant's home.[22]

The 'normalization' of rape in these new studies led second-wave feminists in particular to argue that *any* woman was potentially a victim, *any* man a potential rapist, and rape could occur *any*where.[23] These studies produced a profile of the 'average' rapist, victim, and 'crime'/act and found each to be alarmingly *normal*.[24] Second-wave feminist studies suggest not only that the rapist is little different to other offenders but could *potentially* be any man. Griffin popularized the normality of the rapist in her article, 'The All-American Crime',[25] and Brownmiller indicated 'the typical American rapist might be the boy next door'.[26] The relative *normality* of rapists has been a common finding across post-1960 texts.[27]

This *normalization* provided a knowledge base for feminists and others to lobby for rape law reform to remove old assumptions or myths about the offence. The rape trial became a particular site of struggle after many complainants described they had been raped twice—once by the assailant and again by the legal system.[28] These knowledges also provide a background to evaluate the large-scale 'progressive' reforms that have occurred over the past 50 years including to the substantive offence definitions, evidence, and procedural rules (discussed in Chapter 3). While law reforms have recalibrated the offence to better align with the 'reality' and improve the experience of complainants in the criminal justice system, a large body of literature has recognized that this has not brought about significant practical changes to the prosecution of trials. As we noted in Chapter 1, attrition at

[20] See, eg, NSW Standing Committee on Social Issues, *Sexual Violence: The Hidden Crime. Inquiry into the Incidence of Sexual Offences in NSW—Part 1.* Report No 6 (Legislative Council of NSW 1993).

[21] See, eg, medico-legal texts include such citations: Hayman and Lanza (n 18) 480; Ann Wolbert Burgess and Lynda Holmstrom, 'Rape Trauma Syndrome' (1974) 131 The American Journal of Psychiatry 981, 981; Douglas Ringrose, 'Sociological, Medical and Legal Aspects of Rape' (1975) 4 Criminal Law Quarterly 440, 440.

[22] See, eg, Susan Brownmiller, *Against Our Will: Men, Women and Rape* (Simon & Schuster 1975) 185–86; Amir (n 2).

[23] See, eg, Brownmiller (n 22) 185–86.

[24] See, eg, Amir (n 2) ch 18.

[25] Susan Griffin, 'The All-American Crime' in Leroy Schultz (ed), *Rape Victimology* (Charles C Thomas 1975).

[26] Brownmiller (n 22) 174.

[27] See, eg, Bonney, 'Interim Report No. 1' (n 14); Law Reform Commission of Victoria (n 14).

[28] Russell, *The Politics of Rape* (n 7).

all points in the criminal justice system (reporting, investigation, prosecution) remains high—including high numbers of successful appeals in the event of a conviction. It has been said that this 'justice gap' is more a 'justice chasm'.[29] Given the significant energies and resources invested in rape law reform globally, how is this apparent failure to be explained? We next discuss three broad arguments attempting to grapple with this conundrum.

3. The Patriarchal, Masculine Logic of the Law

There has now long been a tradition of scholarship critiquing positivist methods of legal reasoning, objectivity, and neutrality.[30] Critical race scholars and feminist legal theorists have argued that the law tells particular 'stock stories' which pose as neutral while excluding other narratives.[31] In the context of rape, a body of feminist work argues that modern rape laws do not address female violation or sexual autonomy because they were never designed to do so, the laws being developed from older property laws which protected male interests—including those of fathers and husbands.[32] Tracing the remarkable continuity in how rape trials are conducted across decades—despite significant law reform—demonstrates that requirements developed from these older property offences steeped in patriarchy continue to be the benchmark from which the 'true rape' is assessed.[33] A diverse group of 'radical' feminists go further arguing law reform failure results from law being underpinned by particular types of sexuality that exclude the feminine, making it incapable of responding effectively to the harm of rape.

Some of the better-known critiques argue, variously, that women's subjectivity is denied by the law because it is based on *heterosexuality*,[34] *masculine*,[35]

[29] Liz Kelly, Jo Lovett, and Linda Regan, 'A Gap or Chasm? Attrition in Reported Rape Cases' (Research Study 293, Home Office 2005).

[30] See, eg, Carol Smart, *Feminism and the Power of Law* (Routledge 1989); Regina Graycar and Jenny Morgan, *The Hidden Gender of the Law* (Federation Press 1990); Margaret Davies, *Asking the Law Question* (5th edn, Thomson Reuters 2023); Rosemary Hunter, 'Analysing Judgments from a Feminist Perspective' (2015) 15 Legal Information Management 8; Rosemary Hunter, 'The Power of Feminist Judgments?' (2012) 20 Feminist Legal Studies 135.

[31] See, eg, Symposium, 'Legal Storytelling' (1989) 87 Michigan Law Review 2073; Mari Matsuda, 'Looking to the Bottom: Critical Legal Studies and Reparations' (1987) 22 Harvard Civil Rights-Civil Liberties Law 323; Robyn West, 'The Difference in Women's Hedonic Lives: A Phenomenological Critique of Feminist Legal Theory' (1987) 3 Wisconsin Women's Law Journal 81; Patricia Williams, *The Alchemy of Race and Rights: Diary of a Law Professor* (Harvard UP 1991); Rae Kaspiew, 'Rape Lore: Legal Narrative and Sexual Violence' (1995) 20 Melbourne University Law Review 350.

[32] Brownmiller (n 22) ch 2; Clark and Lewis (n 6); Herman Schwendinger and Julia Schwendinger, *Rape and Inequality* (Sage 1983); Quilter, 'From Raptus to Rape' (n 1).

[33] Quilter, 'From Raptus to Rape' (n 1); Brownmiller (n 22) ch 2.

[34] Brownmiller (n 22); Clark and Lewis (n 6); Nicola Gavey, *Just Sex?: The Cultural Scaffolding of Rape* (Psychology Press 2005); Nicola Gavey, *Just Sex?: The Cultural Scaffolding of Rape* (2nd edn, Routledge 2018).

[35] Catherine MacKinnon, 'Feminism, Marxism, Method and the State: An Agenda for Theory' (1982) 7 Signs 515; Catherine MacKinnon, 'Feminism, Marxism, Method and the State: Toward Feminist Jurisprudence' (1983) 8 Signs 635.

patriarchal,[36] *phallocentric*,[37] and/or *'possessive'*[38] sexuality or *'sexual indifference'*.[39] For example, MacKinnon argues that society privileges the masculine perspective which the law reinforces but does not cause.[40] In terms of rape law, the crime is defined in 'male bodily terms' focusing on 'penetration'.[41] Additionally, the law privileges the male body and adjudicates issues of consent and non-consent in male sexual terms. To demonstrate her point, MacKinnon provocatively reverses the question usually asked in relation to rape:

> Instead of asking, what is the violation of rape, what if we ask, what is the nonviolation of intercourse? To tell what is wrong with rape, explain what is right about sex. If this, in turn, is difficult, the difficulty is as instructive as the difficulty men have in telling the difference when women see one.[42]

For Smart,[43] the entrenchment of a phallocentric[44] model of sexuality means that law as a site of 'sexing' and 'gendering' practices, constructs woman as perpetually 'biological'—a biology that is 'unruly'[45] and which can only be read as 'inviting' or being responsible for rape.[46] For Smart, the rape trial '. . . is a process of disqualification (of women) and celebration (of phallocentrism)'.[47] It testifies to how discourses of heterosex—what Gavey calls the 'cultural scaffolding of rape'—enable trials to reconstitute sexual violation as 'just sex'.[48]

[36] Carole Pateman, 'Women and Consent' (1980) 8 Political Theory 149, Carole Pateman, *The Sexual Contract* (Polity Press 1988); Louise Du Toit, *A Philosophical Investigation of Rape: The Making and Unmaking of the Feminine Self* (Routledge 2009).

[37] Smart, *Feminism and the Power of Law* (n 30); Carol Smart, *Law, Crime and Sexuality: Essays in Feminism* (Sage Publications 1995).

[38] Ngaire Naffine, 'Possession: Erotic Love and the Law of Rape' (1994) 57 Modern Law Review 10; Ngaire Naffine, *Feminism & Criminology* (Allen & Unwin 1997).

[39] Yvette Russell and Joanne Conaghan, *Law and Gender* (OUP 2013); Yvette Russell, 'Woman's Voice/Law's Logos: The Rape Trial and the Limits of Liberal Reform' (2016) 42 The Australian Feminist Law Journal 273.

[40] MacKinnon, 'Toward Feminist Jurisprudence' (n 35) 644.

[41] See also Catherine MacKinnon, 'Sex and Violence: A Perspective' in Catherine MacKinnon, *Feminism Unmodified: Discourses on Life and Law* (Harvard UP 1987); Catherine Mackinnon, 'A Rally Against Rape' in Catherine MacKinnon, *Feminism Unmodified: Discourses on Life and Law* (Harvard UP 1987).

[42] MacKinnon, 'Toward Feminist Jurisprudence' (n 35) 646–47. See also Catherine MacKinnon, 'Rape: On Coercion and Consent' in Catherine MacKinnon, *Toward A Feminist Theory of the State* (Harvard UP 1989).

[43] Smart, *Feminism and the Power of Law* (n 30).

[44] By phallocentric we mean '. . . a specifically discursive series of procedures, a strategy for collapsing representations of the two sexes into a single model, called "human" or "man", but which is in fact congruent only with the masculine . . . Within phallocentric paradigms femininity can only be represented in some necessary relation to masculinity': Elizabeth Grosz, 'Philosophy' in Sneja Gunew (ed), *Feminist Knowledges: Critique and Construct* (Routledge 1990) 150.

[45] Smart, *Law, Crime and Sexuality* (n 37) 229.

[46] ibid 224–25.

[47] Smart, *Feminism and the Power of Law* (n 30) 35.

[48] Gavey 2018 (n 34).

Key legal concepts such as consent are problematic not because of the expressed content of their definitions (although they may also be problematic) but because they are based on heterosexual and patriarchal structures that deny women's subjectivity.[49] For example, relying on stories of the social contract, Pateman argues that patriarchal sex right continued in civil society, meaning that women are not treated as 'individuals' and are therefore excluded from the social contract. In terms of consent:

> Women exemplify the individuals who consent theorists have declared are incapable of consenting. Yet, simultaneously, women have been presented as always consenting, and their explicit nonconsent has been treated as irrelevant or has been reinterpreted as 'consent'.[50]

For du Toit the legal elements of rape (notably sexual intercourse and consent) do not speak to women's sexual subjectivity.[51] The patriarchal symbolic order upon which the law is based distinguishes sex and rape only by whether the woman gives her consent or not to a man *having* intercourse with her. This distinction fails to ask whether the woman *actively desired* the intercourse[52] and how that might be articulated.

The gendered nature of the law means that law reform is likely to fail because it does not challenge the structural coherence of the law, which at its heart fails to acknowledge woman as subject.[53] Devoting considerable energy to law reform including 'tinkering' with key legal concepts (such as consent and the fault element) cannot address a logic that systematically erases the feminine.[54] Some warn 'feminism to avoid the siren call of the law', criticizing the feminist movement for being '"seduced" by law'.[55] Smart argues that law is the wrong arena to address this harm: '[i]t is glaringly obvious that the criminal law does not provide a remedy to sexual abuse, it is increasingly obvious that it causes harm, yet still it is assumed that the solution is to encourage more women and children into the system.'[56] For others, law reforms may be less '"improvements" in the law' as 'adjustments

[49] Mary Heath and Ngaire Naffine, 'Men's Needs and Women's Desires: Feminist Dilemmas about Rape Law Reform' (1994) 3 Australian Feminist Law Journal 30; Rosemary Hunter and Sharon Cowan, *Choice and Consent: Feminist Engagements with Law and Subjectivity* (Routledge-Cavendish 2007); Joanne Conaghan and Yvette Russell, 'Rape Myths, Law, and Feminist Research: "Myths About Myths"?' (2014) 22 Feminist Legal Studies 25; Gavey 2005 (n 34).

[50] Pateman, 'Women and Consent' (n 36) 150.

[51] Louise Du Toit, 'The Conditions of Consent' in Rosemary Hunter and Sharon Cowan (eds), *Choice and Consent: Feminist Engagements with Law and Subjectivity* (Glasshouse 2007); Du Toit, *A Philosophical Investigation of Rape* (n 36).

[52] Du Toit, 'The Conditions of Consent' (n 51) 38–39.

[53] Russell, 'Woman's Voice/Law's Logos' (n 39) 296.

[54] Du Toit, *A Philosophical Investigation of Rape* (n 36).

[55] Smart, *Feminism and the Power of Law* (n 30) 160.

[56] ibid 161.

designed to "soften" or mitigate the essential (masculine) nature of law'.[57] What law reform does not do is challenge a system that erases female subjectivity and only allows her to be represented as the lacking side of the binary.

While we do not analyse the trials through this theoretical lens, in particular, we have sympathy with the argument that tinkering with consent definitions or implementing special measures do not get to the heart of why rape trials are so traumatic for victims.

4. The Translation to Practice Problem

A second line of argument pragmatically recognizes that reforming the law may *potentially* improve the situation of rape complainants, but it relies precariously on the practices of the law.[58] Rape law reform has been described as:

> . . . a Sisyphean task, with constant pressure leading to reforms, only to have such 'successes' neutralized in practice; the boulder falling back down the mountain.[59]

Similar arguments have been made for decades despite the (ongoing) energies devoted to law reform efforts. The 'translation to practice' or 'implementation gap'[60] has been raised following most law reform efforts in Australia and in the common law world including by feminists, law reform bodies, governments, and other evaluation exercises.[61] The literature is vast and here we overview three main explanations which overlap in various ways.

[57] Russell, 'Woman's Voice/Law's Logos' (n 39) 295.

[58] Carol Smart, 'Feminism and the Law: Some Problems of Analysis and Strategy' (1986) 14 International Journal of the Sociology of Law 109; Clare McGlynn and Vanessa Munro (eds), *Rethinking Rape Law: International and Comparative Perspectives* (Routledge 2010); Julia Quilter, 'Re-Framing the Rape Trial: Insights From Critical Theory about the Limitations of Legislative Reform' (2011) 35 The Australian Feminist Law Journal 23.

[59] Clare McGlynn, 'Feminist Activism and Rape Law Reform in England and Wales: A Sisyphean Struggle?' in Clare McGlynn and Vanessa Munro (eds), *Rethinking Rape Law: International and Comparative Perspectives* (Routledge 2010) 150.

[60] Australian Law Reform Commission, *Family Violence—National Legal Response* (ALRC Report 114, 2010) 1125.

[61] See, eg, NSW Department for Women, 'Heroines of Fortitude: The Experience of Women in Court as Victims of Sexual Assault' (NSW Department for Women Report 1996); Mary Heath and Ngaire Naffine, 'Men's Needs and Women's Desires: Feminist Dilemmas about Rape Law Reform' (1994) 3 Australian Feminist Law Journal 30; Kathleen Daly and Brigitte Bouhours, 'Rape and Attrition in the Legal Process: A Comparative Analysis of Five Countries' (2010) 39 Crime and Justice 565; Patricia Easteal (ed), *Balancing the Scales: Rape, Law Reform and Australian Culture* (Federation Press 1998); Vivien Stern, 'The Stern Review: A Report by Baroness Vivien Stern CBE of an Independent Review into How Rape Complainants are Handled by the Public Authorities in England and Wales' (Government Equalities Office and Home Office 2010); Elisabeth McDonald, *Rape Myths as Barriers to Fair Trial Process* (Canterbury UP 2020).

The 'intentions' of progressive reforms don't control the practices of the law

Adler, one of the early feminist advocates for law reform in the United Kingdom, indicated that the 'intentions' of those who initiated the amendments to rape laws were circumvented in the practices of the courts.[62] Similarly, Smart recognized:

> . . . the main dilemma for any feminist engagement with law reform is the certain knowledge that, once enacted, legislation is in the hands of individuals and agencies far removed from the values and politics of the women's movement.[63]

Legislatures may, of course, 'speak' with different intents to different audiences. Sometimes the intent behind statutory reform is to express normative values for general consumption by the public—such as legislating the meaning of consent as 'free and voluntary agreement', or enshrining the ethical standards contained in communicative or affirmative models of consent. Nevertheless, this criticism of law reform recognizes that the practical impact of reform on the conduct of rape trials is tied to the way judicial officers and legal practitioners perform the law; that the 'uptake' of progressive reforms can't be guaranteed and needs to be operationalized.[64] Legislation is not self-executing.

When the 'gap' is discerned, the problem is often characterized as one that can be solved by better educating key stakeholders[65] about rape myths and misconceptions, trauma, and trauma-informed practices. We note that this is a very different change strategy to one that, say, mandates new practices and prohibits old ones through legislation or professional conduct rules. In recent times, the focus has been on educating police, practitioners, jurors, and judges about rape myths and misconceptions. Practitioners[66] and judges[67] have been a particular focus of law

[62] Zsuzsanna Adler, 'Rape—The Intention of Parliament and the Practice of the Courts' (1982) 45 Modern Law Review 664.

[63] Smart, *Feminism and the Power of Law* (n 30) 164; Lise Gotell, 'Canadian Sexual Assault Law: Neoliberalism and the Erosion of Feminist-Inspired Law Reforms' in Clare McGlynn and Vanessa Munro (eds), *Rethinking Rape Law: International and Comparative Perspectives* (Routledge 2010).

[64] Quilter, 'Re-Framing the Rape Trial' (n 58).

[65] See, eg, ALRC, *Family Violence* (n 60) chs 25–28; Victorian Law Reform Commission, *Improving the Response of the Justice System to Sexual Offences* (Report, 2021); ALRC, *Safe, Informed, Supported: Justice Responses to Sexual Violence* (ALRC Report 143, 2025).

[66] See, eg, Nina Hudson and others, 'Understanding Adult Sexual Assault Matters: Insights From Research and Practice' (Practice Guide, Australian Institute of Family Studies December 2024).

[67] See, eg, Australian Institute of Judicial Administration, 'Papers presented at the "Enhancing Safe Practice: A National Justice Forum on Sexual Assault" (AIJA 2024) <https://aija.org.au/publications/papers-presented-at-the-enhancing-safe-practice-a-national-justice-forum-on-sexual-assault/> accessed 11 July 2025; 'Managing Sexual Assault Hearings' training programme run by the National Judicial College of Australia (NJCA) <https://www.njca.com.au/judicial-education-programs/> accessed 11 July 2025.

reform recommendations calling for specialized (but not mandatory) training.[68] Jurors are the target audience for the ever-expanding suite of statutory jury directions.[69]

While we have some sympathy for the 'gap' explanation, we argue that it is important to look closely at the 'reformed' statute books and identify, with some precision, what it is that progressive reforms seek to do. As we explain in Chapter 3, having reviewed 50 years of progressive rape law reforms, there are very few reforms that actually exclude rape myths or prohibit rape trial practices that are known to cause distress to complainants.

Inconsistent implementation or uptake by practitioners

Another related argument is that there has been 'inconsistent' implementation of reformed laws in practice, producing inter-trial variation—an issue we discuss at various points in this book, including Chapter 9. While it might be anticipated that there is trial-to-trial variation, in our dataset we found troubling differences between how individual judges operationalized the law including failing to give relevant jury directions. Inconsistent implementation has been an ongoing concern for law reform bodies with, for instance, an early Victorian Law Reform Commission report stating:

> The statute books are littered with provisions that have never been properly implemented because once the legislation was adopted; nobody bothered to make the necessary adjustments at the level of *organizational practice*. Another limitation of relying on legislation is that the legislative process is slow and *somewhat unpredictable*.[70]

As just one of many examples, Cockburn's study of the implementation of Tasmania's 2004 reformed communicative and affirmative consent models found they were largely unsuccessful, with practitioners and judges failing to engage with the positive consent standard and continuing to resort to evidence of resistance and 'inferred' consent.[71]

[68] See, eg, Women's Safety and Justice Taskforce (Qld), 'Hear Her Voice: Women and Girls' Experiences across the Criminal Justice System' (Report No 1, Vol 3, Queensland Government 2022) 603–27; ALRC, *Safe, Informed, Supported* (n 65) ch 7.

[69] See Chapter 3 at p. 67.

[70] Law Reform Commission of Victoria, *Rape: Reform of Law and Procedure* (Interim Report No 42, 1991) 16 (emphasis added).

[71] Helen Cockburn, 'The Impact of Introducing an Affirmative Model of Consent and Changes to the Defence of Mistake in Tasmanian Rape Trials' (DPhil thesis, University of Tasmania 2012). See also Olivia Smith, *Rape Trials in England and Wales: Observing Justice and Rethinking Rape Myths* (Palgrave Macmillan 2018); Ellen Daly, *Rape, Gender and Class: Intersections in Courtroom Narratives* (Palgrave Macmillan 2022); and references above at (n 61).

A related argument is that it is only an older 'dinosaur'[72] generation of lawyers and judges that are not implementing reformed laws. Craig's study of Canadian sexual assault trial practices discredits the notion that a 'kinder and gentler approach' is taken by experienced members of the bar now because 'whacking' the complainant is ineffective with modern mores and reformed laws.[73]

It should be noted that inconsistent application of the law is not considered by all to be a failure. The uneven development of law and its application is said to be a site of 'discursive struggle, with contradictory implications' some of which may be used for feminist purposes.[74] For example, Gotell, analysing Canadian reforms around 'affirmative consent', demonstrates these may produce victim-blaming narratives (eg failing to act 'responsibly') but in other circumstances, such as intoxicated complainants, judges may raise the bar on the accused's duty to take reasonable steps to ensure consent.[75] For other scholars, the problem of inconsistent application of the law might turn the lens towards different measures of 'success' from conviction rates to how complainants are treated by the criminal justice system[76] or to focus on alternative restorative justice.[77]

The trial as a whole is 'resistant' to change

Another related argument is that the trial is simply 'reform-resistant'[78] because of the embedded 'rape schema'[79] and/or the continued dominance of rape myths (discussed separately later). The rape schema, which we briefly introduced in Chapter 1, relates to legal requirements that developed when the law was primarily concerned with regulating marriage and property rights, but which were redeployed into the 'new' crime of 'rape' during the seventeenth and eighteenth centuries, without modification, to an offence now ostensibly concerned with

[72] Wendy Tuohy, 'Legal "dinosaurs" the problem, not consent laws, says law reform chair' *The Age* (16 May 2021) <https://www.theage.com.au/national/victoria/legal-dinosaurs-the-problem-not-consent-laws-says-law-reform-chair-20210514-p57s1g.html> accessed 11 July 2025, citing VLRC Chair, Tony North QC.

[73] Elaine Craig, *Putting Trials on Trial: Sexual Assault and the Failure of the Legal Profession* (McGill-Queen's UP 2018) chs 2–3.

[74] Smart, *Law, Crime and Sexuality* (n 37).

[75] Lise Gotell, 'Reassessing the Place of Criminal Law Reform in the Struggle Against Sexual Violence: A Critique of the Critique of Carceral Feminism' in Anastasia Powell, Nicola Henry, and Asher Flynn (eds), *Rape Justice* (Palgrave Macmillan 2015) 61.

[76] Wendy Larcombe, 'Falling Rape Conviction Rates: (Some) Feminist Aims and Measures for Rape Law' (2011) 19 Feminist Legal Studies 27; Anna Carline and Clare Gunby, 'Rape Politics, Policies and Practice: Exploring the Tensions and Unanticipated Consequences of Well-Intended Victim-Focuses Measures' (2017) 56 The Howard Journal of Crime and Justice 34.

[77] Clare McGlynn, 'Feminism, Rape, and the Search for Justice' (2011) 34 Oxford Journal of Legal Studies 825.

[78] McDonald, *Rape Myths as Barriers to Fair Trial Process* (n 61) 3.

[79] Quilter, 'Re-Framing the Rape Trial' (n 58); Susan Estrich, *Real Rape: How the Legal System Victimizes Women Who Say No* (Harvard UP 1987).

protecting women's sexual autonomy.[80] Quilter has previously explained that the schema serves to structure the court's interpretation of evidence into:

> ... a 'logical' series of conclusions steps that might be represented in the following formula:
>
> The location was (not) remote +
> There was (no) physical injury +
> She did (not) recently complain of rape +
> She was (not) of 'good fame'
> = she is (un)believable; she had sex/she was raped.
>
> ... [E]ven where legislative reforms are introduced they are in a sense 'unreadable' as they are circumvented and co-opted back into the 'old story', to the detriment of the female rape complainant.[81]

The rape schema's requirements align closely with what Estrich described as the attributes of a so-called 'real rape': the act is perpetrated by a stranger; is committed in a public place; results in injuries or involves a weapon.[82]

The power of the rape schema lies in subsuming the specificities of any trial into these requirements erasing other information as irrelevant. The requirements of the schema have a highly sedimented history and mean that progressive legislative reforms are co-opted back into this old story. In the adversarial context, prosecution and defence argue reverse sides of the coin—what they leave in place is an acceptance of the schema itself as 'correct' and to the exclusion of other narratives.[83] In Chapter 3, we show that while law-makers may have confronted and rhetorically renounced elements of the rape schema—indeed this is one of the recurring motifs of the progressive reform project—they have very rarely taken the step of legislating for their removal from the courtroom. 'Corrective' jury directions are an exemplar of this preference for *disavowing* rather than *disallowing*.

Several empirical studies have demonstrated the lasting significance of the rape schema in trials—despite these no longer being requirements under 'reformed' laws.[84] McDonald's study of New Zealand trials, which initially focused on the

[80] Quilter, 'From Raptus to Rape' (n 1).
[81] Quilter, 'Re-Framing the Rape Trial' (n 58) 31.
[82] Estrich (n 79); McDonald, *Rape Myths as Barriers to Fair Trial Process* (n 61); Craig (n 73); Rachael Burgin and Asher Flynn, 'Women's Behaviour as Implied Consent: Male "Reasonableness" in Australian Rape Law' (2019) 21 Criminology & Criminal Justice 1.
[83] Quilter, 'Re-Framing the Rape Trial' (n 58).
[84] McDonald, *Rape Myths as Barriers to Fair Trial Process* (n 61); Craig (n 73); Sarah Zydervelt and others, 'Lawyer's Strategies for Cross-Examining Rape Complainants: Have We Moved Beyond the 1950s?' (2017) 57 British Journal of Criminology 551; Rachael Burgin, 'Persistent Narratives of Force and Resistance: Affirmative Consent as Law Reform' (2019) 59 The British Journal of Criminology 296; Rachael Burgin, 'Communicating Consent: Narratives of Sexual Consent in Victorian Rape Trials' (DPhil thesis, Monash University 2019); Anastasia Powell and others, 'Meanings of "Sex" and "Consent": The Persistence of Rape Myths in Victorian Rape Law' (2013) 22 Griffith Law Review 456; Cockburn (n 71).

reform-resistant nature of cross-examination, found 'that the trial process *as a whole* is resistant to legal and procedural change'.[85] As Pether stated:

> But all the speech and the writing, the scholarship and the legislation and the training programs and manuals and the textual artifacts of law reform have changed nothing, except perhaps that a larger number of women in many cultures are reporting rapes, only to experience the various instantiations of the embodied institutional and discursive 'second rape' that is one of the predictors of attribution.[86]

Another related argument is that adversarial tactics, particularly cross-examination strategies that unfairly and unjustly traumatize complainants, continue uninterrupted by law reforms.[87] Scholarship has analysed the discursive techniques and strategies used in rape trials that prevent a woman telling her story, particularly by portraying her as 'inconsistent' and reconstructing rape as sex.[88] Cross-examination techniques widely known to be problematic, including the use of closed questions (rather than open questions or narrative form),[89] focusing on peripheral details and minor inconsistencies,[90] are untouched by law reforms.[91]

Some studies suggest that to produce change we must look beyond the trial process including to 'societal beliefs . . . in order to see consequential change to the decision-making processes in rape trials'.[92] Others argue there is more law reform

[85] McDonald, *Rape Myths as Barriers to Fair Trial Process* (n 61) 480.

[86] Penny Pether, 'What is Due to Others: Speaking and Signifying Subject(s) of Rape Law' (2009) 18 Griffith Law Review 237, 243.

[87] See above (n 61). See also Jessica Kennedy and Patricia Easteal, 'Shades of Grey: Indeterminacy and Sexual Assault Law Reform' (2011) 13 Flinders Law Journal 49; Sharon Cowan, 'Sense and Sensibilities: A Feminist Critique of Legal Interventions against Sexual Violence' (2019) 23 Edinburgh Law Review 22.

[88] Gregory Matoesian, *Reproducing Rape: Domination Through Talk in the Courtroom* (Polity Press 1993); Gregory Matoesian, *Law and the Language of Identity: Discourse in the William Kennedy Smith Rape Trial* (OUP 2001); Susan Ehrlich, 'Perpetuating—and Resisting—Rape Myths in Trial Discourse' in Elizabeth Sheehy (ed), *Sexual Assault in Canada Law: Legal Practice and Women's Activism* (University of Ottawa Press 2012).

[89] Nina Westera and others, 'Sexual Assault Complainants on the Stand: A Historical Comparison of Courtroom Questioning' (2017) 23 Psychology, Crime & Law 15; John Conley M and William M O'Barr, *Just Words: Law, Language, and Power* (University of Chicago Press 2005); Susan Ehrlich, *Representing Rape: Language and Sexual Consent* (Routledge 2001); Louise Ellison, 'Cross-Examination in Rape Trials' (1998) Criminal Law Review 605; June Luchjenbroers and Michelle Aldridge, 'Conceptual Manipulation by Metaphors and Frames: Dealing with Rape Victims in Legal Discourse' (2007) 27 Text and Talk: An Interdisciplinary Journal of Language, Discourse Communication Studies 339; Andrew Taslitz, *Rape and the Culture of the Courtroom* (New York UP 1999).

[90] Patrick Tidmarsh and Gemma Hamilton, 'Misconceptions of Sexual Crimes against Adult Victims: Barriers to Justice' (Trends & Issues in Crime and Criminal Justice No 611, Australian Institute of Criminology 2020); NSW Department for Women (n 61) 167; *Rape Myths as Barriers to Fair Trial Process* at 332; Katrin Hohl and Martin A Conway, 'Memory as Evidence: How Normal Features of Victim Memory Lead to the Attrition of Rape Complainants' (2017) 17 Criminology & Criminal Justice 248, 249. See also Chapter 7.

[91] These practices are discussed further in Chapters 6, 7, and 9.

[92] McDonald, *Rape Myths as Barriers to Fair Trial Process* (n 61) 480; Jennifer Temkin and Barbara Krahe, *Sexual Assault and the Justice Gap: A Question of Attitude* (Hart Publishing 2008); Anna Carline

work to be done, offering further recommendations across the range of substantive, evidential, and procedural rules.[93] We take up such possibilities in Chapter 3.

5. Rape Myths

Since the 1960s, as discussed above, a large body of literature from a variety of disciplines has demonstrated a significant gap between the way the law has constructed rape and its 'reality'. In many studies from the 1960s it was assumed that it was the lack of statistical 'information' that shrouded rape in 'myths'.[94] In these early texts the assumption was that producing an evidence base to understand the 'true' picture of rape would rid us of rape myths—as the true picture emerged, the myths would be overturned. To that end, Estrich's[95] and Russell's[96] books were both written with the aim of 'overturning' the 'old myths' of rape. 50 years on, an extensive body of literature—with very limited exceptions[97]—reflects that far from being overturned, rape myths continue to exert a negative influence at all points of the criminal justice system from reporting and investigation, to prosecution.[98] The ongoing influence of rape myths in criminal trials is said to be a key reason why progressive reforms are undermined and a continuing cause of the failure to deliver justice to complainants.[99] While there is a large body of literature about the

and Clare Gunby, '"How an Ordinary Jury Makes Sense of It Is a Mystery": Barristers' Perspectives on Rape, Consent and the Sexual Offences Act 2003' (2011) 32 The Liverpool Law Review 237; Susan Leahy, 'Bad Laws or Bad Attitudes? Assessing the Impact of Societal Attitudes Upon the Conviction Rate for Rape in Ireland' (2014) 14 Irish Journal of Applied Social Studies 18.

[93] McDonald, *Rape Myths as Barriers to Fair Trial Process* (n 61).

[94] Eg Stanley Brodsky and Marcia Walker (eds), *Sexual Assault: The Victim and the Rapist* (Lexington Books 1976) x; Griffin (n 25) 20; Neil Brooks, 'Rape and the Laws of Evidence' (1975) 23(1) Chitty's Law Journal 1.

[95] Estrich (n 79).

[96] Russell, *The Politics of Rape* (n 7); Russell, *Sexual Exploitation* (n 10).

[97] Helen Reece, 'Rape Myths: Is Elite Opinion Right and Popular Opinion Wrong?' (2013) 33 Oxford Journal of Legal Studies 445; Helen Reece, 'Rape Trials Must be Completely Open' *Spiked* (2013) <https://www.spiked-online.com/2013/02/18/rape-trials-must-be-completely-open/> accessed 11 July 2025; Cheryl Thomas, 'The 21st Century Jury: Contempt, Bias and the Impact of Jury Service' [2020] Criminal Law Review 987. Both studies have been roundly criticized, respectively see Conaghan and Russell, 'Rape Myths, Law, and Feminist Research' (n 49); Ellen Daly and others, 'Myths about Myths? A Commentary on Thomas (2020) and the Question and Jury Rape Myth Acceptance' (2023) 7 Journal of Gender-Based Violence 189.

[98] Temkin and Krahe (n 92); Zsuzsanna Adler, *Rape on Trial* (Routledge 1987); Estrich (n 79); Jennifer Temkin, *Rape and the Legal Process* (Sweet & Maxwell 1987); Helenna Kennedy, *Eve Was Framed* (Chatto & Windus 1992); Daly and Bouhours (n 61); Stern (n 61); Sarah Bright and others, 'Attrition of Sexual Offence Incidents Through the Victorian Criminal Justice System: 2021 update' (Crime Statistics Agency 2021); Brigitte Gilbert, 'Attrition of Sexual Assaults from the New South Wales Criminal Justice System' (Report No 170, NSW Bureau of Crime Statistics and Research 2025).

[99] Elish Angiolini, 'Report of the Independent Review into The Investigation and Prosecution of Rape in London' (Crown Prosecution Service 2015); Australian Institute of Family Studies and Victoria Police, 'Challenging Misconceptions about Sexual Offending: Creating an Evidence-Based Resource for Police and Legal Practitioners' (2017); Hudson and others (n 66); Lori Haskell and Melanie Randall, 'The Impact of Trauma on Adult Sexual Assault Victims' (Justice Canada 2019); Jennifer Temkin,

impact of rape myths in a variety of contexts,[100] our focus is on the influence that such myths have on the criminal trial.[101]

What do we mean by 'rape myths'?

Martha Burt is often credited with first using the phrase 'rape myths', defining them as 'prejudicial, stereotyped and false beliefs about rape, rape victims and rapists'.[102] According to a widely cited definition, rape myths are 'descriptive or prescriptive beliefs about rape (ie about its scope, causes, context, and consequences) that serve to deny, downplay or justify sexually aggressive behavior that men commit against women'.[103] Estrich contrasted the flawed 'real rape' concept (discussed above) with 'simple rape', where the features of a 'real rape' (stranger, public place, injury/weapon) are not present.[104]

How closely a rape approximated 'real rape' impacted on whether it progressed through the criminal justice system. In the trial context, rape myths enliven expectations about how the 'true complainant' will act including making an immediate complaint, demonstrating distress, consistently accounting the rape,[105] verbally and physically resisting, and demonstrating injuries. There is also a continuing and deeply embedded myth that women lie about rape. These 'myths' are also referred to as misconceptions[106] or false assumptions.[107] More granular definitions of rape myths impacting the trial have been provided,[108] and in the context of juror

Jacqueline M Gray, and Jastine Barrett, 'Different Functions of Rape Myth Use in Court: Findings From a Trial Observation Study' (2018) 13 Feminist Criminology 205; McDonald, *Rape Myths as Barriers to Fair Trial Process* (n 61); Smith (n 71).

[100] For overviews, see Fiona Leverick and others, 'Rape Myths and Jury Decision Making: An Evidence Review' (University of Glasgow 2025); Lara Hudspith and others, 'The Impact of Rape Myths Education on Jury Decision-Making: A Systematic Review' (2024) 25 Trauma, Violence & Abuse 4062; Fiona Leverick, 'What Do We Know about Rape Myths and Juror Decision Making?' (2020) 24 The International Journal of Evidence & Proof 255.

[101] There is a large body of literature relating to rape myth acceptance scales such as the Illinois Rape Myth Acceptance Scale (IRMAS) (see, eg, Diana L Payne, 'Rape Myth Acceptance: Exploration of Its Structure and Its Measurement Using Illinois Rape Myths Acceptance Scale' (1999) 33 Journal of Research in Personality 27) and the Acceptance of Modern Myths About Sexual Aggression (AMMSA) scale.

[102] Martha R Burt, 'Cultural Myths and Supports for Rape' (1980) 38 Journal of Personality and Social Psychology 217, 217.

[103] Heike Gerger and others, 'The Acceptance of Modern Myths About Sexual Aggression Scale: Development and Validation in German and English' (2007) 33 Aggressive Behavior 422, 423.

[104] Estrich (n 79).

[105] See, eg, Katrin Hohl and Martin A Conway, 'Memory as Evidence: How Normal Features of Victim Memory Lead to the Attrition of Rape Complainants' (2017) 17 Criminology & Criminal Justice 248, 249.

[106] Law Commission (UK), *Evidence in Sexual Offences Prosecutions: A Final Report* (Law Com No 420, 2025) 4–5; ALRC, *Safe, Informed, Supported* (n 65).

[107] Hudson and others (n 66).

[108] Law Commission (UK), *Evidence in Sexual Offences Prosecutions* (Consultation Paper No 259, 2023) 38–42; ALRC, *Safe, Informed, Supported* (n 65); Hudson and others (n 66).

studies, there has been discussion of false and prejudicial beliefs about rape and rape victims in terms of beliefs that blame the victim-survivor, cast doubt on allegations, excuse the accused, and about what 'real rape' looks like.[109]

What does the literature from trials and mock juror studies tell us?

In the context of the rape trial, research has found that rape myths are remarkably resilient to progressive reforms, with several empirical studies of rape trials demonstrating that rape myths continue 'alive and well' in the courtroom despite the law being reformed to reduce the influence of myth-based lines of reasoning.[110] In Australia, the *Heroines of Fortitude Report* analysing trials after the most significant 1981 reforms evidenced that complainants were regularly attacked during cross-examination by questions and themes that relied on rape myths and stereotypes. Similar findings have been made in relation to transcript studies of the County Court of Victoria.[111] Further, Zydervelt and others compared rape trial transcripts from the 1950s in NSW to those in New Zealand (1996–2011) documenting the remarkable continuity over a 50-year period in the leveraging of rape myths and concluding that 'defence lawyers who question rape complainants are merely pursuing the same goals in slightly different ways'.[112] Over the course of this book we will also evidence the continuation of real rape attributes in the trials we examined by both the Crown (Chapter 6) and defence (Chapter 7)—but we argue in the next chapter that they likely continue unabated in courtrooms as no reforms have ever prohibited such myths.

Studies across the common law world provide similar evidence of the preponderance of rape myths. McDonald's studies of New Zealand rape trials reflect the ongoing reliance on rape myths in the questioning process, particularly to challenge complainant credibility with resulting heightened levels of complainant distress.[113] In Canada, Craig's transcript analysis and interviews with practitioners

[109] Leverick (n 100) 257; Gerd Bohner and others, 'Rape Myth Acceptance: Cognitive, Affective and Behavioral Effects of Beliefs that Blame the Victim and Exonerate the Perpetrator' in Miranda Horvath and Jennifer Brown (eds), *Rape: Challenging Contemporary Thinking* (Willan Publishing 2009); Olivia Smith and Tina Skinner, 'How Rape Myths are Used and Challenges in Rape and Sexual Assault Trials' (2017) 26 Social & Legal Studies 441.

[110] See, eg, Daly and Bouhours (n 61); McDonald, *Rape Myths as Barriers to Fair Trial Process* (n 61); Powell and others (n 84); Quilter, 'Re-Framing the Rape Trial' (n 58); Temkin, Gray, and Barrett (n 99). Our own findings on the continued prevalence of rape myths in trials are discussed in Chapters 6 and 7.

[111] See, eg, Burgin, 'Communicating Consent' (n 84); Burgin and Flynn (n 82); Emma Henderson and Kirsty Duncanson, 'A Little Judicial Direction: Can the Use of Jury Directions Challenge Traditional Consent Narratives in Rape Trials?' (2016) 39 University of New South Wales Law Journal 750; Powell and others (84).

[112] Zydervelt and others (n 84) 15.

[113] McDonald, *Rape Myths as Barriers to Fair Trial Process* (n 61); Elisabeth McDonald, *In the Absence of a Jury: Examining Judge-Alone Rape Trials* (Canterbury UP 2022); Elisabeth McDonald, *Prosecuting Intimate Partner Rape: The Impact of Misconceptions on Complaint Experience and Trial Process* (Canterbury UP 2023).

concludes that '[n]otwithstanding reforms to the rules of evidence and the substantive law of sexual assault, many sexual assault complainants continue to experience the criminal justice system as traumatic'.[114] Court observations in England and Wales, prior to major rape law reforms in the UK, found defence barristers drew on rape myths particularly to undermine complainant credibility and victim blaming.[115] Yet more recent court observations of rape trials,[116] following concerted law reform efforts in 1999 and 2003 which included introducing rape shield laws, nevertheless reflect the ongoing reliance in questioning on rape myths—particularly about demeanour, delayed reporting, continued contact with the accused, and lack of physical resistance.[117] These lines of questioning operate to blame victims and excuse perpetrators. Such myths are held in place by broader cultural narratives[118] and deep-rooted gendered cultural scaffolding.[119] While challenges to rape myths were observed in some trials,[120] 'on the whole, myth usage by the defense was insufficiently challenged by the prosecution'.[121]

A large body of research with mock jurors has found that there is 'clear evidence',[122] 'overwhelming evidence',[123] that rape myths impact the way jurors evaluate evidence. The literature recognizes that rape myths may change over time[124] and that people recognize the empirical falsity of certain real rape attributes—such as that most rapes are not perpetrated by strangers but rather by acquaintances.[125] Nevertheless, when confronted with scenarios or case studies, mock jurors fall back on socio-sexual scripts[126]—or gendered heuristics[127]—when asked to deliberate. For example, in scenarios involving acquaintance rapes, mock jurors expect complainants to unequivocally communicate non-consent

[114] Craig (n 73) 219.

[115] Adler, *Rape on Trial* (n 98); Sue Lees, *Carnal Knowledge: Rape on Trial* (Hamish Hamilton 1996).

[116] Smith (n 71); Smith and Skinner (n 109); Ellen Daly, 'Court Observations of English Rape and Sexual Assault Trials: An Intersectional Analysis' (DPhil thesis, Anglia Ruskin University 2021).

[117] Smith and Skinner (n 109).

[118] Daly (n 71).

[119] Smith (n 71).

[120] ibid.

[121] Temkin, Gray, and Barrett (n 99) 222.

[122] Sokratis Dinos and others, 'A Systematic Review of Juries' Assessment of Rape Victims: Do Rape Myths Impact on Juror Decision-Making?' (2015) 43 International Journal of Law, Crime and Justice 36, 47.

[123] Leverick (n 100) 256.

[124] Gavey 2005 (n 34); Conaghan and Russell, 'Rape Myths, Law, and Feminist Research' (n 49).

[125] Louise Ellison and Vanessa E Munro, 'Better the Devil You Know? "Real Rape" Stereotypes and the Relevance of the Previous Relationship in (Mock) Juror Deliberations' (2013) 17 The International Journal of Evidence & Proof 299.

[126] Ellison and Munro 'Better the Devil You Know?' (n 125); Louise Ellison and Vanessa E Munro, 'Turning Mirrors into Windows? Assessing the Impact of (Mock) Juror Education in Rape Trials' (2009) British Journal of Criminology 363; James Chalmers, Fiona Leverick, and Vanessa E Munro, 'The Provenance of What is Proven: Exploring (Mock) Jury Deliberation in Scottish Rape Trials' (2021) 48 Journal of Law and Society 226.

[127] Faye T Nitschke and others, 'The Effect of Heuristic Cues on Jurors Systematic Information Processing in Rape Trials' (2022) 46 Psychology of Women Quarterly 484; Conaghan and Russell, 'Rape Myths, Law, and Feminist Research' (n 49).

particularly through resistance.[128] Some myths may be addressed through education (including expectations around complainant demeanour and delay in reporting[129] and the 'freeze' response[130]) but others—such as the assumption that a complainant will physically resist rape—appear 'unshakeable' despite the guidance provided by expert evidence and/or jury directions.[131] The few studies involving real jurors indicate that 'at least some significant degree of illegitimate reasoning does occur'[132] in relation to sexual offence matters.

Solutions?

A large body of feminist, legal, and governmental literature has recommended the use of expert evidence, jury directions, and calls for (mandatory) education of judicial officers and legal practitioners as methods for overcoming reliance on rape myths.[133] The literature also recommends training on trauma-informed practices for all key stakeholders involved in the criminal justice system.[134] The next chapter will consider the legislative 'faith' that has been placed, particularly in recent times, in jury directions to correct misconceptions or rape myths. As the discussion above reflects, while some myths may be more amenable to change through such initiatives, others seem 'unshakeable'. What is to be made of this?

We think that part of the problem lies in how myths are typically understood.[135] While there is nuance in the scholarly literature as well as governmental reports, much of this literature relies on a conception of myth as falsehood. Jury directions

[128] Ellison and Munro 'Better the Devil You Know?' (n 125); Chalmers, Leverick, and Munro (n 126).

[129] Ellison and Munro 'Better the Devil You Know?' (n 125).

[130] Chalmers, Leverick, and Munro (n 126).

[131] Ellison and Munro 'Better the Devil You Know?' (n 125) 314–15; Louise Ellison and Vanessa E Munro, 'Of "Normal Sex" and "Real Rape": Exploring the Use of Socio-Sexual Scripts in (Mock) Jury Deliberation' (2009) 18 Social & Legal Studies 291; Chalmers, Leverick, and Munro (n 126).

[132] Yvette Tinsley, Claire Baylis, and Warren Young, '"I Think She's Learnt Her Lesson": Juror Use of Cultural Misconceptions in Sexual Violence Trials' (2021) 52 Victoria University of Wellington Law Review 463, 470. cf Thomas (n 97).

[133] See, eg, ALRC, *Family Violence* (n 60) chs 25–28; Victorian Law Reform Commission, *Improving the Response of the Justice System to Sexual Offences* (Report 2021) 395–410; ALRC, *Safe, Informed, Supported* (n 65) ch 7.

[134] Amanda-Jane George and others, 'Specialist Approaches to Managing Sexual Assault Proceedings: An Integrative Review' (Australian Institute of Judicial Administration and Commonwealth Attorney-General's Department 2023) 220–21; Eva McKinsey and others, 'Trauma Informed Judicial Practice from the Judges Perspective' (2022) 106 Judicature 34, 39; Anne Murphy and Kate Lumley, 'Trauma-Informed Courts: Guidance for Trauma-Informed Judicial Practices' (Judicial Commission of New South Wales 2022); Women's Safety and Justice Taskforce (Qld), 'Hear Her Voice: Women and Girls' Experiences across the Criminal Justice System' (Report No 2, Queensland Government 2022) recs 27, 28, 66; Haskell and Randall (n 99); Melanie Randall and Lori Haskell, 'Trauma-Informed Approaches to Law: Why Restorative Justice Must Understand Trauma and Psychological Coping' (2013) 36 Dalhousie Law Journal 501.

[135] See Julia Quilter, 'Getting Consent "Right": Sexual Assault Law Reform in New South Wales' (2020) 46 The Australian Feminist Law Journal 225.

become a measure to 'myth bust' or produce more positive or 'truthful' understandings of rape or how complainants respond to rape. There is, however, a second meaning of myth as a traditional story, usually concerning the early history of a society or explaining a natural phenomenon. Barthes analyses the use of the word myth to indicate an excess of significations.[136] For Barthes, myths are 'received' rather than encoded or interpreted, with the audience receiving myths not as a construction of reality but rather as natural or necessary.[137] Myths, in this sense, 'are deeply embedded tropes, narratives and structures for understanding and making sense of the world, often operating in unconscious ways. In terms of sexual relations, senses of male identity, entitlement, possession, authority, desire, lust, power, patriarchy, and so on, have deep historical roots in this more embedded sense of myth'.[138] Jury directions are unlikely to problematize these deeply embodied socio-sexual scripts or gendered heuristics as the mock-jury studies discussed above have also found.

As we will also argue in the next chapter, the legislative forms in which law reform around definitions of consent and the suite of educative jury directions that are being rolled out around the common law world, do not prohibit the very scripting that lies at the heart of prosecution and defence questioning in rape trials. While juries can, and probably do, bring rape myths (and 'real rape' expectations) into the courtroom, they are not the only trial participants to do so. Lawyers (both prosecutors and defence lawyers) carry a large share of the responsibility, as discussed above. Both sides regularly build their cases around the presence/absence of 'real rape' attributes, and in so doing, they further entrench the problematic myths and stereotypes that reform has (ostensibly) attempted to 'write out' of rape trials. We will argue in this book that the most enthusiastically adopted legislative measure for rape myth correction—statutory jury directions, typically given at the end of the trial—may be misguided and far too little too late.

We will also argue that it is an error to conclude that the limited *practical* change in the conduct of rape trials and the associated negative experiences that complainants continue to report (described above), proves that statutory reform doesn't 'work'. In the next chapter, we interrogate very closely what 'progressive' rape law reforms require—and what they leave untouched.

[136] Roland Barthes, *Mythologies* (Annette Lavers tr, Jonathan Cape 1972).
[137] Quilter, 'Getting Consent 'Right'' (n 135) 16.
[138] ibid. See also David J Hayes, 'Are Rape Myths "Myths"'? (2024) 44 Oxford Journal of Legal Studies 156; Conaghan and Russell, 'Rape Myths, Law, and Feminist Research' (n 49).

3

The Australian Rape Law Reform Project Since the 1970s

1. Introduction

The 1970s is commonly identified as the decade when the first steps towards 'progressive' rape law reform were taken, even if in some jurisdictions the resulting legislation was not enacted until the early 1980s. In this chapter, we aim to lay the foundations for our characterization of a 50-year (and counting) statutory reform programme to transform rape law and the rape trial away from their troubled pasts. We sketch an account of the major features of rape law reform over the decades. We focus on the jurisdictions we have studied most closely—NSW and Victoria—but we also give due recognition to selected developments in other states and territories where they have led the way in innovations that have become part of the architecture of 'modernized' rape laws in Australia. Our aim is not to chart every change to the laws governing criminal offences, trial procedure, and rules of evidence over a span of many decades, but to draw attention to a number of noteworthy features—and to provide a foundation for distinguishing between the promise and the reality of change and transformation.

The architecture of rape law reform

We consider it useful to break down the amorphous concept of 'progressive rape law reform' into more discrete categories in terms of the aspect of the laws governing rape trials that have been the focus of legislative attention. This includes: (i) changes to the *substantive definition* of the crime of rape; (ii) changes to the *procedures* governing the conduct of rape trials; and (iii) changes to the *rules of evidence* operative in rape trials. This triptych for understanding what we refer to as the 'architecture' of rape law is not a perfect framework for categorizing all of the ways in which legislatures have sought to influence trials. For example, it doesn't easily accommodate the introduction (and recent exponential growth) of statutory directions designed to educate or 'correct' juries about a range of rape myths and stereotypes. For convenience—and on the basis that jury directions may be seen as

Reforming Rape Trials. Julia Quilter and Luke McNamara, Oxford University Press.
 DOI: 10.1093/9780198948155.003.0003

a 'soft' form of legislative regulation designed to influence how jurors receive, process, and deploy certain types of evidence—we treat them as part of the subset of evidence rule reforms.

The three categories will help us to illustrate the multifaceted nature of statutory reforms and the resulting *architecture* of modernized (or modernizing) rape law. It is important to acknowledge that the language of 'architecture' is a retrospective characterization. It is not meant to suggest a systematic and pre-planned programme of legislation, designed at a point in time and then executed in an orderly sequenced way over the decades. The truth of statutory reform in this area (and many others) has been much more messy, episodic, and unpredictable. Time and again, law-makers have had their attention drawn—by sexual violence prevention advocates and activists and/or media attention around a reported criminal trial—to an unreformed aspect of rape law (broadly defined) or a reform that has failed to meet expectations. Gap-filling, incremental refinement, correction—these have occurred in big ways and small, many times over the years.

By including an element of chronology and periodization in the account offered in this chapter, we hope that, in addition to showing the different *dimensions* of rape offence and trial laws that have been amended, we can also reveal something of the shifts in priority and preoccupation. The pace and scale of change, across substantive, procedural, and evidentiary laws, has been uneven. In most states and territories, the cumulative story of rape law reform over time consists of both relatively sweeping changes to multiple parts of the architecture of rape law,[1] which made changes to substantive, procedural, and evidentiary laws, as well as discrete changes to a single aspect of the law defining the crime of rape or the law governing the conduct of rape trials—such as the prohibition on an unrepresented accused from personally cross-examining the complainant.[2] Some aspects of rape law architecture have been the subject of perennial refinement over the decades, while the attention paid to others has been ephemeral. For example, attempts to align legal and ethical conceptions of consent have occurred at regular intervals over the full 50-year span, from the abolition of 'deemed consent' through marital immunity in the 1970s in some jurisdictions, to a nationwide adoption of 'affirmative consent' as best practice in the 2020s. By contrast, the rules of evidence have remained largely untouched since the 1990s.

Drivers of change

We also want to draw attention to the epistemological, political, normative, and institutional drivers of change. As discussed in Chapter 2, from the 1960s, a range

[1] See, eg, Crimes (Rape) Act 1991 (Vic).
[2] See, eg, Criminal Procedure Amendment (Sexual Offence Evidence) Act 2003 (NSW).

of disciplines created 'new' knowledges about rape by analysing the 'rape situation' through statistical methods. This afforded fresh vantage points for naming the distance between rape as a social phenomenon and rape as a subject of criminal law and criminal trials. We also acknowledge the important role of feminist and lived experience activism (in various forms) as pivotal and recurring influences on statutory change—from the Women's Electoral Lobby (WEL) in the 1970s,[3] to the Reclaim the Night marches that attracted thousands in the 1980s (and continue to this day),[4] to the work of Saxon Mullins and Rape and Sexual Assault Research and Advocacy (RASARA) in the late 2010s,[5] and the March4Justice protests of the early 2020s.[6] The larger objectives behind reform campaigns have been: gender equality in the protections offered by the criminal law (including for married women); respect for the sexual autonomy and bodily integrity of women; a move away from victim blaming, shaming, and retraumatization in criminal trials; and a desire for an accused person's criminal responsibility to be assessed on its merits, without the benefit of deeply gendered and unfair rape myths and stereotypes that shift scrutiny to complainants.

Another dimension of this part of the story is that, unlike many areas of the criminal law which have, for decades, been captive to hurried 'law and order'-style criminal law making, driven by executive government,[7] many of the statutory reforms to rape laws since the 1970s have been derived from evidence-based, deliberative, consultative processes involving independent reviews by law reform commissions or other inquiry bodies. This is so even where a catalyst for reform has been the controversy and activism produced by a single case, the publicity around which signalled larger inadequacies in rape laws at the time. Two recent examples are the non-convictions of the man accused of raping Saxon Mullins—the catalyst for the most recent round of reform in NSW in 2021[8]—and the man accused of raping Brittany Higgins—which prompted a national conversation, a protest movement

[3] Women's Electoral Lobby, 'WEL History' <https://www.wel.org.au/wel_history> accessed 11 July 2025; Marian Sawer, Making *Women Count: A History of the Women's Electoral Lobby in Australia* (UNSW Press 2008).

[4] See, eg, Canberra Rape Crisis Centre, 'Reclaim the Night Canberra 2024—Event Information' (2025) <https://crcc.org.au/reclaim-the-night-canberra-2024-event-information/> accessed 11 July 2025.

[5] Tiffanie Turnbull, 'Saxon Mullins: The Woman Changing Australia's Rape Laws' *BBC News* (Sydney, 2022) <https://www.bbc.com/news/world-australia-61714818>; RASARA, 'About us' <https://www.rasara.org/about> accessed 11 July 2025.

[6] Angela Woollacott and Michelle Staff, 'Friday Essay: Sex, Power and Anger—a History of Feminist Protests in Australia' *The Conversation* (26 March 2021) <https://theconversation.com/friday-essay-sex-power-and-anger-a-history-of-feminist-protests-in-australia-157402> accessed 11 July 2025.

[7] Russell Hogg and David Brown, *Rethinking Law and Order* (Pluto Press 1998); Luke McNamara and others, 'Understanding Processes of Criminalisation: Insights From an Australian Study of Criminal Law-Making' (2021) 21 Criminology and Criminal Justice 387.

[8] Turnbull (n 5).

(March4Justice), and multiple inquiries including a referral that resulted in the Australian Law Reform Commission (ALRC)'s recently released report.[9]

We also recognize that courts—especially appellate courts—have played a part in the changed face of Australia's rape laws over the decades. In some instances, the courts' endorsement of a regressive aspect of rape law,[10] or adoption of a narrow interpretation of a reformed legislative provision,[11] has served to catalyse (further) statutory reform. At other times, the courts have led an aspect of progressive reform (with legislatures later following),[12] or strongly articulated a 'modern' position that speaks to the ethics of reformed laws by rejecting rape myth-based assumptions (and associated grounds of appeal).[13]

Persons accused of rape tend not to feature explicitly in accounts of rape law reform, but it is important to recognize that an abiding influence (constraint) on the contours of rape law reform has been concern to protect the rights of the accused. The challenge has been to respond to the justice demands of feminist activists and victim-survivors—without eroding the presumption of innocence or diminishing the need for the prosecution to establish guilt beyond reasonable doubt.

We think that consideration of all of these drivers is important to understanding why particular problems with the law (and its operation), and particular solutions, were prioritized at different times. As we will see, in the Australian federal context, a further dynamic at play has been the influence of campaigns advanced, and statutory reforms achieved, in other states and territories. Inter-state/territory borrowing has been a recurring feature of rape law reform since the 1970s. (Sometimes the 'source' jurisdiction has been outside the federation, including England and the USA.) Australian jurisdictions are often loosely categorized into 'common law' states and territories (NSW, Victoria, South Australia, and the Australian Capital Territory)—although this label is increasingly a misnomer, given how much of the criminal law in these places (including on rape) is now the product of statute—and 'Code' states and territories (Queensland, Western Australia, the Northern Territory, and Tasmania), where the primary criminal law statute is modelled, to a lesser or greater extent on the Criminal Code produced for Queensland by Sir Samuel Griffith in 1899.[14] To an extent, this divide has been reflected in the pace or focus of rape law reform. Queensland has moved only recently to implement widescale statutory reform, and Western Australia is poised to follow suit following

[9] Australian Law Reform Commission (ALRC), *Safe, Informed, Supported: Justice Responses to Sexual Violence* (ALRC Report 143, 2025).

[10] See, eg, *Mobilio* [1991] VR 339 where 'consent' induced by fraud as to the asserted 'medical' nature of a procedure was regarded as consent.

[11] See, eg, *Lazarus* [2017] NSWCCA 279, where the Court interpreted 'steps' taken to ascertain consent as including thought processes.

[12] See, eg, *Clark* (unreported, NSWCCA, 17 April 1998), defining consent as free and voluntary agreement.

[13] See, eg, *Harper v R* [2022] NSWCCA 211.

[14] Geraldine Mackenzie, 'An Enduring Influence: Sir Samuel Griffith and His Contribution to Criminal Justice in Queensland' (2002) 2 QUT Law Review 53.

the wide-ranging recommendations of a Law Reform Commission of Western Australia (LRCWA) report.[15] The Northern Territory has also tended to be off the pace in the move towards modernized rape laws across the federation,[16] but a report from the Northern Territory Law Reform Committee has recommended that at least some aspects of the modern rape law architecture that has emerged in recent years be adopted—including affirmative consent and educative jury directions.[17] As noted above, instances of statutory reform have sometimes been driven by factors or events local to a particular state or territory, and this has sometimes triggered momentum for change in other states and territories.

Under the Australian Constitution, criminal law statutes are primarily made by legislatures of the six states and two territories. National harmonization has never been achieved for rape law (nor indeed for criminal law generally).[18] However, at intervals over the last 50 years, federal government-level national initiatives have been significant parts of the rape law reform story—from the Royal Commission on Human Relationships (RCHR) (1977)[19] to the ALRC's report on *Safe, Informed, Supported: Reforming Justice Responses to Sexual Violence* (2025).[20] Even without formal harmonization, one thing we attempt to show in this chapter is that, especially in recent years, there has been a growing convergence on the key features, or desirable 'architecture', of a contemporary set of rape laws.

Modes of statutory influence

In this chapter, we look beneath the surface of the progressive rape law reform label, and identify what we introduced in Chapter 1 as the *mode of statutory influence* that different legislative interventions have involved. This is related to the architecture of rape law, introduced above, but of a different order. It is axiomatic that regulation (broadly conceived) through legislation is multi-modal in that it can attempt to influence behaviour and adjudication outcomes in a variety of ways. Legislative styles of influence may be placed on a loose spectrum from coercion at

[15] Law Reform Commission of Western Australia (LRCWA), *Project 113: Sexual Offences* (Final Report, 2023).

[16] By way of illustration, the ALRC noted that the Northern Territory was the only jurisdiction not to have legislated for an absolute prohibition on sexual 'reputation' evidence, and to still use the statutory language of 'chastity': ALRC, *Safe, Informed, Supported* (n 9) 384–85. We note that the Northern Territory has been a leader in allowing for pre-recording of the complainant's evidence: Evidence of Children Amendment Act 2007 (NT).

[17] Northern Territory Law Reform Committee, *Inquiry Into Affirmation Consent in Sexual Offences* (Final Report No 49, 2023).

[18] Arlie Loughnan, '"The Very Foundations of Any System of Criminal Justice': Criminal Responsibility in the Australian Model Criminal Code' (2017) 6 International Journal for Crime, Justice and Social Democracy 8.

[19] Parliament of the Commonwealth of Australia, *Royal Commission on Human Relationships* (Final Report, Australian Government Publishing Service 1977).

[20] ALRC, *Safe, Informed, Supported* (n 9).

one end (including mandates and prohibitions) to non-binding 'regulation' at the other end, where legislation is enacted to inform, guide, and educate. And there is much in between these two extremes.

Legislation can authoritatively change the boundaries of a legal category, such as the definition of a criminal offence. Adjustments to the fault (*mens rea*) element for rape, away from a purely subjective concept of knowledge to include an objective ('reasonable belief') component, provide an example. Legislation can also enable choice by offering a range of acceptable options. For example, complainants may now choose to give evidence in the traditional way (in person in the courtroom) or they may choose to give evidence using alternative arrangements (such as from a remote location via CCTV). The procedure for giving evidence is not mandated. The options are validated (and courts are required to offer them). The complainant is *entitled* to them.

Legislation can also *prohibit*. A clear example of this is the total ban on questions about/evidence of a complainant's sexual 'reputation'.[21] However, as we will show, and contrary to what is often assumed, law-makers have rarely engaged the power to prohibit in the context of rape law reform. Most statutory attempts to modernize or transform rape trials have pursued more subtle and qualified means. Even where strong statutory language is incorporated into substantive offence definitions—such as the 'communicative consent' high-water mark that 'a person does not consent' if 'the person does not say or do anything to communicate consent'[22]—there is no guarantee that the sound ethical values that underpin such language will set the terms of the adversarial contest of the trial. Indeed, one of the curious features of Australian rape law reform to which we draw attention in this chapter is just how much time (and how many words) have been spent trying to legislatively perfect a concept that is not strictly something that the prosecution must prove: consent. Of course, the *absence* of consent *is* an element that must be proven beyond reasonable doubt, and defining what consent is *not* has equally been a law reform obsession—in the form of statutory 'vitiating' factors, discussed below.

There is an important difference between declaratory *disavowal* of rape myths in the courtroom and practices which distress and traumatize complainants (with potential effects on both complainant experience and trial outcome), and *disallowance* of those rape myths and practices. On closer inspection, the story of progressive rape law reform in Australia involves a great deal of the former, and relatively little of the latter. Our focus in this chapter is laying out enough of the detail of multiple statutory amendments over 50 years to substantiate this characterization, and to support the contention that while a reformed statutory provision may be well suited to discursive circulation outside the courtroom (and positively beneficial as

[21] See, eg, Criminal Procedure Act 1986 (NSW), s 294CB(2); Evidence Act 1929 (SA), s 34L(1)(a).

[22] See, eg, Crimes Act 1958 (Vic), s 36AA(1)(a); Crimes Act 1900 (NSW), s 61HJ(1)(a); Criminal Code 1899 (Qld), s 348AA(1)(a).

a means to validate and support the experiences of victim-survivors and educate the wider community about ethical sexual activity), it may be unlikely to prevent rape myths from entering the courtroom or otherwise transform the way in which rape trials are conducted. The implications of this proposition for our overall assessment of whether the project of rape trial transformation-through-law should be regarded as having 'failed' will be explored across the chapters that follow.

2. Influential Events

As we explained in Chapter 2, there were important scholarly precursors to rape law reform activism in the 1970s, including 'new' knowledges from a variety of disciplines that drew attention to the gulf between how the law constructed the offence and the 'reality' of rape (exposing what more recently has been described as the 'epistemic injustice' of criminal laws on rape at the time[23]), and the emergence of powerful feminist critiques of both social and legal constructions of sexual violence. Feminist grassroots organizations and activism also played a hugely important role.[24]

It is not possible to do justice to all the influences that prompted concerted activism and lobbying for rape law reform in Australia. Here we draw attention to five influential events[25] which contributed to country-wide reform momentum in the second half of the 1970s and early 1980s.

The Michigan Criminal Sexual Conduct Act 1974

In the context of the emergent feminist anti-rape movement in the USA, one of the first organizations to 'turn to law'[26] was the Michigan Women's Task Force on Rape, established in 1973. This group was the driving force behind the Criminal Sexual Conduct Act 1974 (Michigan), widely regarded as the first attempt by a common law jurisdiction to effect wholesale reform to sexual offence laws. Key changes included: making the offence (renamed 'criminal sexual conduct') gender neutral; replacing the offence with a series of graded sexual offences; defining force and consent; limiting the rape in marriage immunity; removing the requirement for corroboration; and limiting the admissibility of evidence of the complainant's sexual history.[27] Michigan's legislation was regarded as a radical game-changer at

[23] Emily CR Tilton, 'Rape Myths, Catastrophe, and Credibility' (2024) 21 Episteme 408.

[24] Marilyn Lake, *Getting Equal: The History of Australian Feminism* (Allen & Unwin 1999).

[25] See also Advisory Group on the Law of Rape, 'Report of the Advisory Group on the Law of Rape' (Home Office 1975) which led to the enactment of the Sexual Offences (Amendment) Act 1976 (UK).

[26] Rose Corrigan, *Up Against a Wall: Rape Reform and the Failure of Success* (NYU Press 2013).

[27] Virginia Nordby, 'Reforming Rape Laws—the Michigan Experience' in Jocelynne A Scutt (ed), *Rape Law Reform: A Collection of Conference Papers* (Australian Institute of Criminology 1980);

the time. It embodied two of the main objectives of the rape law reform movement over time: to reduce the burden of scrutiny and judgement traditionally imposed on the complainant, and to shift the focus to the accused's actions and culpability. Michigan's Criminal Sexual Conduct Act 1974 became a popular touchstone for rape legislative reform initiatives in other jurisdictions, including Canada[28] and, as we will see, some Australian jurisdictions.

The Sydney Rape Crisis Collective (1974)

Australia's first rape crisis centre was established in Sydney in 1974 to provide support to women who were victim-survivors of sexual violence:

> Operating at a time where marital rape was legal, workplace sexual harassment and sexism was condoned, and hospitals were unable or unwilling to support victim-survivors, the volunteers at the organisation would drive all over Sydney, picking up women who had suffered abuse. They would then take them to the Sydney Women's Liberation House in Glebe to offer counselling and medical assistance.[29]

It quickly became a model for the establishment of rape crisis centres elsewhere in Australia.[30] In addition to their massive contribution to creating support services for sexual violence victim-survivors, rape crisis centres were (and remain) influential actors in advocacy for criminal law reform.[31]

The Royal Commission on Human Relationships (1977)

Another important influence on the trajectory of law reform in Australia was the RCHR. With broad terms of reference, the Commission held a wide-ranging inquiry into personal and social changes impacting human relationships including,

Kenneth A Cobb and Nancy R Schauer, 'Michigan's Criminal Sexual Assault Law' (1974) 8 Journal of Law Reform 217.

[28] Julian V Roberts and Robert J Gebotys, 'Reforming Rape Laws: Effects of Legislative Change in Canada' (1992) 16 Law and Human Behavior 555.

[29] Olivia Cleal, '"Full Stop to Sexual Violence': Full Stop Australia Commemorates 50 years of Operation' Women's Agenda (2024) <https://womensagenda.com.au/latest/full-stop-to-sexual-violence-full-stop-australia-commemorates-50-years-of-operation/> accessed 11 July 2025.

[30] Sydney Rape Crisis Collective, *Handbook for Rape Crisis Centres* (Everywoman Press 1975).

[31] M Carmody, 'Site of Struggle—The Development of Sexual Assault Services in New South Wales, Australia' (DPhil thesis, University of New South Wales 1995); Suzanne Egan, 'Excavating Feminist Knowledges and Practices in the Field of Sexual Assault Service Provision: An Australian Case Study' (2019) 74 Women's Studies International Forum 169.

in the Final Report, devoting Part VII to 'Rape and Other Sexual Offences'.[32] The RCHR called for a 'completely new approach to sexual offences'[33] and offered an impressive suite of 57 reform recommendations across all three parts of the architecture of rape law.

On the substantive law of rape, the Commission recommended: limiting the marital immunity; broadening 'sexual penetration' to other violating acts; and redefining the offence away from the focus on 'consent' and towards a focus on the unlawful means used to accomplish the act of sexual penetration (eg violence, threats, false pretences). This proposal bore similarities to the Michigan model of graded offences but went further by recommending that sexual offences be dissolved into the criminal law's general assault categories. The procedural and evidentiary reforms recommended by the Commission included: requiring that courts be closed during a complainant's committal evidence; preventing cross-examination on prior sexual acts except with the leave of the judge; prohibiting evidence of the complainant's sexual reputation or moral character; making complaint evidence inadmissible subject to the general rules of evidence; abolishing the corroboration rule; and prohibiting the publishing of material that identified the complainant.

Many of the legislative reforms recommended by the RCHR now form part of Australian rape laws.

The Women's Electoral Lobby (WEL) Draft Bill (1977)

By the time of the RCHR, Australian feminist activists were already advocating for large-scale reform directed at both the substantive laws defining rape and problematic practices of rape trials. In 1977, influenced by the Michigan reforms, and following the publication of the RCHR's Final Report, the Sydney Women's Electoral Lobby (WEL), which had formed in 1972, drafted a report and draft bill that would overhaul the law of rape in NSW and provided it to the NSW Attorney-General.[34] The WEL stated that the Draft Bill was a result of four years of research into the operation of rape laws in Australia, the USA, England, and West Germany.[35] Its main features were: a gender neutral definition including by broadening what amounted to 'sexual intercourse'; adoption of the Michigan model of graded violence-focused offences; a list of 10 types of behaviour by the accused person that could be relied

[32] Parliament of the Commonwealth of Australia (n 19) vol 5, 189–95, 233.

[33] ibid vol 5, 159.

[34] Women's Electoral Lobby, *Women's Electoral Lobby Draft Bill on Sexual Offences and Other Recommendations on Sexual Offences Law Reform* (1977).

[35] New South Wales Department of the Attorney-General and of Justice, Criminal Law Review Division, 'Supplement to the report of the Criminal Law Review Division of the Department of the Attorney-General and of Justice into rape and other sexual offences' (Parliamentary Paper No 250/1976–77) 38.

on to establish a lack of consent (eg use of force or threat of violence, surreptitious administration to the victim of an intoxicating substance, exploitation of a position of authority or trust). The WEL Draft Bill would also make changes to trial procedure including that leave be required to admit sexual history evidence; use of 'paper' committals; the routine use of non-publication orders in relation to the accused and complainant; and the availability of support persons for complainants when giving evidence.

The WEL Draft Bill provided a major impetus for wholescale rape law reform in NSW. Along with work undertaken within the NSW Government by the Criminal Law Review Division,[36] the WEL Bill influenced the first major rape law reform statutes enacted by the NSW Parliament in 1981 (discussed below).

National Conference on Rape Law Reform (1980)

The impetus for a *national* rape reform agenda in Australia was ignited when an alliance between the Australian Institute of Criminology (which had been established in 1973), the Tasmanian Law Reform Commission, and the University of Tasmania Law School, with support from the Governments of Tasmania and NSW, the federal Attorney General, and the NSW Law Foundation,[37] led to the organization of the National Conference on Rape Law Reform. The conference, which took place in Hobart, Tasmania, from 28–30 May 1980, was attended by over 200 people with representation from a range of groups such as the ALP Women's Committee, the WEL, judges, members of the legal profession, women's and victim's advocates, social workers and health workers, government representatives, police officers, and academics. All states and territories were represented, both amongst attendees and in the jurisdiction-specific reform issues addressed in papers presented at the conference.

The stated aim of the conference was to focus on the 'reform of the law of rape; to evaluate changes introduced in some Australian jurisdictions; and to take advantage of the introduction of new laws in the United States'.[38] 16 resolutions were ultimately passed, and these significantly influenced the direction of future reform. Resolution 1 stated:

[36] New South Wales Department of the Attorney-General and of Justice, Criminal Law Review Division, 'Report of the Criminal Law Review Division of the Department of the Attorney-General and of Justice into rape and other sexual offences' (Parliamentary Paper No 249/1976–77); New South Wales Department of the Attorney-General and of Justice, Criminal Law Review Division (n 35).

[37] See Jocelynne A Scutt (ed), *Rape Law Reform: A Collection of Conference Papers* (Australian Institute of Criminology 1980) vi.

[38] ibid vii.

> THIS CONFERENCE AGREES THAT Australian laws and procedures relating to rape and sexual assaults are seriously defective, and should be urgently modified so as to protect the victims of rape, encourage the reporting and prosecution of offences (with concurrent treatment for victims and offenders) and educate the community generally towards condemnation of sexual violence and harassment in all its forms. Such reforms should be consistent with fair protection of the rights of accused persons.[39]

Other resolutions addressed specific questions of substantive law: abolishing the marital immunity; adopting gender-neutral statutory language; introducing graded offences based on levels of violence; and broadening the act beyond sexual penetration. In relation to the laws of evidence, resolutions called for: limitations on the cross-examination of complainants about past sexual behaviour; exclusion of complaint evidence; and abolition of the corroboration warning.

In addition to the resolved matters, the conference also considered: whether courts should be closed during proceedings; whether non-publication orders should be used to protect names of victims; and whether victims should have separate representation, advice and assistance.

Looking back at this national conference, it is striking how much it framed the agenda for rape law reform in the years that followed. For example, in NSW, where the work of the Criminal Law Review Division and the WEL was already underway, the conference had an immediate effect. At the request of the Premier, the NSW Women's Advisory Council produced a position paper based on the conference resolutions.[40] This position paper was used for further consultation, and was the basis for the first significant wave of statutory rape reform in NSW via the Crimes (Sexual Assault) Amendment Act 1981 (NSW).[41] In Tasmania, while the (then) Tasmanian Law Reform Commission had received a reference in 1979 in relation to rape and sexual offences, it was after the National Conference that a consultation paper based on the resolutions was prepared and circulated to stakeholders. The Commission's final report in 1982[42] made 24 recommendations largely based on the Conference resolutions, which led eventually to the passage of the Criminal Code Amendment (Sexual Offences) Act 1987 (Tas).

The rest of this chapter presents an overview of the reformed architecture of rape law that emerged from the late 1970s. The account is not comprehensive but is designed to illustrate key features—across substantive law, procedure, and

[39] ibid xxiii.

[40] New South Wales Women's Advisory Council to the Premier, *Position Paper on Reform of New South Wales Rape Legislation* (1980) 4, 5. The Council further consulted with a range of groups, including the National Council of Women, the Women Lawyers Association, the Country Women's Association, and the Union of Australian Women.

[41] New South Wales, *Parliamentary Debates*, Legislative Assembly, 18 March 1981, 4761, 4758–59 (Neville Wran, Premier).

[42] Tasmanian Law Reform Commission, *Rape and Sexual Offences* (Report No 31, 1982).

evidence—and to draw attention to the *modes of statutory influence* preferred by law-makers.

3. Reforms to Substantive Criminal Law

In the 1970s, in both 'common law' states like NSW and the 'Code states' like Queensland, the definition of the offence was essentially the same: 'carnal knowledge' of a woman (by a man) 'against her will', noting that the latter had begun to be expressed as 'without her consent',[43] even though expectations persisted that this be established by evidence of force and resistance. The act was limited to penile-vaginal penetration and could only be committed by a man against a woman. The prosecution was required to prove that the accused knew that the other person did not consent.[44] Early reform attention was focused on:

(i) the exclusion of forms of sexual violation other than vaginal penetration by a penis (and the associated 'gendered' nature of the definition);
(ii) the marital immunity which denied protection and justice to married women;
(iii) the treatment of non-consent as synonymous with the use of force; and
(iv) the high fault standard of subjective knowledge of the absence of consent.

Gender neutrality and broadening sexual penetration

An early subject of legislative change was the gendered and limited language of 'carnal knowledge'. South Australia was the first jurisdiction to move to broaden the scope of the offence of rape, first by defining 'carnal knowledge' as including penetration of a woman or man's anus,[45] and then by adopting the language of 'sexual intercourse' as the relevant conduct, and defining it to include the insertion of a penis into a person's mouth.[46]

Achieving cross-jurisdictional consistency on this aspect of the substantive law of rape was a slow process.[47] Gender-neutral language that includes penetration of the vagina, anus, or mouth is, however, now a standard feature of the architecture of Australian laws.[48] While it is now firmly entrenched, it is worth noting that the move to legislate gender neutrality did attract some criticism on the basis that the

[43] *Kilby v R* (1973) 129 CLR 460.
[44] *DPP v Morgan* [1976] AC 182.
[45] Criminal Law (Sexual Offences) Amendment Act 1975 (SA).
[46] Criminal Law Consolidation Act Amendment Act 1976 (SA).
[47] ALRC, *Family Violence—National Legal Response* (ALRC Report 114, 2010) 1130–31.
[48] See, eg, Crimes Act 1900 (NSW), s 61HA; Criminal Code 1924 (Tas), s 2B.

approach can 'conceal the fact that *most* sexual harm is gender-based, perpetrated by males against females'.[49]

A crime of violence

In a multi-decade context where incrementalism has been more common than radical change, it is noteworthy that, influenced by the Michigan model, a number of the early Australian law reform proposals advocated a deliberate shift from the sexual nature of the crime towards its violence. For example, in 1981, NSW abolished the common law offence of rape and replaced it with a set of three graded 'sexual assault' offences based on the level of violence inflicted:

- Category 1: inflicting grievous bodily harm with intent to have sexual intercourse;
- Category 2: inflicting actual bodily harm with intent to have sexual intercourse;
- Category 3: sexual intercourse without consent.[50]

A similar suite of violence-focused offences was adopted in the Australian Capital Territory in 1985, in line with the RCHR's recommendations.[51]

The experiment was short-lived in NSW. Evaluations of the 1981 amendments conducted by the NSW Bureau of Crimes Statistics and Research (BOCSAR) identified issues with the operation of the newly amended offence categories.[52] In particular, the majority of cases (approximately 85%)[53] in the post amendment group involved offences where little or no injury was inflicted. Almost three quarters of cases presented to police were instances of sexual intercourse without consent. By comparison, the more serious offences of inflicting actual bodily harm or grievous bodily harm with intent to have sexual intercourse were rarely charged. The focus

[49] Peter R Rush, 'Criminal Law and the Reformation of Rape in Australia' in Clare McGlynn and Vanessa Munro (eds), *Rethinking Rape Law: International and Comparative Perspectives* (Routledge 2010) 237; Elisabeth McDonald, 'Gender Neutrality and the Definition of Rape: Challenging the Law's Response to Sexual Violence and Non-Normative Bodies' (2019) 45 University of Western Australia Law Review 166.

[50] Crimes Act 1900 (NSW), ss 61B–61D; as amended by the Crimes (Sexual Assault) Amendment Act 1981 (NSW) (since repealed).

[51] Crimes Act 1900 (ACT), pt IIIA, as amended by the Crimes (Amendment) Ordinance (No 5) 1985 (Cth). (At the time the Commonwealth Parliament had the power to make criminal laws for the Territories.) See now Crimes Act 1900 (ACT), ss 51–54.

[52] Roseanne Bonney, 'Crimes (Sexual Assault) Amendment Act 1981 Monitoring and Evaluation: Interim Report No 1—Characteristics of the Complainant, the Defendant and the Offence' (New South Wales Bureau of Crime Statistics and Research 1985) 3–4.

[53] ibid 43.

on the level of harm inflicted did not reflect most instances of rape, and had failed to change the focus in trials from the issue of consent.[54]

By the end of the 1980s, NSW legislators had reverted to a three-tiered offence structure: a model that positioned non-consensual sexual intercourse as the primary sexual offence—although the terminology of 'sexual assault' (rather than rape) was retained—with a more serious aggravated sexual assault offence where the non-consensual sexual intercourse was accompanied by inflicted or threatened injury (or other aggravating factors).[55] A less serious offence of 'indecent assault' (now called 'sexual touching') applied to non-consensual sexual contact of a non-penetrative nature. The third tier was the offence of 'act of indecency' (now 'sexual act').[56]

Although terminology and definitions vary, all other Australian jurisdictions have a primary offence of non-consensual sexual intercourse.[57]

Towards a 'modern' concept of consent and non-consent?

We noted in Chapter 2 the development of a body of feminist scholarship that challenged the consent orientation of rape offence definitions, and we have just discussed the adoption of an alternative legislative approach in some jurisdictions, based on the violence employed by the perpetrator. Nonetheless, proving that sexual activity took place in a context where one person was not consenting remains the centrepiece of the law of rape in Australia. Differentiating between consensual and non-consensual sex—as a matter of criminal law and criminal responsibility—has been a preoccupation of law reformers, and the subject of voluminous additions to the statute books. Early (and continuing) progressive reform initiatives focused not on decentring consent, but on clarifying and detailing what the *absence* of consent 'looks' like. From the late 1970s, law-makers began to address the marital immunity, and then to create lists of factors or circumstances which were to be regarded as 'vitiating' consent. These have been incrementally expanded over the decades. Legislative efforts to enact a positive concept of consent began in the late 1980s and were taken up widely in the 1990s and 2000s. Statutory reform to both aspects of consent law has continued through the 2020s.

[54] ibid 42–3. See also Roseanne Bonney, 'Crimes (Sexual Assault) Amendment Act 1981 Monitoring and Evaluation: Interim Report No 2: Sexual Assault—Court Outcomes: Acquittals, Convictions and Sentence' (New South Wales Bureau of Crime Statistics and Research 1985).

[55] See now Crimes Act 1900 (NSW), ss 61I, 61J.

[56] See now ibid ss 61KC, 61KE. The Australian Capital Territory has retained the graded violence-centred offences: Crimes Act 1900 (ACT), ss 51–54.

[57] Crimes Act 1900 (ACT), s 54; Crimes Act 1900 (NSW), s 61I; Criminal Code 1983 (NT), s 192; Criminal Code 1899 (Qld), s 349; Criminal Law Consolidation Act 1935 (SA), s 48; Criminal Code 1924 (Tas), s 185; Crimes Act 1958 (Vic), s 38; Criminal Code 1913 (WA), ss 325–326.

This endeavour has been the subject of numerous statutory amendments over the years, and to do justice to the full details would require a chapter of its own. Instead, we offer an overview of the main priorities in the move to perfect the law that surrounds a key component of the prosecution case in rape trials: proving non-consent.

Marital immunity

One of the earliest focal points of feminist lobbying for reform in the 1970s[58] was the common law marital immunity: a man could not commit the crime of raping his wife.[59] The immunity was essentially a form of deemed consent: a woman was assumed to always consent to sex with her husband, a proposition which was morally and politically intolerable.[60] South Australia was again the first jurisdiction to move on the common law marital immunity, albeit in a very limited way: an accused was only precluded from relying on the presumption of consent if their rape of their wife was aggravated by acts or threats of actual bodily harm, 'gross indecency', or 'calculated' humiliation.[61] Victoria's initial 'abolition' was also partial, applying only to men who were no longer living with their wives.[62] NSW effected a full abolition in 1981.[63] While all states and territories eventually followed, curiously, South Australia was the last Australian jurisdiction to legislate a total abolition of the marital immunity.[64]

'Vitiated' consent (or statutory indicators of non-consent)

The next focus of consent reform focused on subverting event characteristics which had traditionally been assumed to be indicative of consent, and therefore a barrier to proving the element of non-consent. For example, the Crimes (Sexual Assault) Amendment Act 1981 (NSW) added the following provision to the Crimes Act 1900 (NSW): 'a person who does not offer actual physical resistance to sexual intercourse shall not, by reason only of that fact, be regarded as consenting to the sexual intercourse.'[65]

58 This focus was influenced by developments in overseas jurisdictions: eg Criminal Sexual Conduct Act 1974 (Michigan); Sexual Offences (Amendment) Act 1976 (UK).

59 Lisa Featherstone, 'Criminalising the Husband and the Home: Marital Rape Law Reform, 1976-1994' in Alana Piper and Ana Stevenson (eds), *Gender Violence in Australia: Historical Perspectives* (Monash University Publishing 2019).

60 Jocelynne A Scutt, 'Consent to Rape: The Problem of the Marriage Contract' (1977) 3 Monash University Law Review 255.

61 Criminal Law Consolidation Act 1935 (SA), s 73(3)–(5) as amended by the Criminal Law Consolidation Act Amendment Act 1976 (SA) (since amended).

62 Crimes (Sexual Offences) Act 1980 (Vic).

63 Crimes (Sexual Assault) Amendment Act 1981 (NSW); now Crimes Act 1900 (NSW), s 61KA.

64 Criminal Law Consolidation (Rape) Amendment Act 1992 (SA).

65 Crimes Act 1900 (NSW), s 61D(3)(d), since renumbered; now s 61HI(4). In addition, the 1981 reforms listed three other vitiating factors: mistaken identity, mistake about being married, and submission due to threats or terror (the latter of which had a longer history in NSW rape law).

The statutory lists of 'vitiating' factors have grown over time. One such factor is where the victim-survivor was intoxicated at the time of the rape. We single out this particular 'vitiating' factor for more detailed attention here because of our specific interest in how intoxication evidence operates in rape trials—a topic we discuss more fully in Chapter 8.

In 1987, Tasmania became the first Australian jurisdiction to add a person's intoxication as a circumstance that could vitiate consent. The Criminal Code Amendment (Sexual Offences) Act 1987 (Tas) added a new s 2A to the Criminal Code 1924 (Tas) which modified the existing general definition of consent ('consent which is freely given by a rational and sober person so situated as to be able to form a rational opinion upon the matter to which the consent is given') by listing three sets of vitiating factors: force, fraud, or threats; 'being overborne by the nature of position of another person'; and where a person is '*so affected by liquor or drugs* ... as to be incapable of forming a rational opinion ...'[66]

Victoria followed in 1991. In addition to adding a new positive definition of consent (discussed below), the Crimes (Rape) Act 1991 (Vic) included intoxication as one of the circumstances in which consent might be vitiated. In its current form, s 36AA(1)(g) of the Crimes Act (Vic) provides: 'Circumstances in which a person does not consent to an act include ... the person is so affected by alcohol or another drug as to be incapable of consenting to the act.'

In 2007, NSW added a differently worded intoxication provision to its list of consent vitiating factors: 'The grounds on which it may be established that a person does not consent to a sexual activity include ... if the person has sexual intercourse while substantially intoxicated by alcohol or any drug.'[67] In 2021, NSW adopted the Victorian formulation.[68]

Legislatures in all Australian states and territories, except Western Australia, have adopted some form of statutory provision on intoxication as a consent vitiating factor.[69] The LRCWA has recently recommended that intoxication be included in an expanded list of vitiating factors, using the Victorian model of statutory language.[70]

This example of intoxication as a possible vitiating factor offers an opportunity to pause and reflect on the significance of an assumption that has prevailed in rape law reform for decades: that it is possible to *perfect* the statutory account of consent by a list of circumstances where it is deemed to be absent ('vitiated'). While we have sympathy for the strategy of communicating a rich and ethical conception

[66] Emphasis added.

[67] Emphasis added. Crimes Act 1900 (NSW), s 61HA(6)(a), as inserted by Crimes Amendment (Consent—Sexual Assault Offences) Act 2007 (NSW), sch 1 item 1 (since repealed).

[68] See now Crimes Act 1900 (NSW), s 61HJ(1)(c).

[69] For details, see Chapter 8 at p. 171.

[70] LRCWA (n 15) 64.

of consent via criminal law, we have been cautious about assuming that such statements necessarily translate into the realities of everyday rape trials.

Nonetheless, the lists have continued to grow.

The current state of legislative 'best practice' on this aspect of the rape law architecture is illustrated by the changes made to the Criminal Code 1899 (Qld) by the Criminal Law (Coercive Control and Affirmative Consent) and Other Legislation Amendment Act 2024 (Qld), following recommendations from the Women's Safety and Justice Taskforce.[71] This Act made multiple changes to Queensland rape laws, including a 14-entry, 600+ word list of 'circumstances in which there is no consent'.[72] A significant inclusion (and now regarded as an important part of Australia's 'best practice' rape law architecture) is s 348AA(1)(a)—'a person does not consent' if 'the person does not say or do anything to communicate consent'—a version of which was already in place in Victoria,[73] Tasmania,[74] and NSW.[75]

In theory, such a provision—underpinned by the concept of 'communicative consent' and recognition of the 'freeze' response to sexual violence—looks like it could be a game-changer in the way in which the contest over consent is pursued in rape trials. Much will depend on whether prosecutors take up the opportunity that the legislature has provided and whether and how trial judges direct juries on what is involved in proving non-consent. Noting that Victoria is the only jurisdiction with a long history of such a provision, the available evidence from that state is not encouraging. As we explain in Chapters 6 and 7, in the Victorian rape trials we analysed, s 36AA(1)(a) was largely invisible, and complainants were still routinely challenged during cross-examination on why they had not more effectively manifested their asserted non-consent by words and actions. On the defence case, silence and passivity still spoke of consent. Cockburn reached similar conclusions in her study of rape trials in Tasmania.[76]

On a generous reading, increasingly long lists which declare circumstances where consent may previously have been assumed, but are now treated as circumstances of *non*-consent,[77] might be regarded as a positive sign of change. On this

[71] Women's Safety and Justice Taskforce (Qld), 'Hear Her Voice: Women and Girls' Experiences across the Criminal Justice System' (Report No 2, Queensland Government 2022).

[72] Criminal Code 1899 (Qld), s 348AA.

[73] The provision was first introduced in 1991 in the form of a jury direction, and refined over the years. See now Crimes Act 1958 (Vic), s 36AA(1)(a).

[74] Criminal Code 1924 (Tas), s 2A, as amended by the Criminal Code Amendment (Consent) Act 2004 (Tas).

[75] Crimes Act 1900 (NSW), s 61HJ(1)(a), as amended by the Crimes Legislation Amendment (Sexual Consent Reforms) Act 2021 (NSW), When introducing this amendment, the Attorney General said that it 'addresses the issue of the "freeze" response, where a person may not physically or verbally resist an assault. Silence does not mean consent, nor should consent be inferred when a person remains unresponsive. Consent is something which must be actively communicated': New South Wales, *Parliamentary Debates*, Legislative Assembly, 20 October 2021, 7509 (Mark Speakman, Attorney-General).

[76] Helen Cockburn, 'The Impact of Introducing an Affirmative Model of Consent and Changes to the Defence of Mistake in Tasmanian Rape Trials' (DPhil thesis, University of Tasmania).

[77] For a summary, see ALRC, *Safe, Informed, Supported* (n 9) Appendix D, 651–54.

analysis, such lists reflect (and encourage) better informed and more enlightened community attitudes on what should be regarded as *criminal* sexual violence. Legislation of this sort can no doubt be usefully engaged in education campaigns, but our concern in this book is more limited: do they play a role in transforming the conduct of rape trials?

Although there is drafting variability across the Australian jurisdictions, most non-consent lists are now expressed in a way that characterizes the sexual activity as non-consensual if it occurred in one of the listed circumstances. But, for this recharacterization to be realized, at least two things need to happen. The prosecution needs to *engage* the provision, and the prosecution must establish beyond reasonable doubt that the circumstance existed. However, it may be risky to attempt to establish that, for example, the complainant was asleep at the time of sexual penetration (where this is contested) or 'froze'—that is, said or did nothing (where this is contested). In many rape trials, statutory markers of non-consent will not loom as the 'trump card' that they are ostensibly drafted to be. As we will see in the chapters to follow, we found that prosecutors are more likely to attempt to prove the element of non-consent by highlighting traditional (and problematic) manifestations of non-consent (and 'real rape').

Legislating a positive conception of consent

Normally, in a criminal law context, legislation defines elements that must be proven by the prosecution. One of the idiosyncratic features of rape law reform in Australia is that law-makers have attempted to do the opposite. Alongside lists of non-consent factors, legislators have attempted to articulate in statutory form the very thing said to be missing in a sexual encounter that amounts to rape: consent.

While statutory formulations of consent predate the progressive era of rape law reform,[78] the first Australian jurisdiction to design a positive statutory definition of what consent *is*, rather than relying only on a list of circumstances indicative of non-consent, was Victoria. A decade after NSW made major changes in 1981, Victoria introduced its first wide-ranging rape law reform statute: the Crimes (Rape) Act 1991 (Vic). This statute quickly came to be regarded as having set the standard for progressive rape law reform in Australia.[79] One of the notable changes effected by the 1991 Act was the addition of a definition of consent as 'free agreement'[80] (followed by a list of 'circumstances in which a person does not freely agree to an act', of the sort discussed earlier).

In the to-and-fro of NSW and Victoria competing for the mantle of the most progressive rape law reform jurisdiction, this time it was NSW that was slow to

[78] See, eg, Criminal Code 1924 (Tas) s 1, discussed in *R v Schell* [1964] Tas SR 184.

[79] David Brereton, '"Real Rape", Law Reform and the Role of Research: The Evolution of Victorian Crimes (Rape) Act 1991' (1994) 27 Australian and New Zealand Journal of Criminology 74.

[80] Crimes Act 1958 (Vic) s 36 (since amended).

move. It was another 16 years before the Crimes Amendment (Consent—Sexual Assault Offences) Act 2007 (NSW) amended the Crimes Act 1900 (NSW) to expressly provide for a positive definition of consent. In its current form, s 61HI(1) states: 'A person consents to a sexual activity if, at the time of the sexual activity, the person freely and voluntarily agrees to the sexual activity.'[81] The phrase 'free and voluntary agreement' has come to be regarded as the best practice formulation and has been widely adopted.[82] Western Australia will be the last jurisdiction to legislatively enshrine such a definition when it implements the recommendations of the LRCWA's recent report.[83]

On the one hand, it is remarkable that it will have taken more than 30 years for all Australian states and territories to achieve something as elementary as a statutory definition of consent, given that, in its negative form (ie non-consent), this concept is the primary touchstone for defining rape and other sexual offences. On the other hand, while it may well perform an important communicative function outside the courtroom, including in education campaigns,[84] it is not self-evident that this positive statutory definition does progressive work in trials.

In Chapter 6, we will explain that in the rape trials we analysed it was rare for prosecutors to actively engage the concept of 'free and voluntary agreement' in framing the Crown case. We are also equivocal about what effects the long lists of vitiating factors or 'circumstances where there is no consent' have on the conduct of trials. To take just two examples, we will see that evidence that the complainant was highly intoxicated does not necessarily mean that they will be considered 'so affected . . . as to be incapable of consenting.'[85] Further, a statutory edict that a complainant who 'said or did nothing' did not consent will mean little if the prosecution does not engage this statutory 'tool' to make its case,[86] or if the defence contends—contrary to the complainant's account that she 'froze' out of fear and trauma—that she was a willing participant who expressed her consent by words and actions.[87] The argument we will advance further in later chapters of this book, with the aid of analysis drawn from trial transcripts, is that there is very little in the architecture of contemporary rape law in Australia that *prohibits* the (rape myth-laden) narratives that have traditionally dominated rape trial discourse, or that *demands* their recalibration.

[81] We note that by the time this amendment was made the NSW courts had already moved to adopt the consent as 'free and voluntary agreement' formulation: *Clark* (n 12) (Simpson J).
[82] See ALRC, *Family Violence* (n 47) 1150; ALRC, *Safe, Informed, Supported* (n 9) 317.
[83] LRCWA (n 15) 40.
[84] See, eg, 'Consent Can't Wait' (Australian Government, 2024) <https://www.consent.gov.au/> accessed 11 July 2025.
[85] See Chapter 8.
[86] See Chapter 6 at pp. 130–131.
[87] See Chapter 7 at p. 144.

The fault element for rape

From the 1970s, one of the elements of the common law definition of rape that attracted scrutiny was the entirely subjective fault element of *actual* knowledge of the other person's non-consent. Criticism intensified after the House of Lords decision in *DPP v Morgan*,[88] in which it was held that an honest—even if unreasonable—mistaken belief in consent could negative criminal responsibility. Calls began to be made for a statutory adjustment of the fault element so that it incorporated an objective component. This was already the case in the Code jurisdictions. Here, knowledge is not an element of the offence of rape in the way that it is in the common law jurisdictions, and for an accused to avoid conviction on the basis of a mistaken belief in consent, the mistake must be both honest and *reasonable*.[89]

In the common law jurisdictions, the first step was to expand the *mens rea* for rape, extending statutory 'knowledge' to include recklessness (as foresight of the possibility that the other person was not consenting). In NSW, this was part of the first wave of rape law reforms in 1981.[90] The common law jurisdictions were initially reluctant to take the further step of introducing some sort of objective standard, but over time momentum began to shift. Statutory adjustment of the subjective formulation of knowledge or recklessness first took place in NSW in 2007, with Victoria following in 2014.[91] While drafting approaches vary, essentially this hybrid approach to *mens rea* requires the accused to have 'reasonable grounds' for believing that the other person was consenting.[92]

By about 2020, calls for a further refinement of the fault element for rape coalesced around 'affirmative consent' as the new gold standard for statutory reform of the law governing the fault element for rape.[93] Although the phrase is used in a variety of ways in media and scholarly discourse,[94] including as a synonym for communicative consent, in Australian law and law reform discussions it has come to refer more specifically to the obligations of the 'seeker' of consent, with communicative consent aligned to the 'giver' of consent. Although problematic on a variety of fronts—including the highly gendered nature of a sexual event inherent in the distinction, and its incompatibility with the notion of consent as (mutual)

88 [1976] AC 182.

89 See, eg, Criminal Code 1913 (WA), s 24.

90 Crimes (Sexual Assault) Amendment Act 1981 (NSW).

91 See now Crimes Act 1900 (NSW), s 61HK(1)(c); Crimes Act 1958 (Vic), s 36A.

92 See Wendy Larcombe and Others, 'I Think it's Rape and I Think He Would be Found Not Guilty': Focus Group Perceptions of (un)Reasonable Belief in Consent in Rape Law' (2016) 25 Social & Legal Studies 611.

93 Anthony North, 'Legislating Consent in Sexual Relations: How Significant is the Move to Affirmative Consent?' (2023) 48 Alternative Law Journal 5. Some have argued for an even higher standard outside the criminal law context; see, eg, Theodore Bennett, 'Hell Yes?: Enthusiastic Consent as a Legal Standard for Sexual Consent' (2024) 49 Alternative Law Journal 255.

94 Lisa Featherstone and others, *The Limits of Consent: Sexual Assault and Affirmative Consent* (Springer 2024) ch 2; ALRC, *Safe, Informed, Supported* (n 9) 319.

free and voluntary agreement—we apply what has become the conventional usage in Australian law.

As with the complainant-focused 'communicative consent' concept (discussed above), Tasmania is credited with being the first Australian jurisdiction (more than 20 years ago) to attempt to legislate for an expectation of active steps to ascertain whether the other person is consenting.[95] NSW first introduced a version of what is now referred to as 'affirmative consent' in 2007 at the same time that a 'reasonableness' dimension was added to the fault element of 'knowledge'.[96] The Crimes Act 1900 (NSW) was amended to provide that, in determining whether the accused 'knew' that the complainant was not consenting (recalling that this was deemed to include having 'no reasonable grounds' for a belief in consent), the trier of fact must consider 'any steps taken' by the accused to ascertain consent. A narrow reading of this provision by the NSW Court of Criminal Appeal in *Lazarus*,[97] and the subsequent public advocacy of the complainant in this case, Saxon Mullins, catalyzed further change. Not only was the inadequacy of the NSW 'steps taken' formulation exposed, the events sparked a national conversation about sexual violence, the trial experiences of complainants, and the desirability of the law meaningfully reflecting the ethical standards of affirmative consent. They also contributed to another nation-wide rape law reform wave that spanned the next decade, engaging every Australian jurisdiction in some form of inquiry.[98] The idea of 'affirmative consent' has been enthusiastically embraced in multiple jurisdictions, including NSW and Victoria. Section 61HK(2) of the Crimes Act 1900 (NSW) now states: 'a belief that the other person consents to sexual activity is not reasonable if the accused person did not, within a reasonable time before or at the time of the sexual activity, say or do anything to find out whether the other person consents to the sexual activity.'[99]

These recent developments occurred after the timeframe of our trial transcript studies, and so it remains to be seen how legislative reforms based on affirmative consent will be operationalized. We think it will be necessary to distinguish between the symbolic and expressive benefits of legislative endorsement of the ethics of affirmative consent and the work the legislation can realistically be expected to do in rape trials. As part of the framework for assessing criminal responsibility, provisions like s 61HK(2) mean only that if an accused person wants to assert in a trial (whether through their own evidence or by submissions made by their lawyer) that they had a belief in consent that was *reasonable*, that assertion will need to be accompanied by information about something they said or did to

[95] Criminal Code 1924 (Tas), s 14A, as amended by the Criminal Code Amendment (Consent) Act 2004 (Tas).

[96] Crimes Amendment (Consent—Sexual Assault Offences) Act 2007 (NSW).

[97] *Lazarus* (n 11) [168].

[98] For an overview, see ALRC, *Safe, Informed, Supported* (n 9) 8–9, 190, 317.

[99] Crimes Act 1900 (NSW), s 61HK(2). See also Crimes Act 1958 (Vic), s 36A(2).

ascertain consent. We note that in rape trials it is rare for the accused to mount an offence based exclusively on the fault element—that is, that they honestly and reasonably (even if mistakenly) believed the complainant was consenting. In the majority of rape trials, the defence asserts that the sexual activity was consensual. It is therefore unrealistic to expect that the statutory adoption of a form of affirmative consent, even if seen as integral to a new best practice standard for progressive rape law in Australia, will shift the focus of intense scrutiny from the complainant to the accused.

4. Procedural Reforms

From the very beginning of the progressive reform period in Australia (and even before) it was recognized that, in addition to the impacts of substantive offence definitions and evidentiary rules, the *procedures* associated with rape trials were also a source of distress and potential injustice for victim-survivors. Without understating the importance of procedural reforms, in this part of the chapter we want to draw attention to some of the implications of a rape trial reform approach that is oriented towards making the complainant's experience less awful, through accommodations or 'special measures' that sit on top of, without supplanting, the substantive content of the adversarial trial.

The most active periods for legislative reform of this type were the 1990s and 2000s, but procedural reforms have been enacted over the course of the full 50 years since the progressive era began in the 1970s. Changes have sometimes been part of a wide-ranging reform package and sometimes a discrete piecemeal change, including in response to problems illustrated by a specific case.

We organize our discussion around *general* measures that apply in all rape trials, and *specific* measures that might be offered to individual complainants depending on the circumstances of the trial and the evidence that parties seek to admit. In the overview that follows, we draw most of our statutory examples from the two jurisdictions that have been the focus of our empirical work: NSW and Victoria.

General measures

The first legislative moves to improve complainants' experience of rape trials were to protect complainants from adverse publicity, embarrassment, and stigma by protecting their identity and limiting the visibility of their court appearance and testimony to the general public. In the 1970s limited reforms were made in Tasmania, South Australia, Western Australia, and Queensland to enable the court to prohibit the publication of complainants' names; and, in Queensland and Victoria, a power to close the courts during a complainant's evidence was legislated. Over time, a set of standard accommodations has become commonplace and relatively uniform across the country.[100]

Closed courts during a complainant's evidence

In 1991, Victoria introduced a limited discretion to close the courtroom to protect complainants if having an open court would cause 'undue distress or embarrassment' to the complainant.[101] In 1999, NSW embraced *in camera* proceedings, subject only to the court directing otherwise where the complainant consents or there are special reasons in the interests of justice for an open court.[102]

Alternative arrangements for giving evidence

Alternative arrangements for giving evidence—such as from a remote location via CCTV, the use of screens in the courtroom, or special seating arrangements—now operate in most rape trials across Australia. When first introduced in Victoria, the availability of alternative arrangements for witnesses to give evidence in sexual offence proceedings was limited to instances where the court was satisfied that the witness in giving evidence was likely to 'suffer severe emotional trauma' or 'be so intimidated or stressed as to be severely disadvantaged as a witness'.[103] Such arrangements are now generally framed as an *entitlement* rather than requiring the discretion of the court.[104]

Support person

Complainants in NSW have been entitled to have a support person with them while they give evidence since 2005 in NSW,[105] and since 2009 in Victoria.[106] This is now a routine accommodation in all jurisdictions.[107]

Protection of complainant anonymity

Prohibitions on publication of the name of the complainant are one of the core components of the special measures that apply to sexual offence trials. In NSW (since 1987) and Victoria (since 1991), it has been a criminal offence to publish any matter which is likely to identify the complainant.[108]

[100] See generally, ALRC, *Safe, Informed, Supported* (n 9) 416.

[101] Crimes (Sexual Offences) Act 1991 (Vic). See now Open Courts Act 2013 (Vic), s 30(2)(d).

[102] Crimes Legislation Amendment (Sentencing) Act 1999 (NSW). See now Criminal Procedure Act 1986 (NSW), s 291.

[103] Crimes (Rape) Act 1991 Act (Vic), s 37C. See now Criminal Procedure Act 2009 (Vic), s 360.

[104] See, eg, Criminal Procedure Act 1986 (NSW), s 294B(3).

[105] Criminal Further Amendment (Evidence) Act 2005 (NSW). See now Criminal Procedure Act 1986 (NSW), s 294C.

[106] Criminal Procedure Amendment (Consequential and Transitional Provisions) Act 2009 (Vic); see now Criminal Procedure Act 2009 (Vic), ss 360(c), 365.

[107] See ALRC, *Safe, Informed, Supported* (n 9) 416.

[108] Crimes (Personal and Family Violence) Amendment Act 1987 (NSW); see now Crimes Act 1900 (NSW), s 578A. Crimes (Sexual Offences) Act 1991 (Vic); see now Judicial Proceedings Reports Act 1958 (Vic), s 4(1A).

Specific measures

Prohibition on personal cross-examination by the accused

In all jurisdictions, there is a statutory prohibition to protect complainants from being personally cross-examined by the accused—in the relatively rare case where the accused is unrepresented. This is an interesting example of a phenomenon that has occurred at intervals over the years: a single trial that brings to attention an aspect of the conduct of rape trials that imposes an unreasonable burden on the complainant; it catalyses prompt reform in the jurisdiction in question; the reform becomes part of the expected architecture of modern rape law; and, over time, the reform is taken up by all or most of the other Australian jurisdictions.[109] Legislation now provides that the complainant cannot be cross-examined or re-examined by the accused but may be examined by a person appointed by the court.[110]

'Re-use' of complainant's evidence at retrial

In 2005, NSW legislated to allow a recording of the complainant's trial evidence to be used at a retrial rather than require the complainant to endure the ordeal of having to give evidence a second time.[111] This measure was also triggered by a single high-profile case (in which the complainant indicated that she could not face giving evidence at a planned retrial),[112] and has now been adopted in some form in all jurisdictions.[113]

Considering procedural reform

Procedural reforms have been welcome and important—and net contributors to an improved complainant experience (and enhanced process justice). However, it is important to recognize their limitations in terms of the ambitious goals of *transforming* rape trials. For complainants, the intensity of the experience of giving evidence is likely to mediated by some of these measures (such as giving evidence from a remote location via CCTV), and this can reduce traumatization. However, the substantive nature of the interrogation to which complainants are exposed is

[109] For details of this story, which began in NSW, see New South Wales Law Reform Commission, *Questioning of Complainants by Unrepresented Accused in Sexual Offence Trials* (Report No 101, June 2003); Criminal Procedure Amendment (Sexual Offence Evidence) Act 2003 (NSW). See also ALRC, *Safe, Informed, Supported* (n 9) 368.

[110] See Criminal Procedure Act 1986 (NSW), s 294A; Criminal Procedure Act 2009 (Vic), s 356.

[111] Criminal Procedure Amendment (Evidence) Act 2005 (NSW). See now Criminal Procedure Act 1986 (NSW) pt 5, div 3-4.

[112] *Skaf (Bilal) and Skaf (Mohammed)* [2004] NSWCCA 37; see Lisa Davies, 'What We Learnt from Skaf Case' *The Sydney Morning Herald* (2013) <https://www.smh.com.au/national/nsw/what-we-learnt-from-skaf-case-20130118-2cyma.html> accessed 11 July 2025.

[113] See, eg, Criminal Procedure Act 2009 (Vic) pt 8.2, div 7; see ALRC, *Safe, Informed, Supported* (n 9) 282.

unaltered by procedural reforms. This is not because the procedural reforms have 'failed'. The evidence we present in Chapter 5 suggests that they are mostly operating as intended. Rather, it is because they have not been designed to alter the substance of the trial event. *That* requires recalibration of the rules of evidence—and the boundaries of permissible examination and cross-examination which they set. It is to this third part of the architecture of rape law reform to which we now turn.

5. Reforming Evidence Rules

If the starting point for substantive offence reform in the 1970s was a very immature and qualified concept of consent (and non-consent), considered to be 'redeemable', the first priority of the push to modernize *evidence rules* was to undo extant special rules that operated to the disadvantage of complainants and created barriers to successful prosecution. As we explained in Chapter 2, the default position at common law had long been that the evidence of (female) rape complainants was inherently suspect, reflecting a deep-seated distrust of women as perverse liars prone to making false allegations which threatened innocent men.[114] Three rules were most significant:

- the requirement for 'prompt complaint' on the basis that 'delayed' complaint signified that the woman's testimony was unreliable, and the need for a warning if the complainant's report was not made immediately;
- the need for 'corroborative evidence' (ie evidence independent of the complainant) without which the judge was required to give a warning to the jury about the dangers of convicting on the woman's testimony alone because of the 'ease' of making a rape accusation; and
- the 'twin myths'[115] of sexual 'reputation' evidence and sexual history evidence (that would otherwise have been regarded as irrelevant and/or hearsay) was admissible because sexual 'reputation' was deemed relevant to consent and reliability, and sexual experience with the accused was understood as relevant to consent. Sexual experience evidence with other persons was relevant to credibility. The common law premise was that only the 'good' or 'chaste' complainant was believable (or could be raped).

[114] Julia Quilter, 'Re-Framing the Rape Trial: Insights From Critical Theory About the Limitations of Legislative Reform' (2011) 35 The Australian Feminist Law Journal 23; Julia Quilter, 'Rape Trials, Medical Texts and the Threat of Female Speech: The Perverse Female Rape Complainant' (2015) 19 Law Text Culture 231.

[115] *Bull v The Queen* (2000) 201 CLR 443, 457–58.

As discussed in Chapter 2, these rules were major contributors to why complainants often felt like *they* were on trial, describing the experience of giving evidence as a 'second rape'.

Moves to limit the use of complainant sexual 'reputation' and experience evidence in rape trials (widely referred to as 'rape shield' laws) were amongst the earliest statutory reform events in Australia, influenced again by Michigan's Criminal Sexual Conduct Act 1974. In 1976, Western Australia legislated to provide that no evidence as to the complainant's sexual history, disposition, or reputation could be adduced, by way of cross-examination or otherwise, without the leave of the court.[116] Victoria, South Australia, and Tasmania were also early movers on this aspect of rape law reform.[117]

Given these early moves, and the attention paid to this aspect of rape law by the RCHR,[118] it is unsurprising that the topic of evidence rules was prominently discussed at the National Conference on Rape Law Reform in 1980. It is noteworthy that rape shield laws were just one of the options considered for addressing the unfairness of complainants being cross-examined about their sexual histories. The National Conference also considered: whether complainants should be subject to cross-examination at all; whether complainants should have separate representation, advice, and assistance; and whether questions related to sexual behaviour should be prohibited on the grounds that the breadth of a person's sexual experience has no bearing on truthfulness.[119] Of these options, rape shield laws have been adopted as the primary mechanism for excluding (certain types of) rape myth-based evidence from rape trials.

As noted earlier, all Australian jurisdictions except the Northern Territory have legislated an outright prohibition on evidence about the complainant's so-called sexual 'reputation'.[120] In the next part of this chapter we review the laws that restrict the admissibility of evidence of a complainant's sexual history or experience.

Restrictions on sexual experience evidence

Most states and territories have adopted what has been described as a 'discretionary' leave model:

116 Evidence Act Amendments Act (No 1) 1976 (WA).

117 Rape Offences (Proceedings) Act 1976 (Vic); Evidence Act Amendment Act 1976 (SA); Evidence Act (No 3) 1976 (Tas).

118 Parliament of the Commonwealth of Australia (n 19) para 27.

119 Scutt, *Rape Law Reform* (n 37) 214.

120 See, eg, Criminal Procedure Act 1986 (NSW), s 294CB(2); Criminal Procedure Act 2009 (Vic), s 341.

> These discretionary models generally consist of a presumptive prohibition, an enhanced relevance test, and a threshold for leave (including a non-exhaustive list of factors which need to be considered when assessing whether that threshold has been met).[121]

Under this model, illustrated by the Criminal Procedure Act 2009 (Vic), Pt 8.2, Div 2, the judge retains a residual discretion to admit the evidence (or allow the questioning designed to adduce it).[122] The court must not grant leave for the evidence to be admitted:

> ... unless it is satisfied that the evidence has substantial relevance to a fact in issue and that it is in the interests of justice to allow the cross-examination or to admit the evidence, having regard to—
> (a) whether the probative value of the evidence outweighs the distress, humiliation and embarrassment that the complainant may experience as a result of the cross-examination or the admission of the evidence, in view of the age of the complainant and the number and nature of the questions that the complainant is likely to be asked; and
> (b) the risk that the evidence may arouse in the jury discriminatory belief or bias, prejudice, sympathy or hostility; and
> (c) the need to respect the complainant's personal dignity and privacy; and
> (d) the right of the accused to fully answer and defend the charge.[123]

The NSW model, first introduced in 1981,[124] is regarded as the most restrictive of Australia's rape shield laws—described by the ALRC as an 'exclusionary' model.[125] Under the regime established by s 294CB of the Criminal Procedure Act 1986 (NSW), admission of sexual experience is prohibited,[126] unless its subject matter falls within one of the legislative 'gates'[127] *and* 'the probative value of the evidence outweighs any distress, humiliation or embarrassment that the complainant might suffer as a result of its admission'.[128] The prima facie *prohibition* on sexual experience evidence and the absence of a residual discretion to admit, has attracted criticism[129] and calls for statutory amendment, but, to date, successive NSW Governments have preferred to leave the legislation in place.

[121] ALRC, *Safe, Informed, Supported* (n 9) 387.
[122] Criminal Procedure Act 2009 (Vic), s 342.
[123] ibid s 349. For an overview of other jurisdictions, see ALRC, *Safe, Informed, Supported* (n 9) 385–87.
[124] Crimes Act 1900 (NSW), s 409B (since relocated), as amended by the Crimes (Sexual Assault) Amendment Act 1981 (NSW).
[125] ALRC, *Safe, Informed, Supported* (n 9) 387.
[126] Criminal Procedure Act 1986 (NSW), s 294CB(3).
[127] See ibid s 294CB(4)(a)–(f).
[128] ibid s 294CB(4).
[129] See, eg, *M v R* (1993) 67 A Crim R 549; *Jackmain v R* [2020] NSWCCA 150.

The strong NSW model of rape shield law has come to be regarded as the Australian high-water mark of legislative attempts to rewrite the rules of the rape trial. It was something of a shock, then, when in 2025 the ALRC—in the context of an inquiry primarily motivated by a desire to improve the quality of justice delivered to victim-survivors of sexual violence—recommended that the NSW rape shield laws should be wound back and replaced by a 'discretionary' leave model.[130]

In Chapter 5, we share our findings on how the current laws have been operating in NSW, which provide a basis for challenging the characterization of the NSW rape shield law model as having gone 'too far'. Here, we draw attention to the wider implications of the ALRC's recommendation. If it was implemented, it would be the first time, to our knowledge, that a component of the architecture of progressive law reform had been undone. We think it is telling that this proposal relates to one of the few aspects of *evidence law* that has been the subject of progressive reform, and underscores long-standing resistance to altering the fundamental rules that govern rape trials. The wind-back recommendation also speaks to something that has been insufficiently acknowledged in the literature on rape law reform: the tendency to treat the rights of the accused as inherently in tension with attempts to restrict the sorts of evidence that can be relied upon in rape trials to challenge the veracity of the complainant's allegation. In our assessment, this construction has contributed to a general reluctance to exclude evidence—even where it is underpinned by discredited rape myths and stereotypes. In this respect, sexual history evidence, and evidence of counselling communications (which we turn to next) are the exceptions. Other rape myth-informed evidence has not been the subject of legislative reform to prohibit or restrict its admission. Instead, lawmakers have preferred more benign modes of statutory influence: most notably, arming trial judges with educative jury directions to balance or 'neutralize'[131] the impact of rape myth-based evidence on jury deliberations and decision-making. We consider this rapidly expanding component of the modern architecture of Australia's rape laws in the final part of this chapter.

Counselling communications privilege

A decade or so into the progressive rape law reform era, a new challenge began to emerge. Defence lawyers began to seek access to records of counselling sessions

[130] ALRC, *Safe, Informed, Supported* (n 9) 387.

[131] This term is adopted from judicially endorsed language to describe the intended effect of another (analogous) technique to address myths and misconceptions—counter-intuitive expert evidence: see *Jacobs v R* [2019] VSCA 285 and *MA v R* (2013) 40 VR 546, referring to the following passage from New Zealand Law Commission, *Evidence: Evidence Code and Commentary* (Report No 55, vol 2, 1999) 67: 'The purpose of such evidence is to restore a complainant's credibility from a debit balance because of jury misapprehension, back to a *zero or neutral balance*' (emphasis added).

that the complainant may have had with a rape crisis centre or other health service. Cossins described the practice as 'an alternative way of obtaining access to the same type of "bad character" evidence that rape shield provisions were designed to address . . . .'[132] In response to lobbying from rape crisis and victim support organizations, law-makers began to enact legislation which restricted access to admission of such evidence. All Australian jurisdictions have legislated for some form of qualified privilege in relation to communication records, which have been modified and improved over time.[133] For example, in NSW and Victoria, courts are required to ensure that the complainant is aware of the provisions and is given a reasonable opportunity to seek legal advice.[134] Unusually (but entirely appropriately) in the rape trial context, the complainant has standing to appear in proceedings to determine an application for access to records.[135]

Improper questions

All Australian jurisdictions have introduced legislation designed to prevent the asking of 'improper' questions during cross-examination, more or less based on s 41 of the Uniform Evidence Law.[136] Although not originally designed as a rape law reform measure, the 'improper question' mechanism for controlling questioning came to be seen as an important measure for improving the complainant's experience of giving evidence (or, to use the language we have adopted in his book, to enhance process justice). In NSW, legislation was strengthened for precisely this reason. When introducing the bill that became the Criminal Procedure Further Amendment (Evidence) Act 2005 (NSW), the NSW Attorney General, Bob Debus, noted that the reforms were important 'because improper questions asked of them in cross-examination are one of the most distressing aspects of the court process for sexual assault complainants.'[137]

[132] Anne Cossins, 'Contempt or Confidentiality?: Counselling Records, Relevance and Sexual Assault Trials' (1996) 21 Alternative Law Journal 223, 223.

[133] Criminal Procedure Act 1986 (NSW), pt 5, div 2; Evidence (Miscellaneous Provisions) Act 1958 (Vic), pt II, div 2A. See generally ALRC, *Safe, Informed, Supported* (n 9) 374–75.

[134] Criminal Procedure Act 1986 (NSW), s 299; Evidence (Miscellaneous Provisions) Act 1958 (Vic), s 32CD.

[135] Criminal Procedure Act 1986 (NSW), s 299A; Evidence (Miscellaneous Provisions) Act 1958 (Vic), s 32CE. Legal Aid NSW has established a Sexual Assault Communications Privilege Service (SACPS) to provide legal advice and representation to complainants in relation to the privacy of their counselling records: Legal Aid New South Wales, 'Sexual Assault Communications Privilege Service' <https://www.legalaid.nsw.gov.au/my-problem-is-about/victims-rights/victims-support-scheme/sexual-assault-communications-privilege-service> accessed 11 July 2025. In addition, the service provides education to increase the awareness of the privilege in the legal and medical professions.

[136] See ALRC, *Safe, Informed, Supported* (n 9) 358–63. See also ALRC, *Uniform Evidence Law* (ALRC Report No 102, 2005) 144–57.

[137] New South Wales, *Parliamentary Debates*, Legislative Assembly, 23 March 2005, 14900 (Bob Debus, Attorney General).

A question is 'improper' (and a 'disallowable question') if it is 'misleading or confusing'; 'unduly annoying, harassing, intimidating, offensive, oppressive, humiliating or repetitive'; put in a 'tone that is belittling, insulting or otherwise inappropriate'; or 'has no basis other than a stereotype'.[138]

Provisions like s 41 are an interesting mode of statutory influence. In the Uniform Evidence Act formulation that applies in NSW and Victoria, the wording ('must disallow') suggests that the legislature has imposed something akin to a statutory obligation to *prohibit* offending questions. The *potential* for statutory restrictions on improper questions to change the nature of rape trial cross-examination of complainants is evident, and this is significant in a context where law-makers have generally been disinclined to restrict the types of evidence admitted in rape trials. On one (admittedly ambitious) reading of s 41, it might be said that judges have an obligation to disallow questions that have no basis other than a rape myth (stereotype)—such as that a 'genuine' victim-survivor of sexual violence complains immediately, or that there is a 'correct' way for a person to behave after a rape. To date, there is little evidence that s 41 has been used in this way,[139] a conclusion which is also supported by the findings we present in Chapter 7.

From warnings that evoked rape myths to jury directions that 'correct' them

We have left until last the aspect of the architecture of rape laws in Australia which has arguably undergone the most dramatic transformation—the guidance offered by trial judges to juries. As noted earlier in this chapter, in the 1970s, judges were effectively required to *reinforce* rape myths and systemic biases against complainants by warning jurors: about the danger of convicting on the basis of the uncorroborated evidence of the complainant; that any 'delay' in complaint could provide a basis for weakening the credibility of the complainant; and that 'inconsistencies' in the accounts provided by the complainant at different points might raise doubts about the veracity of the allegation. 50 years later, most Australian jurisdictions have introduced a long list of statutory directions that *correct* rape myths of this type. At a discursive level, and with reference to the wider symbolic, communicative, and educative functions of the criminal law,[140] this represents a massive reversal in the law's relationship to rape myths. However, in terms of transforming

[138] See Evidence Act 1995 (NSW), s 41; Evidence Act 2008 (Vic), s 41.

[139] See Anne Cossins, *Closing the Justice Gap for Adult and Child Sexual Assault: Rethinking the Adversarial Trial* (Palgrave Macmillan 2020) 432; ALRC, *Safe, Informed, Supported* (n 9) 363.

[140] See generally RA Duff, *Punishment, Communication and Community* (OUP 2000); James Chalmers and Fiona Leverick, 'Fair Labelling in Criminal Law' (2008) 71 Modern Law Review 217; Cass Sunstein, 'On the Expressive Function of Law' (1996) 144 University of Pennsylvania Law Review 2021.

rape trial practice, there is a sting in the tail of this mode of statutory influence, as we will explain.

Corroboration

Abolition of the traditional corroboration warning was recommended by the RCHR in 1977, identified as a priority at the National Conference in 1980, and was the subject of rape law reform from the 1980s.[141] Over time legislation evolved from *declaring* that the old common law direction was no longer required, to *prohibiting* the giving of such a direction.[142] In Chapter 9, we report findings which suggest that, despite the strong legislative language, a version of the corroboration warning (the so-called 'single witness' warning) was observable in some of the NSW trials we analysed.

'Delay'

Australia's first corrective jury direction for sexual offence trials was introduced in NSW in 1981.[143] It was designed to educate the jury about how they should (and should not) consider evidence that suggested the complainant did not complain at the first opportunity. The trial judge was required to advise the jury that the absence of a complaint or a 'delayed' complaint did 'not necessarily indicate that the allegation that the offence was committed is false', and that 'there may be good reasons' why a person might hesitate or refrain from complaining.[144]

Differences in accounts

Interestingly, it would be another several decades before law-makers turned again to the corrective jury direction as a method for reducing the influence of rape myths in trials. In the mid-2010s, the Parliament of Victoria introduced a jury direction to question an assumption which has been a core feature of criminal trials (including rape trials) for a long time: that differences (or 'inconsistencies') in the accounts given by a witness at different times were indicative of fabrication.[145] In essence, the direction advises the jury that this is not necessarily so. At the time of its introduction, the new direction was described by the Victorian Attorney

[141] Eg Crimes (Sexual Offences) Act 1980 (Vic); Crimes (Sexual Assault) Amendment Act 1981 (NSW); Acts Amendment (Sexual Assaults) Act 1985 (WA).

[142] Eg Criminal Procedure Act 1986 (NSW), s 294AA; Evidence Act 2008 (Vic), s 164(4).

[143] Crimes Act 1900 (NSW), s 405B(2) (since relocated), as amended by the Crimes (Sexual Assault) Amendment Act 1981 (NSW).

[144] See now Criminal Procedure Act 1986 (NSW), s 294; and Jury Directions Act 2015 (Vic), s 52. For an overview of laws in all Australian jurisdictions, see Julia Quilter, Luke McNamara, and Melissa Porter, 'The Most Persistent Rape Myth? A Qualitative Study of 'Delay' in Complaint in Victorian Rape Trials' (2023) 35 Current Issues in Criminal Justice 4, 5.

[145] Jury Directions Act 2015 (Vic), s 54D, amended by the Jury Directions and Other Acts Amendment Act 2017 (Vic).

General as an important amendment to assist in dispelling the myth 'that a real victim would remember all the details of an offence, and describe that offence consistently each time, to any person, in any context'.[146] NSW followed suit in 2018.[147]

On the face of it, this was a textbook example of evidence-based law reform. The messages contained in legislation were updated to reflect what is known in the scientific literature about memory, recall, and trauma[148]—instead of allowing the law and its practices to embody unquestioned but deeply problematic gendered assumptions and misconceptions, and to impose unfair expectations on complainants giving evidence. In Chapter 9, we share our findings on the operation of this direction.

Recent expansion of jury directions

Enthusiasm for statutory jury directions as a 'solution' to the continued circulation and influence of rape myths in trials has notably increased in recent years. In 2021, NSW added five new directions to the two already in existence.[149] In 2022, Victoria added a similar suite of new directions to those already contained in the Jury Directions Act 2015 (Vic).[150] Also in 2022, South Australia significantly expanded the scope of directions relating to consent contained in the Evidence Act 1929 (SA).[151] In 2024, Queensland, a jurisdiction which had never before enacted a statutory jury direction for sexual offence trials, added nine directions to the Evidence Act 1977 (Qld).[152]

The momentum continues. Western Australia and the Northern Territory are expected to introduce a suite of directions soon,[153] and the ALRC has recently recommended that:

[146] Victoria, *Parliamentary Debates*, Legislative Assembly, 22 February 2017, 298 (Martin Pakula, Attorney General).

[147] Criminal Procedure Act 1986 (NSW), s 293A, as amended by the Criminal Legislation Amendment (Child Sexual Abuse) Act 2018 (NSW).

[148] Lori Haskell and Melanie Randall, 'The Impact of Trauma on Adult Sexual Assault Victims' (Justice Canada 2019) 23; Katrin Hohl and Martin A Conway, 'Memory as evidence: How Normal Features of Victim Memory Lead to the Attrition of Rape Complainants' (2017) 17 Criminology & Criminal Justice 248, 261–62; Ronald P Fisher, Martine Powell, and Haley Dawson, 'Inconsistency, Omissions and Confidence as Indicators of the Accuracy of Sexual Assault Victim's Recollections' in Nadine Deslauriers-Varin and Craig Bennell (eds), *Criminal Investigations of Sexual Offenses* (Springer International Publishing 2021).

[149] Criminal Procedure Act 1986 (NSW), pt 5, div 1, sub-div 3, as amended by the Crimes Legislation Amendment (Sexual Consent Reforms) Act 2021 (NSW).

[150] See the Jury Directions Act 2015 (Vic), pt 5, divs 1–5, as amended by the Justice Legislation Amendment (Sexual Offences and Other Matters) Act 2022 (Vic).

[151] Evidence Act 1929 (SA), s 34N, as amended by the Statutes Amendment (Stealthing and Consent) Act 2022 (SA).

[152] Evidence Act 1977 (Qld), pt 6B, div 3, as amended by the Criminal Law (Coercive Control and Affirmative Consent) and Other Legislation Amendment Act 2024 (Qld). See also Evidence (Miscellaneous Provisions) Act 1991 (ACT), ss 80B–80C.

[153] LRCWA (n 15) ch 10; Northern Territory Law Reform Committee (n 17) ch VI.

> The Standing Council of Attorneys-General should establish an appropriately funded expert multi-disciplinary working group to produce a model bill containing judicial directions to address myths and misconceptions in sexual offence trials, to be enacted by each state and territory (the Model Jury Directions Bill).[154]

As things stand, although there is inter-jurisdictional variation, jury directions in Australia cover a broad range of topics. In addition to statutory directions on substantive offence elements (such as those on consent and 'reasonable belief in consent' in Victoria[155]), the following rape myth 'corrections' are offered in one or more jurisdictions:

- non-consensual sexual activity may occur in different circumstances, including between people who know each other, are married, or in a relationship;
- non-consensual activity can occur in many circumstances and is not always perpetrated by a stranger in a public area;
- non-consensual sexual activity may occur between people who are of the same or different sexual orientation, and people of any gender identity;
- non-consensual sexual activity may occur between people who have previously had consensual sex of the same or a different kind;
- a person is not to be regarded as having consented because they 'froze', or did not say or do anything to indicate that they did not freely and voluntarily agree;
- there is no typical, normal, or proper response to non-consensual sexual activity;
- a person is not to be regarded as having consented because they did not verbally or physically resist;
- the absence of violence or injury or threats is not indicative of consent or a lack of truthfulness;
- none of the following provide a basis for assuming a person consented to sexual activity: a person's appearance, clothing, alcohol/drug use, location, flirtatious conduct, or employment as a sex worker;
- continuation of a relationship, or post-event communication with the accused does not necessarily mean the allegation is false;
- differences in a complainant's account are common and not necessarily indicative of a lack of truthfulness;
- there may be good reasons for 'delayed' complaint and this is not necessarily indicative of fabrication; and

[154] ALRC, *Safe, Informed, Supported* (n 9) 253.
[155] Jury Directions Act 2015 (Vic), ss 46–47.

- trauma effects people in different ways, and the presence or absence of emotion or distress is not necessarily indicative of a lack of truthfulness.

It is, of course, too early to predict how the availability of newly created jury directions will impact on the operation of rape trials. In Chapter 9, we report our findings on the operation of the *two* directions that were operative in NSW and Victoria at the time of our transcript studies (ie the 'delay' direction, and the differences in account direction). Here we caution against overstating the capacity of jury directions to transform rape trials. Jury directions represent a deliberately cautious *mode of statutory influence* on rape trials. Jury directions prohibit nothing; they seek to guide and educate, and balance or *neutralize* the rape myths that may still underpin much of the evidence that is adduced in trials. Juries are told only that a particular circumstance or aspect of the complainant's behaviour does not *necessarily* ('of itself') indicate consent or falsity. Juries are *not precluded* from relying on the evidence of that circumstance or behaviour to conclude that the complainant consented and is now lying—and lawyers are not prevented from inviting this conclusion.

Part of the appeal of jury directions, we suggest, is that they are relatively palatable to all parties and stakeholders. They contain powerful messages that have been voiced by victim-survivors and sexual violence support services and prevention advocates for decades, and which are consonant with scientific expert knowledge. And yet they place no restrictions on the admissibility of any type of evidence, including questions in cross-examination that evoke the very rape myths that the direction purports to 'correct' or 'balance' or 'neutralize'. If law-makers had sought to *prohibit* such questions, a hostile reaction from parts of the legal profession (and the judiciary) could have been anticipated. Jury directions steer a middle course. Whether they are a vehicle for rape trial transformation in the direction of enhanced process justice and outcome justice for victim-survivors of sexual violence is open to debate.

6. Conclusion

Although rape laws in Australia have never been harmonized across the federation, and there are still inter-jurisdictional differences, the law reform momentum is clear and strong: all states and territories have moved, or are in the process of moving, to a common architecture of modern or progressive rape law. In some respects, this architecture is an impressive achievement. If the significance of 50 years of statutory reform was measured in terms of the number of words added to (or changed in) legislation, there could be no denying the enormity of Australia's rape law reform programme since the 1970s. Even if the assessment was undertaken on the more discerning basis of sentiments and values expressed 'then and now', a positive assessment could still be sustained. The messages contained in the contemporary statute books of most of Australia's states and territories—explicit and implicit—are undeniably more positive than they were compared to those embedded in the common law and legislation five decades ago. Knowledge now resides in legislation that more accurately understands the nature of sexual violence and which is less judgmental of people who make accusations of sexual violence and who turn to the criminal law and the courts for justice. But if the evaluation is more sharply focused on the extent to which legislation *demands* that the rape trial be conducted differently, in line with the *ethics* of modern legislation, a much more qualified picture emerges. The empirical findings presented in this book provide support for this subdued assessment of what has been achieved through statutory reform to date.

Where new ways are *required*, they are largely about the procedures (and civility) by which trials are conducted. This, we suggest, is largely a *veneer* of progressive change rather than a deep transformation of the nature of the rape trial contest. Modernized rape laws are more edifice than transformative architecture. The large majority of rape myths and stereotypes that have traditionally been engaged to impede access to justice for victim-survivors are as welcome as ever in contemporary rape trials.

Complainants now have access to *procedural* arrangements that will temper the distress of the ordeal. The *substantive* definition of the offence of rape has been thoroughly overhauled, including embracing the concepts of communicative and affirmative consent. But the plain truth is that these improvements were never designed to dramatically change the *evidence* in rape trials, or prevent parties from engaging rape myths to advance their position. In theory, they may reorient the focus of scrutiny from the accuser to the accused but, for the most part, a different, 'better' approach to trials is encouraged rather than required.

In terms of the *content* of rape trials, very few of the 'sins' of the past are now banned. Our survey of the architecture of reformed rape laws in this chapter has identified just five rules that could meaningfully be characterized as *prohibitions*: on publicly identifying the complainant; on members of the public accessing the courtroom while the complainant is giving evidence (ie 'closed courts'); on the accused personally cross-examining the complainant; on questions about sexual 'reputation'; and on the traditional corroboration warning. Legislation limiting access to counselling communications and the admissibility of sexual experience evidence *approaches* prohibition in some jurisdictions, but in most states and territories, the protections afforded to complainants are qualified and subject to judicial discretion.

It is certainly the case that higher standards of courtesy and polite communication are expected compared to the 1970s, but, for the most part, lawyers for the accused remain free to run the defence case in the traditional way: by challenging the complainant's credibility on character grounds, disputing their allegation because it does not accord with the culturally understood attributes of a 'real rape' or a 'true victim', and accusing them of lying about what the defence characterizes as a consensual sexual encounter. Few of the features of the contemporary architecture of rape laws described in this chapter interrupt these practices. Not because they 'fail', but because they were never intended to do so. When it comes to rape myths and stereotypes, legislatures have generally preferred relatively benign modes of statutory influence, such as a conception of 'improper' questions, which applies to all trials and which regulates *form* rather than *substance*, and jury directions that are instructive—but do not bind decision-makers, foreclose questions, or exclude evidence. Large investments are being made in elaborate jury directions regimes—including the Model Jury Directions Bill recently proposed by the ALRC[156]—with the aim of reducing the risk that jurors will bring rape myths and stereotypes into trials through the 'back door'. Meanwhile, no attempt has been made in any Australian jurisdiction to legislatively curtail the capacious concept of 'relevance',[157] which is the *front door* by which many rape myths enter the courtroom through questions asked of complainants during cross-examination (discussed in Chapter 7)—and, to some extent, as we explore in Chapter 6, via questions asked by the prosecution during evidence-in-chief. Assessed against the standard of improving both process justice and outcome justice for victim-survivors of sexual violence, we think this is a serious deficit in the architectural design of contemporary rape laws in Australia.

These are not flaws or oversights, but active decisions on the part of law reform bodies, legislators, and to some extent the judiciary; along with the influence exerted by other institutions, including the legal profession and civil society organizations concerned with speaking up for the rights of the accused. The 'unreformed' aspects of rape law to which we have drawn attention here may or may not be the subject of future statutory recalibrations. In this chapter, we have attempted to communicate an account of what *has* changed over the last 50 years, so that this legal reality (rather than an abstract and romanticized narrative of progressive rape law reform) can be used as a touchstone for understanding what we learned when we undertook close empirical studies of rape trials in two jurisdictions—Victoria and NSW. Australia's two most populous states are generally regarded as having exerted a heavy (progressive) influence on the parameters of rape law reform across the country since the 1970s. Jurisdiction-specific differences need to be respected, but we are confident that there are lessons to be learned from transcript analyses and other qualitative methods (explained in the next chapter) in these two states, and that our findings will resonate elsewhere. This is especially so when the other Australian jurisdictions have largely adopted the same rape law architecture (or are in the process of doing so).

156 ALRC, *Safe, Informed, Supported* (n 9) 253.
157 Evidence Act 1995 (NSW), s 55; Evidence Act 2008 (Vic), s 55.

The normative position that we have advanced here, based on 50 years of Australian rape law reform, is just the beginning of what we aim to achieve in this book. Our highest priority is to offer some much-needed illumination to the practices of contemporary rape trials. One of the paradoxes of the modernizing project is that while the content of rape laws *on the books* has become more visible and better known over time, how laws *operate* in trials is now *less* visible and open for scrutiny, partly as a result of laudable efforts to shield victim-survivors from public scrutiny, stigma, and distress. Access to trial transcripts is not easily achieved (as we explain in the next chapter), and we approached it as a precious opportunity to contribute to reducing this opacity, including by 'hearing' the voices of complainants—who are largely silenced by the rules designed to protect their anonymity, and the social risks associated with deciding to publicly identify themselves. Most importantly in the context of this book, access to transcripts has afforded us the opportunity to create an evidence base for testing our normative claims about what should be regarded as the 'true' story of rape law reform since the 1970s.

4

Windows to Rape Trial Practice

1. Introduction

Given the questions that we set out to answer in this book, it was inevitable that the traditional tools of the lawyer and legal academic would only take us so far. Tracking the details of statutory amendments over time is important, as is consideration of the things that law-makers said at the time of enactment. And the wider context out of which the reform agenda has emerged (discussed in Chapter 3) is also important. But we learn next to nothing about how laws are affecting the conduct of trials from analysing bills, statutes, second reading speeches, and parliamentary debates—aside, perhaps, from some references to past 'failures' that the new law is designed to correct. Appellate decisions give us important insights into how laws are being interpreted—and this can be an important *part* of understanding whether the ambitions of a particular reform are being realized. For example, as discussed in Chapter 3, the 2017 decision in *Lazarus* prompted the NSW Parliament to undertake further statutory amendments in 2021.[1]

We don't underestimate the importance of appellate review in interpreting and shaping the law. Indeed, as we explain below, systematic analysis of a body of Australian appellate case law forms part of the research design of the work we have undertaken. But only a proportion of rape trials result in appeal, and the topics that are scrutinized are typically very discrete. Appellate decisions, therefore, offer only a partial glimpse of what is happening in courts on a daily basis. We knew that further lines of inquiry and richer data sources would be required to get to the heart of this book's concerns.

Such realizations are neither new nor unique to attempts to understand sexual violence laws. This book is firmly located in the traditions of empirical legal research,[2] and law and society (or socio-legal) scholarship, which seeks to understand and evaluate how laws *operate* in the world.[3] As Darian-Smith has put it 'law has a life beyond law texts'.[4]

[1] *R v Lazarus* [2017] NSWCCA 279. See Chapter 3 at p. 58.
[2] See Peter Cane and Herbert M Kritzer (eds), *The Oxford Handbook of Empirical Legal Research* (online edn, Oxford Academic 2010).
[3] Naomi Creutzfeldt, Marc Mason, and Kirsten McConnachie, *Routledge Handbook of Socio-Legal Theory and Methods* (Routledge 2019).
[4] Eve Darian-Smith, *Laws and Societies in Global Contexts: Contemporary Approaches* (Cambridge UP 2013) 3.

Reforming Rape Trials. Julia Quilter and Luke McNamara, Oxford University Press.
 DOI: 10.1093/9780198948155.003.0004

Reform-oriented socio-legal research regards the moment of statutory enactment as just the beginning of a (potential) change. Statutory reforms are rarely 'self-executing' and what happens in practice—in the everyday decisions and actions of justice system participants—is the measure of success (or otherwise). Even recognizing the symbolic and wider educative effects of published rape law reforms, inspired words in a statute book are unlikely to mean much to victim-survivors of sexual violence unless they have some discernible effect on the experience of being a complainant in a rape trial; that is, by improving what we have identified as the dual barometers of reform impact—process justice and outcome justice.[5] Empirical inquiry into how new laws are operationalized is increasingly recognized as a critical component of law reform programmes, including those designed to improve access to justice and reduce justice system retraumatization for victims of sexual violence.[6] But this can be easier said than done.

2. Barriers to 'Open Justice'

An important dimension of the legitimacy of the judicial system is the principle of open justice.[7] It has been described as 'fundamental to the integrity of and confidence in the administration of justice'.[8] The High Court of Australia has explained the rationale in simple terms: 'court proceedings should be subjected to public and professional scrutiny'.[9] It might be assumed to follow that empirical research into the workings of courts should be relatively easy. But this is not the case. While the principle of open justice has long-facilitated public access to courtrooms, researchers face a long list of barriers, both formal and informal. Hanley and Payne have observed that the 'organisational priorities' of institutions of criminal justice administration 'do not generally include facilitating external research despite the need to examine the operation and implications of justice processes'.[10] Courts may be less 'closed research sites' than prisons and police forces, but there are nonetheless barriers to research that are at odds with the image and rhetoric of 'open justice'.[11]

[5] See Chapter 1 at pp. 15–16.

[6] See, eg Australian Law Reform Commission (ALRC), *Safe, Informed, Supported: Justice Responses to Sexual Violence* (ALRC Report 143, 2025) 164–69.

[7] ALRC, *Traditional Rights and Freedoms—Encroachments by Commonwealth Laws* (ALRC Report 129, 2015) 231.

[8] New South Wales Law Reform Commission (NSWLRC), *Open Justice: Court and tribunal information: access, disclosure and publication* (Report 149, 2022).

[9] *Hogan v Hinch* (2011) 243 CLR 506 [21].

[10] Natalia Hanley and Jason Payne, 'The Ethics of Contemporary Criminal Justice Research' in Bruce M Smyth, Michael A Martin, and Mandy Downing (eds), *The Routledge Handbook of Human Research Ethics and Integrity in Australia* (Routledge 2024) 228.

[11] ibid.

One of the major barriers for researchers (in Australia and many other jurisdictions) is that access to court documents—including transcripts of proceedings—is heavily restricted, either by the rules governing eligibility to request and receive court documents, or the price tag of them, or both. Parties to proceedings and their lawyers are entitled to obtain a copy of transcripts, for a fee. Courts *may*, in their discretion, release transcripts to non-party applicants, such as a journalist or researcher, but typically, there is no clear published procedure by which non-parties can apply for transcripts. Ad hoc correspondence with relevant authorities (such as heads of bench or court registrars) is required, and, in the absence of explicit criteria, requests must seek a benevolent exercise of discretion. In addition, the fees are usually high. For example, *if* permission for a non-party to access transcripts was granted in NSW, a typical full transcript in a rape trial could run to 500 pages, with a price tag of approximately $7,500.[12] This is not a uniquely NSW or Australian problem. Researchers elsewhere who have managed to negotiate some form of access to rape trial transcripts have highlighted the challenges and compromises involved.[13]

The idea that researchers should have a right to request court documents appears to be slowly gathering some momentum in Australia,[14] but the difficulties of designing a project on court operations that is both methodologically rigorous and feasible remain a disincentive to work of this sort.

Researchers who want to study *sexual offence* trials face significant additional hurdles. As explained in Chapter 3, measures to protect the privacy of complainants in rape trials were amongst the earliest measures taken to reduce the risk and burdens associated with reporting a crime of sexual violence and participating in the prosecution of the alleged offender. They include prohibitions on identifying the complainant and 'closed court' arrangements when the complainant is giving evidence.[15]

These barriers and restrictions mean that compared to what is conveyed by the idea of 'open justice', the reality is rather different. The 'truth' of what goes on in criminal courts involving sexual offence prosecutions is only viewable from selective and partial windows.

[12] Criminal Procedure Regulation 2017 (NSW), sch 2, pt 1, [11].

[13] See, eg, Elaine Craig, *Putting Trials on Trial: Sexual Assault and the Failure of the Legal Profession* (McGill-Queen's UP 2018) 18–19; Rachael Burgin, 'Communicating Consent: Narratives of Sexual Consent in Victorian Rape Trials' (DPhil thesis, Monash University 2019) 59.

[14] See Conclusion of this chapter.

[15] See Chapter 3 at pp. 59–60.

3. Finding the Way 'in' to Trials

As discussed in Chapter 2, there is a large (and ever-growing) body of English language literature from common law jurisdictions on rape laws, rape trials, and rape myths, but only a small portion of it is empirical in nature. Researchers often struggle to find ways 'in' to observe and analyse the day-to-day operation of trials. This is one of the reasons that research employing various forms of trial *simulation* has proliferated—particularly where the research aim is to understand (or predict) the influence of rape myths on juries in rape trials.[16] In many jurisdictions, it is a criminal offence to disclose—or solicit the disclosure of—the contents of jury deliberations on the basis that secrecy is an essential element of the integrity of the jury system.[17] The result is what has been described as a 'jury-sized hole' in our understanding of criminal trials.[18] In a very small number of exceptions, researchers have been given permission to question, interview, or survey real jurors after a real trial, either in studies focused on sexual offence trials[19] or in wider studies that included juries from sexual offence trials.[20]

The barriers described here have not diminished scholarly interest in the part played by juries in rape trials, but have redirected researchers towards experimental methods using 'mock juries'. Leverick, Chalmers, and Munro have described the essence of 'mock jury' studies: 'members of the public recruited to act as jurors in (often highly realistic) case simulations'.[21] The format that most closely resembles real rape trials (sometimes referred to as 'trial reconstruction') is where participants ('jurors') watch a live or video-recorded scripted courtroom performance by actors playing the roles of judges, prosecutors, defence lawyers, and witnesses before participating in deliberation and reaching a verdict.[22] This model is time consuming and labour intensive. This may explain why, as Ross has

[16] For an overview, see Fiona Leverick, 'What Do We Know about Rape Myths and Juror Decision Making?' (2020) 24 The International Journal of Evidence & Proof 255.

[17] Eg Jury Act 1977 (NSW), s 68A; Juries Act 1974 (England and Wales), s 20D.

[18] Jacqueline Horan and Mark Israel, 'Beyond the Legal Barriers: Institutional Gatekeeping and Real Jury Research' (2016) 49 Australian & New Zealand Journal of Criminology 422; Lewis Ross, 'The Curious Case of the Jury-Shaped Hole: A Plea For Real Jury Research' (2023) 27 The International Journal of Evidence & Proof 107.

[19] Judy Cashmore and Lily Trimboli, 'Child Sexual Assault Trials: A Survey of Juror Perceptions', Crime and Justice Bulletin No 102 (NSW Bureau of Crime Statistics and Research 2006).

[20] Yvette Tinsley, Claire Baylis, and Warren Young, '"I Think She's Learnt Her Lesson": Juror Use of Cultural Misconceptions in Sexual Violence Trials' (2021) 52 Victoria University of Wellington Law Review 463; Benjamin Spivak and others, 'The Impact of Fact-Based Instructions on Juror Application of the Law: Results from a Trans-Tasman Field Study' (2020) 101 Social Science Quarterly 346; Cheryl Thomas, 'The 21st Century Jury: Contempt, Bias and the Impact of Jury Service' [2020] Criminal Law Review 987.

[21] James Chalmers, Fiona Leverick, and Vanessa E Munro, 'Why the Jury Is, and Should Still Be, Out on Rape Deliberation' (2021) 9 Criminal Law Review 753, 754.

[22] Eg Louise Ellison and Vanessa E Munro, 'Of "Normal Sex" and "Real Rape": Exploring the Use of Socio-Sexual Scripts in (Mock) Jury Deliberation' (2009) 18 Social & Legal Studies 291; James Chalmers, Fiona Leverick, and Vanessa E Munro, 'The Provenance of What is Proven: Exploring (Mock) Jury Deliberation in Scottish Rape Trials' (2021) 48 Journal of Law and Society 226.

observed, '[t]he majority of such studies involve an experimental stimulus that is very different from the experience of participating in a real trial'.[23] Many studies are now conducted online, where participants read (or watch) a vignette or transcript, and provide answers to questions—simulating deliberation and decision-making, without interacting with other 'jurors'.[24] Some mock jury studies utilize rape myth acceptance scales which are also used to research attitudes in the wider community.[25]

Notwithstanding their limitations, and questions about their 'ecological validity',[26] mock jury studies, in their various forms, make a contribution to understanding the sort of factors that may (and may not) influence jury decision-making in rape trials. But they are less of a window into what is happening in rape trials than they are a partial proxy, offering 'useful glimpses'[27] into what might be happening in one discrete part of the criminal trial (being jury deliberations).

Our interest in what is happening in rape trials is much wider than that, including the parts of the trial when the complainant gives evidence (such as the questions they are asked), when the lawyers make submissions, and when the judge provides direction to the jury. On the last of these trial components, we note that some mock jury research investigates the impact of judicial directions and other forms of rape myth education on juror attitudes and decision-making.[28]

Observation and transcript studies

The most common methods of researching what is happening during the 'body' of the trial—that is, the giving of evidence (which is critical to complainant experience) as well as lawyers' submissions and trial judges' directions—have been *court observation* and *transcript analysis*.

Court observation is a valuable qualitative social science method that involves researchers sitting in the courtroom during proceedings, which become a dynamic

[23] Lewis Ross, 'Mock Juries, Real Trials: How to Solve (Some) Problems With Jury Science' (2024) 51 Journal of Law and Society 324.

[24] Eg Thea Gumbert-Jourjon, 'Unreasonable Doubts? The Impact of Rape Myths and Legal Misconceptions on Mock-Juror's Decisions in Sexual Assault Trials' (DPhil thesis, University of New South Wales 2023); Cassandra Starosta, Evelyn Maeder, and Craig Leth-Steenson, 'The Role of Complainant/Defendant Gender and Form of Sexual Assault on Jurors' Perceptions of Prototypicality and Verdicts' (2025) 40 Journal of Interpersonal Violence 696.

[25] See Sofia Persson and Katie Dhingra, *Rape Myths: Understanding, Assessing and Preventing* (Emerald Publishing Limited 2022) ch 3.

[26] Ross, 'The Curious Case of the Jury-Shaped Hole' (n 18) 108.

[27] Ellison and Munro, 'Of "Normal Sex" and "Real Rape" (n 22) 292.

[28] Eg Lara Hudspith and others, 'The Impact of Rape Myths Education on Jury Decision-Making: A Systematic Review" (2024) 25 Trauma, Violence & Abuse 4062; Yazhi Pang, Kari Davies, and Yong Liu, 'Changes in Certitude, Adherence, and Attitude: Immediate Effects of Rape Myth Intervention on Jurors in a Mock Trial' (2022) 19 International Journal of Environmental Research and Public Health. See also Leverick, 'What Do We Know about Rape Myths and Juror Decision Making' (n 17).

'field' of data collection. Given that audio-recording is generally prohibited in courtrooms,[29] court observations are usually manually recorded, ranging from selected verbatim accounts of oral exchanges to researcher descriptions of, and reflections on, what they are seeing, and these data are later analysed for what they reveal about the subject(s) of inquiry.

During the past decade, court observation has been employed in several studies of rape trials, with a focus on the nature, prevalence, and impact of rape myths, and mainly in the United Kingdom.[30] Herriott has explained the appeal of court observation methods as follows:

> Court observations . . . enabled collection of rich, qualitative data to capture the complexities of the trial process. Observations allow comprehensive analysis of how myths are constructed within the adversarial environment as well as behavioural and linguistic examination of parties present.[31]

Smith has noted that while much valuable data can be collected during court observations, it is impractical to attempt to make a verbatim record of all that is said, and that 'if all speech is paramount', obtaining official transcripts is preferable.[32]

We assessed that it was essential to our aims to have a full record of what was said by trial participants: complainants and other witnesses, lawyers, and judges. This was especially so in relation to the long and often complex series of questions and answers that constitute complainant examination-in-chief and cross-examination, as well as the often-detailed directions that trial judges give to juries. We were keen to investigate whether the form and substance of questions, the space afforded to complainants to tell their story, and the nature of the guidance provided by judges to juries had changed in ways consistent with the narrative of incremental progressive reform and improvements.

Acknowledging that in many jurisdictions courts are closed to the public during the complainant's evidence and special permission from the judge to observe will be required, court observation favours researcher *access* to the courtroom over *data comprehensiveness* (in terms of words at least). In the case of transcript studies

[29] See, eg, Court Security Act 2005 (NSW), s 9 which creates a criminal offence with a maximum penalty of 12 months imprisonment.

[30] Olivia Smith, *Rape Trials in England and Wales: Observing Justice and Rethinking Rape Myths* (Palgrave Macmillan 2018); Jennifer Temkin, Jacqueline M Gray, and Jastine Barrett, 'Different Functions of Rape Myth Use in Court: Findings From a Trial Observation Study' (2018) 13 Feminist Criminology 205; Ellen Daly, *Rape, Gender and Class: Intersections in Courtroom Narratives* (Palgrave Macmillan 2022); Michele Burman and others, 'Impact of Aspects of the Law of Evidence in Sexual Offence Trials: An Evaluation Study' (Scottish Government Social Research 2007).

[31] Charlotte Herriot, 'Attack as the Best Form of Defence? Rape Myth Construction in the Adversarial Trial in England and Wales' in Madhumita Pandey (ed), *International Perspectives on Gender-Based Violence* (Springer International Publishing 2023) 17.

[32] Olivia Smith, *Researching English Sexual Violence Trials Using Court Observation Methods* (Sage Publications 2020) 11.

the priority is reversed. Transcripts offer something approaching a comprehensive record of words spoken during the trial. Craig explains:

> Though written transcripts are hard to obtain and do not represent an exact version of the interactions among trial participants, the trauma of a trial is still better evidenced by the transcript than what is written about the case by a judge. The power dynamics between the various parties, the humiliating exposure of the personal, and the overall cruelty of the process can emerge clearly from a transcript's account of the words spoken, the questions asked and answered, and the emotions recorded. The microscopic level at which complainants are cross-examined is demonstrated by the transcripts in a way that simply could not be captured in a judicial decision.[33]

And, of course, for jury trials, there is no publicly available written 'judicial decision' from which insights about the trial might be gained. If a trial results in a conviction, the judge's sentencing remarks *may* be publicly available, but these will tell us next to nothing about how the trial was conducted. Appellate judgments, where they exist, may be a richer source, but only in relation to the discrete issue(s) under appeal, and never a substitute for the honesty and relative completeness of trial transcripts.

The catch, as alluded to by Craig, and discussed above, is that the availability to researchers of transcripts from rape trials is severely restricted by the general rules governing standing to access court documents and the costs of purchasing transcripts. Additionally, rape trial researchers are required to respect the strict legal protections that safeguard the privacy of the complainant. Such restrictions are not insurmountable but the conditions of access can sometimes be onerous. For example, Burgin has explained that a condition of permission to access transcripts from rape trials in the County Court of Victoria was that she was required to read the transcripts on the premises of the Victorian Government Reporting Service and take away only de-identified notes.[34]

As a result, transcript studies of rape trials have been relatively rare, especially in comparison to mock jury studies. The only UK rape trial research based on transcript analysis of which we are aware is Dowd's study of (parts of) the transcript in a single case from Northern Ireland.[35] Craig's mixed methods study of sexual assault trial lawyering in Canada included analysis of transcripts from 20 trials.[36]

[33] Craig (n 13) 19.

[34] Burgin (n 13) 69. A similar approach was required for Sharon Cowan, Eamon P H Keane, and Vanessa E Munro, 'The Use of Sexual History Evidence and "Sensitive Private Data" in Scottish Rape and Attempted Rape Trials' (Briefing Report, The University of Edinburgh 2024).

[35] Eithne Dowds, '"I presume she wanted it to happen": rape, reasonable belief in consent, and law reform in Northern Ireland' (2022) 73 Northern Ireland Legal Quarterly 74.

[36] Craig (n 13).

More transcript studies have been undertaken in Australia and New Zealand. The earliest we have identified was a Western Australian study of 38 rape trials in the 1970s, focused on the impact of new statutory restrictions on sexual experience and 'reputation' evidence.[37] In the 1980s, the NSW Bureau of Crimes Statistics and Research (BOCSAR) completed a series of transcript studies to assess the impact of the major reforms introduced by the Crimes (Sexual Assault) Amendment Act 1981 (NSW) (discussed in Chapter 3).[38] In 1997, the Victorian Rape Law Reform Evaluation Project's work on the operation of that State's first major suite of progressive rape law reforms—the Crimes (Rape) Act 1991 (Vic)—included transcript analysis of the trial judge's directions in 27 rape trials.[39] The methodology for Quilter's doctoral research included analysis of transcripts from 25 NSW rape trials from the 1990s.[40]

More recent transcript research includes studies based on 10 rape trials in Victoria,[41] and Burgin's doctoral research study of 15 rape trials in Victoria.[42] In another study, transcripts from 21 contemporary New Zealand rape trials were compared with trials transcripts from 21 NSW trials from the 1950s.[43] Limited quantitative transcript analysis has also been done as part of the work undertaken by recent law reform commission inquiries into rape and sexual offence trials.[44] In 2020, the NSW Law Reform Commission (NSWLRC) undertook a limited examination of transcripts from 16 trials, and lamented that it had been 'unable to undertake a comprehensive examination of trial transcripts within the scope of this review'.[45]

The largest transcript analysis study in Australia remains the landmark *Heroines of Fortitude* report which analysed the proceedings of 111 trials finalized in the

[37] See Liza Newby, Rape Victims in Court—the Western Australian Example' in Jocelynne A Scutt (ed), *Rape Law Reform: A Collection of Conference Papers* (Australian Institute of Criminology 1980).

[38] These are discussed in Chapter 3 at p. 50.

[39] Melanie Heenan and Helen McKelvie, 'The Crimes (Rape) Act 1991: An Evaluation Report' (Rape Law Reform Evaluation Report No 2, Department of Justice Victoria 1997).

[40] Julia Quilter, 'Re-inventing rape: an analysis of legal, medical, feminist and governmental discourses' (DPhil thesis, Monash University 2000).

[41] Anastasia Powell and others, 'Meanings of "Sex" and "Consent": The Persistence of Rape Myths in Victorian Rape Law' (2013) 22 Griffith Law Review 456; Emma Henderson and Kirsty Duncanson, 'A Little Judicial Direction: Can the Use of Jury Directions Challenge Traditional Consent Narratives in Rape Trials?' (2016) 39 University of New South Wales Law Journal 750.

[42] Burgin (n 13).

[43] Sarah Zydervelt and others, 'Lawyer's strategies for cross-examining rape complainants: Have we moved beyond the 1950s?' (2017) 57 British Journal of Criminology 551; Nina Westera and others, 'Sexual assault complainants on the stand: a historical comparison of courtroom questioning' (2017) 23 Psychology, Crime & Law 15.

[44] Queensland Law Reform Commission, *Review of consent laws and the excuse of mistake of fact* (Report No. 78, 2020) ch 3; Law Reform Commission of Western Australia (2023 The Law Reform Commission of Western Australia, *Project 113: Sexual Offences* (Final Report, 2023); Joe Clare, 'Project 113: Sexual Offences Statistical Analysis Report' (Independent analysis, Law Reform Commission of Western Australia 2023).

[45] NSWLRC, *Consent in relation to sexual offence* (n 8) 9.

District Court of NSW in 1994–95.[46] This study is an exemplar of what can be learned about the operation of rape trials from systematically reviewing the questions asked (and answers given) of complainants (and other witnesses), and has been a major touchstone for our own research on this topic. It was the first large Australian study to provide compelling evidence that the emerging narrative of 'transformed' rape trials as a result of 'progressive' law reform might not be matched by the day-to-day working of the criminal courtroom. While sobering (and still incredibly important) in this respect, the report showed what sophisticated empirical analysis with a sizeable dataset could produce.

McDonald's recent studies of rape trials in New Zealand have made an important contribution to the rape law reform literature, and another source of encouragement about the importance of transcript analysis, as well as a valuable influence on our research design.[47] McDonald and colleagues analysed 30 rape trials from the Auckland and Whangārei District Courts finalized in the period 2010–2015, and 10 rape trials from the Sexual Violence Court Pilot (2017–2018), one of the first specialist lists for sexual offences in the common law world.[48]

4. Research Design

This book draws on two discrete trial transcript studies: (i) a study of transcripts from 33 rape trials in the state of Victoria and; (ii) a study of 75 sexual offence trials in the state of NSW.

The Victorian trials

We set out to identify a non-representative purposive sample of rape trials that could play two roles: as a dataset for our investigation of intoxication evidence in rape trials;[49] and as a dataset for work we were commissioned by the Victorian Law Reform Commission to undertake, focused on:

[46] NSW Department for Women, 'Heroines of Fortitude: The experience of women in court as victims of sexual assault' (NSW Department for Women Report 1996). Researchers listened to audio recordings of trial proceedings.

[47] Elisabeth McDonald, *Prosecuting Intimate Partner Rape: The Impact of Misconceptions on Complaint Experience and Trial Process* (Canterbury UP 2023); Elisabeth McDonald, *In the Absence of a Jury: Examining judge-alone rape trials* (Canterbury UP 2022); Elisabeth McDonald, *Rape Myths as Barriers to Fair Trial Process* (Canterbury UP 2020).

[48] Sue Allison and Tania Boyer, 'Evaluation of the Sexual Violence Court Pilot' (Gravitas Report, 2019). See also Amanda-Jane George and others, 'Specialist Approaches to Managing Sexual Assault Proceedings: an Integrative Review' (Australian Institute of Judicial Administration and Commonwealth Attorney-General's Department 2023) 90-99.

[49] Australian Research Council Discovery Project: 'Intoxication Evidence in Rape Trials: A Double-Edged Sword?' (DP200100101).

- the types of evidence that featured in trials, including whether evidence was 'word-against-word' only, or whether there was corroborating evidence;
- the presence of expert evidence in relation to matters at issue in the trial;
- the nature of complainant cross-examination, including questioning techniques directed at challenging the credibility of the complainant, and the truthfulness of her account;
- whether myths and misconceptions about sexual harm and victimization feature in rape trials;
- judicial interventions (whether self-initiated or in response to objections from counsel) during complainant cross-examination;
- the impact of the new fault element (applying from 1 July 2015) of 'no reasonable belief in consent', including whether this reform has shifted the focus away from the complainant's behaviour, and towards the accused, and the 'steps taken' to obtain consent; and
- the operation of the Jury Directions Act 2015 (Vic), particularly Part 5 'Sexual Offences'.

The following inclusion criteria were applied: (i) prosecution of a single defendant on a charge of rape, whether with or without other charges; (ii) tried in the County Court of Victoria after a plea of not guilty; (iii) trial conducted during the period 2013–2020; and (iv) evidence of complainant and/or defendant intoxication (by alcohol and/or other drugs (AOD)) at the time of the alleged offence. AOD consumption is a factor in a large proportion of sexual violence incidents and rape trials.[50] Consequently, although it does not feature in all rape trials, intoxication evidence (in a variety of forms) is typical rather than exceptional. Therefore, we were confident that, even with this specific inclusion criterion, our dataset would not contain atypical cases, and would provide a robust foundation for exploring a wide variety of aspects of rape trials. Applying these criteria, we first identified eligible Victorian cases from amongst those which were in the public domain, courtesy of appellate decisions and reported sentencing remarks. Additional eligible cases were identified via communications with the VLRC, and with the Victorian County Court, Office of Public Prosecutions, and Victoria Legal Aid (conducted on our behalf by the VLRC).

These searches produced a sample of 33 trials that took place in the County Court of Victoria between 2013 and 2020. The trials related to conduct that occurred between 1985 and 2018. In all cases, the complainants were women and the accused persons were men. The accused gave evidence in 42% of the trials.

[50] See the sources listed in Chapter 8 at pp. 169–170 (the sources are referenced at nn 4 and 5).

Our sample of 33 trials included 22 trials resulting in a guilty verdict on at least one charge of rape; nine trials with a not guilty verdict; and two trials in which a verdict of acquittal was entered on appeal.

The NSW trials

As with Victoria, we again set out to identify a dual-purpose sample that could contribute to our intoxication evidence research and the larger ambitions of work we were commissioned to complete by the NSW Department of Communities and Justice focused on issues such as cross-examination approaches, prosecution responses, and judicial questioning/directions, and encompassing the following research questions:

- What is the experience of complainants of sexual offences in the conduct of the trial?
- Are legislative and privacy protections for the complainant adhered to in the conduct of sexual offence trials? Do these protections offer sufficient support?
- What are some of the common themes in the cross-examination of complainants?
- Do lawyers and judges comply with rules of evidence? Which rules are/are not complied with?
- What support mechanisms are offered to and/or used by complainants (eg giving evidence by CCTV, being assisted by a support person)?
- Are there any improvements that could be made—both to law and procedure—to improve the complainant experience?

We began the sample selection process with a BOCSAR-provided list of 741 sexual offence trials (involving 2,197 charges) finalized in the NSW District Court between 2014 and 2020. Again, we did not attempt to create a representative sample. Rather, in consultation with BOCSAR, we applied purposive (criterion) sampling to produce a sample that could feasibly be analysed within the prescribed timeframe, and which exhibited a degree of diversity with respect to factors such as: the nature of the offence(s) charged;[51] the trial outcome (ie guilty of one or more charges or not guilty); whether the trial was a jury trial or conducted by a judge alone; location of the trial; whether the complainant was female or male; and inclusion of both Aboriginal and non-Aboriginal complainants. So that part of the sample could also be used for our study of intoxication evidence in rape trials, we

[51] We were asked to include not only charges of rape (or 'sexual assault' as this offence is known in NSW), but also other adult sexual offences, such as aggravated sexual assault and indecent assault (now known as 'sexual touching'): Crimes Act 1900 (NSW), ss 61KE-61KF.

also took into account whether trials featured evidence of AOD use by the complainant and/or accused.

Where possible, we chose the number of trials for the sample that roughly reflected the proportion of the total number of trials in the list provided by BOCSAR featuring each relevant variable. This exercise was undertaken before we received any trial transcripts. This meant that the contents of trial transcripts had no influence on the creation of the study sample.

The result was a sample of 75 trials that took place in the District Court of NSW between 2014 and 2020, and which related to conduct that occurred between 2003 and 2018. All trials involved a male accused, with a male co-accused in two cases, and a female co-accused in one case. In 72 trials, there was a single complainant, and in three trials there were two complainants. In five trials the complainant was male.

The 75 trials involved 302 charges. The number of charges per trial ranged from one to 16. Overall, the largest number of charges (141) were for sexual assault (ie rape). There were 37 aggravated sexual assault charges and 54 charges for indecent assault. In some trials the accused was charged with sexual offences and non-sexual offences (eg assault occasioning actual bodily harm). 63 trials (84%) featured evidence of AOD use by the complainant and/or accused. The accused gave evidence in 56% of trials.

In 30 trials (40% of the total sample) the accused was convicted of at least one sexual offence. In 39 trials (52%) the accused was found not guilty on all charges. In six trials (8%) the accused was convicted only of a non-sexual offence charge (eg common assault).

Limitations of transcripts and our samples

In our assessment, and as we have explained earlier in this chapter, transcripts are a very rich window into the operation of rape trials, and transcript analysis is an essential component of the multiple research methods required to assess the impact of statutory reforms to rape law, evidence, and procedure. However, they do not offer us a completely 'true' and complete account of what is going on in trials,[52] and cannot on their own tell us how and why rape trials are conducted in the way they are, and whether statutory law reforms have efficacy. Transcripts (ie words on a page or screen) are effective for communicating the words that are spoken in the courtroom (although they are imperfect in this respect), but they cannot communicate tone, emotion, mood, atmosphere, etc—all of which are important to

[52] Emma Cunliffe, 'Untold Stories or Miraculous Mirrors? The Possibilities of a Text-Based Understanding of Socio-Legal Transcript Research' (2013) <http://dx.doi.org/10.2139/ssrn.2227069>, accessed 11 July 2025.

the experience of complainants and other participants in a trial. Researchers who have had access to audio recordings have rightly noted the additional benefits of being able to hear the sounds of the trial, including 'complainant pauses, silence and displays of emotion' and 'the tone, style, pace and volume' of the voices of complainants and other witnesses, lawyers, and judges.[53] In addition, transcripts tell us next to nothing about the many other points in the justice system that can have a significant impact on the experience of victim-survivors, such as reporting to, and communicating, with police, liaison with lawyers and court staff in the pre-trial period, and post-trial experiences.

It is important, therefore, that research on complainant experience employs a range of methods, including the court observation and mock jury methods discussed above, as well as interviews with victim-survivors/complainants, lawyers and judges, and other justice system and sexual violence support service stakeholders.[54]

Both the Victorian and NSW samples were non-representative samples. They include only a subset of the total number of trials conducted during the relevant period that would have met our case eligibility criteria. For the Victorian sample (reflecting the manner in which eligible cases were identified—see above), the sample was skewed towards cases in which the trial resulted in a finding of guilt.

Another limitation was that it proved difficult to obtain a transcript for all trials that was 'complete'—defined for our purposes as inclusive of counsel's opening remarks, all oral evidence, counsel's closing addresses, and the trial judge's summing up. The *minimum* requirement for inclusion in both of our datasets is that our transcript holding for the case included the complainant's cross-examination.

In NSW, in 49 of the 75 trials we had a complete trial transcript. In 10 trials we were missing the opening addresses of counsel, in three trials we were missing the closing addresses of counsel, and in six trials we were missing the trial judge's summing up. We had the complainant's courtroom evidence for all 75 trials, and the accused's courtroom evidence for all trials in which they gave evidence (56% of trials).

The problem of incomplete records was more pronounced in the Victorian study. We obtained prosecution and defence closing addresses for only 4 of the

[53] McDonald, *Rape Myths as Barriers to Fair Trial* (n 48) 8. See also NSW Department for Women (n 47).

[54] For example, Elena Campbell and others, '"This Is My Story. It's Your Case, But It's My Story": Interview Study' (KPMG and RMIT Centre for Innovative Justice 2023); Patricia Cullen and others, 'Voices from the frontline: Qualitative perspectives of the workforce on transforming responses to domestic, family and sexual violence' (ANROWS Research Report 21/2022); Anna Carline, Clare Gunby and Jamie Murray, '"And that's why street-wise complainants now always give evidence behind screens, live": exploring the intensive affects of the courtroom' in Kirsty Duncanson and Emma Henderson (eds), *Courthouse Architecture, Design and Social Justice* (Routledge 2022); Craig (n 13); Wendy Larcombe and others, 'Reforming the Legal Definition of Rape in Victoria—What Do Stakeholders Think?' (2015) 15 QUT Law Review 30; Jennifer Temkin, 'Prosecuting and Defending Rape: Perspectives From the Bar' (2000) 27 Journal of Law and Society 219.

33 cases. We obtained the trial judge's summing up and directions to the jury (the 'charge' as it is known in Victoria) in six cases. In one case we did not obtain the complainant's evidence-in-chief (which had been given in the form of a VARE).[55]

Finally, it is important to be clear that transcript analysis of the sort we have undertaken provides no basis for suggesting any correlation between the features of rape trials to which we draw attention in the following chapters and trial outcomes. There are far too many variables to speculate on such matters. In particular, jury deliberations are secret and not transcribed. The words spoken in the jury room do not feature in even the most complete of trial transcripts. Of course, as we argued in Chapter 1, the verdict is not the only measure of the 'success' of a rape prosecution. Where supported by the words contained in the transcript, we *have* commented on events (such as lines of questioning during cross-examination) that appear to bear on the complainant's courtroom experience.

Ethics approval and confidentiality measures

Approval for the collection and analysis of trial transcripts was granted by the University Human Research Ethics Committee[56] in accordance with the Australian Code for the Responsible Conduct of Research.[57]

Strict conditions of ethics approval and the permission to access transcripts granted by the County Court of Victoria and the District Court of NSW, included the use of secure methods for transfer and storage of electronic files containing daily trial transcripts and measures to ensure that the anonymity of complainants and other trial participants was maintained.

De-identification of transcripts at the earliest opportunity was a key part of this process. Transcripts were obtained from the County Court of Victoria by staff from the VLRC, and from the NSW District Court by staff from BOCSAR, and securely delivered to us. De-identification involved the redaction from all pages of a transcript of the complainant's personal identifying information, information specific to the incident (such as location), and identifying information about defendants, witnesses, judges, and lawyers. Once de-identification was completed, the original transcripts were stored in a secure cloud server location. Only the redacted versions of the transcripts were shared with and read by research team members, and subjected to analysis.

[55] VARE refers to a Visual and Audio Recording of Evidence, pursuant to div 5 of pt 8.2 of ch 8 of Criminal Procedure Act 2009 (Vic).

[56] University of Wollongong Human Research Ethics Committee Approval 2020/376.

[57] National Health and Medical Research Council, Australian Research Council, and Universities Australia, 'Australian Code for the Responsible Conduct of Research' (2018).

Each trial was given a unique alphanumeric code (eg V1, V2, N1, N2 etc). Participants in the trial were assigned a sub-alphanumeric code (eg V1C for the complainant in the first trial in our Victorian dataset; or N7A for the accused in the seventh NSW trial).[58]

In addition to the formalities of ethics approval compliance and adherence to the Australian Code for the Responsible Conduct of Research, we were always cognizant of our wider ethical responsibilities given the especially sensitive nature of the data to which we had privileged access. Analysis of transcripts from past criminal trials unavoidably involves proceeding without the usual first step of obtaining the consent of the complainant, the accused, witnesses, or lawyers and judges—whose words are recorded within them. As McDonald has observed, prior consent from complainants is neither feasible nor appropriate.[59] Transcripts occupy an unusual, and somewhat uncomfortable, position as (heavily controlled) public records of the administration of justice and as chronicles of personal trauma, and this gives rise to additional layers of ethical responsibility for researchers.[60] Aware that there can be no guarantee that our transcript analysis won't cause further distress to victim/survivors of sexual violence, we have been vigilant about respecting the humanity of the person whose life and integrity is so often the centre of rigorous courtroom scrutiny: the complainant. Without wanting to patronize (or essentialize) the complainants whose testimonies we read, we do want to record that we were regularly struck by their strength and power—all the more noteworthy given the heavily constrained and often hostile environment in which they were attempting to 'speak out'.[61]

Researcher well-being is an important part of a framework for the ethical conduct of research on sexual violence, including the work on rape trials undertaken for this book.[62] Practices of self-care and peer-care for members of the research team were adopted throughout the project, and especially during the periods of close reading of transcripts, including de-identification, coding, and the selection of transcript extracts for inclusion in chapters.

[58] In extracts from transcripts, we have used the following abbreviations to identify who is speaking: C = complainant; A = accused; W = witness; TJ = trial judge; P = prosecutor; and D = defence counsel. Where the participants are obvious from the context (eg cross-examination of the complainant involves defence counsel asking, and the complainant answering, questions) we have used the simple form of Q & A to denote the speaker.

[59] McDonald, *Rape Myths as Barriers to Fair Trial* (n 47) 24.

[60] Craig (n 13) 19; McDonald, *Rape Myths as Barriers to Fair Trial* (n 47) 23–24; Marina Veličković, 'Ethical Challenges of Using Trial Transcripts for Research Purposes: A Case Study of the International Criminal Tribunal for the Former Yugoslavia' (2024) 11 London Review of International Law 381.

[61] Tanya Serisier, *Speaking Out: Feminism, Rape and Narrative Politics* (Palgrave Macmillan 2018).

[62] Tina Skinner and others, 'A Focus on Ethics and Researcher Wellbeing' in Rachel Forester-Jones (ed), *Research Handbook on Ethics in Social Research* (Edward Elgar Publishing 2023); Rebecca Campbell, 'Revisiting Emotionally Involved: The Impact of Researching Rape. Twenty Years (and Thousands of Stories) Later' in Miranda A H Horvath and Jennifer M Brown (eds), *Rape: Challenging Contemporary Thinking—10 Years On* (2nd edn, Routledge 2022).

Coding and qualitative analysis

This book draws on analysis of over 40,000 pages of transcript from 108 trials. The transcript length differed considerably from trial to trial, ranging from 100 pages to over 1,300 pages. This was the product of several variables, including the number of witnesses, the length of time the complainant gave evidence (this being, typically the longest phase of the trial), and the number and duration of *voir dire* legal arguments. The average length of a trial transcript was approximately 400 pages.

Data was qualitatively analysed using deductive coding.[63] This required the prior development of a 'codebook' that consisted of a pre-defined set of nodes and sub-nodes based on the aims and research questions of the Victorian and NSW studies, respectively, and our knowledge of the multiple legislative provisions which are intended to frame rape trials in each jurisdiction, particularly those introduced to improve the complainant's experience and reduce the influence of rape myths. The Victorian codebook was developed first. It contained 85 items across 11 main categories. In drafting the NSW codebook, we benefited from our prior creation and use of the Victorian codebook, although adjustments were made to reflect the different project parameters of the two commissioned projects.[64] It contained 219 items across 27 main categories.

Once drafted, the codebooks were uploaded to the software package NVivo (version 12 plus). De-identified trial transcripts were then uploaded to the same project file. For both studies, transcripts were manually coded by one of the authors, or another member of the research team under our supervision. Each transcript file was read in full, with a determination made as to whether a passage should be assigned one or more of the predetermined codes. Notwithstanding its deductive nature, this process still involves an exercise in interpretation and judgement. Therefore, although not necessarily required for qualitative analysis, in order to maximize consistency, we conducted an intercoder consistency exercise to trial the codebook and our application of it.[65] This exercise (involving independent coding of the same trial transcript by each member of the research team, followed by comparison and discussion) informed codebook refinement, and harmonization of coder interpretations, before proceeding to code all transcripts for all trials in the sample.

In a qualitative study of the sort in which we were engaged, coding is a means to an end. It is a way of capturing the presence or absence of selected anticipated

[63] Andrea J Bingham and Patricia Witkowsky, 'Deductive and Inductive Approaches to Qualitative Data Analysis' in Charles Vanover, Paul Mihas, and Johnny Saldana (eds), *Analyzing and Interpreting Qualitative Research: After the Interview* (Sage Publications 2021).

[64] Our NSW codebook also benefited from input of a Research Advisory Panel convened by BOCSAR to guide our NSW commissioned research.

[65] See Cliodhna O'Connor and Helene Joffe, 'Intercoder Reliability in Qualitative Research: Debates and Practical Guidelines' (2020) 19 International Journal of Qualitative Methods 2.

features of rape trials. This, in turn, facilitates systematic analysis of those features, isolation of illustrative examples of the feature in question, and comparison across trials in the sample.

We also created coding 'notes' for each trial that we read and coded. This ensured that unanticipated features, or wider reflections prompted by the coding exercise, could be captured and incorporated into later analysis and synthesis of findings.

In our experience, coding of trial transcripts was a partly iterative and cumulative process. That is, as we moved from one trial to the next, we were influenced by what we had read in the previous trial (or the one before that), and/or the reflections this earlier reading generated about our larger concerns for the courtroom implementation of rape law reforms. In this way, our readings of each trial were both discrete and interconnected. To put it another way, our qualitative research involved an approach which embraced the continuities between reading, coding, analysis, and synthesis (as well as discussion with peers in a collaborative research team). We regard these approaches as strengths rather than weaknesses. Although some methodologists would argue for strict separation between *analysis* (including coding) and *interpretation*, we embrace the view that 'these closely related processes overlap and interact . . .'[66]

For the larger NSW study, we also used the NVivo classifications facility to record basic descriptive information about each trial, such as: court location; gender of trial participants; number and type of sexual offence charges; relationship between complainant and accused; setting in which the alleged sexual offences occurred; mode by which the complainant gave evidence; whether a support person was present; and whether DNA evidence was admitted.

Use of transcript extracts in this book

Consistent with the primarily qualitative nature of our transcript studies, in this book we make extensive use of anonymized extracts from trial transcripts. We believe this approach is warranted for two inter-related reasons. Having had the rare privilege to read and analyse a significant number of rape trial transcripts, we believe we have an obligation to offer as large a window as possible into what occurs in the courtroom. Much may be familiar to courtroom 'insiders' (including judges and lawyers) but the specifics of what is said during witness examination and cross-examination in rape trials very rarely enters into the public domain. Secondly, the words spoken in rape trials—especially to and by complainants—have authenticity and considerable power, and in our assessment they are an essential component of

[66] Allen Trent and Jeasik Cho, 'Interpretation in Qualitative Research: What, Why, How' in Patricia Leavy (ed), *The Oxford Handbook of Qualitative Research* (2nd edn, OUP 2020) 958.

communicating and illustrating our key findings about the operation of rape trials. Their inclusion also affords the reader an opportunity to assess whether the observations, claims, and suggestions made in this book are substantiated by the available evidence.[67]

Other data sources

Although transcripts from 108 trials are the primary data source for the analysis presented in this book, our research design included two other components. Both were adapted specifically to the topic with which this project began: how does intoxication evidence operate in rape trials? We learned a great deal about this question from our transcript analyses, but we determined that valuable additional insights could be drawn from analysis of appellate decisions involving appeals from rape trials, and interviews with lawyers with experience acting in rape trials.

Our appellate decisions dataset consisted of 102 decisions handed down in the decade from 2010 to 2019 (drawn from all Australian jurisdictions) that involved an appeal against conviction on a rape charge and where intoxication of the complainant formed part of the evidence in the case. Although appellate decisions are not representative of rape trials generally, they provide an additional perspective, noting that appellate courts play an important role in interpreting legislation, influencing future criminal law enforcement and courtroom practices, and communicating with and educating the wider community.

We conducted interviews with 15 lawyers from Victoria and NSW with experience acting in rape trials, either as prosecutors, defence lawyers or both. We sought to get beneath the surface of questions asked about intoxication, and submissions made by lawyers, in rape trials (revealed by transcripts), and develop a better understanding of the motivations and strategic considerations behind examination and cross-examination practices that we identified through transcript analysis. Anonymity was a condition of ethics approval.[68] Interview data was subjected to thematic content analysis. Coding was largely inductive (ie without reliance on predetermined codes), with the aims of our intoxication evidence study serving as touchstones for analysis.

[67] To clearly distinguish extracts from transcripts used in this book, the words spoken are both identified as quotes *and* italicised.

[68] Ethic approval for the interviews was granted by the University of Wollongong Human Research Ethics Committee Approval 2020/416.

5. Conclusion

As we reflect back on how we went about the work that has laid a strong foundation for the insights and arguments of this book, we recognize that we have been working at an interesting time in the evolution of empirical research on sexual offence trials in Australia, and transcript analysis research in particular. As we noted in Chapter 1, we benefited from fortuitous timing and commissioned research opportunities in Victoria and NSW. These meant that the barriers that had traditionally challenged aspiring transcript researchers were less imposing for us. At the same time, we take some credit for the improving landscape, having advocated for enhanced researcher access to transcripts through law reform inquiry submissions and our liaison activities with courts and governments. In 2024, the Queensland Parliament took an important step towards facilitating researcher access to transcripts from sexual offence trials when it acted on a recommendation from the Queensland Women's Safety and Justice Taskforce[69] that a procedure should be established to allow researchers to request access to sexual offence trial transcripts *and* apply for a waiver of the usual fees. The NSWLRC has also recommended that legislation be introduced that facilitates researcher access to transcripts.[70]

We are confident that the chapters that follow in this book substantiate the claims we have made in this chapter about the value of transcript analysis as a mechanism for illuminating how contemporary rape trials are conducted in Australia. As we explained in Chapter 3, an enormous amount has changed over the last 50 years when it comes to the statutory architecture that is meant to frame rape trials. With access to transcripts from more than 100 Victorian and NSW trials, we have been afforded a precious opportunity to shed much-needed light on what has changed for the better—and what has not—and to consider the implications for the future of rape law reform in Australia, and in common law jurisdictions around the world.

[69] Women's Safety and Justice Taskforce (Qld), 'Hear Her Voice: Women and Girls' Experiences across the Criminal Justice System' (Report No 2, Queensland Government 2022) recs 81–82, 364.

[70] NSWLRC, *Open Justice* (n 8) 91.

5

Special Measures for Rape Trials

1. Introduction

As discussed in Chapter 3, from the earliest rape law reform efforts in Australia, significant energies have been focused on improving the experience of rape complainants in the criminal justice system. The emphasis has been on reducing retraumatization, or, to use the terminology we have adopted in this book, to improve the ability of the rape trial to deliver process justice. The literature reviewed in Chapter 2 explains that rape trials are unique criminal trials, particularly in terms of the impact they have on the person who is the alleged victim-survivor of sexual violence—that is, the complainant. Many victims of crime, especially violent crime, will find the experience of appearing in a trial as a witness confronting. In rape trials, the risk of retraumatization is even higher, including because the complainant is expected to provide intimate details of the rape, and is likely to be cross-examined in ways that make them feel as if *they* are on trial.

In this chapter, we report our findings on how the *procedural* architecture of contemporary rape trials was operating in the trials we analysed. These aspects of progressive rape law reform have been designed to reduce retraumatization and improve the capacity of complainants to give their best evidence. As we explained in Chapter 3, many of these procedural reforms were legislated as complainant *entitlements*, such as the right to a support person, or as *prohibitions*, such as the ban on an unrepresented accused personally cross-examining the complainant. It was perhaps unsurprising then to observe that the raft of special measures designed to improve the complainant's experience was *generally* operating as intended. The findings presented in this chapter support the main argument advanced in this book about the significance of the *mode of statutory influence* represented by different components of progressive rape law architecture. Procedural changes are largely *mandated*—subject in most instances to the complainant's preference. We found that lawyers and judges generally played by these rules. Where the rules required that certain special measures be adopted, this is usually what occurred. But we also observed oversights and missteps (and technological inadequacies and failures) that meant that some complainants did not receive the full benefit of the more trauma-informed trial experience that reformed legislation promises them.

Reforming Rape Trials. Julia Quilter and Luke McNamara, Oxford University Press.
 DOI: 10.1093/9780198948155.003.0005

In this chapter, we also share our findings on one of the oldest special measures for rape trials: the evidence law restrictions commonly known as 'rape shield' laws; that is, the prohibition on sexual 'reputation' evidence, and the restriction of sexual experience evidence. As we explained in Chapter 3, this is one of the rare occasions when law-makers have opted for strong modes of statutory exclusion—where evidence that is likely to distress the complainant (and which will often engage rape myths) is presumptively excluded. We found that Victorian and NSW rape shield laws were generally operating as intended in the trials we analysed. This is noteworthy in a context where studies of the operation of sexual history laws in other jurisdictions have made more negative assessments about whether change has been achieved,[1] and it underscores the importance of attending to the specificity of legislative form and of undertaking jurisdiction-specific empirical studies.

2. The Operation of Procedural Measures

General measures

Many of the procedural measures introduced by statutory reform over the past 50 years apply *generally* in all rape trials. Although their statutory expressions differ by jurisdiction, there is a high degree of uniformity about the availability of such measures in Australia. These include the complainant's entitlement to give evidence via alternative arrangements and to be accompanied by a support person, as well as *mandatory* closed courts and automatic prohibitions on publishing the name of the complainant.

Unsurprisingly, given their mandatory nature (and consistent with previous research[2]), we found that the general measures for protecting the complainant were operative in the majority of the Victorian and NSW trials we analysed. Courts were typically closed during a complainant's evidence, the prohibition on identifying the complainant was adhered to, and it was routine for complainants to give evidence from a remote location via CCTV. In the majority of trials, the complainant had a support person with them. Although there were some gaps and failures (the significance of which we return to below), the wide adoption of these general measures is noteworthy in the context of our wider aims of assessing whether and how progressive rape law reforms have been implemented. This is especially so in a context where studies in other common law jurisdictions have produced mixed findings on the operation of special measures.[3]

[1] See, eg, Joanne Conaghan and Yvette Russell, *Sexual History Evidence and the Rape Trial* (Bristol UP 2023).

[2] Sarah L Deck and others, 'An Examination of Implementation of Special Measures in Child Sexual Assault Trials and the Problems that Arise' (2022) 34 Current Issues in Criminal Justice 188, 203.

[3] See, eg, in England and Wales: Rabiya Majeed-Ariss and others '"Could Do Better": Report on the Use of Special Measures in Sexual Offence Cases' (2021) 21 Criminology & Criminal Justice 89;

Court closure

One of the early reform measures employed to protect the confidentiality of the complainant and to reduce distress was the mandated practice of closing the court to members of the public while the complainant is giving evidence—whether in the courtroom or from a remote location.[4] This measure has been in operation in Victoria and NSW since the 1990s,[5] and so we expected to observe excellent compliance with a special measure that is firmly established. What we found was high levels of compliance, with some notable exceptions.

In Victoria, the power is available to the court if it is 'necessary to avoid causing undue distress or embarrassment to a complainant'.[6] While this provision relies on the discretion of the court, in the trials we analysed the court was routinely closed. In one trial, on one day, the prosecutor forgot to make the request, and the trial judge consequently did not make the order. This oversight was rectified at the beginning of the next day before the complainant recommenced her evidence.

Court closure in NSW is mandatory 'unless the court otherwise directs' on 'the request of a party to the proceedings' and there must be 'special reasons in the interests of justice' or the 'complainant consents' to the court remaining open.[7] Courts were *routinely* closed in the trials we analysed, but we observed variation in how this was done. While most judges initiated an order closing the court, some judges called for applications to do so and, occasionally, there was uncertainty about the mandatory nature of the order, and the circumstances in which it applied:

TJ: Mr Crown is there any reason for the complainant's evidence to be in closed court?
P: No your Honour. The provision actually says--
TJ: No that is all right. I just didn't know whether there had been a previous order in the other trial made but here we don't have her giving evidence in person so I do not see a problem.

We don't want to overstate the significance of rare instances like this one (where confusion was soon remedied) but it represents an early illustration of one of our overall findings: there was more trial-to-trial variability than there should be—both in terms of the practice of how trials were conducted and knowledge

Ruth Durham and others, 'Seeing Is Believing: The Northumbria Court Observers Panel'. Report on 30 rape trials 2015–16 (Northumbria Police & Crime Commissioner 2017); Anna Carline, Clare Gunby, and Jamie Murray, '"And That's Why Street-Wise Complainants Now Always Give Evidence Behind Screens, Live": Exploring the Intensive Affects of the Courtroom' in Kirsty Duncanson and Emma Henderson (eds), *Courthouse Architecture, Design and Social Justice* (Routledge 2022).

[4] Criminal Procedure Act 1986 (NSW), s 291; Open Courts Act 2013 (Vic), s 30(2).
[5] See Chapter 3 at p. 59.
[6] Open Courts Act 2013 (Vic), s 30(2)(d).
[7] Criminal Procedure Act 1986 (NSW), ss 291(1), (3).

of applicable laws. We also observed instances of (at least rhetorical) 'push-back' against the trajectory of progressive reform. In one trial, the judge criticized the closed court requirement:

> *... in circumstances where the evidence is being given in a closed circuit television room or by pre-recorded evidence and I think it's in the interests of justice that people who have an interest in the proceedings, for example, the family of an accused person, be present to know the basis on which their family member is either acquitted or convicted. I think there is a good reason in public policy and in the administration of justice for that to occur, especially so when there is absolutely no chance that this complainant will ever be in a courtroom to have to confront the accused, but there is no discretion in that section. So it's a closed court except for the media.*[8]

The judge ultimately complied with the legislative requirements, but this incident, and the one previously mentioned, prompted us to reflect that variations in judicial application of the law have the capacity to contribute to complainant distress and undermine progressive reform. A successful transformation of the rape trial requires consistency and predictability about how the complainant will be protected. These expectations can be confounded by the high degree of autonomy exercised by trial judges in the Australian criminal trial system, especially, as we will see, when ostensibly progressive legislation vests the judge with a broad discretion as to whether they should intervene to influence the 'shape' of a rape trial.[9]

While courts were routinely *ordered* to be closed in the trials we examined, the procedure for doing so could be ineffective. Courts are usually closed 'manually' after being ordered to be closed by the judge, and this is implemented through a combination of the court officer proclaiming that the court is 'closed' to members of the public and hanging a physical 'closed court' sign on the court entrance door. This process was not foolproof. In one trial, the judge interrupted cross-examination of the complainant:

> *TJ: Can I just interrupt you there. Officer, the door to the closed court—sheriff's officer, someone's left the door open in the closed court. There's no one present in court, but it should be closed, thank you. Yes, you continue, Mr [defence counsel].*

In other trials, members of the public wandered in and out of the courtroom and judges had to remind them of the closed court arrangements and ask them

[8] The last part of this statement is a reference to the provision that allows the media to be present if the complainant is giving evidence from a remote location: Criminal Procedure Act 1986 (NSW), s 291C.

[9] For example, see the discussion of the 'improper question' statutory regime in Chapter 9 at p. 206.

to leave. Sometimes other lawyers, unrelated to the proceedings, entered and left the courtroom (presumably because they assumed their matter was being heard in that courtroom). Sometimes it was difficult for the judge to manage the closed courtroom environment, particularly when the trial involved a large number of persons:

> *TJ: When the personae dramatis is as large as it is yesterday, it's easy for other individuals to be in the Court and that not be apparent.*

These infringements of the mandatory closed rules were minor, and the way they were handled demonstrates the commitment of the judges to ensuring that this special measure operates as intended. However, from the point of view of maximizing process justice for the complainant, they are failings that should (and could) be avoided. The measure is designed to maximize the privacy afforded to a complainant in giving evidence, with the dual hope that it improves the quality of evidence and reduces trauma to the complainant in engaging with the criminal justice system. Even minor infractions can cause complainant distress as the following statement from a prosecutor reveals:

> *Before the witness comes on, I've been instructed that the complainant has been distressed by seeing people come in and out of the courtroom during the proceedings, despite the proceedings being in camera.*

Another feature we observed was that some judges took a rather liberal approach to exempting individuals from the prohibition on entry to the courtroom.[10] These included the accused's partner or parents, lawyers and readers, as well as law students and school students. Occasionally the prosecution objected to such persons being permitted to stay during the complainant's evidence. In one trial, the prosecutor objected to the accused's partner remaining in the courtroom, but the judge overruled the objection and permitted that person's presence. In a different NSW trial, a judge suggested the accused had a general '*entitlement*' to a support person, despite there being no foundation for this in legislation; in another, the judge purported to justify granting an exemption to the accused's current partner on the basis of the need for '*equilibrium*' given that the complainant had access to a support person (which, as discussed below, is a legislative entitlement in NSW).[11]

A further observation about the operation of the closed court special measure is that exemption (and media access) decisions were rarely preceded by consultation with the complainant about their preferences—as might be expected in

[10] In Victoria there is an express power to exempt: Open Courts Act 2013 (Vic), s 30(1)(b).

[11] In NSW, the accused only has a *right* to a support person if they are a 'vulnerable person' (ie a child or a cognitively impaired person): Criminal Procedure Act 1986 (NSW), s 306ZK(6).

line with the aspiration of making trials as trauma informed as possible (acknowledging that this is not legislatively required). Also the complainant is usually not informed about who has been granted an exemption and allowed to remain in the courtroom during their evidence. Where the complainant gives evidence from a remote location via CCTV (as typically occurred in the Victorian and NSW cases we analysed—see below), the primary issue for judge and counsel appeared to be whether the complainant could *see* the person(s) via the AV link to the court:

> TJ: *Yes. I think it's appropriate for the person who is present in court [ie accused's current partner] to remain. . . .The only issue I suppose is whether she is visible to the complainant.*
>
> P: *If she could possibly move a bit to her right hand side, should assist your Honour.*

We contend that even if the complainant does not 'see' the person, such exemptions have the capacity to undermine the complainant's privacy. This is especially so if the complainant learns later who was in the courtroom, which may lead to a sense of violation at having been required to share intimate and distressing details in front of a larger audience than they had been led to expect.

We also saw examples of what we regard as best practice, such as in the following trial, where the trial judge provided the complainant with important information about the closed court arrangements:

> TJ: *In the Court room at the moment Ms [redacted], there's no member of the public, it's, the Court room is closed. The only people in the Court room are the jury; Mr [defence counsel]; the lawyers and the Court staff. All right?*
>
> C: *Yes, your Honour.*

In trials where closed court exemptions are requested, it would be preferable if the complainant was consulted on their views. The judge should then explain to the complainant precisely who will remain in the courtroom, and why they have been granted an exemption.

Automatic prohibition on publication of name of the complainant

As discussed in Chapter 3, an early protection introduced to enhance complainant privacy was to prohibit any publication of the complainant's name, or any information that could identify them. The prohibition applies automatically—it does not require a separate non-publication order.[12] Breach of the prohibition is a criminal offence in NSW and Victoria.[13]

[12] See *Carrington v R* [2021] NSWCCA 257 [8]–[9].
[13] Crimes Act 1900 (NSW), s 578A; Judicial Proceedings Reports Act 1958 (Vic), s 4(1A).

Given that this prohibition has been in place for decades, we would expect to observe perfect compliance—and we did find that court transcripts expressly recorded the prohibition on publication in almost all of the trials we analysed. Typically, the restriction was referred to as a non-publication order (even though, technically, no such order is required) and there was occasional confusion on the part of the judge and/or counsel about the legal basis for the prohibition. In the following instance it fell to the prosecutor to advise the judge about the automatic nature of the prohibition:

> P: *Coming to the non-publication, there is a statutory prohibition of any matter, as you would be aware, that identifies the complainant in relation to prescribed--*
> TJ: *You want a non-publication in relation to the complainant?*
> P: *There's a statutory non-publication--*
> TJ: *And anything that might tend to identify--*
> P: *There's a statutory provision in relation to that under s 578A of the Crimes Act. That prohibition under 578A(2) extends to any matter which is likely to lead to the identification of the complainant.*

In other instances, there appeared to be a fundamental misunderstanding of the law that applied:

> TJ: *Has there been a non-publication order made in the matter of [Accused's name]? I'm just looking at the name of the complainant.*
> P: *Well, there has not been. No, but--*
> TJ: *Should there be?*
> P: *Yes, probably. They're former husband and wife.*
> TJ: *Is that necessary, then, or?*
> P: *I don't think it's--*
> TJ: *It's usually in relation to children.*
> P: *Yes. Yes.*
> TJ: *Look, I'll make a tentative one at this stage. I'll make one at this stage but it can always be--*
> P: *Yes, your Honour.*
> TJ: *I make a non-publication order in relation to name of the accused and the complainant.*

Having observed judge-to-judge variability in her study of Canadian rape trials, Craig pointedly remarked that there is an 'expectation that all trial judges who preside over sexual assault trials possess a minimum threshold of *basic* legal knowledge'.[14] It is incumbent on counsel and judges to be familiar with all parts of the

[14] Elaine Craig, *Putting Trials on Trial: Sexual Assault and the Failure of the Legal Profession* (McGill-Queen's UP 2018) 191 (emphasis in original).

laws that govern rape trials, including special measures such as the prohibition on revealing the identity of the complainant. This may seem like a relatively minor example, but it goes to a larger finding from our transcript studies. A judge's solid understanding of the rules (with the assistance of counsel), and attention to detail in how they are operationalized in all aspects of the trial, are essential to ensuring that the complainant has access to the 'reformed' courtroom that they have been promised.

Where there are gaps in knowledge or execution in a given trial, process justice is compromised. Even the modest rape trial transformation that progressive reforms are designed to achieve will be thwarted unless all components of the modern architecture of rape laws are in play—including relatively minor procedural arrangements. While we don't ultimately subscribe to the *implementation gap* account of why rape law reform continues to fail victim-survivors of sexual violence,[15] our findings suggest that trial-to-trial inconsistency in terms of familiarity with, and adherence to, reformed rape laws is making a contribution.

It is largely beyond the scope of trial transcript analysis studies to offer insight on the effectiveness of prohibitions outside the courtroom unless they are the subject of comment during proceedings. This occurred twice in the 108 trials we analysed. In one instance, a photographer took a photo of the complainant *in the courtroom* causing the complainant distress. The judge admonished the person responsible and threatened to deal with them by way of contempt proceedings. In another, it was brought to the court's attention that a photo of the complainant had been published. Although pixelated, the complainant was still identifiable.

Alternative arrangements

In the NSW and Victorian trials we analysed, it was routine for complainants to give their evidence using alternative arrangements,[16] most commonly by attending a remote location and 'appearing' in the courtroom via CCTV. This has become a cornerstone of trauma-informed best practice for rape trials in Australia. While a small number of complainants elected to appear in court in person (and give their evidence from the traditional witness box) the large majority exercised their right to avoid the distress of personal appearance in the same location as the accused.[17]

[15] See Chapter 2 at p. 26.

[16] Criminal Procedure Act 1986 (NSW), s 294B; Criminal Procedure Act 2009 (Vic), s 360(1).

[17] While it was not a focus of our research, we note that past studies have produced mixed results on whether appearance via CCTV, or using other alternative arrangements, diminishes the quality and impact of the complainant's evidence. See, eg, Carline, Gunby, and Murray (n 3); Majeed-Ariss and others (n 3) 100–01; Louise Ellison and Vanessa E Munro, 'A "Special" Delivery? Exploring the Impact of Screens, Live-Links and Video-Recorded Evidence on Mock Juror Deliberation in Rape Trials' (2013) 23 Social and Legal Studies 3; Yvette Tinsley and Elisabeth McDonald, 'Use of Alternative Ways of Giving Evidence by Vulnerable Witnesses: Current Proposals, Issues and Challenges' (2011) 42 Victoria University of Wellington Law Review 705.

While it appeared that all complainants had *access* to alternative arrangements, the logistical and technological planning and execution for remote location CCTV evidence was deficient in some trials. If the complainant is giving evidence from a remote room (as they are likely to be), it is essential that they have access to all relevant documents about which they are going to be examined. In the majority of the trials we analysed, remote location rooms were prepared to a high standard. This achieved a relatively seamless integration of the remotely located witness into the courtroom and the trial. However, in some trials, examination-in-chief and cross-examination were impeded by the fact that relevant exhibits, statements, and other documents were not to hand (or were difficult to navigate) in the remote location from which the complainant was giving evidence.

The most common flaws and complications were technological. Some were at the minor end of the scale and related to AV set-up. The following exchange is illustrative:

P: *I wonder before that's done if it's not asking too much, whether we can have the witness' head a bit lower so that we can see everything.*
TJ: *So possibly move your chair back a bit further.*
P: *No, further. No, that's . . .*
TJ: *We're just chopping off the top of your head at the moment. You're lowering the chair, are you?*
C: *I'm trying to.*
TJ: *All right. I think that's better. Is everybody happy with that? Yes, all right.*

At other times the courtroom camera was not ideally located, sometimes resulting in the complainant being able to see the accused. These might seem like trivial matters, but they undermine the very rationale for offering alternative arrangements to the complainant: to reduce the distress of giving evidence. It shouldn't fall to the complainant to move position or adjust furniture in the moment just before they are about to be questioned. Given that technology-facilitated evidence is now mainstream in Australia rape trials, it is reasonable to expect that appropriate checks are done before the complainant is called.

A bigger problem was that the technology infrastructure in some trials was not always reliably fit for purpose—an issue that previous studies in a number of jurisdictions have also identified.[18] Again, this has the capacity to impede trauma-informed best practice and exacerbate complainant distress. At times the sound quality was inadequate, or the AVL link was temporarily lost. Often there was only one fixed camera directed at a single bar table location, which meant that, between

[18] See, eg, Olivia Smith, *Researching English Sexual Violence Trials Using Court Observation Methods* (Sage Publications 2020) 30–33; Elisabeth McDonald, *Rape Myths as Barriers to Fair Trial Process* (Canterbury UP 2020) 118–19; Nina Westera and others, 'Special Measures in Child Sexual Abuse Cases: Views of Australian Criminal Justice Professionals' (2020) 32 Current Issues in Criminal Justice 224; Deck and others (n 2) 199.

examination-in-chief and cross-examination, counsel had to swap positions so that the questioner could be seen by the complainant. Occasionally, the location of the remote room, including in the following trial, meant that people could be seen walking past, behind the complainant, leading the trial judge to say:

> *I don't know where we're linked to but it's a terrible remote witness room . . . Having people wander past like . . . It looks like a shopping mall. It's just not appropriate.*

While such instances were rare amongst the trials we observed, they shouldn't happen at all.

Another negative aspect of the use of a remote location was that the complainant was sometimes required to take on 'duties' which would not have been expected of them had they given evidence personally in the courtroom. For example:

> P: *Can you maybe just hold those up just to confirm we're looking at the same photographs? Yes, thank you.*
> TJ: *Just try not to knock the microphone, Ms [complainant]?*
> C: *Sorry.*
> TJ: *That's okay.*
> C: *If you just . . .*
> TJ: *If you just get the witness to describe things rather than hold it up? It may be difficult to hold it up, I suspect.*

In other trials, the complainant was asked to take responsibility for operating equipment for playing and pausing CCTV footage on which she was being questioned. Such expectations seem to us inconsistent with the trauma-informed ambition of contemporary trials.

The largest technological challenge we observed was when counsel sought to show CCTV or other video footage during examination-in-chief or cross-examination of the complainant. This footage needed to be displayed simultaneously in the courtroom and the remote location, and it was important that those in the court (especially the jury) were able to see the video and the complainant (on a screen) at the same time. Some courtrooms were simply not adequately equipped. Granted, such a situation requires a more sophisticated technological set-up than usual, but the technology need is not uncommon and should be anticipated and addressed in advance. In one case, the technological hurdle appeared so insurmountable that the complainant was asked by the prosecutor's instructing solicitor whether she might be willing to give her evidence in person in the courtroom as a 'solution' to the CCTV footage challenge. The complainant maintained her preference for giving her evidence from the remote location, and another (stop-gap) solution was found. Clearly, it should not fall to the complainant to compensate for deficiencies of technology or forward planning. That the frustration (and extensive delays) could have been avoided was acknowledged by the judge:

TJ: If we had thought about this, I could have lobbied for this to be in the court with the pop-up screens, couldn't I? Next time - unless either of you want to make the call - we could possibly move the whole trial to a court with screens.

In another, we observed the opposite: the court considered the option of moving a complainant who wanted to give her evidence in person in court to a remote location, to address technological challenges. The screen on which video footage was to be played during her evidence could not be viewed from the witness box. However, a solution was found and the complainant remained in the courtroom. More disturbingly, in the same trial, defence counsel also proposed relocation of the complainant to the remote location room because of an asserted concern that her visible distress 'live' in the courtroom—when she was being questioned while shown taxi CCTV footage and stills of the complainant and the accused during the alleged rape—was unfair to the accused. The problem, in the submission of defence counsel, was that the complainant's extreme emotional distress in the courtroom could be so prejudicial to the accused as to warrant the dismissal of the jury. To manage this risk, the remote location could provide some 'distance':

D: [The complainant's reactions] . . . are not so palpable in the remote [location] - there's that distance, and that's my submission in a sense, ***that that's why those provisions are designed to be there.*** *Well, they're obviously designed for protection of the complainant, but in a circumstance like this it may be more appropriate that she gives her evidence from a remote facility, given the nature of this graphic, pornographic material that she's going to be required to watch over and over again and comment on.*[19]

This bold attempt to misappropriate the special measure of remote location CCTV evidence, to the *accused's* benefit, was not rejected out of hand by the trial judge:

TJ: I will speak to her in a moment when she comes back into court about the need for her to let me know if she's too upset to go on for any reason at all, if she's feeling upset either emotionally or physically.
D: Yes, Your Honour.
TJ: Now, I can also say to her that if it transpires that she does feel very upset physically or emotionally, there is an option available to her, I'd only put it in these terms at this stage, of giving evidence from what we call a remote facility, another room and her image would be seen by the jury. I'll explain that much her and we'll see how we go.

[19] Emphasis added.

In the end, the complainant gave her evidence in court, including during the showing of the video footage. Nonetheless, the incident is troubling. Frankly, it is absurd and unfair to suggest that the complainant should somehow be expected to moderate her emotional state and demeanour at the very time that she is being questioned about a traumatic event, interrogated by defence counsel in cross-examination, *and* closely scrutinized by the jury for her honesty and believability. (We say more about showing a complainant such footage in advance in Chapter 6.)

These examples serve as a reminder about the need to be vigilant about respecting the *purpose* of special measures like remote location CCTV: to support the well-being of the complainant.

Support persons

Another special measure introduced nearly 20 years ago to reduce trauma to complainants is the right to be accompanied by a support person while giving evidence (whether in court or in the remote location).[20] Although trial transcripts are not a perfect record of whether a support person was in attendance, it was common for the judge to recognize that person's presence on the record, which leads us to conclude that most complainants in the NSW and Victorian trials we analysed had a support person.[21]

As with other special measures, we observed instances where the complainant's entitlement to a support person was not fully understood or respected. In some trials, the prosecution made an *application* for permission to have a support person present, and the judge treated the measure as a matter for objections and ruling if required. In one NSW trial, defence counsel objected to the support person sitting next to the complainant in the witness box (in the courtroom). The judge took up a suggestion from the prosecutor that the complainant be asked to begin without the support person by her side, and that '*we make a start and see how we go*':

> *TJ: It certainly would be preferable - if she is minded to be strong enough to come and give evidence in Court, unless there is a sign she really needs it, and we are all in agreement, particularly when there is opposition to it, I think it is better to proceed and see how we go, particularly in view of [defence counsel's] opposition to it.*

There appeared to be no legal basis for this decision, noting that the statutory entitlement is to have the support person 'present near' and 'within the complainant's sight, when . . . giving evidence'.[22] An accused may only object on the

[20] Criminal Procedure Act 2009 (Vic), ss 360(c), 365(1); Criminal Procedure Act 1986 (NSW), s 294C.

[21] This contrasts with studies from other jurisdictions, where, in some courts, the support person was not always permitted to sit with the complainant in the remote location: see, eg, Majeed-Ariss and others (n 3) 101; Durham and others (n 3) 19–20.

[22] Criminal Procedure Act 1986 (NSW), s 294C(1).

limited grounds that the suitability of the person chosen, 'is likely to prejudice the accused person's right to a fair trial' (eg the person chosen is a witness in the proceedings)[23]—a circumstance that did not arise in this trial.

Towards reliable good practice

Though small in number, the gaps and errors that we have described in this part of the chapter suggest that the entitlement to special measures that are designed to minimize the risk of retraumatization of the complainant are not as universally established as they should be. In the scheme of all the things that make rape trials traumatizing for complainants, *procedural* measures of the sort discussed in this chapter are very modest adjustments to the running of a trial. They should be guaranteed for all complainants in all trials in all courtrooms. The basic trauma-informed practices, which have been established by statutory reform for the better part of two decades or more, should be routine best practices. Their availability should not be vulnerable to the misunderstandings of the judge or counsel, or defence attempts to subvert or misappropriate them. They should not be reliant on amenable counsel or a favourable ruling from the trial judge, or good fortune (such as in relation to the availability of appropriate technology in the courtroom to which the trial has been allocated). Each criminal trial is, of course, a unique event, and deserves to be treated as such. However, some procedural aspects of rape trials occur with such regularity and/or are of such significance for the complainant (a uniquely positioned witness/non-party to proceedings) that they warrant reliable arrangements to guarantee best practice for minimizing distress. This is especially so in relation to the location and technology-related logistical matters that arise from complainants giving evidence from a remote location via AVL.

Specific measures

In addition to the generally available measures just discussed, another important dimension of the reformed procedural architecture of rape trials is that legislatures have provided for additional measures that may be available depending on the circumstances of the trial and the evidence that parties seek to admit. Specific measures include: a prohibition on complainants being personally cross-examined by an accused;[24] rules that allow the re-use of evidence in retrials;[25] and additional protections for the giving of evidence by vulnerable witnesses.[26] The rights of

[23] ibid s 294C(4).
[24] Criminal Procedure Act 1986 (NSW), s 294A; Criminal Procedure Act 2009 (Vic), s 357.
[25] Criminal Procedure Act 1986 (NSW), pt 5, divs 3–4; Criminal Procedure Act 2009 (Vic), pt 8.2, div 7.
[26] Criminal Procedure Act 1986 (NSW), pt 6; Criminal Procedure Act 2009 (Vic), pt 8.2, div 6.

the complainant under such measures may be absolute, such as the right not to be cross-examined by the accused. Others are an entitlement that may be limited, based on the court's discretion and the balancing of considerations such as 'the interests of justice'—such as the power to use recorded evidence from a trial at a subsequent trial, which is subject to the court's authority to compel a complainant to give evidence at the subsequent trial.

Most of the specific measures were only rarely operative in the trials we analysed, but where they were engaged, they appeared to operate largely as intended. In the few instances where legislative provisions regarding appropriate support for vulnerable complainants were engaged, they appeared to operate effectively and with high levels of compliance with statutory requirements. This included the use of witness intermediaries, the holding of ground rules hearings, and the recording of the complainant's police interview and its playing as part of the complainant's evidence-in-chief. Examination and cross-examination practice was more variable. However, in one trial, where the complainant had a cognitive impairment, we observed what we would regard as best practice. Most notably, following a ground rules hearing, with active input from the witness intermediary, the dynamic of the complainant's cross-examination was noticeably different to that of other trials we observed, including by virtue of being more logical and clear in the sequencing of questions, and less adversarial.

Recorded evidence in a retrial

We offer further detail on this specific measure because it occurred with some frequency in the trials we analysed (approximately 10%). The rules that provide for the use in a retrial of a recording of the complainant's evidence from the first trial appeared to be operating as intended, and meeting the policy objective of reducing complainant trauma by removing the burden of having to give evidence *again* in a retrial.

Sometimes the practice was hampered by the technological challenges discussed above. The sound quality of pre-recorded evidence was at times suboptimal, creating listening challenges for the judge, lawyers, and jurors. Sometimes there was equipment failure or disc non-recognition or the disc being cued to the wrong location. Pre-recorded evidence often requires editing. This posed its own challenges, including the need for negotiation between counsel over edits, and the question of what to tell the jury about footage that reflected edits, potentially confusing time stamps etc.

As with other special measures, good practice was not universal. In one trial, the judge appeared to undermine the policy animating the recorded evidence innovation by inviting the jury to consider the fact that the complainant's evidence took the form of the playing of a recording from an earlier trial as a weakness in the Crown's case, because the jury had not had the opportunity to see the complainant personally:

> *It may be the witnesses' demeanour or behaviour while giving the evidence, particularly during cross-examination, may have been able to assist you in determining whether you accept the evidence of the witness beyond reasonable doubt. Whether, in some way, the absence of the witness deprives you of some assistance in evaluating the evidence is really a matter for speculation. If, however, you feel in some way that you have been deprived of that assistance, then it is a matter that you take into account in determining whether the Crown has proved its case beyond reasonable doubt.*

Admittedly, this was another rare instance, but it adds further weight to our concern that some rape trials are conducted in ways that are at odds with the trajectory of progressive rape law reform, and which deny complainants the full benefits and protection of the procedural special measures that have been introduced to nudge the rape trial in the direction of trauma-informed best practice.

Overall, our findings confirm that the use of recorded evidence is a clear advance on requiring a complainant to return to give evidence a second (or even third) time where there is a retrial (or for other reasons such as where a trial is aborted). It appears to us that it may also have positive effects over and above the primary rationale of reducing the complainant's burden (and trauma) of having to give evidence again. For example, recorded evidence is typically edited prior to being played at the subsequent trial, and this facilitates the exclusion of lines of questioning (and associated answers) that are determined, at the second trial, to be unfair to the complainant or otherwise inappropriate, prejudicial (to the accused), or inadmissible.

3. The Operation of Evidentiary Special Measures: Sexual Reputation and Experience Evidence

As discussed in Chapter 3, the admission of (and cross-examination on) evidence of the complainant's so-called sexual 'reputation', and/or their sexual experience or history, has long been regarded as having the capacity to retraumatize *and* to introduce rape myths into the trial. Such evidence is frequently irrelevant to the facts in issue, and only draws relevance by relying on myths about the assumed relationship between so-called sexual 'reputation' and/or prior sexual behaviour and a person's willingness to consent to sexual activity.[27]

Some of the earliest rape law reform measures in Australia were designed to sever this nexus by introducing what were colloquially known as 'rape shield' provisions. Victoria first legislated to this effect in 1976, with NSW following in 1981.[28]

[27] Clare McGlynn, 'Rape Trials and Sexual History Evidence: Reforming the Law on Third-Party Evidence' (2017) 81 The Journal of Criminal Law 367.

[28] See Chapter 3 at p. 63.

'Rape shield' provisions typically prohibit questions about sexual reputation and restrict questions about sexual experience. The specific statutory formulas differ across Australian jurisdictions, but NSW and Victoria both contain a total prohibition on the admission of evidence of the sexual reputation of the complainant.[29] On sexual experience evidence, NSW is usually understood as having the strictest regime in Australia. The NSW 'exclusionary' model[30] provides for a presumptive exclusion, subject only to a discrete and limited set of statutory exceptions or 'gates'.[31] To be admissible, the evidence must both fall within one of the gateways *and* the judge must assess that the probative value of the evidence outweighs any distress, humiliation, or embarrassment that the complainant might suffer as a result of admission. Victoria's is a 'discretionary' model involving presumptive prohibition with a residual judicial discretion to admit based on an enhanced relevance test ('substantial relevance') and in the 'interests of justice' having regard to various criteria.[32]

Gaps in our sets of transcripts, especially in Victoria,[33] hampered our ability to undertake a comprehensive assessment of how 'rape shield' laws were operating in the trials we analysed, but we had a sufficient foundation for a number of observations.

We observed high levels of compliance with the prohibition on 'reputation' evidence. This part of the architecture of 'reformed' rape laws, at least, appears to be solidly embedded in Victoria and NSW—in law *and* in practice.

Our conclusions about the operation of restrictions on sexual experience evidence are a little more equivocal. Overall, we observed high levels of compliance with the required *legislative procedures*: applying for leave to admit, including pre-trial application by the party seeking admission; submissions from both sides; and a judge's ruling that records the nature and scope of the evidence to be admitted where leave has been granted.[34] Further, during the trials, counsel generally followed the rules by complying with the judge's ruling in terms of the scope of permitted questions. Transgressions were met with appropriate objections, and further rulings were made where there was non-compliance. We note that these generally positive findings differ from studies of the operation of rape shield

[29] Criminal Procedure Act 1986 (NSW), s 294CB(2); Criminal Procedure Act 2009 (Vic), s 342 (previously referred to as reputation for 'chastity').

[30] Australian Law Reform Commission (ALRC), *Safe, Informed, Supported: Justice Responses to Sexual Violence* (ALRC Report 143, 2025) 387.

[31] David Brown and others, *Criminal Laws: Materials and Commentary on Criminal Law and Process of New South Wales* (8th edn, Federation Press 2025) 685. See also Law Commission (UK), *Evidence in Sexual Offences Prosecutions: A Final Report* (Law Com No 420, 2025) 105–07.

[32] Criminal Procedure Act 2009 (Vic), s 349.

[33] In particular, we did not have transcripts of all pre-trial applications and rulings: see Chapter 4.

[34] See Criminal Procedure Act 1986 (NSW), s 294CB(8); Criminal Procedure Act 2009 (Vic), ss 342, 344.

laws in other jurisdictions, which have observed non-compliance or inconsistent compliance.[35]

We found that legislative compliance does not translate into routine exclusion. In NSW, where our transcript holdings were the most complete (and so basic quantification is possible), some form of sexual experience evidence was admitted in approximately 50% of trials—a finding consistent with previous studies in Australia and elsewhere.[36] This is noteworthy in a context where the NSW 'exclusionary model' of rape shield laws is considered to be the most restrictive in Australia, and previous research has found that Victoria's 'discretionary' model laws have, in practice, offered limited protection against intrusive questioning.[37]

Total prohibition on evidence of sexual reputation

In Victoria, we observed no instances in which complainants were cross-examined about their sexual reputation. In NSW, despite the complete prohibition, sexual reputation evidence was raised in three trials. In two it was ruled inadmissible and in the third, there was an objection to a question asked and the question was not pressed by the defence. Of course, the question had already been asked, and it is possible that even though no answer was required, distress may have been caused to the complainant and her credibility damaged in the eyes of the jury.

Victorian legislation also provides that 'sexual history evidence'[38] is not admissible to 'support an inference that the complainant is the type of person who is

[35] See, eg, Olivia Smith, *Rape Trials in England and Wales: Observing Justice and Rethinking Rape Myths* (Palgrave Macmillan 2018) 105; Craig (n 14); McDonald (n 18) ch 5; Liz Kelly, Jennifer Temkin, and Sue Griffiths, 'Section 41: An Evaluation of New Legislation Limiting Sexual History Evidence in Rape Trials' (Report 20/06, Home Office Online 2006) 8; Durham and others (n 3) 38; Sharon Cowan, Eamon PH Keane, and Vanessa E Munro, 'The Use of Sexual History Evidence and "Sensitive Private Data" in Scottish Rape and Attempted Rape Trials' (Briefing Report, The University of Edinburgh 2024). For a multi-jurisdiction overview, see Conaghan and Russell (n 1), esp ch 4.

[36] Patricia Easteal, 'Sexual Assault Law in Australia: Contextual Challenges and Changes' in Geetanjali Gangoli and Nicole Westmarland (eds), *International Approaches to Rape* (Policy Press 2011); Mary Heath, 'The Law and Sexual Offences Against Adults in Australia', Issues Paper No 4 (Australian Centre for the Study of Sexual Assault 2005); Sarah Zydervelt and others, 'Lawyer's Strategies for Cross-Examining Rape Complainants: Have We Moved Beyond the 1950s?' (2017) 57 British Journal of Criminology 551, 565; Rape Crisis Network Ireland, 'Previous Sexual History Evidence and Separate Legal Representation' (Position Paper, 2012); McDonald (n 18) ch 5; Craig (n 14); Smith (n 35) ch 4.2; Kelly, Temkin, and Griffiths (n 35); Durham and others (n 3); McGlynn (n 27) 374.

[37] Easteal concluded that the 'substantial relevance' test is open to interpretation and influenced by rape myths: Easteal (n 36) 22.

[38] As defined in Criminal Procedure Act 2009 (Vic), s 340: 'sexual history evidence means evidence that relates to or tends to establish the fact that the complainant—(a) was accustomed to engaging in sexual activities; or (b) had freely agreed to engage in sexual activity (other than that to which the charge relates) with the accused person or another person.'

more likely to have consented to the sexual activity to which the charge relates'.[39] This provision does not provide for an absolute prohibition, but significantly restricts the admission of such evidence.[40] We found no evidence that sexual history evidence was being admitted for this purpose in the Victorian trials we examined. We did find, however, that the restrictions on admissibility may be operating in ways not necessarily intended by the legislature, including to restrict evidence that the prosecution seeks to admit. In one trial, the prosecution sought to lead evidence of the complainant's virginity prior to the alleged rape—a reference to her virginity being contained in her Video and Audio Recorded Evidence (VARE). The defence sought to have that evidence excluded. The trial judge initially ruled that the evidence could be admitted. That ruling, however, was revisited after defence counsel later re-agitated the issue and sought its exclusion. Defence counsel argued that the complainant's asserted virginity was '*incapable of challenge by the defence*', and the admission of the complainant's reference to virginity would have '*an enormous prejudicial impact on the accused man*'.

The trial judge ruled that the evidence relating to virginity was inadmissible:

> *TJ: I agree that the evidence is relevant and probative as to consent and the other issues raised by [the prosecutor], but the risk of unfair prejudice is high and in my view outweighs the probative value. The risk of prejudice lies in the likely perception by the jury that the complainant was indeed a virgin. That likely prejudice is increased by reason of the inability of the defence to challenge the evidence. Consent is the real issue in this trial, not whether the complainant was a virgin, and as I say, although that has some relevance, it is outweighed by the risk of prejudice to the accused. Therefore the answer to question 197 should be excluded from the VARE.*

In another case, the prosecutor sought to lead evidence of the complainant's sexual activity with her boyfriend prior to the alleged rape to explain the presence of a second Y chromosome DNA profile found following forensic swabs taken from the complainant. Defence counsel had not sought to cross-examine the complainant on her sexual activity and preferred to leave the issue of the second DNA profile 'hanging', arguing it would be prejudicial for the prosecution to introduce such evidence. The trial judge determined that the prejudice outweighed the probative value and refused the admission of the evidence.

[39] Criminal Procedure Act 2009 (Vic), s 343.

[40] It being subject to separate tests for admission including the 'special circumstances' test in s 352.

Restrictions on evidence concerning the complainant's sexual experience

As explained earlier, the required pre-trial application process was followed in most of the trials we observed in which parties sought to admit sexual experience evidence. On some occasions, the defence only made their application after the trial had commenced, but in most cases the correct procedure was followed thereafter. In one trial, the defence made three applications during the prosecution's examination-in-chief, but without disclosing the extent of the questions defence counsel wanted to ask the complainant. In the absence of the jury, the prosecutor pushed back against this strategy, and the judge strongly admonished defence counsel:

> *TJ: . . . s 293 [the then NSW 'rape shield' provision] is not a tactical section; s 293 is a section for the protection of a witness, a complainant. It is for the purpose of avoiding any unnecessary embarrassment, undue embarrassment, humiliation, and also it is there to protect the integrity and past of a witness. And it . . . in all effect, really should be a pre-trial issue. Right now the Crown is boxing with shadows, because at the moment she still does not - nor do I - have a real understanding of the evidence you are seeking to adduce, and how far into the complainant's history, and the relationship you are wanting to delve. And I do not think it is fair [for] . . . the Crown to have to answer the case, really, in reply . . .*

When defence counsel pressed that the rape shield laws were not only concerned with the complainant's well-being, but also required consideration of '*unfair prejudice*' to the accused, the judge emphasized that the impact on the Crown case was also relevant:

> *TJ: Well, put it this way. I will not be forcing the Crown to close until I have your full s 293 application, because right now you know what you want to adduce evidence on. It is not arising out of the chief of the complainant. You know where you want to go and, in all fairness, it needs to be put before the Court for the application to be determined.*

While compliance with the application process was the norm in our trials, we also observed trials in which there was no application before a sexual experience question was asked, including instances of prosecutor non-compliance. In such cases, either counsel objected to the question asked, or the judge intervened, with the matter addressed in the absence of the jury.

Our impression is that questioning of the complainant about past sexual activities, after leave had been granted, was closely monitored. For example, in one trial, defence counsel's proposed questions regarding past sexual activities were carefully scrutinized in advance by the trial judge, with input from the prosecutor. The questions were then revised to make them less 'brutal'. Ultimately, it was decided (based on a suggestion from the prosecutor) that the questions first be asked during a 'Basha inquiry',[41] which essentially affords an opportunity for the questions and answers to be previewed in the absence of the jury. If necessary, adjustments can be made before the witness is questioned in front of the jury. Our reading of the transcript of that inquiry suggests that the cross-examination was measured and in accordance with the agreed approach.

In another trial, cross-examination on sexual activity began to stray outside the agreed parameters, but was quickly closed down after a prosecution objection and the matter was discussed in the absence of the jury. The defence wanted to assert that the absence of sexual activity between the complainant and her husband signalled an 'unhappy marriage', and defence counsel suggested that the *absence* of sexual activity was not caught by the rape shield restriction. The prosecution contested this submission and the trial judge ruled that cross-examination should be confined to questions about the state of the complainant's marriage generally, rather than about sexual activity. During cross-examination, defence counsel pushed the limits set by the trial judge, and the prosecutor objected:

D: *Your relationship with your husband wasn't very good at this time either, was it, as of July 31 last year?*
C: *It wasn't good? What do you mean? It wasn't good?*
D: *Did you tell your sister that your marriage was a loveless marriage?*
C: *No, I did not.*
D: *Did you tell your sister that your marriage relationship had ceased?*
P: *Your Honour, I interrupt at this stage. I object to this line of questioning on the basis of its relevance to the fact in issue, Your Honour.*

A discussion followed in the absence of the jury, at the end of which defence counsel agreed to ask no further questions on this topic.

We offer two reflections on this trial. On the one hand, it shows that, with vigilance from the prosecution and the trial judge, even a boundary-pushing defence counsel can be constrained. This also occurred in another trial, where the judge interrupted cross-examination of the complainant to warn defence counsel that their line of questioning (including the suggestion that it was not uncommon for the complainant to allow female and male friends to sleep in her bed) might be veering into prohibited territory. After a brief discussion in the absence of the complainant, defence counsel indicated that they would not continue the line of questioning.

[41] *R v Basha* (1989) 39 A Crim R 337.

On the other hand, we note that defence counsel's inappropriate line of questioning about the state of the complainant's marriage was ultimately interrupted on the basis of a *relevance* objection. This prompts us to ponder why the proposed line of questioning was not proactively disallowed, noting that in earlier discussions, the trial judge had expressed reservations about the relevance of the topic that the defence wanted to pursue, but offered no ruling, before the discussion reverted to the application of Victoria's rape shield laws. In Chapters 7 and 9, we discuss the implications of the broad approach to relevance in Australian evidence law, including the opportunities it creates for engaging rape myth-based lines of cross-examination. Here we note that, as a matter of law, where a party seeks to admit sexual experience or activity evidence, a threshold issue that should precede consideration of the operation of rape shield laws is whether the evidence has first been assessed as meeting the test for relevance.[42]

* * *

Our analysis suggests that the legislative restrictions on sexual experience evidence in NSW and Victoria, although not entirely foolproof, were operating as intended. In this regard our findings differ from those in other jurisdictions. To be clear, complainants were asked questions about sexual experience in the trials in our study. Our point is that counsel and judges appeared to generally play by the 'rules' (with some exceptions noted above). Applications were made, submissions taken, and pre-trial rulings delivered including about the scope of questions. Where counsel strayed from those 'rules', objections were forthcoming or the judge shut-down the line of questioning. While complainants were still regularly asked questions about sexual experience it should be remembered that the provisions in NSW and Victoria regulating sexual experience evidence were never designed to prohibit *all such questions*—that *was* the choice made by the early drafters only in relation to prohibiting questions on sexual reputation. In the context of our examination in Chapter 3 of different modes of statutory influence, the progressive reforms to prohibit sexual reputation evidence are unique. The legislative drafting route in relation to sexual experience evidence was different but nonetheless important: to produce a special architecture to control and limit questions on such evidence (a 'restrictive model'). These rules appear to be having a material effect on the contents of cross-examination which in turn has implications for complainant experience (process justice) and trial outcomes (outcome justice). Of course, as we will explore in Chapter 7, the same cannot be said for cross-examining complainants about rape myths.

[42] *R v Burton* [2013] NSWCCA 335 (Simpson J).

4. Conclusion

Special measures now have a long history as an important part of the architecture of modernized Australian rape laws. Our analysis of transcripts from Victoria and NSW rape trials revealed that most special measures—including general and specific *procedural* measures, and the evidentiary rules governing evidence of the complainant's sexual 'reputation' and sexual experience and activity—were operating as intended. Our sense is that they make an important contribution to making the experience of giving evidence less traumatizing than it has traditionally been. But we also saw instances where complainants were denied the full benefit of the special measures to which they were entitled for a variety of reasons—including misunderstandings or lack of knowledge about the applicable laws and expected arrangements, as well as the technological inadequacies of the assigned courtroom or remote location for CCTV evidence.

Rape trials constitute a large proportion of the caseload of the County Court of Victoria and the District Court of NSW, and the special measures discussed in this chapter have been in place for many years. In these circumstances, there is no valid excuse for the flaws, missteps, and failings that we have documented in this chapter. And we don't think it is enough to point to the fact that such blemishes were rarely observed across more than 100 trials. This is true, but all complainants are entitled to be confident that the available mechanisms for minimizing trauma will be in operation in the trial that matters most to them.

Alongside these *procedural* measures, we also observed solid compliance with the *evidentiary* special measures that are designed to significantly reduce the likelihood that complainants will be asked distressing questions about their past sex lives. The (almost) complete absence of questions about sexual 'reputation' shows what a *prohibition* mode of statutory influence can achieve—and invites consideration of whether other categories of rape myth-based evidence might be treated similarly. We consider this idea further in Chapter 10.

The laws on sexual experience evidence do not go this far; they were always intended to restrict (not prohibit) lines of questioning via a rigorous scrutiny process, which was on display in most of the trials we examined: pre-trial application, submissions and rulings based on statutory criteria, followed by vigilance during questioning of witnesses to ensure everyone 'plays by the rules' during the trial. Mindful that some previous studies have made more negative assessments of whether sexual history evidence regimes are operating as intended, and noting our relatively modest (and sometimes incomplete) sample of trial transcripts, we are hesitant about characterizing NSW and Victorian rape laws as unequivocal success stories of the progressive rape law reform project of the last 50 years.

Another explanation for our caution is that, as we were finalizing this chapter, the Victorian Court of Appeal handed down its decision in *Bloomfield v R*, an appeal against an interlocutory ruling.[43] Reading this judgment served to remind us that the parameters of rape shield laws continue to be contested, and the protections afforded to complainants remain susceptible to judicial constructions that may be out of sync with the trajectory of progressive rape law reform. By majority, the Court of Appeal overturned the trial judge's *disallowance* of a defence application to cross-examine the complainant about certain sexual activities. The relevant sexual activities related to two prior allegations of rape made by the complainant. The defence argument in favour of leave to cross-examine the complainant can be summarized as follows: because the complainant, it was alleged, had lied about two past rape allegations, she had a tendency to fabricate; therefore, the evidence would support the defence case that her allegation against the accused was fabricated. A full account of the evidence is not possible here but, suffice to say, it was by no means established that the two previous allegations were false.[44]

The majority reasoned that there was 'an inference to be drawn' that it was 'improbable that [the complainant] was raped or sexually assaulted' on each of these occasions by different men.[45] The evidence thereby met the heightened test of 'substantial' relevance to a fact in issue[46] and it was in the 'interests of justice' to permit the cross-examination. Any distress, humiliation, or embarrassment to the complainant would be 'relatively minor'.[47] In dissent, Walker JA held that the relevant cross-examination about the complainant's prior sexual activities did not go to a fact in issue and could only impugn her credit, and was thereby not permitted.[48]

Given the 'high incidence of sexual violence', a factor included in statutory guiding principles for the interpretation of law applicable to sexual offence trials,[49] including in circumstances where women are intoxicated (as this woman was),[50] we find the majority's reasoning alarming, because it undermines the protections that should be afforded to complainants about past sexual activity. We also note that the majority reasoning about the complainant's (un)believability is reminiscent of the deeply entrenched rape myth that women lie about rape.[51] As we will show in Chapter 7, this gendered stereotype was detectable beneath the surface of complainant cross-examination in almost every one of the contemporary trials we analysed. As we argue in Chapter 10, appellate courts have an important role in challenging rape myths; they should not be engaging them.

[43] *Bloomfield (a pseudonym) v The King* [2025] VSCA 98.
[44] ibid [27], [71].
[45] ibid [78], [84].
[46] ibid [86]
[47] ibid [86]–[87].
[48] ibid [112], [137]–[139]; see Criminal Procedure Act 2009 (Vic), s 352(b).
[49] Criminal Procedure Act 2008 (Vic) s 338(a).
[50] In Chapter 8 we analyse the challenges faced by complainants who were intoxicated at the time of the rape.
[51] See Chapter 2 at p. 33.

An additional basis for anxiety about the stability of rape shield laws in Australia comes from an unlikely source: the recent report of the Australian Law Reform Commission (ALRC), *Safe, Informed, Supported: Justice Responses to Sexual Violence*.[52] We regard the NSW 'exclusionary' approach to sexual experience evidence as an exemplar of what a strong mode of statutory influence looks like. As we noted in Chapter 3, the ALRC has recommended that it be replaced with a 'discretionary leave model for the admission of sexual history evidence, consistent with the approach adopted in all other jurisdictions'.[53] The Commission acknowledged that it had insufficient time to adequately consult on the effectiveness of the existing provision[54]—and did not undertake any evaluative work (including trial transcript analysis) regarding the operation of the current provision (despite its strong recommendation on the importance of such evaluations in other areas).

There is a certain irony in the fact that the latest inquiry into further modernizing the architecture of Australian rape law in the direction of genuinely trauma-informed approaches, with a commitment to reducing the influence of rape myths and misconceptions, has recommended 'roll back' of arguably the high-water mark reform of the last 50 years. The pursuit of national harmonization does not justify erosion of what has been achieved to date in some jurisdictions.[55] The implication carried by the Commission's recommendation is that NSW rape shield laws are imbalanced—in favour of complainant well-being. Our findings challenge this characterization. Strong restrictions on sexual experience evidence have a unique capacity to alleviate retraumatization of complainants and reduce myth-based reasoning in trials, while still respecting the rights of the accused by allowing the defence to ask questions that adduce relevant evidence.

* * *

The findings presented in this chapter underscore what can be achieved, in terms of rape trial transformation, by strong modes of statutory influence, including *prohibitions* and *entitlements*. As we will show in coming chapters, when it comes to the substance of examination-in-chief and cross-examination, Australian law makers have largely eschewed this approach, preferring more benign modes of statutory influence. This leaves a lot of room for problematic rape myths to circulate in trials, and limits the capacity of reforms to materially improve the access of victim-survivors to a trial forum that delivers both process justice and outcome justice.

52 ALRC (n 30).
53 ibid 385.
54 ibid 387.
55 See Guzyal Hill and Jonathan Crowe, 'Harmonising Sexual Consent Law in Australia: Goals, Risks and Challenges' (2023) 49 Monash University Law Review 1, 8, 10–11; discussed also in ALRC (n 30) 85.

6

Framing the Crown Case

The Influence of 'Real Rape' Attributes

1. Introduction

As described in Chapter 3, the progressive rape law reform narrative suggests that rape laws and trials have been *transformed* to rid trials of rape myths and reduce retraumatization of complainants. As discussed in Chapter 2, a large body of feminist and other scholarship has systematically demonstrated the disconnect between rape myths and the reality of rape including how complainants respond to rape. It might be expected that this context—of significant law reform and improved understanding of rape—should assist the prosecution to prove a charge of rape without relying on the rape schema[1] or 'real rape' attributes. Our analysis of Victorian and NSW rape trials found little evidence that this is so.

Much of the blame for deploying rape myths in the courtroom tends to be attributed to defence counsel (and in Chapter 7 we present findings which confirm that such practices are common). In this chapter, we show that prosecutors play a part too—by placing front and centre in the Crown case many of the real rape attributes that research has discredited, including by relying on evidence of resistance, distress, and immediate complaint.[2] While there is nothing to prohibit the prosecution framing the case in this way, the upshot is that the old rape schema is left intact. We also reveal that when the prosecution *does* challenge rape myths, this tends to take the form of attempting to explain why *on this occasion* the complainant's conduct deviated from rape myth-based expectations, which leaves the myth undisturbed or even consolidated.

Before we turn to these two dimensions of the prosecution's part in the continued circulation of rape myths in trials, and consistent with our interest in both

[1] See Chapter 1 at p. 9 and Chapter 2 at pp. 29–30.

[2] Previous rape trial studies in common law jurisdictions have produced similar findings. See, eg, Olivia Smith, *Rape Trials in England and Wales: Observing Justice and Rethinking Rape Myths* (Palgrave Macmillan 2018) 64; Elisabeth McDonald, *Rape Myths as Barriers to Fair Trial Process* (Canterbury UP 2020) 48; Elaine Craig, *Putting Trials on Trial: Sexual Assault and the Failure of the Legal Profession* (McGill-Queen's UP 2018) ch 5; Ellen Daly, *Rape, Gender and Class: Intersections in Courtroom Narratives* (Palgrave Macmillan 2022) ch 2.

Reforming Rape Trials. Julia Quilter and Luke McNamara, Oxford University Press.
 DOI: 10.1093/9780198948155.003.0006

process justice and outcome justice, we discuss features of prosecution practice that are misaligned with trauma-informed best practice.

2. Examination-in-Chief Questioning: Trauma Informed?

Recognition of the need to improve the courtroom experience of complainants and reduce retraumatization has been a focus of rape law reform efforts, including the special measures discussed in Chapter 5. Added to these special protections, the literature recognizes that how complainants are questioned in the courtroom is important to reducing retraumatization and producing best evidence.[3] We found that, generally, prosecutors (and judges) make a concerted effort to ensure that the courtroom is a less foreign, hostile, and daunting place for complainants than it has traditionally been. This was evidenced in the generally courteous approach to complainants, including in modes of address, as well as being sensitive to the complainant's needs while giving evidence—such as being responsive to distress and the need for breaks.[4]

While we observed examples of best practice from some prosecutors, there was considerable trial-to-trial (prosecutor-to-prosecutor) variation. These divergent practices have implications for whether complainants can be confident that their examination-in-chief will be conducted in the most trauma-informed way possible.

Form of questioning

An important aspect of a trauma-informed courtroom is to ensure that complainants are able to tell their story in their own language and manner.[5] The Australian Law Reform Commission (ALRC) heard recently that complainants 'felt that they did not have agency, choice, or voice'.[6] This is particularly important when recounting intimate details of a rape. There is a large body of research that shows that questioning style has the capacity to enhance the provision of best evidence, and can contribute to a complainant being afforded 'room' in the trial to tell their story

[3] See, eg, Mark R Kebbell, Steven Deprez, and Graham Wagstaff, 'The Direct and Cross-Examination of Complainants and Defendants in Rape Trials: A Quantitative Analysis of Question Type' (2003) 9 Psychology, Crime and Law 49; Louise Ellison and Jacqueline Wheatcroft, '"Could You Ask Me That in a Different Way Please?" Exploring the Impact of Courtroom Questioning and Witness Familiarisation on Adult Witness Accuracy' (2010) 11 Criminal Law Review 823.

[4] We observed some rare moments of discourtesy including where the prosecutor had failed to learn how to pronounce the complainant's name.

[5] Elena Campbell and others, '"This Is My Story. It's Your Case, But It's My Story": Interview Study' (KPMG and RMIT Centre for Innovative Justice 2023).

[6] ALRC, *Safe, Informed, Supported: Justice Responses to Sexual Violence* (ALRC Report 143, 2025) 100.

in their own voice.[7] Allowing evidence to be given in narrative form is understood to be best practice for both children and adults.[8] Thirty years ago, the *Heroines of Fortitude* report encouraged this approach.[9]

Section 29(2) of the Evidence Act 1995 (NSW) and the Evidence Act 2008 (Vic) allows evidence to be given in narrative form, either on the court's own motion, or on application by the party that called the witness. In the trials we analysed, there were no instances where the prosecution applied for (or the court ordered) the complainant to give evidence in narrative form.

The use of open-ended questions is another mechanism that is known to enhance best evidence including ensuring accuracy of memory.[10] In a number of the trials we analysed, the complainant was prompted by a series of open-ended questions during evidence-in-chief, such as: '*What happened then?*'; '*What happened next?*'; '*So what happened*'; '*and then?*'. This afforded the complainant space to tell their story in 'their voice'. Notably, in such trials there were few objections by defence counsel. For example, in one trial, the complainant and the accused had known each for some years before the events that were the subject of the trial. The complainant was afforded room to provide a lengthy explanation of prior events that contextualized her fear of the accused. At one point the complainant asked the prosecutor if she should continue to which the prosecutor said, '*You're on a roll, please keep going*'. There was no objection by defence counsel to this approach.

While the adoption of open-ended questions appeared to enhance the quality of a complainant's evidence during examination-in-chief, this was not consistently adopted across the trials we observed. In some trials, the prosecution adopted a closely controlled step-by-step question and answer format. We observed that one of the weaknesses of this approach was that complainants were sometimes unable to recall the specific detail being sought, and so responded '*I don't remember*'. For example:

> Q: *Do you remember getting in the car?*
> A: *No. Yes, I do, but I don't remember where I went.*
> Q: *What is the next thing you do remember?*
> A: *I remember that I met up with three boys and then they were in my car and then the next thing I know is that we somehow got to the silver sedan motor vehicle.*

[7] See Chapter 2 at p. 31.

[8] ALRC (n 6) 272; Martine Powell, 'Investigative Interviewing: #askgoodquestions' (2020) 42 InPsych 16; Kimberlee Burrows and Martine Powell, 'A Prosecutor's Guide to Improving Child Witness Interviews About Alleged Sexual Abuse: A View From the Australian Context' (2013) 5 Investigative Interviewing: Research and Practice 12.

[9] NSW Department for Women, 'Heroines of Fortitude: The Experience of Women in Court as Victims of Sexual Assault' (NSW Department for Women Report 1996) 141.

[10] Kebbell, Deprez, and Wagstaff (n 3); Burrows and Powell (n 8); Powell (n 8).

Q: *Again we will take that step by step. You remember meeting up with three boys. Do you remember how you met them?*
A: *No, I don't.*

The expectation that the complainant *should* remember such details does not align with the scientific literature on memory and trauma,[11] particularly where the complainant was intoxicated at the time of the events they were asked to recall[12]—a topic we consider further in Chapter 8.

'Signposting' was another good questioning practice we observed in examination-in-chief in some trials. This involves expressly advising the complainant when the prosecutor is about to move from one topic to another, and when examination-in-chief is nearly at its end. Introducing structure and clarity in this way reduces the risk of the complainant becoming confused, and offers some reassurance to the complainant they are progressing through the evidence-in-chief phase. Signposting is good practice and could be adopted more routinely by the prosecution.

Detailed questioning: location, sexual acts, body parts, and positions

It is well known that being asked to provide precise and intimate details—about the location where the rape occurred, and about sexual acts and body parts—in front of strangers is challenging and retraumatizing for complainants when giving evidence in a criminal trial.[13] While prosecutors generally attempted to be sensitive, including by acknowledging the personal nature of the questioning or apologizing for asking about such intimate matters, detailed questioning of this sort was commonplace in the trials we analysed. Table 6.1 offers examples of topics and questions.

We also observed questioning about details of the sexual acts which did not appear relevant to the charge, and may have been distressing and embarrassing for the complainant to answer. For example, complainants were questioned about:

- whether the accused had ejaculated;

[11] See, eg, Katrin Hohl and Martin A Conway, 'Memory as Evidence: How Normal Features of Victim Memory Lead to the Attrition of Rape Complainants' (2017) 17 Criminology & Criminal Justice 248; Shazia Akhtar and others, 'The "Common Sense" Memory Belief System and its Implications' (2018) 22 The International Journal of Evidence & Proof 289; Lori Haskell and Melanie Randall, 'The Impact of Trauma on Adult Sexual Assault Victims' (Justice Canada 2019).

[12] See generally, Heather D Flowe and Anna Carline (eds), *Alcohol and Remembering Rape: New Evidence for Practice* (Palgrave Pivot 2021).

[13] See, eg, McDonald (n 2) 90–91; NSW Department for Women (n 9) 130–32, 141–42.

- on what location of the complainant's body the accused ejaculated;
- what part of the complainant's breast the accused had touched;
- how the accused touched the complainant's breast, such as '*squeezed*' or '*sucked*' (in one trial the complainant was asked to stand and demonstrate to the jury how the accused had touched her breasts);
- whether the accused's penis was hard or soft during forced oral sex; and
- the length of time the sexual intercourse had lasted and how the accused was moving during sexual intercourse.

Reflecting on these findings, we are prompted to ask *why* prosecutors consider it appropriate and necessary to ask questions of this sort? In addition to the risk of retraumatizing the complainant, there is also a risk that the complainant's credibility in the eyes of the jury will be adversely impacted. The very asking of the question likely assigns relevance to the (minute) detail requested, and the complainant's common response of '*I don't remember*' underscores the complainant's imperfect recall.

We also observed a lack of sensitivity by some prosecutors to the complainant's (sexual) language choices or understanding of anatomy. In some trials, prosecutors required complainants to use 'formal' terminology for anatomy or sex acts which

Table 6.1 Questions on specific details asked during examination-in-chief

Topic	Illustrative Questions
Location of the rape	*Can you tell us what the lighting conditions were like?Can you tell us where the bed was in relation to the door?What was in your room at that time furniture-wise?So where was your head oriented on the bed?Are you able to say if… there were bedclothes on the bed? Where were they?*
How clothing was removed	*Do you remember how your underwear was removed?When you say your underwear [was] then pulled to the side, what part of your underwear was pulled to the side?And did you say those things to him before he unzipped your vest?In relation to your top garments, did he take your bra off as well as the top?*
Position of body parts	*Where were your legs?Where were your hands at the time?Do you know what position his body was in?How were you on the bed?*
Timing and duration	*How long was he putting his penis into your vagina for?Was it fast or slow?How long did this whole episode last?How long did he do that for [touching your breast]?*

were not always understood or used by the complainant. For example: ejaculate rather than *cum*; penis rather than *dick*; sperm rather than *cum*; oral sex rather than *giving head*; have sex rather than *fook*. The following extract from examination-in-chief in one trial illustrates the effect that this style of questioning can have on the complainant:

> Q: *When you said during the interview that you gave him head, what did you mean by that?*
> A: *Oral - is it oral - oral sex.*
> Q: *And could you tell us how you gave him oral sex, what did you do?*
> A: *Gave him head, so when he asked me - like when I said I'll do it, that's what I did, gave him oral sex and then after just laid there.*
> Q: *I'm sorry to ask you for these details, but your mouth was involved, what part of his body?*
> A: *His penis.*
> Q: *Was it hard or soft?*
> A: *Hard.*
> Q: *Do you know what I mean by the word ejaculate?*
> A: *Can I have a break?*
> Q: *Of course.*

The prosecution must always prove beyond reasonable doubt the elements of the offence including the conduct element (ie sexual intercourse). However, in the many trials where the accused conceded that sexual intercourse occurred, but claimed it was consensual (the majority of trials we analysed), we doubt the appropriateness of the sorts of questions we have discussed here. They will often be unnecessary and likely to increase the complainant's distress. While there is nothing preventing the prosecution from asking these types of questions, they sit uneasily with the trajectory of reforms designed to improve the experience of complainants in trials and reduce retraumatization.

Viewing of CCTV footage

Although such evidence is rare, in a small number of the trials we analysed, the prosecution planned to play a recording of CCTV footage which included interactions between the complainant and the accused that constituted the alleged rape. A question arose as to whether the complainant should be given the opportunity to view the footage ahead of time, with the aim of reducing the shock and distress of seeing the footage for the first time while in the witness box. In one trial, defence counsel was opposed to the complainant being allowed to do so. After extensive submissions and discussion, the trial judge adopted what we consider to be an appropriate trauma-informed approach, ruling that the complainant should be given a chance to watch the footage ahead of time to help prepare her for its contents:

> TJ: *She is shown in the video naked and taking part in sexual acts in the taxi with the accused. It will be embarrassing and probably distressing for her to see the footage, and in the circumstances it is appropriate that she should not see it for the first time in front of the jury. The setting in which she does see it for the first time should be an appropriate one in the presence of, for example, [the solicitor instructing the prosecutor].*

Audio evidence, such as a recording of a pretext call between the complainant and the accused, also has the potential to cause distress. In one case, the trial judge was alert to this possibility and forewarned the complainant—albeit, in court, immediately prior to the audio being played:

> P: *All right. Now, I want to play these two records, Your Honour. And I want you to listen to them, please, Ms [complainant]. Then I will ask you some more questions after listening to those two phone calls, all right?*
> TJ: *Have you heard those phone calls since you made them?*
> C: *No, I've read them.*
> TJ: *Okay. It can sometimes be a bit of a shock to hear your voice again, so just be ready for that.*

The complainant *did* become distressed, and the trial judge intervened appropriately by calling a break:

> TJ: *... [The prosecutor] wants [to ask] you some questions before we play the third recording, so what I might do is just give you a bit of a break. As I said, it is – it's sometimes a shock, isn't it, to hear your voice on the recording when you haven't heard that before. So we will just give you a bit of time. Can you take a break, members of the jury....*

Although the trial judge handled the issue well when it arose, we think it would have been preferable if the complainant had been forewarned, before the trial commenced, and given an opportunity to hear the recording.

We realize that the correctness of the watch in advance approach may be questioned, and not just by defence lawyers. In the context of our interviews with lawyers about intoxication evidence,[14] when asked whether they would offer a

[14] See Chapter 8.

complainant an advanced screening of CCTV footage that was to be admitted at trial, one prosecutor said:

> *No, because... that probably amounts to coaching. I mean, you know, I would show a complainant their text messages because they've sent them, they would know about it, but CCTV... – it's a different thing.... [A]t the end of the day you have to be very fair and you can't show... a complainant evidence which she would not be privy to because that might affect the evidence that she gives in court.*

The prosecutor acknowledged that there was a difficult 'balance' to be struck between their duty to the court and the responsibility to avoid retraumatizing the complainant:

> *Yeah, because you can actually see people becoming... very triggered and they're completely traumatised because they can see themselves in a light that... probably they just didn't imagine and, you know, it's an hour before they were sexually assaulted. So it is traumatic, it's traumatising, but they're the rules within which I work, I can't change that.*

We consider that a trauma-informed courtroom should adopt, as routine practice, advanced viewing by the complainant of CCTV footage that includes images of themselves and the accused, and advance listening to audio that includes the voices of the complainant and the accused. A protocol to this effect would be preferable to an approach that requires trial-by-trial contestation and judicial adjudication. We acknowledge that there may be tensions here with the rigours of an adversarial system, including the expectation that matters that go to potential forensic advantage should be assessed on a case-by-case basis, with opportunities for counsel to make submissions. However, from the perspective of creating an environment of sensitivity and respect for complainants, and minimizing distress and retraumatization, we believe that advance viewing is desirable. As we argued in Chapter 5, all complainants are entitled to be reassured (in advance) that they will receive the benefit of measures designed to minimize their retraumatization. In our view, that applies equally to special protections that have been legislated (such as giving evidence from a remote location via CCTV) and other trauma-informed practices, like the chance to preview distressing video or audio evidence.

3. Rape Myths and the Crown Case

How the prosecution frames the Crown case is significant, including because it signals the importance of certain evidence to the jury. While we acknowledge the overriding duty of prosecutors to ensure a fair trial, and to adduce all relevant evidence,[15] in the trials we examined, the Crown case was often framed in a formulaic way. This included adducing evidence of questionable utility, even if it satisfied the broad definition of 'relevant' evidence.[16] Not only does this have the capacity to extend the duration of the trial, including the complainant's time 'on the stand', but we believe that some categories of evidence provided avenues for rape myths to be invoked. These included evidence about clothing; evidence from medical examinations including DNA evidence; and CCTV and digital communications evidence.

Clothing

Questioning a complainant about the clothing worn at the time of the alleged offence has long been a 'stock' cross-examination technique—engaging the rape myth that there is a relationship between 'sexually provocative' attire and consent.[17] While such lines of questioning may be less common today, and less inclined to explicitly shame and blame women for the rape based on what they were wearing at the time, it continues to feature in rape trials.[18] Clothing-based myths and stereotypes now feature on the list of educative jury directions that have been legislated in Australian jurisdictions in recent years.[19]

Given this history, we were surprised to see that in a number of the trials we analysed, the prosecution asked the complainant a number of questions about clothing and underwear. Recognizing that this *will* sometimes be important information given the facts of the case, there were trials where it was not obvious to us that the clothing details mattered. In one trial, the prosecutor asked the complainant seven questions about her underwear (including its location in a photograph, colour, and brand). In another, the prosecutor asked the complainant 27 questions about what she was wearing (a '*onesie leopard print*'), and when it was removed by the accused (in a car in an alleyway). This focus has the capacity to distress and confuse the complainant:

[15] Office of the Director of Public Prosecutions (NSW), 'Prosecution Guidelines' (ODPP NSW 2021) [2.2]–[2.3]; Director of Public Prosecutions Victoria, 'Policy of the Director of Public Prosecutions for Victoria' (DPP Victoria 2023) [21].

[16] Evidence Act 1995 (NSW), s 55; Evidence Act 2008 (Vic), s 55; discussed further in Chapter 9 at p. 213.

[17] The *Heroines of Fortitude* report found that just under half of complainants (44%) were asked detailed questions about the clothing worn at the time of the alleged offence: NSW Department for Women (n 9) 162–65. See also McDonald (n 2) 286–92.

[18] See Sarah Zydervelt and others, 'Lawyers' Strategies for Cross-Examining Rape Complainants: Have We Moved Beyond the 1950s?' (2017) 57 British Journal of Criminology 551.

[19] See, eg, Criminal Procedure Act 1986 (NSW), s 292E, as amended by the Crimes Legislation Amendment (Sexual Consent Reforms) Act 2021 (NSW). See also Chapter 3 at p. 69.

Q: *Once you got to the alleyway, is that what you're saying--*
A: *Yes.*
Q: *--your clothing came off?*
A: *Yes.*
Q: *I'm asking you just to restrict yourself to before then. Were you fully clothed up until you arrived at the alleyway?*
A: *Hold on one second.*
Q: *Sorry, you don't understand the question?*
A: *No, I don't.*

While it is clearly not the intention of the prosecution to draw attention to clothing so as to engage a rape myth about inferred consent, there is a risk that questioning on the topic during examination-in-chief, especially lengthy questioning, reinforces the idea that attire *is* relevant to consent and provides a platform for cross-examination on this topic.

Medical evidence

As we explained in Chapter 2, the idea that the signs of a 'true' rape can be found on the victim-survivor's body is one of the oldest and most enduring rape myths. It underpinned the expectation of physical resistance and the search for evidence of physical injuries that verified the complainant's attempts to resist. As a consequence, medical examination of the complainant's body came to be regarded as an important part of investigation and evidence gathering. In Chapter 3, we discussed the range of ways in which rape laws have been re-written to displace the focus on resistance—including modernized definitions of consent,[20] and educative jury directions.[21]

Nevertheless, DNA and/or other forms of medical evidence were led in the majority of the trials we analysed. This was so even though the identity of the accused was typically not in issue, and sexual intercourse was often conceded. In most trials, what was in dispute was whether or not the complainant consented to the act(s) in question. It is well known that medical evidence is equivocal or neutral in relation to the question of consent—even where the complainant sustained injuries.[22] This knowledge featured prominently in the evidence of medical expert witnesses and closing submissions of prosecutors. For example, '*The doctor could not comment on whether or not the injuries around the anus were caused by consensual penetration*'.

[20] Eg Crimes Act 1900 (NSW), s 61HI(4).
[21] Eg Jury Directions Act 2015 (Vic), s 47D.
[22] See Chapter 2 at p. 21.

We appreciate that the prosecution may choose to adduce 'neutral' medical evidence, anticipating that, as the NSW Court of Criminal Appeal has observed, 'a jury will usually expect a complainant to be medically examined'.[23] However, there is also a line of authority from the same court that suggests that 'the calling of inconclusive medical evidence is undesirable and should be avoided if defence counsel will agree to make no comment on the Crown's failure to call the doctor'.[24] Of course, defence agreement may not be forthcoming. However, there remains a risk that routinely calling such evidence will reinforce the myth that a 'true' complaint of rape can be known by evidence of physical injury (and resistance).

CCTV/digital media communications

Here we group together two further categories of evidence: CCTV recordings—from one or more of the many places that fixed CCTV cameras are installed (including licensed premises, public streets, and common areas of apartment buildings); and records of digital media communications—text messages and social media posts sent or shared (or received) by the complainant. Such evidence was another routine feature of many of the trials we analysed, the utility of which was not necessarily obvious.

CCTV evidence—typically footage which depicted the complainant at some point prior to the alleged rape (as distinct from footage of the actual rape, discussed earlier)—*may* provide some contextualization of events. However, we think that careful consideration is required to identify whether, on balance, such evidence may impliedly reinforce stereotypes about sexually provocative behaviour and inferred consent as well as myths about intoxication and consent (the latter we consider further in Chapter 8). For example, in one trial, the complainant was shown a large quantity of (video only) footage taken from CCTV cameras at a club where she had interacted with the accused. The prosecutor paused the recording a number of times to ask the complainant what the accused was saying in the 'scene' depicted. Her most common answer was '*I don't remember*'.

Records of text messages and other digital communications are routinely collected during police investigations, and evidence of this sort was admitted in 66% of the 108 trials we analysed. In some trials, this evidence was engaged to support the Crown case (and the complainant's allegation) including where it was said to contain an admission by the accused. More commonly, however, digital communications evidence was utilized by the defence to facilitate rape myth-based cross-examination of the complainant, including: characterizing content as 'flirtatious' (and a basis for inferring consent); using content as a touchstone for suggesting

[23] *KE v R* [2021] NSWCCA 119 [112] (N Adams J).
[24] *Adams v R* [2018] NSWCCA 303 [101] (Campbell J).

inconsistency in accounts; and interpreting content as characterizing a complaint as 'delayed' or incomplete.[25]

In fairness to prosecutors, recognizing their responsibility to adduce all relevant evidence, this aspect of the trials we observed is not so much the result of a failure to reimagine how the Crown case should be framed and made, as a reminder of the broad parameters of relevant evidence (a topic we consider further in Chapter 9). Nonetheless, we do think the routine inclusion of digital communications evidence requires reconsideration, particularly where it relates to communications that took place days or weeks before the alleged rape, and given that there is often very little appreciation of the nuances and idiosyncrasies involved in authoring and reading text messages and social media posts. Digital communication evidence is fertile ground for the invocation of rape myths in trials.[26]

4. 'Real Rape' Attributes

In addition to the possibility that rape myths may enter the courtroom through evidence that is routinely admitted but not always necessary, we found that examination-in-chief was a point in the trial when rape myths were engaged in a more direct way. It was common for the prosecution to frame the Crown case in ways that reflected the rape schema that we introduced in Chapters 1 and 2. The *presence* of 'real rape' attributes—including resistance, immediate complaint, and complainant distress—was highlighted, presumably because this was regarded as a strength of the Crown case. Yet the continuation of such lines of questioning seems at odds with the narrative of progressive rape law reform oriented towards positive, communicative, and affirmative concepts of consent. We start by drawing attention to the relative invisibility of the reformed concept of consent in the Crown case in the trials we analysed.

The concept of consent

As discussed in Chapter 3, concerted efforts have been made over the past 50 years to 'perfect' the concept of consent, and transform it in accordance with an ethic of free agreement and communication. We found little evidence of this transformation on display in the framing of the Crown case. By this we do not mean simply that phrases such as 'communicative model' or 'communicative consent' did not appear in the transcripts (although this is certainly the case), but also that the lines

[25] See Chapter 7 at p. 152.

[26] See Julia Quilter and others, 'Text Messages and Social Media Posts as Evidence in Rape Trials: A New Entry Point for Rape Myths?' (2026) Crime, Media, Culture https://doi.org/10.1177/1741659026 1429130 accessed 30 March 2026.

of questioning pursued by the prosecution rarely showed any trace—explicit or implicit—of the idea of consent as 'free and voluntary agreement', involving communication between the parties to the sexual act. At most, we observed cursory mention in opening and/or closing addresses by the prosecution that the legal definition of consent means 'free and voluntary agreement'. This was sometimes accompanied by a version of the following statement: '*Furthermore the law says that a person who does not offer actual physical resistance to sexual intercourse is not, by reason only of that fact, to be regarded as having consented to the sexual intercourse*'; and, depending on the facts, a reference to legislated consent 'vitiating' factors (use of force or threats by the accused; that the complainant was asleep etc).

On the rare occasion that agreement did feature in examination-in-chief, it formed part of short sentences such as:

Q: Did you consent or agree to him putting his penis inside your vagina?
A: No.
Q: Did you consent or agree to any sexual contact with the accused man that night?
A: No.

To be clear, we are not suggesting that the simplicity of these questions is improper; it may well be forensically advantageous. Rather, we are drawing attention to the fact that such an approach involves no amplification on the meaning of consent, and tends to assume that the meaning is mutually understood by the questioner and answerer (and the jury). The silent or minimalist approach to the meaning of consent that we observed in most trials stands in contrast to the energy (and volume of statutory words) that has been devoted to modernizing the concept of consent that is said to be at the heart of contemporary rape laws.[27]

We saw only glimpses of active prosecution engagement with an aspect of modernized rape laws that has been taken up in a number of Australian jurisdictions, and we referred to in Chapter 3 as the high-water mark of communicative consent: that an indicia of non-consent is where the complainant did not say or do anything to communicate consent.[28] Legislation to this effect was in operation in Victoria at the time of the trials we analysed.[29] The following two extracts are examples of where prosecution questioning implicitly evoked this concept of communicative consent:

Q: Now at any point, did you do anything?
A: Only after he came.

[27] See Chapter 3 at p. 51.
[28] See Chapter 3 at p. 54.
[29] See, eg, Crimes Act 1958 (Vic), s 36AA(1)(a). Such a provision was only adopted in NSW in 2021: Crimes Act 1900 (NSW), s 61HJ(1)(a), as amended by the Crimes Legislation Amendment (Sexual Consent Reforms) Act 2021 (NSW).

Q: *What did you do?*
A: *I told him he needed to leave. I had made it clear that I'd been awake and I told him he had to leave and I got upset and sad.*
Q: *When you told him to leave, was that the first time you'd said anything since the time he got on that second couch?*
A: *Yeah.*

* * *

Q: *Were you still on your back on the bed?*
A: *Yes.*
Q: *Had you said anything to him at that point?*
A: *No.*
Q: *Had you moved your body at all at that point?*
A: *No.*

These are good-practice examples of what progressive reform of the concept of consent makes possible in terms of a fresh approach to adducing evidence of non-consent. However, in the Victorian trials we analysed, such an approach was exceptional rather than routine. More commonly, the prosecution engaged a decidedly unreformed idea of non-consent as resistance.

Resistance

The expectation that victim-survivors of sexual violence must demonstrate their lack of consent through resistance is one of the oldest and most thoroughly discredited rape myths, and has been the subject of multiple forms of legislative 'correction'. It was striking, then, to see that examination-in-chief questions were regularly framed around the old understanding of non-consent as resistance. In the majority of trials we analysed, the prosecution elicited evidence from the complainant of verbal and physical resistance. The prosecution regularly questioned the complainant about what they *said* or *did* in response to the accused's actions; for example, '*did you say "no"?*'; '*did you scream?*'; '*did you try to push him off?*'. Many questions adduced evidence from the complainant of verbal resistance such as saying '*no*', '*stop*', crying out, screaming, and crying, including trials where the complainant gave evidence that they had done so on multiple occasions. In one case, the complainant '*At least 20 times or more*' told the accused she did not want to have sex with him. Prosecution questioning also elicited evidence from the complainant of physical resistance such as pushing, biting, scratching, kicking, struggling, and fighting back.

Understandably, where complainants *did* say 'no', or *did* physically resist, the prosecution's questions sought to amplify this fact. For example:

Q: *What did you do in response to that [the accused forcibly kissing the complainant], if anything?*
A: *I fought very hard and closed my mouth as hard as I could and he continued to push his mouth onto me and was biting my lips to open my mouth and I kept trying to move away....*
Q: *Did you do anything in relation to that action?*
A: *I was fighting him and fighting.*
Q: *When you say you were fighting him and fighting him, how were you fighting him? What were you doing?*
A: *Trying to punch him off me, trying to pull his hair but his hair was so short I couldn't get a grip.*

* * *

Q: *What were his hands doing, do you recall?*
A: *Holding me down. Just on the, on the shoulders.*
Q: *And what were you doing?*
A: *I couldn't do anything, I - he was too strong I couldn't, I couldn't get him off.*
Q: *Did you try?*
A: *Of course I did.*
Q: *How?*
A: *Um tried to push him off and I couldn't get him off.*
Q: *Did you say anything?*
A: *No.*
Q: *Why not?*
A: *'Cause my kids were asleep in the room, I can't wake 'em up. I didn't want them to come in and see what was going on.*

In the following case, the trial judge joined a resistance-focused line of questioning from the prosecutor:

Q: *Did you say anything to him?*
A: *I asked him to stop.*
Q: *And what, when you say you asked him to stop, what did you say?*
A: *Can you stop.*
TJ: *And was that the second time you said stop, after he made that comment, is that right?*
A: *Yes.*
TJ: *All right.*
Q: *All right. And did you say softly or loudly or what?*
A: *In a loud voice.*
Q: *All right?*

A: And I was holding him away from me. So, like – 'cause I was laying down, so he was on top. So, I was pushing him away from me.
Q: All right. And when you said stop the first time, how loud was it the first time?
A: I'd say it was loud enough, because he asked me to put my voice down because of his housemate.
TJ: And when you say you were pushing him away, can you just describe – again, I know you did something with one of your hands there, was it one hand, two hands or just explain what you did?
A: With two hands. So, I tried to move him away from me.
TJ: And where [were] your hands on him?
A: On his chest. His chest, towards that area.

Of course, such lines of questioning are not seeking to criticize the complainant, or to express *approval* of rape myths. The prosecution is trying to mount the strongest case—and anticipate how the complainant is likely to be cross-examined. The complainant is also entitled to give *their* account of what occurred—including the fact that they said 'no' or tried to push the accused away, if that is what occurred. Recognizing these matters, we nonetheless draw attention to three implications of resistance-focused case framing.

First, and most obviously, there is a disconnect between the sort of language used and encouraged by prosecutors—which is evocative of the (unreformed) idea of rape as defined by *force*. The use of words and phrases such as '*resist*', '*struggle*', '*fight back*', and, in one trial, even the old common law language of '*against her will*', further sediments assumptions about the 'true' complainant, in the face of decades of reform directed at moving the rape trial to focus on the absence of free and voluntary agreement.

Secondly, with prosecution questions heavily focused on what the complainant was *doing*, very little attention was paid to what the complainant was thinking or feeling, or to what communication had (or had not) occurred in relation to agreement to engage in the sexual activity. In one illustrative trial, the complainant attempted to explain that at a point in time when she was being raped by the accused in his taxi, she was trying to memorize the accused's taxi licence number (on display on the car dashboard) for the purposes of identifying him in a later report, which speaks to her *lack of agreement*. However, the significance of this appeared to be lost. The prosecutor's next question began with '*Let's take a step back a little bit*', and then the prosecutor redirected the complainant back to the topic of why she had felt unable to physically resist.

Finally, although well-intentioned, we wonder about the impact of prosecution questions that seemed to imply (or could be perceived—by the complainant and/or the jury—to imply) that the complainant could have done more to resist. For example:

Q: *At any point did you yell or try and hit him or anything like that?*
A: *No, I did try push him away but every time I did raise my voice or try hit him he would have – his temper would escalate....*
Q: *Did you say anything other than stop, that you can remember?*
A: *No, I can't remember.*

* * *

Q: *... did you continue the whole time, or was there a point where you did not ... resist?*
A: *Resist. By the end I couldn't physically resist. I didn't have the physical strength to keep resisting physically.*

* * *

Q: *Now up to this stage had you screamed out at any point in time?*
A: *I was trying – no I didn't scream I don't think, I remember at some time I thought I was seeing people walking by and I tried to call out but I don't think any noise was coming out, I don't think I was making a sound.*

Such lines of questioning tend to validate—rather than disrupt—the assumption that the best evidence of non-consent is resistance, and risk conveying to the complainant (and to the jury) that they did not act as a 'true' victim would have. While the complainant is here afforded the opportunity to explain their response, they are inevitably framed as someone who 'failed' to resist—which sits very uncomfortably with the values of progressive rape law reform.

Complainant distress

Despite the rule's foundation in the dubious assumption that there is only one emotional response that a 'true' victim will display, it remains the case that, as a matter of law, evidence of the complainant's observed distress in the aftermath of the alleged rape is admissible. It may be relevant for two purposes: to 'enhance the *credit* of the complainant' and to 'support the *occurrence* of the offending'.[30] It can strengthen the complaint if it implicates the accused and is reasonably explicable only on the basis of the rape having occurred.[31]

It was therefore unsurprising that in many of the trials we analysed, the prosecution led evidence from a variety of witnesses (friends, family members, ambulance officers, police officers, medical experts), and text messages and other digital communications records, that at a time proximate to the alleged sexual offence,

[30] *R v Churchill* [2025] HCA 11 [3].
[31] *R v Gulliford* [2004] NSWCCA 338 [151].

the complainant displayed distress. Evidence was elicited from witnesses about the complainant's demeanour. Witnesses used a variety of terms to describe the state the complainant was in: '*crying*', '*sobbing*', '*upset*', '*anxious*', '*distressed*', '*distraught*', '*frazzled*', '*dishevelled*', '*shaking*', '*traumatized*', '*scared*', '*frightened*', '*terrified*', '*bewildered*', '*shocked*', '*shut off*', '*confused*', '*hyperventilating*', '*nervous*', '*shaky*', '*sombre*', '*serious*', and '*embarrassed*'. For example:

Q: *Describe the female when you saw her?*
A: *She was distressed, she was crying, she was sort of getting herself together... Uber.*

***

Q: *Now how was [the complainant] when you first saw her in that room?*
A: *Devastated. She was...*
Q: *Why do you say – what was it about her that she was either doing or saying or her appearance that made you think she was devastated?*
A: *It's just her emotions had taken over, she was just crying and crying and she wasn't talking. I was asking her most of the questions and she would kind of just give me one word answers. So when I noticed she was like that, I just decided to get her home.*

Evidence of distress also featured prominently in the prosecution's closing address to the jury. For example:

> *You can also further use that material when you have regard to her distressed condition, when she was telling people, the manner in which she was doing it, and you'll remember that both her father and [witness name redacted] described her as hysterical on the Thursday night. So it goes to the truth of what she's saying; that is, that the allegation is not likely to have been fabricated and more likely to be accurate.*

We don't underestimate the seriousness of evidence of the complainant's observed distress. However, the prevalence of distress evidence in contemporary rape trials seems at odds with one of the central motifs of progressive rape law reform: that it is unfair to judge the complaint against a deeply flawed and inaccurate notion that a 'true' victim behaves in a particular way. What are the implications for the victim-survivor whose post-event demeanour displays anger or stoic silence, or who masks the trauma with a veneer of light-heartedness?

It would be unfair to lay blame for the perpetuation of discredited stereotypes and assumptions at the feet of prosecutors when the practice of adducing distress evidence as part of the Crown case is entirely consistent with the case law. So long as distress evidence is regarded as *strengthening* the Crown case, there is little incentive for prosecutors to move away from it. Indeed, they might be criticized for doing so. The problem lies with the state of the law on the admissibility of distress evidence, which seems to us to be in real tension with the more progressive judicial and legislative messages to be found elsewhere, including appellate authority and recently introduced statutory jury directions that emphasize that there is no typical, proper, or normal response to non-consensual sexual activity.[32]

Immediate complaint

Another discordant note in Crown case framings in the trials we analysed is evidence of prompt or immediate complaint. Against the long history of assuming that the true complainant could be known by the speed of her complaint, we noted in Chapter 3 that this rape myth was one of the early targets of progressive rape law reform—albeit, via 'corrective' jury directions rather than prohibition of this category of evidence. However, throughout this period there has been no change to the evidence rules, which still provide that complaint evidence is admissible (as an exception to the hearsay rule) to prove that the offence occurred *and* to enhance the complainant's credibility.[33] It is perhaps not surprising then that, in the trials we analysed, where it was available, the prosecution relied on evidence of prompt complaint. Complaint evidence came from a wide variety of sources including friends, siblings, parents, relatives, police, 000 calls, ambulance officers, and medical examiners, as well as through records of text messages and other digital communications. The following extract illustrates how the prosecution drew attention to evidence that the complainant's behaviour conformed neatly to the traditional common law (and discredited) expectation of an immediate formal complaint. The witness was a motorist who was flagged down by the complainant when she ran from the hotel where the alleged rape occurred:

Q: *What happens next, Mr [redacted]?*
W: *I wind the window down and see what the problem was.*
Q: *When you wound your window down did you ask her any questions, or did you speak to her?*
W: *I didn't have time. As soon as I opened the window, she told me to call the police 'cause she'd been raped.*
Q: *Were they the first words that she spoke to you?*
W: *Yes.*
Q: *What did you do at that point, Mr [redacted]?*
W: *She kept telling me to ring 000 and ring the police, so I got me phone out and I rung 000.*

32 Eg *Harper v R* [2022] NSWCCA 211 [118] (Button J). See also Criminal Procedure Act 1986 (NSW), s 292B; Jury Directions Act 2015 (Vic), s 47E.

33 Evidence Act 1995 (NSW), s 66(2); Evidence Act 2008 (Vic), s 66(2); *Papakosmas v R* (1999) 196 CLR 297; *WS v R* [2023] NSWCCA 52 [31].

Cognizant of the assessments that are made by prosecutors about the forensic benefits of utilizing such evidence in a given trial, here we draw attention to the wider implications of continuing to afford a special status to evidence of prompt complaint. These include the risk of validating the rape myth that the 'true' victim-survivor will immediately complain; and providing a platform for the defence to cross-examine the complainant and witnesses as to whether the complaint *was* 'immediate' and whether it may have been flawed in other respects or 'incomplete'. We explore these rape myth-based lines of cross-examination more fully in Chapter 7, but here we want to draw attention to the fact that *both* parties—prosecution and defence—play a part in the circulation of rape myths associated with the timing and content of a victim-survivor's report of what has happened to them.

In a number of trials we analysed, evidence of this sort featured prominently in the prosecution's closing address to the jury. For example:

> *On her version, the accused is literally still in the premises when she sends the text messages to [a friend]. He leaves shortly before their arrival. That's important. That means she has acted in a way you might think somebody who has suffered this sort of attack could be expected to act. She's not delayed, she's not prevaricated, she sought assistance from her friends as soon as she could conceivably do so. Now, that might be an important feature in your considerations.*

The language used here is strongly reminiscent of the way in which the old expectation of 'immediate' complaint was communicated to jurors—prior to the advent of progressive rape law reform. Its use suggests that a strong prosecution case is still considered to be one that maps onto the rape schema, and the attributes of a 'real rape'.

We wonder how jurors are supposed to process evidence and submissions that reify evidence of prompt complaint, when they may also be directed by the judge that 'people may react differently to sexual offences and there is no typical, proper or normal response to a sexual offence' and 'some people may complain immediately to the first person they see, while others may not complain for some time and others may never make a complaint'.[34] The incongruency is not a product of lawmaker error or oversight. Jury directions of this sort represent a particular mode of statutory influence.[35] As we explain further in Chapter 9, statutory jury directions are designed to *accompany* rather than displace evidence that engages rape myths. This is an important part of the story of why prosecutors continue to highlight evidence of immediate complainant.

[34] Jury Directions Act 2015 (Vic), s 52(4). See also Criminal Procedure Act 1986 (NSW), s 294.
[35] See Chapter 3 at p. 71.

Supportive (or 'corroborative') evidence

Against the perception that rape trials are uniquely 'word-on-word' cases (ie the only available evidence comes from what is said by the complainant and accused), and noting the statutory abolition of the common law warning about the dangers of convicting on the uncorroborated evidence of the complainant,[36] we found that other supportive evidence was introduced by the prosecution in the large majority of Victorian and NSW trials we analysed. This included documentary evidence (such as photographs, medical reports, records of text messages, and other digital communications) and testimony from witnesses, police officers, medical, DNA, forensic and other experts. Given the culturally embedded myth that complainants lie about rape,[37] it is probably unsurprising that, even if not technically required, supportive evidence featured prominently in the Crown case, and in closing addresses. For example:

> *Now, importantly, members of the jury, the complainant's evidence doesn't stand alone, and the Crown urges you to take into account the other evidence in the trial that supports her. Firstly, you have the evidence of what the complainant told other witnesses after the offences occurred.... Now, the complainant is also supported, you might think to a strong degree, to a very strong degree by the physical evidence in the case and that is her observable injuries...*

* * *

> *There are some aspects of this case that have the pure ring of truth to them. This is not just a case of word on word because the complainant's word is supported by a number of different pieces of evidence in such a way that you can be confident beyond reasonable doubt that the sexual intercourse took place in the way she described it.*

These examples illustrate powerfully a key finding of this chapter: there is a considerable distance between the progressive rhetoric of reformed rape laws—including the conviction that a complainant's allegation no longer needs corroboration—and the reality of how the Crown case is constructed in contemporary rape trials. In drawing attention to these features of the Crown case in trials in this study, we are not suggesting that prosecutors have actively sought to engage rape myths or conceptions of 'real rape'. We acknowledge that the prosecutor in a trial may consider the evidence relevant to facts in issue or may reasonably anticipate that the defence will attempt to do so. However, in a context where the prominence of 'real rape' attributes was a notable feature of trials in this study, it is important to recognize that

[36] See Chapter 3 at p. 68.
[37] See Chapter 2 at p. 33.

this was not simply a product of defence strategy and lines of cross-examination (matters to which we turn in the next chapter). Rather, the prosecution plays a part in reinforcing the importance of these attributes.

5. Challenging (or 'Negativing') Rape Myths

Having devoted a good portion of this chapter to explaining how the prosecution regularly *engaged* rape myths in the trials we analysed, it is appropriate to register that we also observed instances where the prosecution *challenged* rape myths on which the defence might rely. The most direct and unambiguous instances of this practice were on the topic of the significance to be attached to the absence of physical injuries on the complainant's body. The most common way for the prosecution to challenge the expectation of injuries as a marker of 'true' rape was to lead evidence from a doctor who performed the medical examination of the complainant to 'explain' the absence of injuries. For example:

> Q: *What does that mean in a medical sense in terms of the absence of injuries . . . ?*
> A: *. . . [It] doesn't preclude a sexual assault from having occurred. It's possible for penile vaginal penetration or digital penetration or even penetration with an object to occur without there being injury, whether it is consensual penetration or non-consensual penetration.*

Direct challenges to other rape myths were less common, but did occur in some trials. In the following example, the prosecutor strongly rebuffed the expectation of resistance in their closing address:

> *The Crown says [the complainant] was very clear about her lack of willingness to have sexual contact with [the accused], but it comes back to are you satisfied whether there was an agreement. Okay. She doesn't have to say no. She doesn't have to fight him off. She doesn't have to physically resist him. The question for you to determine is whether she did, in fact, agree, and very clearly, the Crown says to you, she did not agree.*

A similarly direct approach was sometimes used by prosecutors to challenge the expectation that a 'true' victim always provides an entirely consistent account of what happened, and the suggestion that 'inconsistency' is indicative of fabrication (a rape myth that is frequently engaged by defence counsel, as we explain in Chapter 7). The following, from a closing address, is illustrative:

> *One of the things you'd, no doubt, know is that human memories are not perfect and they don't operate like a video camera and it's not CSI and we can't wind back the*

camera and see everything in high definition and know exactly what happened, but just because human memory doesn't work perfectly, doesn't mean she cannot know what happened in the past. So, just for example, I've outlined to you what [the complainant] said and what other people remember her saying. It's not word perfect, but neither is a human memory capable of remembering exactly what someone said in a period of distress some time ago and, as I said, just because things aren't remembered perfectly doesn't mean we cannot know what happened in the past…

More often, however, the prosecution's approach was to attempt to counteract (or negative) the potential impact of a rape myth by adducing evidence that explained why *this* victim-survivor on *this* occasion did not respond in the way 'expected', in terms of, for example, resistance or immediate complaint:

Q: *What did you mean when you told police, . . . 'There's nothing I could do about it'?*
A: *I just felt so helpless. . . .*
Q: *Why do you say you felt helpless?*
A: *'Cause I didn't know what to do. I just froze.*

* * *

Q: *Why was it that you didn't call the police, first of all, on that day when you woke up . . . ?*
A: *I didn't want to involve the police. I didn't want it to happen. I didn't want my life to fall apart. I didn't want, you know, like this. I didn't want this big thing to happen. I wanted everything to stay the same and wished that it couldn't have happened.*

Noting that, in the majority of trials we analysed, the complainant was accused by the defence of fabricating the allegation of rape (a trial feature we discuss in Chapter 7), prosecutors sometimes attempted to persuade the jury why, on the evidence before them, the accusation of lying should be rejected:

I'd suggest to you that if she were to make up a story, or if someone were to make up a story, you would make up a better story than this. You would make up a story about kicking and screaming, you'd make a triple 0 call, you'd call out to your mother. You wouldn't be sending these kind of vague text messages of, 'Something bad just happened,' to your friend in the middle of the night. And you wouldn't have responded to the accused's text messages in the manner in which you did if you were trying to effectively stitch him up for a false sexual assault. I suggest to you that her story, her version of events is quite understated. She doesn't paint an elaborate picture of things that went on. It has the ring of truth to it.

The 'negativing' practices and interventions illustrated here may well have been strategically sound in the context of the specific trial, but they also tend to consolidate, rather than disrupt, long-held and underlying rape myths—including, in the last example, that women lie about rape and that rape is an 'easy' allegation to make. Mounting a fact-specific 'logical' rebuttal may provide the jury with compelling reasons for understanding why *this* complainant is to be believed—and we don't underestimate the importance of this, in terms of both process justice and outcome justice for victim-survivors. But in the context of the decades-long progressive rape law reform project with which this book is concerned, it speaks to the modesty of what has been achieved and the hold that rape myths still exercise over the courtroom.

6. Conclusion

The many legislative reforms of the past 50 years haven't especially been directed at changing how the Crown case is framed and presented in a rape trial. Understandably, especially from a complainant retraumatization perspective, the prosecution has not been perceived to be 'the problem'. Instead, criticism has largely focused on defence strategies, particularly the damaging impact of cross-examination on complainants—and for good reason (something we turn to in the next chapter). Even so, it might have been expected that the re-making of the law of rape, including via a modernized conception of positive and communicative consent, would translate into a fresh approach to the prosecution of rape trials. The findings of our analysis of Victorian and NSW rape trials suggest that this has not (yet) occurred. Rape myths are still regularly engaged by prosecutors where they are perceived as strengthening the Crown case, and are usually only negatived on a case- (and complainant-) specific basis.

It would be unfair and simplistic to 'blame' prosecutors for the continuation of the practices we observed. Prosecutors are responsible for running the specific trial in which they appear; they are not responsible for achieving systemic change. In addition, structural and institutional forces and constraints (time for preparation being an important one) mean that, against the grain of the narrative of progressive reform, the prosecution cannot simply re-imagine the rape case as it sees fit. Along with the fact that law-makers have made very few incursions into the admissibility of rape myth-based evidence,[38] the Crown case is heavily influenced by the nature of the police investigation that has already occurred, including the types of evidence gathered (eg CCTV footage and mobile phone records) and the

[38] See Chapter 3 at p. 72.

protocols in place for medical examinations of complainants and the production of 'rape kits'.[39] These forms of evidence feature prominently in briefs, and influence the shape of the Crown case.

In all of these circumstances, it is not surprising that we found that rape myths were still very present in the Crown case in the trials we analysed. The findings speak to a conundrum. On the one hand, as Craig has observed, the prosecution's 'duty to ensure a fair process ... includes working to eliminate those forms of discrimination that distort the fact-finding process, or prevent equal access to the criminal justice system'.[40] On the other hand, the prosecutor works within the legal environment created by legislators and judicial interpretations. For all the ways in which it has been changed by progressive reform, that environment remains one in which rape myths are largely free to circulate.

[39] In NSW, Sexual Assault Investigation Kits (SAIKs); in Victoria, Forensic Medical Examination Kits (FMEKs).

[40] Craig (n 2) 136.

7

Cross-Examination

'Genuine' Victims, 'Lying' Complainants, and the Resilience of Rape Myths

1. Introduction

In the previous chapter, we demonstrated that it would be a mistake to attribute responsibility for problems in the nature of contemporary rape trials to defence lawyers alone. In the Victorian and NSW trials we analysed, prosecutors played a part in the continued reliance on 'real rape' attributes where they are regarded as present and available to strengthen the Crown case. Nonetheless, it is clear that the point in the trial where the complainant is cross-examined by the defendant's lawyer is a crucial site of inquiry for any assessment of whether rape trials have been transformed by progressive rape law reform. As we discussed in Chapter 2, cross-examination has long been regarded as the most traumatic aspect of a rape trial for a complainant, particularly where it involves intense scrutiny of the complainant's character and conduct, and rape myth-inspired interrogation. It is clear that the lines of questioning to which a complainant is subjected during cross-examination have been a major contributor to complainant distress, retraumatization, and dissatisfaction.[1]

It follows that the question of the manner in which cross-examination is conducted looms large in discussions of how much trials have been transformed since the 1970s—away from complainant character interrogation and retraumatization. Without diminishing the importance of *how* a complainant is questioned—including tone, intensity, and duration—we are most interested in the *content* of cross-examination. It may be accepted that lawyers conducting cross-examination are more consistently polite than they were 50 years ago.[2] We saw evidence of this

[1] Michele Burman, 'Evidencing Sexual Assault: Women in the Witness Box' (2009) 56 Probation Journal 379; Anne Cossins, *Closing the Justice Gap for Adult and Child Sexual Assault: Rethinking the Adversarial Trial* (Palgrave Macmillan 2020); Elisabeth McDonald, *Rape Myths as Barriers to Fair Trial Process* (Canterbury UP 2020); Elena Campbell and others, '"This Is My Story. It's Your Case, But It's My Story": Interview Study' (KPMG and RMIT Centre for Innovative Justice 2023); Ania Moroz and Tamar Dinisman, 'Suffering For Justice: Sexual Violence Victim-Survivors' Experiences of Going to Court and Cross-Examination' (Victim Support 2024).

[2] Virginia Bell, 'Keynote Opening Speech' (Enhancing Safe Practice: A National Justice Forum on Sexual Assault, New South Wales, 2 August 2024); Lisa Featherstone, *Sexual Violence in Australia, 1970s–1980s: Rape and Child Sexual Abuse* (Palgrave Macmillan 2021) chs 2, 6.

Reforming Rape Trials. Julia Quilter and Luke McNamara, Oxford University Press.
 DOI: 10.1093/9780198948155.003.0007

in our reading of transcripts from both Victoria and NSW. However, a witness can be morally impugned, shamed, criticized, traumatized, and silenced by a series of questions delivered with all the characteristics of courteous and respectful discourse. A complainant can also be cross-examined in a way that brings rape myths into the courtroom, without transgressing the rules of evidence or the ethical obligations of barristers.

We have already discussed (in Chapter 5) our findings on the operation of statutory prohibitions on questions and evidence about sexual 'reputation' and statutory restrictions on evidence of past sexual experience. We concluded that although imperfect in their operation, these rare instances, where the legislature has attempted to reshape rape trials using relatively strong modes of statutory influence, have narrowed the parameters of admissible evidence and reduced the distress caused to complainants. Of course, 'slut-shaming' or allegations of promiscuity are not the only ways that complainants can be accused of consenting and lying, or be disrespected and traumatized during cross-examination. These are not the only trial features that progressive statutory reform has purported to address.

In this chapter, we consider other aspects of the content of cross-examination, including lines of questioning that can bring other rape myths into the trial. We will see that in the Victorian and NSW trials we examined, rape myths were frequently invoked, and complainants were regularly scrutinized against a set of standards and expectations drawn from the traditional (unreformed) rape schema (see Chapter 2). In the large majority of trials, these defence practices were oriented towards producing a familiar narrative for the jury's consumption: the complainant is a liar and their allegation of non-consensual sexual violence is a fabrication.

This chapter is presented in two main parts. The first part (section 2) summaries notable features of the trials we analysed, with an emphasis on observed features that sit uncomfortably with the claim that rape trials have been modernized and transformed to both shift the spotlight away from the complainant's conduct and character, and to reduce the presence and impact of the myths, misconceptions, and stereotypes that have traditionally underpinned rape law and practice. The second part (section 3) seeks to account for what we observed: why are complainants still questioned on topics that cause them distress, which they consider unfair, and which seem at odds with the narratives of progressive statutory reform and the associated goal of criminal trials without rape myths?

2. What Is (Still) Happening During the Cross-Examination of Complainants?

Both of our transcript studies were primarily qualitative and the manner in which we present, illustrate, and discuss our findings in this chapter will reflect that. However, while our samples were insufficiently large or representative to provide

Table 7.1 Proportion of NSW and Victorian trials where cross-examination questions engaged selected rape myths

Rape myth-based line of questioning	NSW (n = 75)	Victoria (n = 33)
The complainant did not physically resist	51%	36%
The complainant did not verbally communicate non-consent	53%	55%
The complainant suffered no injuries	49%	33%
No force or threats were used	31%	27%
Pre-event 'flirtation' inferred consent	56%	42%
The complaint was 'delayed'	84%	79%
The complainant offered 'inconsistent' accounts	76%	97%
The complainant is lying	95%	88%

a firm basis for generalizing about Australian rape trials, some basic quantitative data offer a convenient starting point. Table 7.1 summarizes our findings on the proportion of trials in which, on our assessment, the most familiar rape myths were engaged in the trials we analysed. This tabular data summary provides an efficient (and striking) way to communicate one of our headline findings: rape myths feature prominently in the cross-examination of complainants (and in the submissions subsequently made by defence lawyers to juries). This is consistent with the findings of empirical research undertaken recently in other common law jurisdictions. For example, a recent study of the experiences of victim-survivors in England and Wales found that 73% of complainants were asked at least one question associated with a myth or stereotype.[3]

In the following discussion, we will explain and illustrate how cross-examination questioning engages myths and stereotypes about what a 'real rape' looks like, and is used to support assertions that the case at hand departs from these expectations such that the Crown case should be rejected. There are two major consequences of the continuing prevalence of these topics in cross-examination. The first is that it perpetuates the entrenched rape trial dynamic of imposing a heavy burden of scrutiny on the person who is the putative *victim* of a sexual crime, which is known to be a major contributor to complainant retraumatization and the experience of process injustice. The second is that it effectively incorporates rape myths into the

[3] Moroz and Dinisman (n 1) 37. See also Elaine Craig, *Putting Trials on Trial: Sexual Assault and the Failure of the Legal Profession* (McGill-Queen's UP 2018); McDonald (n 1); Ellen Daly, *Rape, Gender and Class: Intersections in Courtroom Narratives* (Palgrave Macmillan 2022).

body of evidence upon which the jury will adjudicate, with potential implications for jury deliberations and verdict (including the risk of outcome injustice).[4]

Expectation of resistance

One of the most basic aims of advocacy and rape law reform since the 1970s was to overturn the traditional common law requirement of evidence of *force*. The traditional common law expectation that a 'genuine' victim will 'resist to the utmost'[5] has been recognized as one of the most egregious causes of injustice for sexual violence victim-survivors, and in need of reform—not just in Australia but across the common law world and beyond.[6] In Chapter 3, we discussed the energy, and number of legislative words, that have gone into reconceiving rape into a crime defined by the absence of consent, where consent is defined positively as free and voluntary agreement. Part of the statutory architecture for this transformation has been the express statutory disavowal of the traditional 'requirements' for proving non-consent, such as evidence of an express 'no', force, threats, physical resistance, or injuries. The move to a consent-focused definition of rape was expected to relieve victim-survivors of the unfair burden of having to prove that, by their words and actions at the time, or by the injuries displayed on their bodies, they had resisted.

Against this background, we were struck by the regularity with which questions carrying an expectation of resistance were asked during complainant cross-examination in the trials we analysed. Some examples were especially outrageous:

> Q: *Why didn't you close your mouth when he's got his penis in it? Are you slack-jawed or something, are you? Sorry, Your Honour. You have no control over your jaw, is that what you're saying?*
> A: *I had no control of my body.*
> Q: *You couldn't bite down on his penis that you didn't want in your mouth?*
> A: *No.*

Other instances were less crass, insensitive (and outrageous), but no less evocative of the expectation that non-consent should be manifested by physical resistance:

[4] For an explanation of process justice and outcome justice, see Chapter 1 at pp. 15–16.

[5] See Julia Quilter, 'From Raptus to Rape: A History of the "Requirements" of Resistance and Injury' (2015) 2 Law & History 89.

[6] Sara Uhnoo, Sofie Erixon, and Moa Bladini, 'The Wave of Consent-Based Rape Laws in Europe' (2024) 77 International Journal of Law, Crime and Justice; David T Johnson art ID no 100668, 'Is Rape a Crime in Japan?' (2024) International Journal of Asian Studies. See also Amy Vorenberg, Jessica Durkis-Stokes, and Jessica C Brown, *Utmost Resistance: Examining Sexual Violence Law in the United States* (Carolina Academic Press 2024).

Q: *So what are you saying? You didn't indicate anything to him to say, don't do it?*
A: *I never once gave him the thought of me wanting to have sex with him.*
Q: *You didn't scream out, stop?*
A: *I did say stop but I didn't scream it.*
Q: *You didn't kick him?*
A: *No.*
Q: *Could have bitten him, could have scratched him, did none of that?*
A: *No, I was in shock.*

* * *

Q: *... [A]t no stage that evening did you do anything to resist engaging in sexual activity with [the accused]?*
A: *Yes I did....*
Q: *Is it not true that if you had used all your strength you could have pushed him off you?*
A: *Um, not in that moment.*

* * *

Q: *Were you offering any resistance at this point in time?*
A: *Resistance as in other than begging him to stop? Physical resistance?*
Q: *Physical resistance?*
A: *No because at that point in time I was trying, I was crying and holding the bed frame.*

* * *

Q: *Yes, now, there doesn't appear to be, and I'm not suggesting you had to, but there doesn't appear to be any pushing back or you getting up or ... ?*
A: *Because I was scared, I was frozen.*

This last example serves to illustrate the disconnect between the (reformed) values expressed in contemporary rape laws and the (unreformed) values and expectations that continue to underpin cross-examination of complainants in rape trials. On this occasion, defence counsel simultaneously acknowledged that the law has changed and no longer requires resistance *and* invoked an expectation of resistance. This supports the main argument advanced in this book: that the narrative of progressive rape law reform to change trials is more rhetorical veneer than substantive transformation. Later in this chapter we reflect on why legislation that ostensibly writes resistance out of the definition of rape has not produced this outcome in the practice of rape trials.

In many trials we observed, the expectation of resistance manifested in cross-examination questioning that evoked an obligation of express oral communication of non-consent. For example:

Q: *I suggest to you, ma'am, that you didn't indicate that you were not consenting. You never said to him, 'No.'*
A: *I did not give him consent to have sex with me.*

Such examples are noteworthy, not only because they illustrate the (unreformed) lines of questioning that persist in rape trials, but because they reveal complainants who are pushing back against the expectation of verbal resistance, and the implication that they did not act in the way that a 'true' victim would have done. Later in this chapter, we return to the question of complainant 'voice' during cross-examination, including to illustrate both the shackles that the conventions of cross-examination impose, and the opportunities that are nonetheless seized by some complainants to tell their story.

A variation on the expectation of verbal resistance that we observed was the suggestion that the complainant had not done so to the requisite degree:

Q: *Do you say that you used your full voice, calling out as loud as you could for [the accused] to stop doing this to you?*
A: *As I could at the time, yes.*
Q: *What do you mean, 'As you could', Ms [complainant]? Did you . . . ?*
A: *Well I couldn't breathe, so it was as loud as I could . . .*
Q: *You say you couldn't call out because you couldn't breathe?*
A: *Yes.*
Q: *So you're saying for this entire time you were being penetrated without your consent, you could not breathe?*
A: *No, not the whole time.*
Q: *Well, there were times, I suggest to you, even on your own evidence that you could have called out forcefully for help?*
A: *I could of, but I didn't.*
Q: *Did you tell him to stop as loud as you could?*
A: *I told him to stop.*
Q: *Did you tell him to stop as loud as you could?*
A: *I don't know what volume I used, but it was enough for him to hear me. Over and over again.*

The aspect of the rape schema (described in Chapter 2) that is arguably most discordant with the narrative of modernized rape law is the reification of evidence of physical injuries. A half-century of progressive change could be expected to have consigned to history the conflation of injury and non-consent. And yet, we observed instances where the absence of injuries was the subject of cross-examination questioning. For example:

Q: *You didn't suffer any injuries as a result of this incident?*
A: *Physical injuries?*

Q: Yes, physical injuries?
A: No.

As with other rape myths engaged during cross-examination, the messages conveyed to the jury by such lines of questioning circulate not only during the time that the complainant is in the witness box. They resonate as part of the narrative communicated to the jury during closing addresses. For example, in a different case, defence counsel told the jury:

> *The point really though remains that beyond the bruise there were no visible injuries at any time . . . no visible injuries at any time that support Ms [complainant]'s complaint.*

Even *before* the era of progressive rape law reform began in the 1970s, one of the common law's few relaxations of the expectation of resistance was where there were threats of violence. For example, prior to the major reforms of 1981, s 63 of the Crimes Act 1900 (NSW)—which established the penalty for (but not the definition of) the crime of rape—also stated that '[t]he consent of the woman, if obtained by threats or terror, shall be no defence to a charge under this section'. Still, we observed trials where defence counsel engaged the absence of threats of violence as a basis for doubting the complainant's assertion that non-consensual sexual activity had occurred. For example:

Q: Through the sexual activity in that room, throughout what happened, it's not your evidence that [the accused] verbally threatened you, did he?
A: What do you mean?
Q: He wasn't verbally—as in saying words that were threatening?
A: No.
Q: No. In fact, what you say, and what you've told the police, is he was, through this activity, whispering compliments to you.

One of the things we hope to draw attention to by illustrating our findings with extracts from trial transcripts is the material effects of the questioning practices we are describing. Of course, words on a page can't tell us what complainants were feeling when asked questions of the sort shown here, but it seems likely that they often produce trauma effects, including surprise, confusion, hurt, anger, distress, and shame.[7] Such questioning can reinforce the deeply troubling stereotype that 'women who are sexually assaulted have only themselves to blame'.[8] The continued reliance on resistance narratives, which is also documented in other recent

[7] See Campbell and others (n 1).
[8] Craig (n 3) 204.

empirical studies,[9] is one of the most stark counterfactuals to the rape trial transformation narrative. To put it mildly, it is troubling that one of the most discredited misconceptions about sexual violence perpetration appears to still be in regular circulation in rape trials.

Accommodating the 'freeze' response?

One of the features of the new 'gold standard' for progressive rape law in Australia is the addition to a growing list of circumstances where sexual activity is characterized as non-consensual, the following: where the person *does not say or do anything* to communicate consent.[10] As explained in Chapter 3, such a provision articulates the communicative model of consent, and recognizes that to 'freeze' can be a 'normal' response to sexual violence.[11] The aim of such legislation is to transform how 'inaction' is engaged in a criminal trial—such that it is no longer evidence of consent, but its opposite: non-consent.

Legislation of this sort was not introduced in NSW until 2021, and so was not yet in operation in NSW at the time we conducted our transcript study. Now that it is in place, can we be hopeful that resistance narratives will finally loosen their hold on rape trials? Time will tell, but the findings of our Victorian transcript study are not encouraging. Such a provision *was* in operation in that jurisdiction ('a person does not consent' if 'the person does not say or do anything to indicate consent to the act'[12]) but it had no discernible effect on the tendency of defence counsel to engage resistance narratives during cross-examination. Several of the examples offered so far in this chapter came from Victorian trials. Lines of questioning during complainant cross-examination that were underpinned by the traditional expectation of a verbalized demonstration of non-consent, which attempted to infer consent on the basis of silence, were common:

> Q: *And you had the opportunity at that stage to say something to him if you did not agree with this?*
>
> A: *I guess so, but I didn't, because I was frozen.*

* * *

[9] McDonald (n 1) ch 7; Rachel Burgin, 'Persistent Narratives of Force and Resistance: Affirmative Consent as Law Reform' (2019) 59 The British Journal of Criminology 296; Daly (n 4); Jessica Schaffer, 'Narratives of Force, Resistance and Mistaken Belief in Consent in South Australian Rape Cases' (2023) 44 Adelaide Law Review 608. See also Eithne Dowds, 'Redefining Consent: Rape Law Reform, Reasonable Belief, and Communicative Responsibility' (2022) 49 Journal of Law and Society 824.

[10] Crimes Act 1900 (NSW), s 61HJ(1)(a), as amended by the Crimes Legislation Amendment (Sexual Consent Reforms) Act 2021 (NSW).

[11] See Chapter 3 at p. 54.

[12] Crimes Act 1958 (Vic), s 36AA(1)(a). A version of this provision was first introduced (as a jury direction) by the Crimes (Rape) Act 1991 (Vic) to s 37(c) of the Crimes Act 1958 (Vic) (since repealed).

Q: *When this incident occurred with [the accused] . . . [d]id you scream when this happened?*
A: *At that time I was just quiet.*
Q: *You didn't make a sound?*
A: *Not at that time.*
Q: *You didn't call out to your brother for help?*
A: *No, not at the time.*

Later in this chapter, we turn to consider why rape myth-based expectations of victim-survivors continue to be voiced in rape trials, in the face of legislation which was designed to prevent or dissuade them. For now, we simply note how confounding it must be for complainants who were aware of (or become educated about) the narrative of progressive rape law reform only to encounter questioning underpinned by the same judgmental expectations that victim-survivors of sexual violence experienced 50 years ago. And not just expectations of verbal and physical resistance.

The expectation of immediate complaint ('delay')

The old common law expectation that the 'true' rape victim will immediately 'raise the hue and cry'[13] was one of the earliest targets of law reform advocates in the 1970s.[14] Its corollary, the assumption that a 'failure to complain immediately' supports 'a presumption of fabrication on the part of the rape complainant',[15] has been the subject of statutory reform in every jurisdiction, most commonly in the form of a 'corrective' jury direction (the use and effectiveness of which we take up in Chapter 9).

On one (rhetorical) level then, the rape myth that 'delay' is indicative of fabrication is regarded as a relic—no longer consonant with what we know about how victims of sexual violence might behave in the aftermath.[16] In the practice of trials, however, the expectation of immediate (and 'perfect') complaint is still very present. Across our Victorian and NSW studies, we observed cross-examination questioning that attempted to draw attention to some form of 'delay' in complaint in more than 80% of the trials we analysed (see Table 7.1). We say *some form* of delay because although 'delay' is usually taken to connote literal temporal delay, the rape myth is actually broader than that. It includes a set of expectations about

[13] Henry Bracton, *Bracton on the Laws and Customs of England* vol 2 (1268) (Samuel E Thorne, tr, Harvard UP 1968) 415; see also Australian Law Reform Commission (ALRC), *Safe, Informed, Supported: Justice Responses to Sexual Violence* (ALRC Report 143, 2025) 147.
[14] See Chapter 3 at p. 68.
[15] ALRC, *Family Violence—National Legal Response* (ALRC Report 114, 2010) 1299.
[16] ALRC, *Safe, Informed, Supported* (n 13) 150.

how the 'true' victim will respond: with a swift complaint, to the 'right' person, and using precise terminology and detail. This means that a suggestion of 'delay' can be operative even in rape trials where there is evidence that the complainant reported promptly. In one case, the prosecutor adopted the term 'incomplete complaint' to capture the breadth of what we have referred to as *versions* of delay in complaint.

We observed cases where 'delay' (in this wider sense) was suggested despite the fact that the complainant reported the rape to someone within minutes, and many cases where the complainant reported to police within 24 hours. These included trials where the veracity of the complainant's allegation was challenged because they:

- did not complain to the *accused* immediately after (including a case where the complainant was asked why she didn't say '*Look, get out of my bed. You've just raped me*');
- did not immediately phone the police after the accused left;
- phoned the Lifeline counselling service rather than the police;
- sought directions to the nearest police station rather than call 000;
- told a work colleague and friend rather than their mother;
- did not, at the first opportunity, say to a parent on arrival home, '*I've been raped*'; and
- ran from a hotel room, flagged down a member of the public, and told a police officer on arrival that she had been raped, but did not at that time say (as later detailed) that the accused had '*licked your vagina*' or '*sucked your breast*'.

The ubiquity of digital communications evidence in contemporary rape trials creates additional expectations of the 'true' complainant: that their post-event text messages will constitute an immediate, precise, and comprehensive record of their allegation.[17] In the following example, the complainant was questioned on the contents of a post-event message she sent to a work colleague/friend:

Q: *You sent her a text, can I suggest, which said, 'I think I was raped'?*
A: *Yes.*
Q: *You didn't say to her, 'I was raped'?*
A: *Yes.*
Q: *You were saying that there was some uncertainty in your mind about what it was that had happened?*
A: *I was confused. I was --*
Q: *And indeed—I'm sorry?*

[17] See Julia Quilter and others, 'Text Messages and Social Media Posts as Evidence in Rape Trials: A New Entry Point for Rape Myths?' (2026) Crime, Media, Culture https://doi.org/10.1177/17416590261429130 accessed 1 April 2026.

A: *I was still intoxicated at the time. I was confused and still trying to work out what had happened. I was trying to piece together in my mind how I got there.*

In such instances, there is no recognition of the many valid reasons for hesitancy in text messages composed after a traumatic event, including the idiosyncrasies of text-based communications, fear associated with disclosure, and the greater tendency of women to use 'lexical hedges' that suggest uncertainty or tentativeness.[18]

The practices we have described here—which expressly or impliedly criticize the complainant for how they reacted to the alleged rape—have at least two potential effects which are at odds with the narrative that suggests rape trials have been transformed by statutory reform. First, complainants who are challenged in this way are likely to feel ashamed or embarrassed and retraumatized by contradictory suggestions: that if they *were* raped, they did not do the 'right thing'; and that their failure is or may be attributable to the fact that they *were not* raped and are lying when they now say they were. Secondly, juries are invited to draw an adverse inference from the 'delay' about the complainant's reliability and credibility as a witness. As we will see in Chapter 9, when delay is suggested in a trial, juries are likely to be offered an educative direction from the trial judge. However, this practice appears to have limited influence on the content (and the experience) of cross-examination, including the likelihood that the complainant will be challenged and criticized for their 'delayed' complaint.

Expectation of consistent accounts

A dimension of the traditional expectation of immediate complaint was that the manner in which the details are subsequently articulated by the complainant should be *consistent*. Inconsistency was regarded as an indicator of lying (a feature that we consider further below). This expectation has been debunked by the literature on memory, recall, and trauma.[19]

It is now well recognized that victims of sexual offences may recount events differently at different times and to different audiences and that such inconsistencies are not necessarily indicative of fabrication or unreliability. This is now reflected in legislation in both Victoria[20] and NSW[21] and elsewhere in Australia,[22] although, as we discuss below, this is legislation of a particular kind. Sometimes referred to

[18] Robin Lakoff, *Language and Woman's Place: Text and Commentaries* (rev edn, OUP 2004) 172; see also Sana Ahmed, 'A Study of Lexical Features and Ideograms in SMS Language: A Gender Based Formal Study' (2021) 3 Competitive Linguistic Research Journal 61; Catrina Brown, 'Women's Narratives of Trauma: (Re)storying Uncertainty, Minimization and Self-Blame' (2013) 3 Narrative Works 1; Zoë D Peterson and Charlene L Muelenhard, 'Was It Rape? The Function of Women's Rape Myth Acceptance and Definitions of Sex in Labeling Their Own Experiences' (2004) 51 Sex Roles 129.

[19] See Chapter 3 at p. 69.

[20] Jury Directions Act 2015 (Vic), s 54D.

[21] Criminal Procedure Act 1986 (NSW), s 293A.

[22] See, eg, Evidence Act 1977 (Qld), s 103ZY.

as 'corrective', it is more accurate to refer to jury directions as guidance that is designed to balance or *neutralize* rape myth-based evidence, rather than prohibit it.

And yet, a cross-examination technique employed by defence counsel in 80% of the Victorian and NSW trials we examined was the deployment of earlier accounts provided by the complainant as a reference point for challenging the veracity of the complainant's trial evidence (and hence, her credibility and reliability as a witness). A variety of earlier accounts were drawn upon by defence counsel for this purpose, including what was said to a complaint witness (such as a friend, person on the scene, or parent), to police, ambulance, or medical officers, what was recorded in a police interview and statement, and the complainant's evidence at the committal hearing (in Victoria).[23]

In a finding that is consistent with previous research,[24] we were struck by how frequently and intensely cross-examination took the form of highlighting differences in accounts given by the complainant at different times in different contexts—not only in relation to central facts in issue, but also precise details, and peripheral matters of no obvious relevance. The expectation that a complainant should be able to recall minutiae, including on distressing details of the event—such as the location of clothes and underwear; the position of hands, arms, and legs (at multiple time points); the angle of the complainant's leg at the time of penetration; or the duration of penetration—is unrealistic and unfair. It is even more unfair when coupled with the cross-examination practice of pointing to asserted 'inconsistencies' between how the complainant described such matters shortly after the event, and how they recall them (if at all) in their trial evidence. For example:

Q: *No, and that's the paragraph [in the complainant's statement] relating to him putting his finger in your vagina, isn't it?*
A: *Yes.*
Q: *In that paragraph you refer to finger, singular, don't you; just one finger?*
A: *To be honest, I don't know whether it was one, two or five.*
Q: *All right. In your evidence - you don't remember how many fingers were placed in you. Is that right?*
A: *No.*
Q: *In your evidence in chief you talked about inserting his fingers into your vagina. Do you remember giving that evidence?*
A: *I recall saying fingers, yes.*

[23] Committal hearings (including the giving of evidence by the complainant) are still part of Victoria's criminal prosecution system. In NSW, committal proceedings take place 'on the papers' and complainants are not required to give evidence.

[24] Mark R Kebbell, Caitriona M E O'Kelly, and Elizabeth L Gilchrist, 'Rape Victims' Experience of Giving Evidence in English Courts: A Survey' (2007) 14 Psychiatry, Psychology and Law 111; McDonald (n 1) 329; Craig (n 3) 31–32.

Q: *But you now say you're not sure whether it was a single finger or it was multiple fingers. Is that right?*
A: *I just said fingers, not meaning one or two. It was just the incorrect wording, fingers.*

The objective of such lines of questioning appeared to be less about clarifying what actually occurred—or directly disputing the account offered by the complainant in evidence-in-chief—and more about 'catching out' the complainant and laying a foundation for characterizing her as, at least, unreliable (ie mistaken), and most commonly, a liar. The strategy behind cross-examination questioning that draws attention to differences in the complainant's account is revealed by the following opening address by defence counsel in one trial:

> *In hearing the evidence, you will hear that the complainant told multiple people what she said occurred early in the morning of [date]. And I would ask you on behalf of [the accused], to listen very very carefully to those versions, and listen carefully to what the complainant is telling all these different people. So for instance, she spoke to ambulance officers, she spoke to police officers, she spoke to a doctor at a hospital, and you'll have her recorded interview. What I would suggest to you is that when you listen carefully, you will start to notice, and you'll start to discern that she provides different versions. In some versions, she doesn't include things that she says in others, and in other versions she adds things that she hasn't referred to before. I will be suggesting to you, and [the accused] tells you that she's making those mistakes because she's not relying on an actual memory of a lived experience, she's making those mistakes because she's getting a fabricated story wrong when she's having to repeat it.*

Here, defence counsel is foreshadowing the evidence that will be adduced by rape myth-inspired lines of cross-examination. Although not technically evidence in a trial, it is likely that the narratives contained in defence addresses to the jury (opening and closing) exert significant influence over how the jury processes the testimony they hear. Hunter and colleagues have noted that, '[i]f it is effective, cross-examination will provide "the ammunition for a persuasive closing address" to the jury'.[25]

Consider the following example of a closing address where other rape myths are engaged—the expectations that a 'true' victim will complain promptly and demonstrate distress:

[25] Jill Hunter and others, *The Trial: Principles, Process and Evidence* (2nd edn, Federation Press 2021) 216, quoting John Stratton, 'Cross-Examination' (The Public Defenders, 1 August 2007) <https://publicdefenders.nsw.gov.au/resources-and-papers/papers-by-public-defenders/cross-examination.html> accessed 11 July 2025.

> *Then we've got the evidence of the number of witnesses, her girlfriends, what the Crown says is complaint evidence. The Crown said to you, that showed her distress. But when did the distress start? You might think that's important, when did she start crying? The Crown said it was almost immediate distress. No, it wasn't.... There was no immediate distress when the light went on. The crying happened later and then all the girlfriends and everyone came in, but it wasn't immediate like the Crown has suggested to you.*

This example serves as a reminder that, as explained in Chapter 6, the continued visibility and influence of rape myths in contemporary trials is attributable to both *prosecution* and *defence* practices. In this instance (and in many others we observed), *both* parties were playing different sides of the same coin. The prosecution was engaging the myth that a 'true' victim is demonstrably distressed immediately after the event to support the *truth* of the allegation (and the guilt of the accused). The defence was characterizing the absence of immediate distress as indicative of the *falsity* of the allegation (and, therefore, the innocence of the accused).

The complainant is lying

The most common culmination of the rape myth-inspired lines of cross-examination discussed in this chapter was a defence assertion that the complainant had fabricated events or the totality of the allegation of rape. We detected an express or implied suggestion that the complainant was lying in some respect in 93% of trials across both the Victorian and NSW studies. In the majority of these trials, the defence offered the jury a suggested motivation for the fabricated allegation. Sometimes the asserted motivation was clichéd and predictable: revenge for an ended relationship or rejection; anger at the accused for alleged infidelity; 'regretted' consensual sex; to conceal consensual sex with another person from a partner/friends/family/local/religious community; or to conceal consensual sex to which she had given 'drunken consent' (a recurring theme which we discuss in more detail in Chapter 8).

In others, the asserted motive was more idiosyncratic (and incredible):

- to obtain compensation from the accused, or victim's compensation, to pay for cosmetic surgery;
- to extract financial compensation from the company that employed the accused;
- to remove the accused (her stepfather) from the family home because he had been preventing her from seeing her boyfriend;
- as an excuse to leave her current boyfriend and return to her old boyfriend;
- to conceal consenting to unprotected sex;

- to conceal consensual sex for which she was paid;
- to strengthen her application for permanent residency in Australia;
- because she was distraught that her GP (the accused) was leaving their medical practice and relocating;
- to facilitate reunification with her (estranged) husband and sons;
- to cover for the fact that she had used her family's holiday caravan without permission; and
- to obtain academic consideration on a university assessment task.

The narrative that characterizes the rape complainant as a 'lying woman' has a very long history,[26] and was intimately connected with the common law's mandatory corroboration warning.[27] Although, as explained in Chapter 3, this requirement has been the subject of incremental statutory erosion, and despite the estimates that only 5% of sexual assault complaints to police are false,[28] our findings suggest that the myth that women lie about rape is as present in trials as it ever was.

Transcript analysis cannot readily discern why a particular 'false allegation' narrative was advanced in a given case, but it is clear enough that this becomes another way of engaging troubling myths and tropes about rape and women who allege rape. Although adapted (or customized) with reference to the specificity of the case in question, many of the 'motivations' we observed in trials in this study are reminiscent of narratives that have long histories, as discussed in Chapter 2. Their potential 'familiarity' with jury members may be perceived as making them more compelling. This may be so even if, on their face, the asserted motivation for a false allegation lacks plausibility. Indeed, in one case, the trial judge observed that making a 'false' allegation to hide consensual sex from her partner (that being the asserted motivation for the complainant's allegation), is a guaranteed way of ensuring that the partner finds out about what the defence says was consensual sex:

> *TJ: The motivation, as I understand it, is she was stewing about the fact that her partner would find out.*
> *D: Yes.*

[26] See Chapter 2 at p. 33.

[27] See *Kelleher v R* (1974) 131 CLR 534; and Chapter 3 at p. 67.

[28] Claire Ferguson and John Malouff, 'Assessing Police Classifications of Sexual Assault Reports: A Meta-Analysis of False Reporting Rates' (2016) 45 Archives of Sexual Behavior 1185; Patrick Tidmarsh and Gemma Hamilton, 'Misconceptions of Sexual Crimes Against Adult Victims: Barriers to Justice' (Trends & Issues in Crime and Criminal Justice No 611, Australian Institute of Criminology 2020); Kate Minter, Erin Carlisle, and Christine Coumarelos, '"Chuck Her on a Lie Detector": Investigating Australians' Mistrust in Women's Reports of Sexual Assault' (Research Report, Issue No 4, ANROWS 2021) 4; ALRC, *Safe, Informed, Supported* (n 13) 99.

TJ: Even though your own client's admission in the interview is that instantly she's saying, 'I hate you, get out'.

D: Yes.

TJ: But this was to avoid her partner finding - she was - I've got it written down, I've been preparing the charge last night, 'Terrified her partner would find out about this unprotected consensual act and that she stewed on this in her room after the sex. She concluded the only way she could avoid her partner learning that she'd cheated on him was to tell an appalling lie, that is to create this account'.

D: That's the motive that's been put, Your Honour, yes so . . .

TJ: Which is, on its face, an absolute guarantee of publication of the fact of intercourse.

D: It is.

TJ: Yes.

The wisdom of advancing speculative motivations for the complainant's allegation may be questionable (particularly in cases where the asserted or implied narrative might be regarded as a considerable stretch) but the move is accurately characterized, we think, as another rape myth-inspired line of cross-examination. Any risk to the defence is substantially reduced by the fact that in such cases it is routine for the defence to request, and the trial judge to give, a 'motive to lie' direction. For example:

TJ: Now, the accused has suggested that [the complainant] had a motive for lying. . . . Let me just remind you that the accused bears no onus to prove a motive to lie. And even if you reject that motive it does not necessarily justify a conclusion that the evidence of the complainant is truthful.[29]

As with the other cross-examination practices discussed in this chapter, there are two reasons to be concerned about the regularity with which complainants are accused of fabrication for an ulterior motive. First, it is a likely contributor to complaint traumatization (process injustice)—noting that it is central to the process by which the *complainant*, rather than the accused, becomes the primary focus of attention and judgment during rape trials.[30] Secondly, it is one of the ways that rape myths enter the courtroom and may influence jurors away from a finding of guilt (outcome injustice). Neither impact is consistent with the image of a transformed rape trial having emerged from decades of progressive law reform.

[29] See Judicial Commission of NSW, 'Onus and Standard of Proof' (2023) <https://www.judcom.nsw.gov.au/publications/benchbks/criminal/onus_and_standard_of_proof.html#p3-625> accessed 11 July 2025 [3-625]. See also, eg, Jury Directions Act 2015 (Vic), s 44L; *Palmer v The Queen* (1998) 193 CLR 1.

[30] See McDonald (n 1) 345.

Complainant voice and pushing back

The final feature of cross-examination to which we draw attention is the constraints that are imposed on the efforts of complainants to find their voice and tell their story. Previous research has identified the opportunity to do so as a high priority for victim-survivors.[31] A number of the cross-examination transcript portions already quoted in this chapter provide a glimpse into the laudable efforts of complainants to challenge the assertion or implication with which they were presented—such as by using the explanatory language of the 'freeze' response or by rejecting the suggestion that they had not verbally resisted loudly enough. We draw attention to the fact that, against the grain of rape myth-informed cross-examination questions, it can be the *complainant* who finds the voice to articulate the progressive meanings and understandings said to be present in contemporary reformed rape laws (but largely invisible in trials). In the following example, the complainant refused to accept defence counsel's characterization of the event as 'having sex'—a colloquialism that carries a heavy implication of consent:

Q: *[The complainant's friend was] right outside your door when you were having sex with [the accused]?*
A: *He was not right outside the door, no, and I did not have sex with [the accused].*
Q: *Well, you did have sex with him, didn't you?*
A: *No.*
Q: *You didn't have sex with him?*
A: *No.*
Q: *So, his penis never went inside your vagina. Is that what you're saying?*
A: *Sex is consensual, and I never had sex with him.*

In another trial, the complaint eloquently voiced the difficulties created by trauma and the social stigma that still surrounds sexual violence victimization:

Q: *But you specifically rang Mr [redacted], you say, to tell him what had happened.*
A: *Yes, ma'am. He was my best friend.*
Q: *And the best that you could do was say, 'Maybe it happened; maybe it didn't'.*
A: *As I mentioned earlier, the conventional idea of what rape was for me--*
Q: *I'm not talking about the conventional idea. I'm talking about what you said to Mr [redacted].*

[31] Clare McGlynn and Nicole Westmarland, 'Kaleidoscopic Justice: Sexual Violence and Victim-Survivor's Perceptions of Justice' (2019) 28 Social & Legal Studies 179; Vanessa E Munro, 'A Circle That Cannot Be Squared? Survivor Confidence in an Adversarial Justice System' in Miranda Horvath and Jennifer Brown (eds), *Rape: Challenging Contemporary Thinking – 10 years on* (2nd edn, Routledge 2022); Campbell and others (n 1); ALRC, *Safe, Informed, Supported* (n 13) 102.

A: *I was traumatised, I was struggling to piece these things together, and I didn't want to make a fuss. I know saying 'someone raped me' is a very heavy thing to say, and I didn't want to say that out loud. It made it real.*

In another, the complainant succinctly broke out of the constraints of cross-examination to educate the court about what is now well known about low rates of reporting of sexual violence:

Q: *You did not ring triple-0, did you?*
A: *No.*
Q: *Having, on your version, just been raped?*
A: *There's a lot of people that never tell police.*

These instances notwithstanding, our overall assessment is that in most trials, the constraints of the question-and-answer convention of cross-examination, and the associated power dynamic, made it very challenging for complainants to push back or challenge what was being put to them. In a number of trials, attempts to 'speak up' or explain were shut down, and the complainant was reminded by defence counsel of the role expected of them. In the following example, the complainant took issue with a line of questioning that attempted to characterize pre-event interactions with the accused as 'flirtatious':

Q: *Well, I suggest to you that you were singing duets with [the accused], at least one at [a bar] and many more at [another bar]. Do you agree or disagree?*
A: *I don't know. If I did it, it was under social pressure....*
Q: *And you, being invited to join someone in a duet, could have said 'no', couldn't you?*
A: *I guess a lot of rape victims could have said 'no'.*
Q: *I'm not asking you about rape. I'm asking you about singing duets.*
A: *One thing leads to another, right?*
Q: *That's a statement. You're here to answer questions, not make statements.*
A: *Okay.*

In another, defence counsel instructed the complainant on how she should give evidence:

Q: *So in other words, it's clear, you wouldn't have given him oral sex unless he had his hands on your head making you do it, correct?*
A: *I wouldn't have given him oral sex if I was able to consent.*
Q: *No, don't...*
A: *... if I was in a fit state.*
Q: *Please, Ms [complainant], don't answer questions with a conclusion. Okay?*
C: *Okay.*

Sometimes the trial judges did the admonishing:

Q: *You're lying. You did send those messages.*
A: *Were you there?*
Q: *I'm suggesting--*
A: *Who are you to say I am lying?*
TJ: *Ms [complainant], just - you just need to answer the questions. Don't ask them.*
A: *I'm offended by this, Judge.*
TJ: *All right. So, your answer is no. Is that right?*
A: *Yes.*

We noted in Chapter 6 that in some trials the prosecution used open questions that afforded complainants the opportunity to tell their story, while in others, a closed question style of examination limited this opportunity. The findings we have presented and illustrated here suggest that cross-examination is an even more constrained part of the trial process for complainants giving evidence. Of course, to a large extent these restrictions flow from the adversarial system and rules of evidence—including those which generally preclude witnesses from expressing opinions, beliefs, or assumptions.[32] However, these findings are important—especially in the context of what is known about victim-survivor experiences of process injustice and being denied the opportunity to tell their story and be heard.

3. Why Are These Things Still Happening?

Sometimes when we have shared our research findings about the cross-examination of complainants with non-legal expert audiences, the understandable response has been: 'Why is this still happening? Why didn't someone intervene?' In Chapter 9, we will consider the parts played (or not played) by trial judges (and prosecutors) in attempting to influence how cross-examination is conducted, but the point we emphasize here is that such questions really go to the disconnect between the transformation that is promised by the narrative of progressive rape law reform and the reality, as revealed by our transcript analyses. It is a disconnect that was identified in NSW a decade or so into the progressive statutory reform era, when the 1990s *Heroines of Fortitude* report documented the persistence of rape myth-based cross-examination questions, including the following headline findings: 70% of complainants questioned about lack of resistance; 84% questioned about lying; 58% questioned about pre-event flirtation or 'sexually provocative'

32 Evidence Act 1995 (NSW), s 76; Evidence Act 2008 (Vic), s 76.

behaviour.[33] The fact that, 30 years on, we are reporting similar findings about how complainants are cross-examined in rape trials really does invite the question: why haven't things changed? In this final part of the chapter, we offer four explanations.

Legislation disavows but does not disallow rape myths

The most important and previously under-appreciated explanation for the continued visibility of rape myths in rape trials generally, and cross-examination questioning specifically, is that very few of the multiple legislative reforms introduced over the decades have been directed at *requiring* changes to the *content* of cross-examination. Courtesy of statutory prohibitions on sexual reputation evidence and restrictions on sexual experience evidence[34] defence lawyers cannot blatantly 'slut shame' the complainant anymore, and they are expected to be polite, but they are otherwise free to interrogate the complainant in the same manner that they did 50 years ago. As we discuss below (and further in Chapter 9), the concept of *relevant* evidence is interpreted so broadly, and the prohibition on *improper* questions is applied so narrowly, that these components of the evidence rules that govern rape trials have not shifted the rape myth orientation of much cross-examination.

Legislation is now replete with strong values about ethical sexual activity and disavowal of the myths and stereotypes that have traditionally impeded justice for victims of sexual violence. But in the context of a trial, neither the reformed legislative conceptions of consent and circumstances of non-consent, nor statutory jury directions, mandate any change to how cross-examination is conducted—what questions are asked, what myths are engaged, what stereotypes are relied on. Our argument is that this is neither an accident nor an oversight. Law-makers have largely resisted the urge to prohibit the invocation of rape myths, preferring more passive ways of influencing the impacts that rape myths have on trials (including the complainant's experience of being cross-examined) and trial outcomes.

Take the example of the resistance expectation, and consider precisely how it has been legislatively disavowed. Section 61HI(4) of the Crimes Act 1900 (NSW) (which has its origins in the first wave of progressive reform in NSW in 1981) states:

> A person who does not offer physical or verbal resistance to a sexual activity is not, *by reason only of that fact*, to be taken to consent to the sexual activity (emphasis added).

[33] NSW Department for Women, 'Heroines of Fortitude: The Experience of Women in Court as Victims of Sexual Assault' (NSW Department for Women Report 1996) 151.

[34] See Chapter 5 at p. 108.

Victoria's equivalent provision states: 'A person does not consent to an act *just because* they do not resist the act verbally or physically'.[35]

Note the location of these provisions—in statutes that define the elements of criminal offences, rather than in statutes governing criminal procedure and rules of evidence—and the phrasing: 'by reason only of that fact'; 'just because'. This drafting is deliberate. There is nothing to prevent the defence from seeking to adduce evidence of a lack of resistance to support the contention that the complainant consented to the sexual activity. Indeed, the legislation assumes that questions to adduce such evidence *will* be asked. There is a statutory sleight of hand at work here: legislation that simultaneously disavows the traditional expectation of resistance, while declining to prohibit its deployment.

The other statutory reform mechanism that is relevant is the jury direction. As we explained in Chapter 3, this approach to modernizing rape trials dates back to the 1980s, and has been enthusiastically embraced and expanded across multiple Australian jurisdictions in the 2020s.[36] In Chapter 9, we discuss more fully our transcript analysis findings on how trial judges engaged the jury directions that were available in NSW and Victoria at the time of our studies. Here, we draw attention to the mode of statutory influence that legislated jury directions seek to exert on trials, and what we regard as another legislative sleight of hand. The 'delay' direction—the first rape myth 'correcting' direction to be introduced in Australia—is illustrative. The NSW direction communicates to the jury that the 'absence of complaint or delay in complaining *does not necessarily* indicate that the allegation that the offence was committed is false' (emphasis added), and that 'there may be good reasons why a victim of a sexual assault may hesitate in making, or may refrain from making, a complaint . . . '.

These are undoubtedly good messages for the jury to hear (and their inclusion in a statute may play an important communicative and educative function outside courtrooms) but they don't go remotely near prohibiting the defence from inviting the jury to regard the complainant's delay as indicative of the fact that they are lying. Victoria's 'delay' direction is more fulsome and informative in 'correcting' the traditional expectation of immediate complainant,[37] but as in NSW, there is no attempt to prohibit lines of cross-examination or closing submissions that suggest to the jury that they should draw an adverse credibility inference from the complainant's 'delay'. Indeed, the 'corrective' direction is predicated on the possibility (our research suggests, likelihood) of this occurring. We develop this analysis of jury directions further in Chapter 9.

Our position is not that jury directions are an undesirable part of the architecture of contemporary rape laws, but that they are a particular (and limited) *mode*

[35] Crimes Act 1958 (Vic), s 36(2) (emphasis added).
[36] See Chapter 3 at p. 69; ALRC, *Safe, Informed, Supported* (n 13) 253–57.
[37] Jury Directions Act 2015 (Vic), s 52, extracted in Chapter 9 at pp. 222–224.

of statutory influence on rape trials. In Chapter 9, we draw on our transcript studies to illustrate how they can be used to their best advantage, and in Chapter 10, we reflect further on their emergence as a prominent part of the new gold standard of reformed rape laws. Our more specific point here, in this chapter on complainant cross-examination, is that jury directions are a mechanism that *presupposes* that rape myths will be engaged in rape trials rather than aiming to exclude them. At most, the aspiration is that the impacts of rape myths on trial outcomes will be reduced or 'neutralized'[38] and perhaps more ambitiously, that over time, defence counsel will come to see less strategic advantage in engaging them—despite a number of the directions being available for the past 40 years. Neither of these possible effects offer much comfort to complainants in rape trials today, who continue to be criticized for their pre- and post-event behaviour and accused of being liars.

Evidence law on 'relevance', 'credibility', and 'improper' questions

One of the grounds on which trial judges can reject a question asked in cross-examination is that it is designed to elicit *irrelevant* evidence. However, 'relevance' is traditionally defined in very broad terms. Evidence is relevant (and questioning adducing it permitted) where, 'if it were accepted, [it] could rationally affect (directly or indirectly) the assessment of the probability of the existence of a fact in issue . . .'[39] In Chapter 9, we look more closely at how trial judges policed relevance in the trials we analysed, but our assessment is that defence counsel are afforded extensive latitude to ask complainants about a wide variety of matters. The fact that rape trials regularly feature questions about pre-event 'flirtation' and post-event behaviour is illustrative of the elasticity of the concept of relevance to a fact in issue. We argue that, in many instances, the case for relevance is predicated on an underlying rape myth—that there is a 'correct' way for a person to behave after being sexually assaulted—which is not rational and should be a priori excluded. This remains an unaddressed dimension of how rape myths enter and influence rape trials.

The cross-examination exception to the credibility rule, which permits questions on matters that 'could substantially affect the assessment of the credibility of the witness',[40] offers wide scope for defence counsel to ask broad-ranging questions of the complainant.[41] In a number of the trials we analysed, we observed that this exception created space for defence counsel to cross-examine the complainant on

[38] For an explanation of our adoption of this term, see Chapter 3 at p. 71.
[39] Evidence Act 1995 (NSW), s 55; Evidence Act 2008 (Vic), s 55.
[40] Evidence Act 1995 (NSW), s 103(1); Evidence Act 2008 (Vic), s 103(1).
[41] Andrew Ligertwood and Gary Edmond, *Australian Evidence: A Principles Approach to the Common Law and Uniform Acts* (6th edn, LexisNexis Butterworths 2017) [7.138]; Stephen Odgers, *Uniform Evidence Law* (20th edn, Thomson Reuters Australia 2025) 900–02.

a broad range of personal history topics, including past substance use, criminal convictions, mental illness, and having had children removed from their care.[42] We imagine that this would have been distressing and embarrassing, and may well have left the complainant wondering what on earth this had to do with their allegation of being the victim of sexual violence. Cross-examination on such matters diminishes process justice and has the potential to adversely impact on outcome justice—depending on how it is used by the jury.

Trial judges have a positive duty to disallow *improper* questions.[43] We address this topic more fully in Chapter 9, but here we note that we observed only limited use of s 41 to disallow questions asked of the complainant during cross-examination—a finding that aligns with previous research.[44] The ALRC recently reported what it described as the 'ineffectual operation' of existing rules on improper questions, 'noting that some defence counsel continue to ask improper questions, prosecutors do not always object (out of concern this may prejudice the jury against the complainant), and judges do not always intervene to disallow improper questions'.[45] In Chapter 10, we consider the potential of a more active approach to regulating improper questions in order to change the nature of cross-examination in rape trials.

None of the three sets of evidence rules discussed here—relevance, the credibility rule, and improper questions—have been customized to address the particular demands of rape trials. They are evidence laws of general application. While not a product of the progressive rape law reform agenda, they are an important part of the legal framework that shapes rape trials. As currently interpreted, they tend to *facilitate* the entry of rape myths into the courtroom, rather than playing a role in excluding or minimizing them. Our analysis of transcripts suggests that *evidence* rules, more so than *substantive offence* definitions, or trial *procedures*, are the most consequential component of rape law architecture for whether rape myths are in circulation in the trial and whether the complainant is retraumatized during cross-examination (noting the inter-relationship between these two trial features). And yet, as we explained in Chapter 3, with the exception of statutory restrictions on sexual reputation and experience evidence, no attempt has been made to customise or 'modernize' the evidence rules that operate in rape trials. The result is the broad parameters of rape myth-influenced cross-examination that we have documented in this chapter.

[42] See Chapter 9 at pp. 217–218.

[43] Evidence Act 1995 (NSW), s 41; Evidence Act 2008 (Vic), s 41.

[44] Sarah L Deck and others, 'Are all Complainants of Sexual Assault Vulnerable? View of Australian Criminal Justice Professionals on the Evidence-Sharing Process' (2022) 26 The International Journal of Evidence and Proof 20, 29.

[45] ALRC, *Safe, Informed, Supported* (n 13) 361.

Relationship to the Crown case

It is easy to malign defence lawyers as responsible for the introduction of rape myths into contemporary trials. This would be both unfair and inaccurate, and would underestimate the difficulty of achieving rape trials without rape myths. We explained in Chapter 6 that we saw little evidence that 'modernized' consent laws (or other aspects of rape law statutory reform) have significantly changed the shape of the Crown case. Where they 'fit', features of the rape schema—and associated rape myths—are relied on to help strengthen the Crown case. With the parameters set in this way, it is hardly surprising that the defence also engages rape myths to their advantage. We observed that, in a given trial, the parties are often playing two sides of the same coin. For example, the Crown may seek to draw attention to the speed with which the complainant reported the alleged rape, while defence counsel may conduct cross-examination in such a way as to draw attention to the incompleteness or lack of specificity in the complainant's account. *Both* are relying on the rape myth that *immediate* complaint is indicative of 'truth'—and that the converse is true.

Limited options for the defence?

One of the explanations sometimes offered for why the entrenched patterns of rape myth-informed cross-examination of complainants persist is that, in a rape trial, there are few options when it comes to defence strategy.[46] Where a decision has been made to plead not guilty, and the best evidence of the accused's guilt is the complainant's account of events, it is perhaps to be anticipated that the defence strategy is likely to involve a challenge to the believability of the complainant's account, including by honing in on 'inconsistencies'.[47] Of course, such an approach is not inevitable or preordained. A defence position based (only) on challenging the Crown's ability to prove the fault element for rape need not involve disputing the complainant's account. However, it is relatively rare for a defence strategy to rely on disputing the fault element for rape, let alone exclusively.[48] There were no such cases in the 108 trials we analysed.

[46] See, eg, Jennifer Temkin, 'Prosecuting and Defending Rape: Perspectives From the Bar' (2000) 27 Journal of Law and Society 219, 231.

[47] In *Reed v R* [2006] NSWCCA 314 [85], Sully J observed that 'there are, in the very nature of things, some sexual assault trials in which *the only practical means* by which the accused person can exercise his right to test the evidence of his accuser is, precisely, by testing in some proper fashion matters of detail, including 'surrounding tangential details' (emphasis added). See Odgers (n 41) 832; also James Glissan, *Advocacy in Practice* (5th edn, LexisNexis Butterworths 2011) 106.

[48] See, eg, Melanie Heenan, 'Trial and Error: Rape, Law Reform and Feminism (DPhil thesis, Monash University 2001) 371; Melanie Heenan and Helen McKelvie, 'The Crimes (Rape) Act 1991: An Evaluation Report' (Rape Law Reform Evaluation Report No 2, Department of Justice Victoria 1997) 191.

In any event, it is clear enough that in many of the trials we analysed defence counsel adopted a tried and true approach to running a defence case in a rape trial (just as the prosecutor often did in running the Crown case). On the one hand, it might be expected that defence counsel will continue to engage methods that have a proven track record of success, where few other options are perceived to exist. On the other hand, we join McDonald in wondering whether there aren't other ways to test the complainant's credibility 'without reinforcing or relying on the general idea that women commonly lie about sex and rape'?[49]

It can be easy to slip into an account that suggests that the problem is one of defence lawyer impropriety. While we certainly observed some instances of cross-examination questions and closing submissions that were outrageous and should never have been asked or made, we don't think such instances are the nub of the problem. Nor do we subscribe to the view that all defence lawyers are consciously weaponizing myths and stereotypes that they know to be false. As we tried to explain in Chapter 2, this is too simplistic an account of what rape *myths* are—including where they come from, and how they circulate and are sustained. Cross-examination of a complainant can be directed to matters like resistance, 'delay', and 'inconsistency' because these form part of the inherited defence 'playbook' for rape trials, rather than because the defence lawyer who does so is on a mission to keep 'rape culture' alive. They remain, in our view, undesirable features of a criminal trial, but we argue that the focus should remain on the legal and material conditions under which rape trials are conducted rather than on condemnation of the defence lawyers, individually or generally. We invite careful and nuanced reflection on the assumption that the rights of the accused would necessarily be compromised if legislation more actively regulated whether and how the defence can deploy the ubiquitous and deeply entrenched line that the allegation is *false* and the complainant is *lying*—and rely on rape myths to this end. We return to this important issue in Chapter 10.

4. Conclusion

In this chapter, we have shown that beneath the narrative of 50 years of progressive law reform, ostensibly designed to weaken the influence of rape myths on the practice of sexual violence laws and the conduct of rape trials, lies a different reality: rape myths are abundant in rape trials, and this has the potential to exacerbate retraumatization of complainants (process injustice), and impact on trial verdicts (outcome injustice). However, we argue that it would be a mistake to conclude that statutory reform has 'failed'.

[49] McDonald (n 1) 426.

The title of this chapter refers to the 'resilience' of rape myths, but on reflection this is something of a misnomer. It suggests that rape myths have been subjected to a serious attempt to eradicate or reduce them, and that they have nonetheless managed to 'survive'. The truth is that few of the many statutory reforms over the years have even attempted to touch the *content* of cross-examination. So it should come as no surprise that the lines of questioning documented in this chapter continue to occur.

The features of contemporary rape trials highlighted in this chapter suggest that while the 'mechanics' of appearing as a witness and being cross-examined in rape trials have been changed for the better in line with *procedural reforms*,[50] the *substance* of what makes cross-examination distressing and unfair for complainants in rape trials has barely been touched. With the exception of questions about sexual 'reputation' and sexual experience,[51] our analysis of transcripts from Victoria and NSW suggests that complainants are likely to be asked the same sorts of questions that complainants were asked in, and prior to, the 1970s.[52] It appears that defence counsel continue to see strategic value in engaging rape myths and stereotypes to impugn the complainant and weaken the Crown case in the eyes of the jury.

Our analysis shows that it is important to interrogate very closely precisely what 'progressive' rape law reforms require—and what they leave untouched. The findings presented in this chapter provide further support for the argument advanced in this book: that there is a mismatch between the celebrated legislative tools of transformation (eg 'perfected' definitions of consent and non-consent; 'educative' jury directions) and the nature of the practices that cry out for transformation—such as rape-myth inspired lines of cross-examination. In Chapter 10, we consider what more can be done to address this mismatch.

[50] See Chapter 5.
[51] See Chapter 5 at p. 108.
[52] Featherstone (n 2) 56, 127; Sarah Zydervelt and others, 'Lawyer's strategies for cross-examining rape complainants: Have we moved beyond the 1950s?' (2017) 57 British Journal of Criminology 551.

8
Intoxication Evidence

1. Introduction

As we explained in Chapter 1, the larger project on which this book reports started with a much smaller one on 'intoxication' evidence in sexual offence trials.[1] We were aware that one of the many ways in which sexual offence laws had been reformed in most Australian jurisdictions over the years was to expressly legislate to interrupt the culturally assumed nexus and rape myths about the relationship between intoxication and consent—a nexus that has impeded justice for victim-survivors of sexual violence.[2] Traditionally, this had made it very difficult, if not impossible, for a person who was intoxicated at the time they were raped to obtain justice via the criminal prosecution system.[3] And this is a systemic rather than a 'niche' problem, given that it is estimated that victim alcohol and/or other drugs (AOD) intoxication is involved in 50 to 75% of all sexual assaults.[4] Perpetrator

[1] This study, 'Intoxication Evidence in Rape Trials: A Double-Edged Sword?', was funded by the Australian Research Council Discovery Project Scheme (DP200100101). See Chapter 1 at pp. 12–13.

[2] Heather D Flowe and John Maltby, 'An Experimental Examination of Alcohol Consumption, Alcohol Expectancy, and Self-Blame on Willingness to Report a Hypothetical Rape' (2018) 44 Aggressive Behavior 225, 226; Clare Gunby, Anna Carline, and Caryl Beynon, 'Regretting it After? Focus Group Perspectives on Alcohol Consumption, Nonconsensual Sex and False Allegations of Rape' (2013) 22 Social & Legal Studies 87; Isabel Grant and Janine Benedet, 'Capacity to Consent and Intoxicated Complainants in Sexual Assault Prosecutions' (2017) 37 Criminal Reports 375; Elaine Craig, 'Sexual Assault and Intoxication: Defining (In)capacity to Consent' (2020) 98 The Canadian Bar Review 70; Emily Finch and Vanessa E Munro, 'The Demon Drink and the Demonized Woman: Socio-Sexual Stereotypes and Responsibility Attribution in Rape Trials Involving Intoxicants' (2007) 16 Social & Legal Studies 591; Emily Finch and Vanessa E Munro, 'Juror Stereotypes and Blame Attribution in Rape Cases Involving Intoxicants: The Findings of a Pilot Study' (2005) 45 The British Journal of Criminology 25.

[3] Liz Kelly, Jo Lovett, and Linda Regan, 'A Gap or Chasm? Attrition in Reported Rape Cases' (Research Study 293, Home Office 2005); Denise Lievore, 'Victim Credibility in Adult Sexual Assault Cases' (Trends & Issues in Crime and Criminal Justice No 288, Australian Institute of Criminology 2004); Natalie Taylor, 'Juror Attitudes and Biases in Sexual Assault Cases' (Trends & Issues in Crime and Criminal Justice No 344, Australian Institute of Criminology 2007).

[4] Australian Bureau of Statistics, 'Personal Safety, Australia: 2021–22(ABS 2023); Australian Institute of Health and Welfare, 'Family, Domestic and Sexual Violence in Australia: Continuing the National Story' (Report No FDV 3, 2019) 17; Antonia Abbey and others, 'Review of Survey and Experimental Research That Examines the Relationship Between Alcohol Consumption and Men's Sexual Aggression Perpetration' (2014) 15 Trauma, Violence & Abuse 265; Heather D Flowe and Anna Carline, 'Alcohol and Remembering Rape: Setting the Scene' in Heather D Flowe and Anna Carline (eds), *Alcohol and Remembering Rape: New Evidence for Practice* (Palgrave Pivot 2021) 2.

Reforming Rape Trials. Julia Quilter and Luke McNamara, Oxford University Press.
 DOI: 10.1093/9780198948155.003.0008

intoxication is also significant with 35% to 75% of perpetrators reporting that they consumed alcohol prior to committing sexual violence.[5]

Even though our research widened to include multiple features of the reformed rape trial—the findings of which are discussed in other chapters in this book—we continued to examine whether statutory reforms on intoxication have changed the way trials are conducted, and reduced the impact of alcohol and drug use-related rape myths and stereotypes. This chapter is devoted to sharing our findings on AOD use and intoxication evidence, as well as demonstrating how they support wider arguments we advance in this book about why statutory reform has not transformed rape trials. We draw on three data sources:

(i) our transcript analysis from the 96 Victorian and NSW trials in our combined samples that featured intoxication evidence;[6]
(ii) our analysis of 102 Australian appellate court decisions involving conviction appeals from rape/sexual assault trials, where there was evidence that the complainant was intoxicated at the time of the alleged offence; and
(iii) our analysis of 15 semi-structured interviews with lawyers from Victoria and NSW with experience acting in rape trials, either as the prosecutor, the defence lawyer, or both.[7]

In the first part of this chapter, we examine aspects of the modern legislative architecture of rape laws in Australia that are directed at intoxication evidence. We have argued in this book that it is important to scrutinize precisely what mode of statutory influence has been engaged by legislation that purports to modernize rape law, and we apply that approach here too. We next report on what our analysis of trial transcripts reveals about what intoxication evidence 'looks like' in rape trials, also drawing on our analysis of appellate decisions and our interviews with lawyers. We then consider what we have learned about whether and how evidence of the complainant's intoxication evidence is used by the prosecution and defence counsel. Finally, we share our findings on what is probably the most consequential way that intoxication evidence affects rape trials: as a basis for attacking the reliability and credibility of the complainant as witness.

[5] Antonia Abbey, Colleen M McDaniel, and Zunaira Jilani, 'Alcohol and Men's Sexual Aggression: Review of Research and Implications for Prevention' in Lindsay M Orchowski and Alan Berkowitz (eds), *Engaging Boys and Men in Sexual Assault Prevention: Theory, Research and Practice* (Elsevier Science & Technology 2022).

[6] There was evidence of AOD consumption by both parties in 58% of these trials, by the complainant only in 22% of trials, and by the accused only in 20% of trials.

[7] For further details on the collection of these data, see Chapter 4 at pp. 83–88, 92.

2. Overview of Legislation

The barrier to justice for victim-survivors presented by intoxication[8] was not a focus of attention during the first 'wave' of rape law reform in Australia in the 1970s and early 1980s. However, it wasn't long before some jurisdictions began to pay more attention to the significance of intoxication evidence, starting with Tasmania in 1987 and Victoria in 1991.[9] In Victoria, a new provision on the meaning of consent included an express statement that a person does not freely consent if '. . . the person is asleep, unconscious, or so affected by alcohol or another drug as to be incapable of freely agreeing'.[10] The Attorney General's second reading speech emphasized that the new formulation of consent 'means real and informed agreement, not the exploitation of a person who does not understand the sexual nature of an act, or *who is incapacitated by a drug*'.[11]

In its current form, as amended by the Justice Legislation Amendment (Sexual Offences and Other Matters) Act 2022 (Vic), s 36AA(1) of the Crimes Act 1958 (Vic) relevantly provides:

> Circumstances in which a person does not consent to an act include . . .
> (g) the person is so affected by alcohol or another drug as to be incapable of consenting to the act;
> (h) the person is so affected by alcohol or another drug as to be incapable of withdrawing consent to the act . . .

When NSW moved to legislate a positive definition of consent in 2007, the complainant's intoxication was added to the list of 'vitiating' factors.[12] In its original form, intoxication was added as a factor that *may* vitiate consent: '. . . if the person has sexual intercourse while substantially intoxicated by alcohol or any drug'.[13] In 2021, this provision was replaced with a new formulation that resembles the current Victorian provision: 'A person does not consent to a sexual activity if . . . (c) the person is so affected by alcohol or another drug as to be incapable of consenting to the sexual activity'.[14]

[8] Note that 'intoxication' may be by way of alcohol and/or another drug: Crimes Act 1900 (NSW), s 428A; Crimes Act 1958 (Vic), s 36AA(1).

[9] See Chapter 3 at p. 53.

[10] Crimes Act 1958 (Vic) s 36(d), as amended by the Crimes (Rape) Act 1991 (Vic) (since further amended and renumbered).

[11] Victoria, *Parliamentary Debates*, Legislative Assembly, 26 November 1991, 1999 (James Kennan, Attorney-General) (emphasis added).

[12] Crimes Amendment (Consent—Sexual Assault Offences) Act 2007 (NSW).

[13] Crimes Act 1900 (NSW), s 61HA(6)(a), as inserted by the Crimes Legislation (Consent—-Sexual Assault Offences) Act 2007 (NSW), as amended by Criminal Legislation Amendment (Child Sexual Abuse) Act 2018 (NSW), sch 1.

[14] Crimes Act 1900 (NSW), s 61HJ(1)(c), as amended by the Crimes Legislation Amendment (Sexual Consent Reforms) Act 2021 (NSW).

Although it occurred over a span of decades—most recently in Queensland in 2024[15]—all Australian states and territories (except Western Australia) have now adopted an equivalent provision as part of their growing legislation on consent and non-consent.[16] Such provisions are undoubtedly powerful on a rhetorical level helping shift the burden of responsibility for the sexual activity away from the intoxicated person (typically, a woman) who has been traditionally 'blamed', doubted, and criticized when she subsequently reports the matter as crime. They are also important at a public discursive level with public education messaging suggesting that 'an intoxicated person cannot give consent'.[17] However, *legally* the provision is more circumspect, and this has significant implications for whether such provisions contribute to rape trial 'modernization'—granted there is a lot of cultural weight for one provision to shift.

None of the Australian legislative provisions *deem* non-consent to have been proven where there is evidence of complainant intoxication. Clearly, this version of statutory influence is not possible given the spectrum of AOD effects captured by 'intoxication', and absent any attempt to legislate a clear and fixed statutory threshold (as is a hallmark of statutory drink-driving offences). The common legislative drafting approach is to combine a strong affirmative statement that a person *does not* consent, with a heavily qualified and indeterminate description of the circumstance in which evidence of a person's intoxication will *prove* non-consent. Although the language varies, the most common Australian formulation provides that: intoxication = non-consent where the person is '*so affected* . . . as to *be incapable of consenting*' (emphasis added). The circularity of this formulation begs the question: what degree of intoxication is required before a person should be regarded as having lost their *capacity* to consent?

Our point is not that this is a case of 'bad' legislative drafting, but rather that it is deliberate. Law-makers have adopted a passive and imprecise mode of statutory influence that leaves a great deal to be determined in the specific evidentiary context of individual trials. As we will see, the same is true of the previous NSW legislative formulation which was operative during our transcript study—where it was said that evidence that the complainant was '*substantially* intoxicated' *may* provide grounds for establishing non-consent. As we will discuss, this type of legislative

15 Criminal Law (Coercive Control and Affirmative Consent) and Other Legislation Amendment Act 2024 (Qld).

16 See Crimes Act 1900 (ACT), s 67(1)(g); Criminal Code 1924 (Tas), s 2A(2)(h); Criminal Code 1983 (NT), s 208GA(2)(c); Criminal Law Consolidation Act 1935 (SA), s 46(3)(d); Criminal Code 1899 (Qld), s 348AA(1)(c). The Law Reform Commission of Western Australia (LRCWA) has recommended the introduction of a provision modelled on the Victorian legislation: LRCWA, *Project 113: Sexual Offences* (Final Report, 2023) rec 8.

17 See, eg, the list provided on: Victoria Police, 'Consent and Consent Laws: Who Cannot Give Consent' <https://www.police.vic.gov.au/consent-laws#who-cannot-give-consent> accessed 11 July 2025.

equivocality leaves much room for AOD use-related rape myths to reverberate in the courtroom.

A parallel development has been the enactment of legislation which aims to limit the opportunity for *defendants* to raise *exculpatory* evidence of their own intoxication.[18] In Australian jurisdictions, and across the common law world, the relevance of evidence that the accused was intoxicated at the time of the alleged offence, and whether it can be relied on to negative voluntariness and/or intent, has exercised minds and promoted debate and disagreement amongst jurists, legislators, and scholars.[19] In Australian jurisdictions, the resolution has been some form of statutory limitation—whether applicable to criminal offences generally, some types of criminal offences (eg basic or general intent crimes), or sexual offences specifically.[20]

The most common approach in the Australian states and territories to limiting the availability of accused intoxication evidence is that it can be taken into account in assessing the (subjective) honesty of an asserted belief in consent, but not in relation to assessing the reasonableness of that belief.[21] NSW legislation goes further, prohibiting regard to evidence of the accused's intoxication in relation to any aspect of the fault element for sexual offences—that is, both subjective (honest belief) and objective (reasonable belief) elements.[22]

3. What Types of Intoxication Evidence Are Led in Rape Trials?

Given the significance that reformed rape laws now attach to intoxication—especially the complainant's intoxication—we were interested in what sorts of evidence are adduced. The following discussion draws on what we learned from our review of appellate decisions (which often featured extracts from first instance trial transcripts), the transcripts in Victoria and NSW, as well as what was revealed by interviews with lawyers.

We found that complainant intoxication evidence (and accused intoxication evidence, when it was present) frequently took the form of self-assessment, as well as third-party witness assessment (including assessment of the complainant by the accused and vice versa). The extent of the complainant's intoxication was

[18] Consistent with the overall aims of this book, our focus in this chapter is on complainant intoxication.

[19] *DPP v Majewski* [1977] AC 443; *R v O'Connor* (1980) 146 CLR 64; Arlie Loughnan, *Manifest Madness: Mental Incapacity in Criminal Law* (OUP 2012) ch 7; David Brown and others, *Criminal Laws: Materials and Commentary on Criminal Law and Process of New South Wales* (8th edn, Federation Press 2025) 174–79.

[20] See generally, Simon Bronitt and Bernadette McSherry, *Principles of Criminal Law* (4th edn, Thomson Reuters 2017) 283–88.

[21] See, eg, Crimes Act 1958 (Vic), s 36B. See also Criminal Code 1899 (Qld), s 348A(3).

[22] Crimes Act 1900 (NSW), s 61HK(5)(b). See also Criminal Law Consolidation Act 1935 (SA), s 268(2).

usually evidenced via answers on what type of AOD had been consumed, the volume of consumption, and over what period of time. The following examples are illustrative:

> Q: *So between [arrival] ... and the others leaving ... a bit after 11, can you recall what you had to drink?*
> A: *I had four cocktails. I had an espresso martini, two white chocolate martinis, and a French martini. Then I've had three shots. There was one called a Jam Donut shot and one called a Wet Pussy shot, and there was one that was with a coffee-based liqueur in it, but I'm not too sure what it was called.*

* * *

> Q: *You had some alcohol at the dance?*
> A: *Yeah.*
> Q: *Can you remember how much you had over the evening until it finished at around about midnight or something?*
> A: *About six or seven.*
> Q: *Of what?*
> A: *Jim Beam and Cola.*
> Q: *They were the normal size cans, were they, you're referring to?*
> A: *Yeah, yeah, they weren't very ...*
> Q: *So, they're a premixed drink, Jim Beam and Cola, correct?*
> A: *Correct, yes.*

Self-assessment isn't limited to quantitative measures of volume and duration of AOD consumption. Questions of the sort illustrated here were often followed by questions that asked the complainant to describe how they were feeling from the effects of the alcohol (or other drugs) that they had consumed. For example:

> A: *At this point I felt it and I was falling over, stumbling. I was just all over the place. I could hear conversations around me but my body just felt, like, useless.*

When complainants were pressed to explain how intoxicated they were at the time of the alleged rape—and where the accused or other witnesses were asked to comment on their impression of the intoxication of the complainant—it was common for answers to engage colloquialisms and slang terminology, such as: '*heaps intoxicated*', '*pretty drunk*', '*messy*', '*smashed*', '*hammered*', '*drunk as a skunk*', '*legless*', '*well lubricated*', '*maggoty*', '*out of it*', '*wobbly*', '*paralytic*', '*jelly*', and '*blotto*'.

These examples are not offered as criticism of the language used by complainants and other witnesses. Rather, they are reproduced to draw attention to the incongruity between, on the one hand, the indeterminate ways in which AOD effects are routinely described in rape trials and, on the other, the seriousness of what is at stake, in a context where the jury must ultimately apply what they have learned about the complainant's intoxication to their deliberations on whether the elements of the offence have been proven beyond reasonable doubt.

Noting that expert scientific evidence to assist the jury features rarely in rape trials (a matter to which we return below) we observed uses of a 'pop' scientific numerical rating scale to 'measure' intoxication. In a number of trials, we observed complainants being asked to (retrospectively) rate their level of intoxication at the time in question on a scale of 1 to 10. For example: '*By the time you went to bed, if nought is not intoxicated at all and 10 is very intoxicated, on that scale of nought to 10 how affected by alcohol did you feel?*' The complainant answered: '*I'd say, yeah, nine, eight or nine*'.

In the following example, it was the trial judge who used the scale, when intervening to ask the complainant about her intoxication on the night in question:

TJ: Can I just ask you something . . . at the time you took the cocaine how affected were you by the alcohol that you consumed?
C: I would describe myself as being drunk.
TJ: If I were to offer you up a scale from one to ten where one is perfectly sober and ten is falling down drunk where would you rate yourself on that scale just before you took the cocaine?
C: I'd probably be about a six.

In Chapter 9, we look closely at the sort of interventions judges made in the trials we analysed. Here, we note that the judge effectively endorsed the self-assessment approach to 'defining' intoxication and numerical rating scales. We found, in our appellate and transcript reviews, that judges sometimes added their own level of imprecision to the question of 'intoxication' by glossing the language used in statutes. For example, the complainant: 'became overwhelmed by alcohol',[23] was in an 'impaired state of consciousness',[24] and was 'inebriated at the time'.[25] Adding further difficulty to the jury's interpretative exercise, judges also used adverbs to try and capture the extent of intoxication, but these were often at odds with the statutory language—'grossly intoxicated',[26] 'heavily intoxicated',[27] and 'extreme intoxication'.[28]

In interviews, a number of prosecutors told us that the 1–10 scale is commonly used in rape trials featuring intoxication evidence. In response to a question about

[23] *Costa v Western Australia* [2019] WASCA 200 [64].
[24] *Hofer v The Queen* [2019] NSWCCA 244 [190].
[25] *R v MCS* [2018] QCA 184 [190].
[26] *Tabbah v The Queen* [2017] NSWCCA 55 [166].
[27] *Agresti v The Queen* (2017) 13 ACTLR 1, 36 [157].
[28] *Hofer* (n 24) [145].

the value of the scale, one prosecutor told us, '*It has no value*'—an assessment that finds support in the literature[29]—but explained that it is used regularly because juries '*tend to find it attractive*'.

Another noteworthy aspect of rape trials featuring evidence of the complainant's intoxication was that attention was drawn—via questioning of witnesses or admission of CCTV footage or both—to how the complainant was 'behaving'. Noting that the key question in issue is typically whether the complainant was intoxicated to the extent of lacking the capacity to consent to sexual activity—a matter of *cognitive* function—this line of inquiry tends to focus on the complainant's ability (or inability) to perform *motor* functions. Examples include observable behaviours like walking, speaking (whether slurring or not), dancing, texting on a mobile phone, calling a taxi, getting in/out of a car, and rolling a cigarette.[30]

The simplistic assumption that motor, mechanical, or physical functions can be regarded as proxies for cognitive impairment is not supported by the scientific literature, which indicates that alcohol impairs cognitive functions before motor impairment.[31] As McGlynn has observed: 'If . . . juries consider complainants to retain capacity simply by reason of their being able to move about and [make] . . . simple decisions . . . then in practice lack of capacity is coterminous with unconsciousness.'[32]

The knowledge that cognitive functions may be impaired *before* motor functions are impaired *should* form part of the evidence in all rape trials where there is evidence of complainant intoxication. However, in the large majority of trials we reviewed—both directly via transcript analysis and indirectly via analysis of appellate decisions—such knowledge was not made available to the jury. Rather, it was assumed that motor function was indicative of the complainant's cognitive capacity, and expert scientific guidance to the contrary was absent.

In a rare exception, an expert witness explained alcohol effects as follows:

> *It can affect decision-making and information processing, and it can also affect what we call motor control, that is the way that people's muscles are controlled.*

[29] Julia Quilter and Luke McNamara, 'The Meaning of "Intoxication" in Australian Criminal Cases: Origins and Operation' (2018) 21 New Criminal Law Review 170; Lauren A Monds and others, 'How Intoxicated Are You? Investigating Self and Observer Intoxication Ratings in Relation to Blood Alcohol Concentration' (2021) 40 Drug and Alcohol Review 1173; Sarah Callinan, 'Alcohol's Harm to Others: Quantifying a Little or a Lot of Harm' (2014) 3 International Journal of Alcohol and Drug Research 127, 132; Elizabeth Manton and others, 'Alcohol's Harm to Others: Using Qualitative Research to Complement Survey Findings' (2014) 3 International Journal of Alcohol and Drug Research 143, 146.

[30] See also Elisabeth McDonald, *Rape Myths as Barriers to Fair Trial Process* (Canterbury UP 2020) 262–64.

[31] Mark Rose and Jon Grant, 'Alcohol-Induced Blackout: Phenomenology, Biological Basis, and Gender Differences' (2010) 4 Journal of Addiction Medicine 61, 70.

[32] Clare McGlynn, 'Feminist Activism and Rape Law Reform in England and Wales: A Sisyphean Struggle?' in Clare McGlynn and Vanessa Munro (eds), *Rethinking Rape Law: International and Comparative Perspectives* (Routledge 2010) 139.

> *That's what makes people—you know, when they're drunk they become unsteady and they can't walk properly and they can't talk properly.* ***That's one of the things that's the last to be affected.*** *So when people drink early on it might affect their personality or their inhibitions or their decision-making or their thinking without necessarily making them look drunk. You know, they can still walk in a straight line and so on. Then as they drink more and more, more and more functions become affected.* ***By the time they can't walk any more, then as I said before, that's one of the last things to be affected, so all the other things have been well and truly affected by the time a person gets to the stage where they can't move properly.***[33]

As noted above, this trial was an outlier amongst those we analysed. We were struck by the regularity with which jurors were required to resolve complex questions without the benefit of expert knowledge on AOD effects. How intoxicated was the person? What did this mean for cognitive functions related to elements of the crime charged (like consent formation)? What did it mean for memory, recall, and the reliability of evidence? Juries were usually told to consider the mostly lay and subjective evidence that they had heard and use their 'common knowledge' to answer these questions. It was also typical for defence counsel to 'step in' and offer their own take on what members of the jury would or should know about AOD effects. Needless to say, these suggestions tended to be partisan rather than neutral, such as the 'knowledge' that intoxication leads to sexual disinhibition. As we will explain in the next section, this often formed an important part of the defence challenge to the Crown's case on non-consent.

For alcohol—the substance that had most often been consumed in the trials we analysed—the challenges that arise from non-expert, anecdotal, and colloquial estimates of AOD consumption and lay impressions about AOD effects were rarely acknowledged. While expert evidence was more common in trials that involved evidence about consumption of 'unfamiliar' drugs, *alcohol* appeared to be treated as a drug where it could be assumed that jurors knew and understood its effects. In a rare exception, in which both the accused and the complainant had been drinking alcohol, the trial judge observed:

> *We haven't got an expert as to the effects of alcohol, the effects of - the elimination rates or the differences in the way a female disposes of alcohol as opposed to a male, we've got none of that on which we can go to the jury.... [The accused] denies being alcohol affected at that point in time but says that he thought, 'She was as drunk as I was' without knowing what on earth that means.*

One of the many disconcerting features of rape trials to which we have drawn attention in this book—and which we explore further in Chapter 9 regarding the

[33] Emphasis added.

practices of judges—is trial-to-trial variability. Furthermore, it is troubling that intoxication evidence—something that features in many trials—is poorly served by expert guidance, and so vulnerable to distortion, speculative interpretation, and exploitation.[34]

4. Proving and Challenging Non-Consent

As we argued in Chapters 6 and 7, against the grain of a narrative of progressive statutory reforms, and a mission to transform rape trials, the prosecution and defence continue to frame their case around rape myths—including expectations of verbal/physical resistance, injuries, distress, immediate complaint, and consistency in accounts. We explained that this was disappointing but not surprising, given that none of the many legislative reforms over the decades have attempted to shift this traditional orientation. Perhaps we *would* see change around the treatment of intoxication evidence, given that there *has* been discrete statutory reform on this aspect of rape law?

We approached this question with caution given that, as noted earlier in this chapter, legislation on complainant intoxication, in particular, is qualified and limited. Overall, we found that the rape myth-oriented dynamic of the evidence adduced in trials remained largely in place. Intoxication evidence tended to serve the interests of the defence, rather than the prosecution, when it came to the issue of proving (and contesting) non-consent.

Prosecution

80% of the trials in our Victorian and NSW transcript studies that featured intoxication evidence, included evidence about the *complainant's* intoxication. Even though they were ostensibly designed to assist the prosecution to prove non-consent, prosecutors rarely engaged the Crimes Act complainant intoxication provisions. We found little difference in this regard between the (old) NSW provision that was operative at the time of our study ('substantially intoxicated') and the Victorian formulation ('so affected . . . as to be incapable of consenting')—that has since been adopted in NSW.

The prosecution sought to unambiguously rely on the relevant statutory provision in only a small minority of cases. Even where the legislation was engaged, the

[34] Some studies suggest that expert evidence may be inconclusive and used to undermine complainant credibility: Cassandra Richards, 'Intoxication: A Drunk Science: Expertise in Cases of Sexual Assault regarding Capacity to Consent' (2020) 2 Canadian Journal of Law and Justice 137; Mary Connell, 'Expert Testimony in Sexual Assault Cases: Alcohol Intoxication and Memory' (2015) 42–43 International Journal of Law and Psychiatry 98.

prosecution did not seek to prove the element of non-consent exclusively on the basis of the complainant's intoxication-related incapacity to consent, but tended to point also to other conduct by the complainant that manifested her non-consent. We saw glimpses of the full potential of the Victorian model being articulated, such as in the following trial judge direction to the jury:

> *The law identifies a number of circumstances where the complainant is deemed or considered not to freely agree or consent to sexual penetration. These circumstances include where the person is so affected by alcohol, or another drug, as to be incapable of freely agreeing.*
>
> *If you are satisfied beyond reasonable doubt that this circumstance existed in relation to Ms [complainant] you must find that she was not consenting. However, you do not need to consider this question only by reference to these particular circumstances. If you are satisfied beyond reasonable doubt on any basis arising from the evidence that the complainant was not consenting then this element will be proven.*

However, our sense is that, in most trials we observed, resort to the legislative provisions on complainant intoxication was limited by a perception (apparently shared by counsel and most judges) that they were only relevant in cases of *extreme* intoxication. This interpretation is evident in the following exchange between the trial judge and the prosecutor in a Victorian trial on whether the complainant intoxication provision was being engaged:

> *TJ: how's the Prosecution putting it [ie the relevance of the complainant's intoxication]?*
> *P: It doesn't put it that highly.*
> *TJ: She [isn't] paralytic when she leaves the [pub], . . . I mean, I don't think she says 'I was so paralytic'.*
> *P: No.*

This interpretation was also reflected in what prosecutors said in interviews about their reluctance to engage the complainant intoxication legislative provision unless the complainant was, in the previous judge's words, 'paralytic'. One prosecutor told us:

> *Quite frankly you have to be basically unconscious for that [ie the threshold of 'substantially intoxicated'] to really get up . . . I mean I think you'd either have to be incredibly, absolutely . . . paralytic or someone got you drunk for that rule to . . . really take on . . . a bit of meaning.*

Another said that '*incapacity is easier to establish*' if the complainant is '*passed out or completely legless*'.[35]

[35] These findings are consistent with the high degree of intoxication viewed as the threshold in a review of Canadian appellate decisions: Grant and Benedet (n 2).

The perception that the complainant's intoxication would only be a 'strength' of the prosecution's case if the level of her intoxication was such as to render her unconscious or asleep at the time of the alleged rape, was a common feature of the various fact scenarios in the trials we analysed.[36] In 58% of the 77 trials (across both studies) which featured complainant intoxication evidence, the prosecution case was that the complainant was asleep (due to being heavily intoxicated or simply asleep) when the rape commenced. We note that, in such situations, the intoxication specific provision is effectively redundant. The list of 'non-consent' factors that is part of the modern architecture of Australian rape law already expressly states that a person cannot consent if they are 'asleep or unconscious'.[37]

One prosecutor told us they would not rely on the complainant intoxication provision unless they had 'empirical evidence':

> *. . . I try not to rely on it unless I've got like really – unless I've got CCTV from someone in a pub where they've like drunk 15 schooners or 15 drinks and you could have a toxicologist say 'Yes, they're substantially intoxicated', then I would rely on it. I think I will never rely on substantial intoxication again unless I have empirical evidence. . . . [I]f there's objective evidence supporting something then the jury is definitely likely to buy it, but if there's no objective evidence supporting it I think you've got no chance.*

As we noted above, the kind of intoxication evidence routinely admitted into rape trials is typically anything but 'objective': it consists of vague, colloquial, and subjective lay assessments. Across both our transcript studies and our appellate review of cases, we observed that it was rare for a toxicologist, pharmacologist, or an AOD expert to be called, especially in the majority of cases where alcohol was the drug that had been consumed. Where such evidence *was* led, the expert was typically disinclined to express (or disallowed from expressing) an opinion on the relationship between the complainant's level of intoxication and the capacity to consent. In only one case in our appellate review did it appear that an expert had touched on the topic of consent, and the nature of that mention was to say that they 'could not venture an opinion as to whether that had deprived the complainant of the capacity to consent'[38]—'*that*' being an estimated blood alcohol in the range of between 0.165% and 0.2% at the time of the alleged rape.

[36] On the relationship between intoxication, sleep, and unconsciousness, see Rosemary Alison Isaacs and others, 'Sleep, Waking and Sleep Inertia in Sexual Assault: A Retrospective Descriptive Study' (2021) 82 Journal of Forensic and Legal Medicine art ID no 102222.

[37] See Crimes Act 1900 (NSW), s 61HJ(1)(d); Crimes Act 1958 (Vic), s 36AA(1)(f).

[38] *Mitic v The Queen* [2011] VSCA 373 [24].

In interview, one prosecutor told us:

I would be very reluctant to [ask an expert to comment on consent] . . . I just think it is dangerous territory to allow an expert to go to that point . . .

Another said:

I don't think any expert would say [whether there was capacity to form consent], they would only talk about whether someone's intoxicated and maybe how they appeared, but the ultimate issue . . . I don't think you'd ever find a pharmacologist to say 'Look, someone substantially impaired cannot consent', you just would not find that.

Along with the high threshold set by the words of statutes, uncertainty about the extent of the complainant's intoxication, and little guidance on the relationship between AOD effects and cognitive functions like consent formation, another challenge is that prosecutors can struggle to position an intoxicated complainant in relation to rape myths about how a 'true' victim of sexual violence should act. A long line of research suggests juries tend to be hard on drunken women, and inclined to 'forgive' accused men who are drunk.[39] Prosecutors are also alive to these stereotypes and attitudes. As one put it:

Look I'm going to be honest with you, . . . you tend to have to work a bit harder . . . because you know that you've got a lot more convincing to do . . . [Y]ou go into it with almost a fatalistic sense where you realise juries are very, very – I mean . . . juries have very gendered views on how women should act and what they should do in certain circumstances, so you kind of have to work harder to try and neutralise that.

We observed that, in some cases, prosecutors tackled this head-on, effectively anticipating that jurors might be inclined to judge the complainant harshly for excessive AOD consumption and failing to act in a responsible and/or rape-preventing manner. For example, in the following trial, during their closing address, the prosecutor underlined the complainant's irresponsible drinking, but appealed to the jury to put that to one side and see it within the context of an exceptional circumstance—a family funeral following a terrible tragedy in the family:

[The complainant] told you that while she was there, she had quite a lot to drink. She became well affected by alcohol . . . [Y]ou might find that the facts of this case

[39] Elena V Stepanova and Amy L Brown, 'Alcohol Priming and Attribution of Blame in an Acquaintance Rape Vignette' (2021) 36 Journal of Interpersonal Violence 1537; Abbey and others (n 4); Flowe and Maltby (n 2) 226; Abbey, McDaniel, and Jilani (n 5); Carline, Gunby, and Beynon (n 2).

are unpleasant. You might think that drinking alcohol to the point where you become drunk and fall asleep is behaviour that's not attractive to you. You're judges in this case, ladies and gentlemen and I ask that what you do is this; you stand back from those reactions to the case, if that's what you have, and you approach the task dispassionately and objectively, as judges. What you're asked to do is to decide whether or not it's proved that [the accused] committed this particular crime upon [the complainant]. Whether or not you approve of her behaviour is, with respect to you, not to the point.

In another case, the Crown played to the fact that the complainant had acknowledged how irresponsible her behaviour had been:

... [S]he was quite candid in answering questions, some of which could on one view of it, have been to her discredit in the sense of she was quite open about how much she drank that night at the dance. She was quite open about continuing to drink at the motel ... The complainant was quite candid about her behaviour then. She didn't deny that she drunk too much and indeed, vomited at some point.

Overall, we found that complainant intoxication provisions like s 36AA(1)(g) of the *Crimes Act 1958* (Vic) play only a very limited role in the prosecution of rape charges where the complainant was intoxicated. Even with extreme intoxication rendering the complainant asleep or unconscious, such cases are regarded by prosecutors as challenging to win. Legislative reform of the sort that has been undertaken to date has not shifted this characterization. As we will explain, there are further impediments to justice for victim-survivors who were intoxicated at the time of the rape. Complainant intoxication evidence—of the sorts that routinely feature in rape trials—offers the defence a variety of strategic options for challenging the prosecution case.

Defence

The first set of observed defence practices to which we draw attention was the pursuit of a line of cross-examination (and accompanying submissions) that suggested that the complainant was *less* intoxicated than they claimed in their evidence-in-chief. For example:

Q: *You appear from the CCTV to be functioning in a normal way?*
A: *Looked to be normal, yes.*
Q: *It wouldn't be, would it, that you're using alcohol as an excuse to cover your behaviour?*
A: *It's not an excuse.*

Q: *And that anything you don't want to answer you're going to say you don't remember or you were drunk?*
A: *It's because I don't remember.*

In this case, notwithstanding evidence from later CCTV footage and several witnesses that the complainant was highly intoxicated to the point of being unable to walk unassisted, vomiting, and being put to sleep on a hotel room floor, the line being advanced by the defence was that, some hours later, the complainant had been woken from sleep by the accused and had consensual sex with him.

In a number of cases, the defence linked the suggestion that the complainant was 'exaggerating' her intoxication to a claim that this was 'cover' for consensual sexual activity that they now regretted:

Q: *What I'm suggesting to you is that you're trying to exaggerate the amount of sleeping tablets you've taken to try and justify why you say you were in a semi-conscious state?*
A: *No.*
Q: *You're using that as a justification for the consensual sexual intercourse that you had with the accused on this evening?*
A: *No, because I didn't have consensual intercourse. I was raped.*

In other trials, the opposite approach was adopted, with defence counsel suggesting that the complainant was *more* intoxicated than they claimed:

Q: *Would you agree with this; that by that late stage, you were off your face?*
A: *I don't know. What is - what's the difference between drunk and off your face?*
Q: *Extremely drunk; I will put it that way?*
A: *I'd say quite drunk but maybe not extremely drunk.*
Q: *You could have been unsteady on your feet?*
A: *Perhaps, but I sway a lot anyway.*
Q: *And you would have been slurring your words?*
A: *I don't know if I actually was. I was getting quite upset.*
Q: *It's a possibility then that you were slurring your words?*
A: *Could have been but I hadn't noticed that myself.*

In light of the legislative provisions on complainant intoxication, it might be considered a risky strategy for the defence to 'talk up' the extent of the complainant's AOD effects. However, our findings suggest that a common defence calculation was that, on balance, there was more to be gained than lost by amplifying the complainant's intoxication.

Counterintuitively—at least with reference to the legislative guidance discussed earlier—such evidence could help the defence to advance their position that the sexual activity that occurred was consensual. This was often linked to a common claim, advanced in cross-examination and defence closing addresses, that AOD consumption produced sexual 'disinhibition' on the part of the complainant, and that, in this state, they in fact consented to what they now seek to characterize as non-consensual. In such instances, it might be said that the defence is enlivening the very assumed nexus between intoxication and consent that the legislation was designed to loosen—noting that such a course was never prohibited, given the limited terms of statutory reform on this topic. One defence lawyer we interviewed described the way in which evidence of the complainant's intoxication offers a foundation for a 'regretted sex' characterization of events:

> *... [I]n the majority of cases where alcohol is a circumstance, it's probably typically a circumstance that favours the defence in the sense that the evidence really doesn't suggest that it's significant enough to have rendered someone incapable of consent. And then practically speaking, it becomes a circumstance by which a complainant may have acted with disinhibition or inconsistent to their kind of sober assessment of the situation.*

When we asked what was meant by disinhibition here, this lawyer answered directly: '*That the complainant would consent to sexual contact that in a sober state they wouldn't consent to.*'

In the trials we analysed, defence counsel used AOD disinhibition lines in different ways. At times, it was to assert generally that the intoxication simply led to a disinhibited state—which thereby implied a logic of consent by the complainant. Such suggestions were sometimes made as a statement of fact about the 'known' effects of a particular drug. For example:

> *Have you heard [of] ... benzodiazepine disinhibition?*
>
> ***
>
> *Did that cocaine reduce your inhibitions that night?*

In the second of these examples, when the complainant rejected defence counsel's characterization of the significance of her cocaine consumption, the trial judge intervened to 'cut to the chase' of what was being suggested:

C: *I don't know what you mean by 'reduce my inhibitions'.*
D: *Well, do things that you would not normally do, sexual things.*
C: *No, I don't - I disagree with that.*
TJ: *I think I'm going to put it bluntly. Ms [complainant], did the cocaine that you had that night and the alcohol that you had consumed cause you to find [the accused] so attractive that you had consensual sexual activity with him?*
C: *No.*

In the context of our observations of the adversarial trial, this style of judicial intervention was relatively unusual. In Chapter 9, we consider further how judges intervened in trials, but our point here is that while the judge, in this instance, clarified the series of propositions being advanced by the defence, there was no disruption of the bona fides of the AOD-based inhibition line of questioning. On the contrary, it might be said to have been implicitly endorsed.

Alcohol disinhibition theory has been discredited in the scientific literature—criticized as a 'largely formal pseudoexplanation'.[40] More recent literature on alcohol myopia theory and alcohol expectancy theory better explains the impacts of alcohol on sexual behaviour. Alcohol myopia theory explains that intoxicated individuals myopically focus on immediate cues, including sexual cues, at the expense of embedded ones.[41] Alcohol expectancy theory describes the near universal beliefs people hold about the expected effects of alcohol such as increased sociability and sexual disinhibition.[42] These theories suggest that while sexual behaviour is complex and affected by many factors (gender, ethnicity, and age[43]), it is men rather than women who report greater sexual disinhibition under the influence of alcohol and drugs.[44]

Another line of questioning we observed carried the suggestion that the complainant's intoxication led to compromised perception and poor decision-making, and that this resulted in consent to sexual activity, to which the complainant would not have consented when sober. For example:

Q: Do you say at this stage you were so intoxicated that you probably weren't thinking straight?
A: I don't understand what you mean by that.
Q: You weren't making decisions and reasoning in the same way that you normally do?
A: I don't think I was doing anything abnormal.
Q: What about joining [the accused] on the bed? That would be abnormal?
A: Yes. . . .

[40] Barbara Critchlow, 'The powers of John Barleycorn: Beliefs About the Effects of Alcohol on Social' (1986) 41 The American Psychologist 751, cited in William H George, Jessica A Blayney, and Kelly Cue Davis, 'Impact of Acute Alcohol Consumption on Sexuality: A Look at Psychological Mechanisms' (2024) 20 Annual Review of Clinical Psychology 307, 319.

[41] See, eg, Abbey, McDaniel, and Jilani (n 5).

[42] See ibid; and Amanda K Gilmore and others, 'Influences of Situational Factors and Alcohol Expectancies on Sexual Desire and Arousal Among Heavy-Episodic Drinking Women: Acute Alcohol Intoxication and Condom Availability' (2013) 42 Archives of Sexual Behavior 949.

[43] Mary E Randolph and others, 'Alcohol Use and Sexual Risk Behavior Among College Students: Understanding Gender and Ethnic Differences' (2009) 35 The American Journal of Drug and Alcohol Abuse 80, 83.

[44] Morten Hesse and Sébastien Tutenges, 'Gender Differences in Self-Reported Drinking-Induced Disinhibition of Sexual Behaviors' (2008) 17 The American Journal on Addictions 293, 293.

Q: *Isn't it possible that in your normal state, in your conscious mind, you wouldn't have done these things but in the state that you were in that night you might have?*
A: *No, I wouldn't have done those things in a drunken state.*
Q: *It's possible on this night that you did; that they occurred consensually?*
A: *I dispute that.*

In many trials we analysed, the proposition that underpins cross-examination of this sort was crystallized in defence closing submissions. For example:

> *So, she may have been in a state where she wasn't thinking clearly [due to AOD consumption]. She may have been in a state where she got involved in something which she later regretted, you might think, or she later realised she probably wouldn't have done, had she been in a sober state of mind. But that's a very different thing from saying she didn't consent to this act of sexual intercourse.*

It was also sometimes contained in the words spoken by trial judges in their summing up and directions to the jury. For example:

> *. . . [T]he evidence that I have just referred to, and [defence counsel] indirectly touched upon, raised the possibility that the complainant may have regretted a decision influenced by having drunk too much to have sex with the accused. Perhaps this regret included a belief that he had taken advantage of her because of this. She may have wanted to avoid the embarrassment of admitting she had too much to drink, agreed to have sex with a man she met for the first time that night who she found out afterwards was married.*

Acknowledging that the trial judge has an obligation to accurately summarize the case advanced by the prosecution and the defence (and associated evidence) it is nonetheless striking to hear a judicial voice so resonant with what we would characterize as versions of 'common knowledge' that blur into (intoxication-related) rape myths. The scientific literature consistently demonstrates that men (rather than women) are more likely to misperceive a woman's behaviour in a sexualized way rather than as 'platonic', *simply because* she is drinking alcohol.[45] Intoxication leads to a 'myopic' focus on immediate 'sexualized cues' increasing a man's misperception of a woman's behaviour as having a sexual intent while ignoring cues that suggest disinterest including blatant refusals.[46]

The proposition that 'drunken consent is still consent' has been a staple of rape trials for decades.[47] Despite the popular narrative that the progressive reform

[45] George, Blayney, and Davis (n 40) 311.
[46] Abbey, McDaniel, and Jilani (n 5) 188–89.
[47] See *R v Bree* [2007] EWCA Crim 804; Phil NS Rumney and Rachel Anne Fenton, 'Intoxicated Consent in Rape: *Bree* and Juror Decision-Making' (2008) 71 Modern Law Review 279.

agenda, and legislative provisions on complainant intoxication in particular, have discredited this proposition, the reality is more tempered. The legislation, on its face, and as operationalized in the trials we analysed, does not seek to prevent reliance on the culturally embedded proposition. Nor has it been consistently disavowed by appellate courts in Australia. Our review of appellate decisions involving complainant intoxication evidence revealed a variety of perspectives. For example, in one case, the South Australian Court of Criminal Appeal found no fault in the trial judge when they told the jury that '[i]t is a common experience that intoxication may reduce a person's inhibitions, may cause them to be more relaxed and outgoing and, in certain circumstances, it may cause them to do things they would not do if they were not intoxicated'.[48] In *Paite v Tasmania*, a majority of the Tasmanian Court of Criminal Appeal took a different approach:

> What is implicit in the appellant's contentions is the suggestion that, perhaps affected by alcohol, the complainant agreed to sexual intercourse, but then quickly regretted her actions and made, and persisted with, a false complaint of rape. In our respectful opinion, it would be wrong to doubt the credibility of the complainant's account based on a generalised notion that alcohol has such an effect. There was no evidence that alcohol may have affected the complainant in that way and, because of the way in which the trial was conducted, it was not a proposition which was put to her so as to give her an opportunity to respond to it.[49]

In the same appeal, Justice Estcourt dissented, concluding that evidence of the complainant's intoxication should have led the jury to have reasonable doubt about whether the Crown had proven the element of non-consent citing 'the possibility of initial alcohol induced euphoria turning into ex post facto regret for her conduct looms in my mind'.[50] That judges of a state appellate court differ on this important topic speaks volumes for the continuing challenges faced by victim-survivors who were intoxicated at the time of their rape, and for the gap that exists between the wider discourse of progressive reform and the rejection of rape myths, and the reality of contemporary law and practice.

In the next part of this chapter, we turn directly to the question of how defence counsel engaged evidence of the complainant's intoxication to challenge their reliability and credibility as a witness. But first we draw attention to a variation on the 'drunken consent' line, observed in a number of trials: the claim that the complainant's intoxication led to an impaired or fragmented memory (or even

[48] *R v Crafter* [2019] SASCFC 25 [72], [77].
[49] (2019) 30 Tas R 73 [124] (Pearce J and Martin AJ).
[50] ibid [59] (emphasis added).

blackout) which has prevented them from recalling that they in fact consented—or, at a minimum, that the prosecution could not exclude the reasonable possibility that the complainant consented. In one illustrative trial, the complainant's evidence was that after having consensual sex with the accused earlier in the evening, she woke from sleep to find the accused penetrating her vagina with his penis. The defence drew attention to her use of the anti-anxiety benzodiazepine medication, Ativan, prescribed for her PTSD, which she had taken (as usual) before bedtime. Cross-examination included the following:

Q: *From your own personal knowledge and what you have been told are you aware that benzodiazepines . . . like the Ativan can cause . . . [side effects like] drowsiness, sedation, impaired balance and weakness?*
A: *Yeah.*
Q: *And that it can also have the effects of you might have to take my word for it at the moment on what it means, a thing called anterograde amnesia, does that ring a bell?*
A: *No.*
Q: *And that's where after an event has passed, you may or may not accept this from me, where after an event has passed despite having been awake through that event a person might forget that it occurred, does any of that ring a bell?*
A: *No.*

The defence later adduced expert evidence verifying that Ativan can cause anterograde amnesia, laying a foundation for the following closing submissions to the jury:

> *The main thing that I would ask you to concentrate on is the affect of Ativan . . . in relation to memory formation and anterograde amnesia. . . . [This] meant that a person could be conscious and awake doing certain things and then not remember them . . . and that is the gap in time immediately preceding her waking up, or claiming to wake up, and saying his penis was in her vagina.*
>
> *What had happened before that? Was she conscious, was she acting, was she consenting, was she giving signs of consent? It is a reasonable possibility, and for those reasons, you must find the accused not guilty of those offences because all of those things would have contributed to his belief that she was consenting, and suggested that it's a reasonable possibility that she was, in fact, freely and voluntarily participating in the acts that occurred.*

In another trial, where the complainant had consumed alcohol and an antidepressant, defence counsel pursued a line of questioning that combined suggestions of *both* disinhibition and partial memory. In addition, in the absence of expert evidence, defence counsel incorporated their own 'expertise' on AOD effects:

> Q: *And you understand that intoxication – heavy intoxication has some effects, including the following. It can affect the way you perceive things – it affects the way you see and hear and understand what's happening, is that fair to say?*
> A: *Yeah.*
> Q: *It can affect the way you remember things, because it can make things hard to remember?*
> A: *Yep.*
> Q: *Yes, and it can distort your memory?*
> A: *Yes, I agree.*
> Q: *It can – I think the term that's sometimes used is disinhibit you, but it can lead you to do things that you wouldn't do when you were sober?*
> A: *Yeah, that's true.*
> Q: *And when you're extremely intoxicated, you can even get to the point of doing things that you later – that you only learned later that you've actually done. Are you aware of that?*
> A: *Yep.*
> Q: *Yes. Have you experienced that?*
> A: *Not really, no,*

These questions provoked no objection from the prosecution and no intervention from the trial judge. They were designed to lay a foundation for suggesting to the jury that it is 'common knowledge' that a person who drinks alcohol and takes antidepressants will become sexually disinhibited and experience impaired memory. This opens up the reasonable possibility—despite the scientific literature noted above—that the hypersexualized complainant had engaged in sexual activity and then forgot having done so.

The contrasts between these various illustrations of defence practice highlights one of our key findings. Intoxication evidence in the 'loose' forms in which it is most commonly presented in rape trials—including complainant self-assessment, unscientific numerical rating scales, and the focus on physical proxies for cognitive effects—is highly *malleable*, capable of being maximized or minimized depending on the case line being advanced by the defence, and amenable to advancing a range of challenges to the prosecution's ability to prove non-consent. And that is before we get to what is probably the greatest opportunity that intoxication evidence offers the defence, and the biggest risk that complainant intoxication evidence can pose to the Crown case: that the reliability of the strongest evidence of non-consent—the complainant's testimony—might be characterized as unreliable due to her intoxication at the time.

5. Reliability and Credibility

When we first conceived a study of intoxication evidence in rape trials, we used the concept of the 'double-edged sword' to hypothesize about the operation of complainant intoxication evidence. We speculated that even if the prosecution case was *strengthened* by legislative gestures in the direction of breaking the culturally assumed nexus between intoxication and consent, it might be *weakened* by the other purposes for which the same evidence might be engaged by the defence. Having found that the prosecution derives very little benefit from the legislative reforms in question, the applicability of our double-edged metaphor was in doubt. We realized that there may only be *one* edge to the sword—one that works to the advantage of the defence. Specifically, we found that evidence of the complainant's intoxication was a powerful tool that the defence could use to challenge the reliability and credibility of the prosecution's main witness.

Prosecutors that we interviewed were fully aware of this risk, given the intense focus in rape trials on the complainant. One said of intoxicated complainants:

> *Gaps in memory, sometimes inconsistencies with other evidence, whether that's other witnesses or evidence like CCTV footage... Without meaning to put it crudely, but the target of [the] defence case is often the credibility or reliability of the Crown case, but in sexual assault trials it invariably relies on the credibility and reliability and honesty of the complainant's evidence.*

Another articulated the risk of focusing heavily on evidence of the complainant's intoxication:

> *[W]ell it's a double-edged sword because... unless you're running [incapacity to consent] you're shooting yourself in the foot by saying they were absolutely drunk because then the drunker they are the less reliable, you're effectively conceding. So you sort of can't have your cake and eat it too. They're either so drunk that they're incapable of consenting or they're not so drunk that they're completely unreliable. You can't... have both.*

This account provides a further explanation for the pattern we observed earlier in this chapter: a disinclination of prosecutors to engage the legislation designed to assist them to prove the element of non-consent.

In the trials in our transcript studies, the complainant's intoxication when the alleged rape occurred (and, sometimes, their AOD use more generally) was exploited by defence counsel in multiple ways to impugn their reliability and credibility. Some of these were discussed in Chapter 7, where we considered the extensive reliance on rape myth-based lines of cross-examination questioning. They include questions that focus on peripheral and minute detail, and questions which seek to highlight (often minor) 'inconsistencies' between the complainant's trial evidence and earlier accounts. The appeal of these general tactics can be heightened in cases where the complainant was intoxicated, because the defence can rely on evidence (or speculation) that the complainant's recall was compromised by AOD-related memory deficits. One prosecutor who addressed this issue when interviewed started by recalling the detailed questions to which one complainant was subjected during cross examination:

> *... and it just became about, well, 'how far were your pants down? How far were they up and what position did you move in? And bearing in mind the room that you were in and, you know, what did you ...' [I]t just becomes this absolute focus on minutiae ... [I]n day-to-day life that doesn't work, let alone when you're intoxicated. ... [B]ecause you're intoxicated, that's seized on. It's almost like a strategic seizing upon because ... in day-to-day life people get things wrong but here they're intoxicated ... and because they've got it so wrong, you know, well maybe she was consenting ... and ... maybe he wouldn't have known that she wasn't consenting. It's about blurring the lines.*

In the balance of this chapter, we focus on the *additional* lines of reliability/credibility attacks which the defence pursued in trials that featured complainant intoxication evidence. We have organized the presentation of our findings around three themes: (i) defence questioning and submissions that emphasized fragmented memories, partial recall, or 'blackouts' said to be associated with AOD intoxication; (ii) questioning and submissions about the complainant's personal history of AOD use; and (iii) the culmination of these lines of scrutiny of the complainant in a request for an 'unreliable evidence' direction.

Memory deficits and 'blackouts'

In the trials we analysed, it was commonplace for complainants to be cross-examined in general terms about impaired memory. For example:

> *Do you accept that your memory of those events that I have suggested did happen are affected by your intoxication on that night?*

***

> *Am I correct, Ms [complainant], in saying that you have no memory of how you got from outside the house to into the bed, is that right?*

Even where the complainant answered in the negative, as often occurred, it is likely that such questions 'primed' the jury to approach with caution the veracity of the remainder of the complainant's testimony.

Another tactic was to ask the complainant a series of detailed questions about events which the complainant had indicated they did not recall due to intoxication. This forced the complainant into an '*I can't remember*' answer, which they were required to repeat multiple times. For example:

Q: *And after you'd been given a jumper wasn't it the case that [the accused] offered you a glass of wine?*
A: *I can't remember.*
Q: *And then you sat up in bed with him and had a glass of wine in bed?*
A: *I don't remember.*
Q: *And in fact you left a glass of wine beside his bedside table that you'd been drinking out of?*
A: *It might have been mine yeah, maybe.*
Q: *So you had a glass of wine in [the accused]'s bed with him?*
A: *I'm not sure where it was that I had it, I don't remember.*
Q: *And [the accused] also had a glass of wine on his side of the bed?*
A: *I don't remember that.*
Q: *And you laid there talking for a little bit to [the accused] in his bed?*
A: *(not transcribable)*
Q: *Sorry?*
A: *I don't remember speaking to him much.*

A variation on this line was adopted in the following trial, a case where the complainant said she was asleep when the accused raped her, while the defence asserted that she was awake, consenting, and suffered from drug-related memory impairment:

Q: *So you don't know how except through basic mechanics he put his penis inside your vagina?*
A: *No.*
Q: *You don't know if he started again by kissing your neck?*
A: *No.*
Q: *Then touching you over your clothes?*
A: *No.*
Q: *Then touching your breasts, vagina, progressing through those stages?*
A: *No, I didn't feel, I didn't feel any of that, no.*
Q: *You don't know whether you reacted to him when he was doing that?*
A: *I didn't feel, I didn't feel anything from him so no.*
Q: *You were under quite a degree of medication?*
A: *Yeah.*
Q: *And that medication sometimes makes you forget what had happened when you were awake?*

A: I don't forget things like that, it's traumatic.
Q: You wouldn't know that, would you, if you've forgotten, is that a no?
A: I know that I wouldn't have forgotten something like that.

This tactic placed the complainant in the difficult (and arguably unfair) position of having to 'admit' that she had no memory of events, most of which, on her account, did not happen. Yet her 'failure' to remember is characterized as a flaw—in her, and in the Crown case—attributable to AOD effects (for which she was responsible). We noted earlier that in more than half of the complainant intoxication trials we analysed, the Crown case was that the complainant was asleep at the time of the rape. In the large majority of trials where this was associated with AOD effects, the defence had access to this kind of ready-made line for attacking the reliability of the complainant and the Crown case.

Defence closing submissions often involved strong encouragement for the jury to entertain doubt, as would be expected, about the complainant's allegation and testimony. In the context of an intoxicated complainant, this was particularly pronounced:

> *She's the one that has to get all the way from innocent to beyond reasonable doubt. And my submission to you, ladies and gentlemen, is that she is simply not good enough. . . .*
>
> *Here's why. She's drunk a lot. She takes a breathalyser sometime the next morning after the police have arrived, we don't know what time. She was either just under or just over. So that's her evidence about her reading sometime during the morning when the police were there. She's had no dinner, no dinner she can remember, anyway. She's drunk two Wild Turkeys, bourbons and Coke of slightly indeterminate number, Wet Pussy shots, and at some stage a police officer in the morning records, '. . . too drunk to make a statement'. So she is a very heavily intoxicated person throughout all this, and probably all the way out through that next morning as well.*
>
> *It's really important, because you're being asked to rely on her . . . And in my submission to you, it's incredibly difficult to trust someone who's that intoxicated. It's just not good enough.*

This passage illustrates a feature of how intoxication evidence commonly featured in the trials we analysed: in the absence of any expert evidence about AOD effects and, in this instance, with non-expert commentary about the significance that the jury should attach to the complainant's intoxication, the jury is encouraged to treat the complainant's intoxication as a barrier to convicting the accused. Added to this is the established legal position that it is 'a common experience that intoxication can have an adverse bearing on a witness's recollection of events'.[51]

[51] *Crafter* (n 48) [72].

In most trials where complainants gave evidence of memory loss, or being asleep (and often woken during the rape), complainants were able—including in the trials noted above—to give sufficient evidence to detail the sexual acts and indicate that they did not consent. Nevertheless, assertions of impaired memory or 'blackout' not only painted complainants as unreliable witnesses, but also provided the basis for a defence claim of 'forgotten' consent.

Scientific and social scientific knowledge on memory

In a context where one of the drivers of statutory reform has been improved scholarly understanding of sexual violence and victimization, it is surprising that contemporary scientific and social scientific knowledge about the relationship between AOD consumption and memory was almost entirely absent from the trials we analysed.[52] The scientific literature indicates that intoxication due to AOD use can have broad ranging effects on the encoding and recall of memory according to the type(s) or combination of drugs involved and the degree of intoxication.[53]

Alcohol is the drug that has been most widely researched in relation to its effects on memory. At higher levels of alcohol intoxication 'partial *(fragmentary)* or full (*en bloc*) memory loss'[54] may occur with women at higher risk of blackouts at lower levels of alcohol than men.[55] The stage of a drug's effects are important: 'an acutely administered substance during its duration of action' will be different to the 'effects of a substance sometime after its immediate drug effects have subsided'.[56]

The scientific literature broadly indicates that intoxication can impact upon the *completeness* of an individual's memory but does not appear to decrease the *correctness* of the information that is reported.[57] The effect of alcohol on recall of *correct details* is related to many factors, including level of intoxication, retention interval length between encoding and recall, and whether free recall or open questions are used (rather than cued or closed questions).[58] Research has found that participants who believed they were alcohol impacted provided more accurate (albeit less complete) information—suggesting people may be more conservative in

[52] See also Lilian Kloft and others, 'Hazy Memories in Courtroom: A Review of Alcohol and Other Drug effects on False Memory and Suggestibility' (2021) 124 Neuroscience and Biobehavioral Reviews 291; Shazia Akhtar and others, 'The 'Common Sense' Memory Belief System and its Implications' (2018) 22 The International Journal of Evidence & Proof 289; Erica Martin and others, 'Tipsy, Trashed, or Totalled? Lay Understanding of Dose-Specific Alcohol Intoxication and the Criminal Justice System' [2024] Psychology, Crime & Law 1, 3.

[53] Kloft and others (n 52); Flowe and Carline, *Alcohol and Remembering Rape* (n 4).

[54] Kloft and others (n 52) 298.

[55] Rose and Grant (n 31) 64; Flowe and Carline, *Alcohol and Remembering Rape* (n 4) 50.

[56] Kloft and others (n 52) 295.

[57] ibid; Theo Jores and others, 'A Meta-Analysis of the Effects of Acute Alcohol Intoxication on Witness Recall' (2019) 33 Applied Cognitive Psychology 334; Heather D Flowe and others, 'Impact of Alcohol and Other Drugs on Eyewitness Memory' in Ray Bull and Iris Blandón-Gitlin (eds), *The Routledge International Handbook of Legal and Investigative Psychology* (Routledge 2020).

[58] Jores and others (n 57) 339–40. In chapter 6 we identified narrative form and 'open questions' as well-suited to allowing the complainant to give their best evidence.

their reporting when they are intoxicated. For example, alcohol-intoxicated persons are more likely to reply '*I don't know*' (a feature we also noted in complainant answers earlier) than sober counterparts, particularly when they are asked cued-recall/closed questions (rather than open/free-recall questions).[59] Studies of how participants encoded a hypothetical rape scenario, while either sober or alcohol intoxicated, indicated that while intoxication decreased the completeness of the participants' recall, there were no alcohol-related effects on recall errors and no evidence that intoxicated women were more prone to incorporating misleading information into their statements.[60] Acknowledging the limitations of experimental studies,[61] they nonetheless suggest that, against the cultural assumption played out in trials every day that intoxication is associated with unreliability and faulty memory, it has been said that intoxicated complainants are 'better than their reputation'.[62]

What is often impacted by intoxication is recall of *peripheral details*—but without bearing upon the correctness of the memories that can be recalled.[63] Research shows that 'memory for emotional events tends to be generally superior compared to neutral events'.[64] However, during a traumatic event, the brain focuses on what is central to survival, so 'does not focus on insignificant and peripheral details' and does not encode these.[65] The sequence of events may also be impacted 'result[ing] in a disorganized and incomplete narrative memory'.[66] Victims of trauma may 'recall only three to five "hotspots" (vivid details) from the event',[67] so memories lacking in detail are to be expected. The modern scientific view of memory is that it is 'fragmentary, time-compressed and prone to errors'.[68]

These understandings of memory—as 'partial', that intoxication appears to impact completeness not accuracy, and that closed questions are known to negatively impede best evidence—all sit at odds with the cross-examination techniques discussed in this chapter (and in Chapter 7). They are also at odds with the 'common

[59] Flowe and others, 'Impact of Alcohol and Other Drugs on Eyewitness Memory' (n 57) 151.

[60] Heather D Flowe and others, 'Alcohol and Remembering A Hypothetical Sexual Assault: Can People Who Were Under the Influence of Alcohol During the Event Provide Accurate Testimony?' (2016) 24 Memory 1042; Heather D Flowe and others, 'An experimental examination of the effects of alcohol consumption and exposure to misleading postevent information on remember a hypothetical rape scenario' (2019) 33 Applied Cognitive Psychology 393.

[61] Experimental studies use relatively low dosages of alcohol (<0.08%), significantly less than the levels of intoxication reported in many of the trials we analysed.

[62] Nadja Schreiber Compo and others, 'Intoxicated Eyewitnesses: Better than Their Reputation?' (2012) 36 Law and Human Behavior 77 cited in Kloft and others (n 52) 298.

[63] Jores and others (n 57) 341.

[64] Kloft and others (n 52) 303.

[65] Lori Haskell and Melanie Randall, 'The Impact of Trauma on Adult Sexual Assault Victims' (Justice Canada 2019) 20.

[66] ibid 22.

[67] Katrin Hohl and Martin A Conway, 'Memory as Evidence: How Normal Features of Victim Memory Lead to the Attrition of Rape Complainants' (2017) 17 Criminology & Criminal Justice 248, 250.

[68] ibid 254; Akhtar and others (n 52) 289–304, 301–302.

knowledges' about the so-called effects of intoxication on memory regularly asserted by lawyers and judges in the trials we analysed. Given the recognized additional challenges of achieving convictions in rape trials where the complainant was intoxicated (see above), it would be preferable if all trials had the benefit of the latest research on AOD effects including on memory, rather than relying on outdated and flawed stereotypes that form part of common knowledge but lack evidence. It is important that instances in which appellate courts have recognized the science behind intoxication and memory become more consistent,[69] *and* that they begin to manifest as expectations of the evidence that should feature in all rape trials where complainant intoxication evidence features.

Utilizing histories of AOD use

So far we have focused on the regular use of evidence of the complainant's intoxication at the time of the alleged rape to challenge the *reliability* of their account of events. Here we draw attention to an ancillary defence strategy: locating the complainant's intoxication on that occasion in a longer history of substance use, which, in turn, is used as the basis for questioning their *credibility*. In Chapter 9, we recognize the wide latitude afforded by the cross-examination exception to the credibility rule—an 'unreformed' aspect of general evidence rules—as one of the reasons why trial judges rarely intervene to protect complainants from traumatizing lines of questioning. Here, we amplify the implications of this latitude for complainants who may have had a history of substance use, including excessive alcohol consumption and illicit drug use.

In some trials, the jury's attention was drawn to this aspect of the complainant's personal history by questions that contained an alcohol use-related description of them (eg '*seasoned drinker*'; '*regular drinker*') or which characterized them as a drug user (eg '*You weren't a stranger to intravenous drugs . . . were you?*' '*Was that an occasion when you shot yourself up with ice?*').

In some trials, defence counsel explicitly referenced the criminal nature of the drug-taking in order to damage the complainant's credibility ('*Your choice was to stay awake to take an illicit substance is it, is that right?*'; '*So it was okay for you to break the law and take drugs?*') or to reference the complainant's past drug offences (eg '*Indeed in 1999 you had a drug conviction, did you not?*').

In some trials, the complainant was subjected to a series of intense questions about past drug use. For example:

[69] See, eg, *Roberts v The Queen* [2012] VSCA 313, [52] (Tate JA); *AWK v Tasmania* [2024] TASCCA 5 [276]–[280] (Wood J, Blow CJ and Martin AJ agreeing).

Q: *You'd been injecting drugs into your body well, well, well prior to [year]. What do you say to that . . . ?*
A: *The only time that I ever injected drugs into my body was with - when [the accused] introduced the ice into the relationship.*
Q: *What about prior to when you met [the accused]?*
A: *I had tried other drugs prior to that, yes.*
Q: *And you had taken drugs intravenously, had you not?*
A: *I had on one occasion, or on one or two occasions, yes.*
Q: *Many occasions, I suggest. What do you say to that?*
A: *I wouldn't suggest many occasions, no.*

From one perspective it might be assumed that such matters are unrelated and irrelevant to the complainant's allegation of sexual violence.[70] However, it is clear that defence counsel will often see advantage in drawing attention to these aspects of the complainant's life and, in the trials we analysed, it was very rare for them to be prevented from doing so. That juries are perceived to be inclined to judge the complainant harshly when such matters are revealed, and disbelieve their accounts of the alleged rape, was acknowledged by one of the prosecutors we interviewed:

> *Look . . . juries tend to be fairly judgmental on complainants who do drugs . . . But I mean the minute you say a complainant has done three or four lines of cocaine or smoked cannabis or done ecstasy, I mean—. . . I think you'll almost certainly get a not guilty.*

Attacks on the complainant's credibility could be amplified where there was evidence that the complainant had not revealed their drug use to the police when reporting the alleged rape. In one trial, the complainant told the police she had taken '*half a sleeping tablet*', but during cross-examination she was asked:

Q: *Are you aware of the results of the blood tests that were done on you?*
A: *No.*
Q: *Are you aware that you had methylamphetamine in your system?*
A: *Yeah, well, I've been - I had been on it for a while, since I was homeless.*

Evidence about past drug use featured heavily in defence counsel closing submissions. Even if in a less judgmental form, such submissions engaged this evidence to raise doubts about the reliability of the complainant's evidence. For example:

[70] In Chapter 9, we discuss the wide parameters for cross-examination that are set by evidence rules on relevance and credibility.

> *You may well feel quite sorry for Ms [complainant]. You may feel some real compassion for her. She was very candid. From her nervousness about giving evidence, to the serious alcohol abuse issues she's had in her past, mental health issues and trauma. But the bottom line is her recall is poor, and at times bizarre. It's not adequate enough to satisfy you to the highest standard of proof known to law.*
>
> * * *
>
> *The problem with the drug ice . . . is that it can make you anxious, it can make you paranoid, and it can make you think that there are things going on around you when really they are not. And you might think ladies and gentlemen that this has a lot to do with this case and the evidence that you have heard over the last week or so.*

Submissions in other trials engaged damning stereotypes of 'drug addicts' and their behaviour, typically as a foundation for convincing the jury that the complainant could not be trusted:

> *. . . [I]t appears that she was heavily using drugs at the time . . . people who you know are using drugs, they'll take whatever drugs they can get their hands on. If they've got a drug addition, they'll take whatever drugs they can get their hands on whenever they can get them. . . . You heard what she said: she was homeless; been running around or moving around from place to place. If people are in the grips of a drug addition, they don't determine the time of day or night to take drugs . . . offered to them; they'll take it whenever they can . . .*

In the following example, in closing submissions, defence counsel disavowed any suggestion that the jury should disbelieve the complainant simply because of substance abuse, while simultaneously, it seems to us, making that very suggestion:

> *The third reason I say you will find the accused not guilty is that the complainant was an ice user. Now that's not a factor that you can determine, say, well she's an ice user therefore that means she's lying about everything, that's not what I'm putting to you members of the jury. But what I'm saying is that you're allowed to use your common sense in assessing her answers to the questions regarding ice use. She has two previous convictions, one possess prohibited drug and another drive car whilst having ice in her blood. You've heard the details of those offences. When she was asked about the possession of ice she gave inconsistent answers. She accepted that she had a syringe in her underwear and she later accepted that she did use a syringe to inject ice. When she was asked whether she was a routine injector of ice, she said no. . . . When asked whether she was a recreational user of ice, she said had been some 20 years before and had used ice previously in her life but that she was no longer an ice user. You're to use your common sense in determining whether or not those answers are truthful or not. She was asked whether she ever took ice voluntarily. You*

consider her answers to those questions in your determination. You may ask yourself why was she so evasive in those answers? What did she have to hide?

In Chapter 7, we reported that it was routine in the trials we analysed for the complainant to be accused of lying. The findings presented here suggest that complainants were especially likely to be characterized as liars if evidence of their past illicit drug use was adduced at trial. We recognize that engaging negative stereotypes about drug users and histories of AOD is a tactic for impugning a witness's credibility that is used generally in criminal trials. However, they have an additional resonance in rape trials, and serve as a reminder that, decades on from the start of the progressive reform era, assessments of the complainant's character and believability is still a centrepiece of the trial. Justice appears even more elusive for complainants who are portrayed in front of the jury as a 'drug user', 'alcoholic', or 'addict' whose credibility is inherently compromised and who, it is suggested, are even more likely to have fabricated the allegation of sexual violence. Cross-examination and submissions about substance use, of the sorts illustrated here, compound the impact of the multiple rape myth-based forms of scrutiny to which complainants are routinely exposed.

Unreliable evidence direction

One of the priorities of the last 50 years has been to break the traditional and deeply problematic nexus between (mainly female) rape victim-survivors and unreliability.[71] Against this background we noted with concern that, in addition to cross-examination questions that criticized the accuracy and quality of an intoxicated complainant's recall, in a number of cases in both Victoria and NSW, the defence sought an 'unreliable evidence' direction. The common law regarded some categories of witnesses as presumptively suspect, and provided for an unreliability warning,[72] the contemporary reach of which is legislated.[73] For example, s 32 of the Jury Directions Act 2015 (Vic) provides that '[t]he prosecution or defence counsel may request . . . that the trial judge direct the jury on evidence of a kind that may be unreliable'. The fact of a person's intoxication is not expressly mentioned in the s 31 list of 'evidence of a kind that may be unreliable', but the list is not exhaustive. The *Victorian Criminal Charge Book* provides examples of unreliable evidence, including '[e]vidence of a witness who was alcohol or drug-affected at the time of the events, whether voluntarily or by the alleged actions of the accused'.[74] Section

[71] See Chapter 2 at p. 34 and Chapter 3 at p. 62.

[72] ALRC, *Uniform Evidence Law* (ALRC Report 102, 2005) paras 18.18–18.19.

[73] Jury Directions Act (Vic), s 32; Evidence Act 1995 (NSW), s 165.

[74] Judicial College of Victoria, 'Victorian Criminal Charge Book' (Judicial College of Victoria 2007) [4.21.21], citing *R v Maple* [1999] VSCA 52; *Hudson v R* [2017] VSCA 122.

165 of the Evidence Act 1995 (NSW) contains a non-exhaustive list, including 'evidence the reliability of which may be affected by age, ill health (whether physical or mental)'.[75] There is authority that evidence from a person who was affected by AOD at the time of the events may fall into this category, or might be regarded as other 'evidence of a kind that may be unreliable'.[76]

In a number of trials we analysed, defence counsel requested, and the trial judge gave, a jury direction to the effect that the complainant's evidence may be unreliable due to their intoxication. The following example is illustrative:

> *I must now warn you about the need for caution when considering [the complainant]'s evidence.*
>
> *I must give you this warning because the evidence [the complainant] gave that she had consumed alcohol in combination with her Pristiq [antidepressant] medication and was highly intoxicated to the extent that she had vomited and then, on her evidence, fallen asleep.*
>
> *My warning to you is as follows. It is the experience of the law that the evidence of a witness who is highly intoxicated may be unreliable. This unreliability can arise due to the effects heavy intoxication can have on a person's perceptions and recollections.*
>
> *The law says every jury must take this potential unreliability into account in determining whether you accept [the complainant]'s evidence at all, and if you do accept it, in whole or in part, and then deciding what weight to give to that evidence.*
>
> *In considering the safety of relying on [the complainant]'s evidence, you should have regard to any supporting evidence led in this trial that you accept, and by supporting evidence, I mean evidence from a source that is independent of [the complainant] and that tends to show the truth of her evidence of the accused's guilt.*

We note that the final part of the direction effectively required the jury to identify 'corroborative' evidence—recalling that, as explained in Chapter 3, the mandatory common law corroborative warning was prohibited as part of early statutory reforms. In Chapter 9, we draw attention to some of the lingering traces of this warning in direction given to juries in contemporary trials.

We offer two observations about the use of the unreliable evidence direction.

First, it lacks the nuance contained in the scientific literature discussed above, which recognizes that intoxication *may* impact the completeness of recall but not necessarily the correctness of memories, and distinguishing between categories of information, such as peripheral details for which there may be impaired recall, and

[75] Evidence Act 1995 (NSW), s 165(1)(c).

[76] See Stephen Odgers, *Uniform Evidence Law* (20th edn, Thomson Reuters Australia 2025) 1628, 1639, 1641. Odgers notes that a range of approaches is discernible in the case law, citing as illustrative: *R v Murphy* [2000] NSWCCA 297; *Diaz v R* [2004] NSWCCA 251.

essential aspects of the rape. The full force of the 'experience of the law' should be tempered by the specificity of expert knowledge.

Secondly, given that 50–75% of rapes are AOD-related and the large majority of rape victims are women,[77] the 'typical' complainant in a rape trial is vulnerable to being treated as presumptively unreliable. In the context of this book's concerns with tracing how long (or short) is the distance that rape laws and rape trials has travelled since the 1970s, the fact the unreliable evidence directions continue to feature in some contemporary rape trials is revealing. It appears that only the unintoxicated woman has escaped the worst category of presumptive unreliability. Her intoxicated sister seems as vulnerable as ever to being typecast as a woman who cannot be believed or trusted.

6. Conclusion

Our findings about how complainant intoxication evidence features in contemporary rape trials aligns strongly with the primary argument advanced in this book: statutory reform has not significantly changed the *substance* of rape trials. Considerable room remains for the engagement of rape myths, and this has troubling implications for both complainant experience (process injustice) and trial results (outcome injustice). To the list of rape myths discussed in previous chapters, we would add a range of AOD-related stereotypes, misconceptions, and assumptions recorded in this chapter. Progressive statutory reforms on complainant intoxication that, ostensibly, seek to break the culturally assumed nexus between AOD and consent, are not operating to shift the focus of scrutiny away from the complainant, or to reduce the influence of intoxication-related myths.

We recognize the value that legislation of this sort is likely to be having outside the courtroom. For example, it provides a foundation for strong educational messages such as the following from the Alcohol and Drug Foundation:

> Recognising and respecting the times when someone is too intoxicated to be able to give consent is part of being a good human.
>
> If you're worried that someone is too intoxicated to consent, they probably are. It's always better to err on the side of caution than risk violating another person.[78]

It is also likely that legislative changes (and surrounding education campaigns) have increased the proportion of trials that feature intoxication evidence—because,

[77] See, eg, Australian Bureau of Statistics (n 4); Australian Institute of Health and Welfare (n 4); Abbey and others (n 4); Flowe and Carline, 'Setting the Scene' (n 4).

[78] Alcohol and Drug Foundation, 'Alcohol and consent' (15 December 2021) <https://adf.org.au/insights/alcohol-and-consent/> accessed 11 July 2025.

consistent with the messages contained in reformed legislation, victim-survivors who were intoxicated at the time of the rape are being encouraged to report, and charges are more likely to be laid and trials pursued in such cases.

But there is a risk here, and we have seen some of the ramifications play out in NSW in recent years. In 2023, the NSW Director of Public Prosecutions was the target of criticism from a small number of judges and commentators in a national broadsheet, *The Australian*, for approving prosecutions that, it was suggested, were never going to result in a conviction and should not have been pursued. A number of the impugned prosecutions involved complainants who had been intoxicated at the time of the alleged rape. The DPP defended her Office's handling of these matters, noting that '[i]t is well known that prosecuting matters involving highly intoxicated complainants involves complex issues of fact and law'.[79] The two most outspoken judges were later disciplined for their comments by a Conduct Division of the NSW Judicial Commission.[80] A review by the NSW ODPP found a high level of compliance with the Prosecution Guidelines[81] in relation to the decision whether to proceed in sexual offence matters,[82] and that the small number of instances where correct procedure had not been followed included matters that 'involved particularly legally and factually complex issues including intoxication of complainants and complexities in the evidence relevant to issues of consent'.[83]

In some respects, this imbroglio can be explained as a combination of unprofessional judicial conduct and an unjustified conservative media beat-up and 'pile on'. But as we reflect on the findings of our research presented in this chapter, we think it also speaks to two things. First, some people (including some judges) still hold an 'unreconstructed' view of rape law and what counts as a prosecutable rape—and an intoxicated complainant does not fit comfortably in this world view. Secondly, the applicable law has changed so little that it remains the case that even for those who embrace the reformed law and the ascendency of a value-set that eschews victim-blaming, the criminal courtroom is still often a hostile environment for a person who was intoxicated at the time they were raped.

[79] ODPP NSW, 'Statement from the ODPP in response to R v Martinez [2023] NSWDC 552' (Media Release, 15 December 2023) <https://www.odpp.nsw.gov.au/publications/news-and-media/Statement-from-the-DPP-in-response-to-reporting-in-The-Australian> accessed 11 July 2025.

[80] Conduct Division of the Judicial Commission of New South Wales, 'Report of Conduct Division of the Judicial Commission of New South Wales: Complaint by Director of Public Prosecutions (NSW) Against Newlinds SC DCJ' (19 August 2024); Conduct Division of the Judicial Commission of New South Wales, 'Report of Conduct Division of the Judicial Commission of New South Wales: Complaint by Director of Public Prosecutions (NSW) Against Whitford SC DCJ' (5 November 2024).

[81] Office of the Director of Public Prosecutions New South Wales, 'Prosecution Guidelines' (ODPP NSW 2021).

[82] Office of the Director of Public Prosecutions New South Wales, 'Sexual Assault Review Report' (ODPP NSW February 2025). One of the authors of this book (Quilter) was an independent reviewer of the report (25).

[83] ibid 2. The Report recommended the establishment of a 'Consent, Sexual Assault and Intoxication Working Group' to consider a range of matters including 'the use of expert evidence at trial to address the impact of intoxication on memory and behaviour' (31).

In recent years (and since our transcript studies), both NSW and Victoria have adopted another form of statutory influence in relation to the rape myth of AOD use as indicative of consent. For example, a direction on 'personal appearance and irrelevant conduct' in s 47G(c) of the Jury Directions Act 2015 (Vic),[84] includes advice to the jury 'that it should not be assumed that a person consented to a sexual act just because the person . . . drank alcohol or took any other drug'. NSW adopted an almost identical direction.[85]

We reserve firm judgement on the likely impact of these new directions, and endorse the view expressed recently by the Australian Law Reform Commission (ALRC) that the operation of these and other new jury directions should be properly evaluated.[86] However, as we explain in Chapter 9, jury directions are a particular (and relatively weak) mechanism for influencing the part played by rape myths in criminal trials—including AOD-use related myths. Certainly, it would be a mistake to assume that the multiple ways in which complainant intoxication is engaged to challenge the Crown's case in trials, revealed in this chapter, will suddenly become off-limits. We have shown that the reductive (and antiquated) view that an intoxicated person is likely to have consented to sexual activity is not the most powerful way that complainant intoxication features in rape trials. Evidence of intoxication opens up other fronts for complainant scrutiny and criticism: around disinhibition, memory, and recall. Alongside the established and frequently engaged defence strategy of painting the complainant as a liar (see Chapter 7), intoxication evidence offers an additional basis for challenging the reliability of the complainant's account: the quality of their recall is degraded by their intoxication.

Our findings on how intoxication evidence features in rape trials has troubling implications for the availability of both *process justice* and *outcome justice*. They point to a significant gap between the protection promised by the narrative of progressive rape law reform to victim-survivors who were intoxicated when they were raped, and the reality of how much evidence of their intoxication will loom as a barrier to justice. The primary argument advanced in this book is that statutory reform has barely touched the multiple ways in which rape myths continue to circulate in rape trials, and which produce traumatization for many complainants. This argument has been powerfully illustrated in this chapter on intoxication evidence. The largely symbolic legislative move to suggest that complainant intoxication may speak to *non-consent*, is swamped by cross-examination tactics and closing submissions that invite the jury to, nonetheless, submit to claims about

[84] As amended by the Justice Legislation Amendment (Sexual Offences and Other Matters) Act 2022 (Vic).

[85] See Criminal Procedure Act 1986 (NSW), s 292E(b), as amended by the Crimes Legislation Amendment (Sexual Consent Reforms) Act 2021 (NSW).

[86] ALRC, *Safe, Informed, Supported: Justice Responses to Sexual Violence* (ALRC Report 143, 2025) recs 3(a)(i), 21.

disinhibition, compromised memory, and dishonesty—on which there is no legislative constraint at all.

In closing, we draw attention to two problematic aspects of the trials we analysed that featured complainant intoxication evidence. The first is the sad irony that the complainant is often the main source of evidence (about AOD consumption) that will be harnessed to their detriment (and that of the Crown case) in the trial. The second is that having done so, the complainant has little control over what the jury is told about the *effects* of that level of intoxication. Moreover, it is rare, especially in cases of *alcohol* intoxication, for the jury to receive the benefit of scientific expertise on AOD effects. Defence counsel are largely unencumbered in their ability to make adverse claims, including about disinhibition, impaired perception, and memory, that do not necessarily align with the scientific literature. And judges largely endorse these renderings of the 'common knowledge' that juries are told they have, and are directed to apply. This is another reason why trials have not been transformed. The *sentiments* that underpin statutory reforms (such as educative jury directions) align closely with expert knowledge, but the *binding rules* that shape the practices of rape trials do not. The space left in trials for intoxication-related rape myths and misconceptions to circulate, and have impact, remains large. It is a serious problem that some trials featured expert evidence on AOD effects, but many did not. This speaks to the wider issue of trial-to-trial variability (considered further in Chapter 9), which undercuts the confidence victim-survivors can have about how their pursuit of justice will play out.

9

Judicial Influences on Rape Trials

1. Introduction

A common and understandable lament sometimes expressed by victim-survivors who have experienced traumatization giving evidence in a sexual offence trial is: Why didn't the judge *do something*... About how I was treated? About the questions I was asked? About the way my character was attacked?[1] There is a 'lawyer's answer' of course, and it starts with an explanation of the role of the judge in the adversarial system governing criminal trials in Australia and other common law jurisdictions. The rules and conventions of this system place constraints on the capacity of the judge and the prosecutor to control or intervene in what defence counsel does during cross-examination. The intervention options that the judge has at their disposal are relatively limited, cross-examination is regarded as a core component of the criminal trial's 'truth-seeking' mission, and wide parameters of cross-examination are considered an important part of the accused-focused conception of a fair trial.[2]

In many ways, these are unsatisfactory responses in that they don't go to the heart of the victim-survivor's legitimate grievance, which is that they were retraumatized—treated unfairly, or with cruelty, suspicion, judgment, and condemnation—by the experience of participating as a complainant in a rape trial. Few would argue that such experiences are compatible with the idea of the progressive statutory reform-driven modern rape trial, or the trauma-informed courtroom.[3] In the context of this book's ambition to explain *why* transformation has not occurred, it is important to focus on the legislative tools that trial judges have

[1] See, eg, Ania Moroz and Tamar Dinisman, 'Suffering For Justice: Sexual Violence Victim-Survivors' Experiences of Going to Court and Cross-Examination' (Victim Support 2024); also Clare McGlynn and Nicole Westmarland, 'Kaleidoscopic Justice: Sexual Violence and Victim-Survivor's Perceptions of Justice' (2019) 28 Social & Legal Studies 179. The converse is also true: when judges have intervened, complainants have expressed appreciation: see, eg, Elena Campbell and others, '"This Is My Story. It's Your Case, But It's My Story": Interview Study' (KPMG and RMIT Centre for Innovative Justice 2023) 86.

[2] *Wakeley* [1990] HCA 23; 93 ALR 79 [20]; see Jill Hunter and others, *The Trial: Principles, Process and Evidence* (2nd edn, Federation Press 2021) 211, 218, 261.

[3] Anne Murphy and Kate Lumley, 'Trauma-Informed Courts: Guidance For Trauma-Informed Judicial Practices' (Judicial Commission of New South Wales 2022); Nicole Bluett-Boyd and Bianca Fileborn, 'Victim/Survivor-Focused Justice Responses and Reforms to Criminal Court Practice: Implementation, Current Practice and Future Directions' (Research Report No 27, Australian Institute of Family Studies 2014). See also Chapter 5 at p. 94.

Reforming Rape Trials. Julia Quilter and Luke McNamara, Oxford University Press.
 DOI: 10.1093/9780198948155.003.0009

at their disposal to influence the 'shape' of rape trials; in particular, the contents of cross-examination and the evidence and knowledge that informs jury deliberation and decision-making.

In Chapter 5, we considered how judges managed court arrangements, and the special rules prohibiting sexual reputation evidence and restricting sexual experience evidence. In this chapter, we share our transcript analysis findings and reflections on other ways in which judges in Victoria and NSW did (and did not) attempt to influence questioning that engaged rape myths or otherwise compromised process justice for the complainant, and potentially impeded outcome justice.

We consider the use of two important parts of Australia's Uniform Evidence Law[4] that has been adopted in both NSW and Victoria: *improper questions* under s 41; and *relevant evidence* under s 55. Although both provisions apply to criminal trials generally, they have the *potential* to change the topics covered in, and the dynamics of, cross-examination of complainants in rape trials. The main driver for the mid-2000s expansion and strengthening of s 41 was concerns about the cross-examination of complainants in sexual offence trials,[5] and the wide boundaries of 'relevance' under Australian evidence laws have long been barriers to keeping rape myths out of the courtroom.

We then turn to consider a mode of judicial influence which dates back to the beginning of the progressive reform era in Australia, and which has recently enjoyed a major surge in popularity: the statutory jury direction—designed to educate jurors about rape myths and misconceptions, and correct or *neutralize* evidence that engages rape myths. As we demonstrated in Chapter 7, such evidence is abundant in rape trials. In this context, the transformative potential of statutory jury directions warrants careful consideration.

Consideration of how these evidentiary components of the statutory architecture governing rape trials are operating is an important dimension of our larger assessment of the impact of 50 years of reform, and whether there is any more scope to legislate for further 'modernization' of the adversarial trial.

2. Disallowing Improper Questions

One of the features of the traditional adversarial trial is a reluctance on the part of trial judges to 'step in to protect witnesses'.[6] When Australia's Uniform Evidence Law came into operation in 1995,[7] trial judges were vested with a *discretion* to

[4] See generally, Stephen Odgers, *Uniform Evidence Law* (20th edn, Thomson Reuters Australia 2025).
[5] See below n 10.
[6] Jill Hunter, 'Battling a Good Story: Cross-Examining the Failure of the Law of Evidence' in Paul Roberts and Mike Redmayne (eds), *Innovations in Evidence and Proof: Integrating Theory, Research and Teaching*' (Hart Publishing 2007) 287.
[7] It now operates in most states and territories (including NSW and Victoria).

disallow a question put to a witness during cross-examination if the question was 'misleading' or 'unduly annoying, harassing, intimidating, offensive, oppressive or repetitive'.[8] In 2005, the NSW Parliament amended the rules on improper questions to create a positive obligation on judges to disallow a question on a broader range of grounds.[9] Although the amendment applied to all criminal trials, the change was directed heavily at improving cross-examination practices in sexual offence trials. It was described by the NSW Attorney General as part of the 'Government's long-term project to improve the circumstances of the victims of sexual assault at trial':[10]

> The amendment in relation to improper questions sets a new standard for the cross-examination of witnesses in criminal proceedings, including by referring, for the first time, to the manner or tone in which a question is asked. It is an important amendment because improper questions asked of them in cross-examination are one of the most distressing aspects of the court process for sexual assault complainants.[11]

At the time, the ALRC described the move from a discretion to a *positive obligation* to disallow improper questions as a way to address traditional judicial reluctance to intervene in cross-examination, and recommended that the NSW model be adopted across Australia.[12]

In its current form, s 41(1) of the Evidence Act 1995 (NSW) provides:

> The court must disallow a question put to a witness in cross-examination, or inform the witness that it need not be answered, if the court is of the opinion that the question (referred to as a ***disallowable question***)—
> (a) is misleading or confusing, or
> (b) is unduly annoying, harassing, intimidating, offensive, oppressive, humiliating or repetitive, or
> (c) is put to the witness in a manner or tone that is belittling, insulting or otherwise inappropriate, or
> (d) has no basis other than a stereotype (for example, a stereotype based on the witness's sex, race, culture, ethnicity, age or mental, intellectual or physical disability).

[8] Evidence Act 1995 (NSW), s 41 (since amended).
[9] Criminal Procedure Further Amendment (Evidence) Act 2005 (NSW).
[10] New South Wales, *Parliamentary Debates,* Legislative Assembly, 23 March 2005, 14899 (Bob Debus, Attorney-General).
[11] ibid 14900.
[12] ALRC, *Uniform Evidence Law* (ALRC Report 102, 2005) 153–54.

The obligation to disallow is not conditional on a prior objection to the question; that is, the judge can (and should) intervene even if not asked to do so by the prosecution.

Prior to 2018 the Victorian version of s 41 was somewhat weaker, in that the judge retained a discretion to allow the question if the judge was satisfied that 'in all the relevant circumstances of the case, it is necessary for the question to be put'.[13] However, the Justice Legislation Miscellaneous Amendment Act 2018 (Vic) (introduced in the middle of the period of our Victorian transcript study) removed this qualification on the obligation to disallow.[14]

Although there are variations, all Australian jurisdictions have a legislative regime for the disallowance of improper questions.[15]

Our findings

In the NSW and Victorian trials we analysed, it was relatively rare for the trial judge to disallow a question asked of a complainant during cross-examination. However, it did occur in some cases—including instances where the judge self-initiated the disallowance, and instances where it was prompted by an objection from the prosecution. Acknowledging that transcript analysis has limitations as a method for seeking to explain *why* a prosecutor or judge acted in a particular way, especially in relation to a 'failure' to object or intervene, we nonetheless consider it noteworthy that we observed considerable trial-to-trial variation in whether and how cross-examination was regulated via the improper question mechanism. We return later in this chapter to consider the implications of the different approaches taken by different judges.

It is important to recognize that the relatively low visibility of s 41 in the trials we analysed is, to a significant extent, attributable to *how* cross-examination was conducted by defence counsel. With some exceptions, questioning was generally conducted in a manner that conformed to contemporary expectations of courtesy, and polite demeanour, consistent with s 41 and the conduct rules and ethical obligations of legal practitioners which operate in Australian jurisdictions.[16]

Given the narrow terms in which the statutory concept of an 'improper question' has been defined and interpreted, it was unsurprising that few questions were disallowed in the trials we observed. Prosecution objections and trial judge interventions were most likely to focus on the *form* of the question, rather than on its substantive content. Cross-examination practices that attracted judicial

[13] Evidence Act 2008 (Vic), s 41(2) (since amended).
[14] See now Evidence Act 2008 (Vic), s 41.
[15] See Australian Law Reform Commission (ALRC), *Safe, Informed, Supported: Justice Responses to Sexual Violence* (ALRC Report 143, 2025) 358–59; and Evidence Act 2025 (WA), s 50.
[16] ALRC, *Safe, Informed, Supported* (n 15) 356.

intervention included: the use of compound questions; questions that were expressed in a confusing way; questions that were vague or lacked specificity or particularity; questions that mischaracterized the complainant's evidence-in-chief, or the contents of earlier statements (eg police statements); or questions that interrupted the complainant before they had finished answering the previous question.

While our focus here is on what we learned about the operation of the s 41 improper question regime, we note that this is not the only possible basis for intervention in cross-examination.[17] Prosecutors sometimes objected, and/or trial judges intervened, when defence counsel breached other trial conventions, including by asking questions that called for speculation, or which combined a question with a comment or submission.

The most likely s 41 ground for intervention was repetition, although even here, defence counsel were generally granted wide latitude. There were many instances where repetitive questioning occurred, but did not attract prosecution objection or judicial intervention. Where it did occur, it was when the question had been asked multiple times (and already answered by the complainant). For example:

D: *It's the case that you went down to get your bags. Is that correct?*
P: *I object to [the question] being asked three times now.*
D: *No, I apologise.*

* * *

D: *I'm going to suggest to you that you visited [the accused] voluntarily on [date redacted].*
TJ: *She's already answered that on three occasions.*
D: *Certainly. Withdrawn.*

Where an intervention occurred, it often resulted not in disallowance, but in an invitation for counsel to rephrase the question, or in the trial judge rendering the question in an appropriate form. For example:

D: *There was another person called [G] that you were not happy about rowing with?*
C: *I never knew [G].*
D: *In fact you told [the accused] that you didn't want to row with [G]?*
TJ: *Just a moment. I reject that question as to form. Firstly, the witness said that he didn't know [G], then you put another question based on him knowing [G], and included 'in fact'.*

17 Trial judges are generally responsible for controlling the questioning of witnesses: Evidence Act 1995 (NSW), s 26; Evidence Act 2008 (Vic), s 26.

D: *If I remove 'in fact'. Can I suggest to you that at some stage you did have a conversation with [the accused] and said something to the effect of, I don't want to row with [G]?*
C: *That is incorrect. I did not know [G].*

The following exchange offers another illustrative (and revealing) example:

D: *You wake up in the morning, the positive effects of alcohol are over, the positive effects of cocaine are now over, you realise what you did last night was not proper considering what's going to happen shortly regarding your marriage status and you blame this guy. You blame [the accused].*
P: *I object, your Honour. There's at least six questions so far been asked continuum without---*
D: *I'll break it down. You wake up the next morning, do you agree with this, feeling the negative side effects of alcohol firstly, don't you?*
C: *A little bit.*
D: *And the negative side effects of cocaine. Correct?*
C: *Yes.*
D: *You remember what you did the night before or, to be fair, the very early hours of that same day, don't you?*
C: *Yes.*
D: *And you're regretting what you've done, haven't you?*
C: *No.*
TJ: *Mr [defence counsel]--*
D: *I note the time also, your Honour.*
TJ: *No. I think the question is just this, isn't it, Ms [complainant], did you make a false complaint against the accused because you regretted having consensual intercourse with him the night before?*
C: *No, I did not.*
TJ: *I think that's the question you were going to ask, Mr [defence counsel].*
D: *Your Honour, I'm so grateful for your preciseness.*
TJ: *Thank you. Would you like to ask another question? You still have time.*

In this case, the judge's intervention—prompted by a Crown objection to a multiple compound question—took the form of reformulating the questions asked of the complainant in cross-examination to go expressly to the heart of what was being suggested by defence counsel. The merit of this judicial intervention was that it cut through layers of innuendo, put the proposition squarely and unambiguously, and gave the complainant the opportunity to give a categorical denial. But it also offers a stark reminder that s 41 is primarily about *form* rather than *substance*. Defence counsel was perfectly free to engage rape myths and stereotypes and an

associated trope of 'drunken consent subsequently regretted'—so long as questions were asked in a 'proper' manner.

Although, as we explain below, we are cautious about embracing the 'under-utilization' account of s 41's operation, our transcript analysis aligns with previous Australian studies that point to the limited use of s 41 to manage questions asked in cross-examination,[18] as well as studies that show that judicial interventions in cross-examination are usually about form and rarely about content.[19]

Certainly, we observed instances of cross-examination questioning that could have attracted s 41 disallowance but did not, and trials where the judge was more vigilant and inclined to intervene than others. One experienced Victorian trial judge recently described herself as 'known for jumping on improper questions from a great height'.[20] Our analysis suggests that, while this might be an apt description of the approach of some judges, there are judges at the other end of the spectrum, and many spread out between these two points. This variability has major implications for the confidence of complainants in a context where they should be guaranteed the trauma-informed standards for which the law provides—a point we take up further below.

The ALRC recently reaffirmed the view it expressed two decades ago: s 41 is under-utilized. The Commission pointed to the 'ineffectual operation of the existing provisions, noting that some defence counsel continue to ask improper questions, prosecutors do not always object (out of concern this may prejudice the jury against the complainant), and judges do not always intervene to disallow improper questions'.[21] It called for a 'culture shift, which could be encouraged through judicial education about the duty to intervene to disallow improper questions'.[22] The ALRC called for 'more consistent intervention by judicial officers, which in turn should deter practitioners from asking improper questions'.[23]

More consistent and robust use of s 41 is clearly desirable from the point of view of minimizing the retraumatization of complainants, and our transcript analyses support the view that there is room for improvement in this regard. In addition, we endorse the Commission's call for further research to determine whether s 41 is 'reducing improper questioning and increasing appropriate judicial intervention'.[24]

[18] See, eg, Sarah L Deck and others, 'Are all Complainants of Sexual Assault Vulnerable? View of Australian Criminal Justice Professionals on the Evidence-Sharing Process' (2022) 26 The International Journal of Evidence and Proof 20, 29.

[19] See, eg, Natalie Martschuk and others, 'Judicial and Lawyer Interventions in Trials of Child Sexual Assault' (2021) 31 Journal of Judicial Administration 3; and Elisabeth McDonald, *Rape Myths as Barriers to Fair Trial Process* (Canterbury UP 2020) 368.

[20] Meryl Sexton, 'Overview of Process in Relation to Sexual Assault Complaints: Before and After Trial—Locating the Trial Process as Part of the Broader Ecosystem' (Enhancing Safe Practice: A National Justice Forum on Sexual Assault, New South Wales, 3 August 2024).

[21] ALRC, *Safe, Informed, Supported* (n 15) 361.

[22] ibid 364.

[23] ibid 364.

[24] ibid 355.

However, we are not necessarily convinced by the under-utilization account of why s 41 has not significantly altered the nature of complainant cross-examination in rape trials. It appears to be a version of the 'poor translation to practice' explanation of failed law reform that we examined in Chapter 2.

We have found no evidence that s 41 was ever intended to do more than control *how* questions are asked, as opposed to *what* questions are asked (ie their content, subject, or topic). In Chapter 7, we explained the frequency with which complainants are asked rape myth-based questions, noting that this has the capacity to produce both process injustice (including retraumatization of the complainant) and outcome injustice. A question that is unfair or upsetting to the complainant because it relies on a discredited rape myth—and expressly or impliedly criticizes them for not having acted as a 'genuine' rape victim would have acted—will typically not be regarded as falling within the definition of an 'improper question', as currently understood. As much has been acknowledged by strong advocates of robust trial judge engagement of s 41:

> Where the question is relevant and 'proper', but to a non-lawyer, and in particular to a complainant, may seem totally irrelevant and designed only to upset them, I gently let the witness know that the question does need to be asked *even if it seems irrelevant to them*, and that they do need to answer.[25]

Judge Sexton's reference to *relevance* is telling. In the next part of this chapter, we draw on our analysis of transcripts to show how the capacious concept of relevance in Australian evidence law and practice provides the wide gate through which rape myth-engaging questions (and the evidence they produce) are allowed to enter contemporary rape trials. Even if s 41 was maximally and consistently utilized in all trials, such questions would continue to be allowed as long as they were asked 'properly'.

Unless s 41 is broadened by the legislature or via expansive judicial interpretation—developments about which we speculate in Chapter 10—it is unlikely that the improper question regimes that operate across Australia will play a significant part in reducing the prevalence of rape myths in trials. Put simply, they were not designed to keep rape myths out of trials. Indeed, as we noted in Chapter 7, and explain more fully below, one of the centrepieces of evidence-related rape law reform in Australia in recent years—the statutory jury direction—is predicated on the *presence* of evidence that engages a broad range of rape myths in trials. It is designed to correct or neutralize such evidence rather than exclude it.

[25] Sexton (n 20) 8 (emphasis added). See also ALRC, *Safe, Informed, Supported* (n 15) 358.

3. 'Relevant' Evidence and the Cross-Examination Exception to the Credibility Rule

If the problem with the statutory rules governing 'improper questions' is that their full potential to improve the way in which rape trial complainants are cross-examined has not been realized, the starting point for our analysis of how *relevance* is assessed in rape trials is different. Over the last 50 years, apart from 'rape shield' laws that govern sexual 'reputation' and experience evidence,[26] no attempt has been made to modify, for the purpose of rape trials, the evidentiary rules governing what counts as relevant (and therefore admissible) evidence. Therefore, our focus here is not on how progressive reforms are operating in practice, but on what occurs under existing general rules on relevance and credibility in criminal trials.

As noted earlier, both NSW and Victoria have substantially adopted the Uniform Evidence Law. The rules on relevance (ss 55–56) and credibility (ss 102–103) contained therein were in operation in the trials we analysed.[27] Under s 55(1), '[t]he evidence that is relevant in a proceeding is evidence that, if it were accepted, could rationally affect (directly or indirectly) the assessment of the probability of the existence of a fact in issue in the proceeding'. In *R v Le*, the NSW Court of Criminal Appeal (NSWCCA) observed: 'This is very broad language, and it suggests . . . a wide rather than a narrow focus to the inquiry whether a proffered piece of evidence has the rational potential which s 55 requires.'[28]

Also relevant to the scope of evidence permitted in trials is the cross-examination exception to the credibility rule. As a general rule, 'credibility evidence about a witness is not admissible' (s 102). However, there is a statutory exception: 'the credibility rule does not apply to evidence adduced in cross-examination of a witness if the evidence could substantially affect the assessment of the credibility of the witness' (s 103(1)). This exception offers wide scope for defence counsel to ask broad-ranging questions of a witness during cross-examination.[29]

These are rules of general application. No adjustment or allowance has been made for rape trials, and progressive rape law reform attention has never been directed at the evidence rules on relevance and credibility. They both ostensibly involve a strong prohibition model of legislative influence (see Chapter 3) and, in theory, could operate to insulate complainants in rape trials from a wide range of questions and topics. However, a great deal depends on the calculations that are

[26] See Chapter 5 at p. 108.

[27] Essentially the same approach is taken in all Australian states and territories: see Fiona Hum, Gregor Urbas, and Ottavio Quirico, *Australian Uniform Evidence Law* (2nd edn, Cambridge UP 2022) ch 3.

[28] *R v Le* [2000] NSWCCA 49 [19]. See also *DPP v Paulino* [2017] VSCA 38 [19]; and Odgers (n 4) 348–50.

[29] Andrew Ligertwood and Gary Edmond, *Australian Evidence: A Principles Approach to the Common Law and Uniform Acts* (6th edn, LexisNexis Butterworths 2017) [7.138]; Odgers (n 4) 951–55.

made about what evidence could 'rationally affect . . . assessment of . . . the existence of a fact in issue', and what evidence could 'substantially affect' assessment of the complainant's credibility.

Our findings

The broad and inclusive parameters set by these evidence rules were on full display in the Victorian and NSW trials we examined. With the exception of determinations on the admissibility of sexual experience evidence (discussed in Chapter 5), the relevance of evidence on a broad range of topics tended to be treated as a given; sometimes a matter for objection, but rarely subjected to exclusion by the trial judge. The following exchanges are illustrative. The first related to a Facebook photo of the accused:

D: *And then again . . . down below there is another little picture - do you remember what that was?*
C: *That's his display picture on Facebook of him and his son.*
D: *It looks like him without a shirt on bending down to his son?*
C: *Yes.*
D: *Did he look good without a shirt on?*
C: *Oh gosh.*
P: *Objection.*
TJ: *What is the objection?*
P: *The relevance.*
TJ: *It is relevant, I'll allow it.*

***

D: *You didn't go to the police?*
C: *I didn't.*
D: *You went to sleep that night?*
C: *No, I couldn't sleep.*
D: *Did you go to bed?*
C: *Yes.*
D: *That was with your partner?*
P: *Your Honour I object. How is that relevant?*
D: *I'm not asking her about any sexual - just where she was, who she was with.*
TJ: *I'll allow it.*

We suggest that the relevance of questions of this sort is doubtful. They are often underpinned by (discredited) rape myths. Therefore, we challenge the proposition that the evidence they seek to adduce can be regarded as evidence that could *rationally* affect assessment of the existence of a fact in issue.

Perhaps reflecting the difference between lay and 'insider' conceptions of relevance in a rape trial context, in some cases it was the *complainant*, rather than the prosecutor or the trial judge, who raised a query about the relevance of a line of questioning. In the following example, defence counsel's questions addressed the complainant's clothing:

D: *... So you have a loose singlet top?*
C: *Yes.*
D: *And loose shorts when you arrived?*
C: *Yes.*
P: *Your Honour, I don't think she said a loose singlet top.*
TJ: *Yes.*
D: *It was a question and she agreed.*
TJ: *Was it a loose singlet top?*
C: *It was fitted but it wasn't particularly -* ***I don't see the relevance of the question, I'm sorry.***
TJ: *Ms [complainant], if the question is asked I suppose unless there is an objection to it on the grounds of relevance can you remember, was it loose or tight?*
C: *I don't remember it being particularly loose or tight.*
TJ: *Okay.*[30]

In another case, the complainant was questioned about the nature of her relationship with a friend ('F'), then located in another country, to whom she claimed to have complained via Snapchat shortly after the alleged sexual offence:

Q: *Did [F] end up coming to Australia ... ?*
A. *Yes.*
Q: *And did you meet up with him?*
A: ***Is that relevant?***
Q: *No, well did you meet up with him.*
A: ***But is that a relevant question?***
Q: *Yes.*
A: ***Then judge, sorry, is that a relevant question?***[31]

This 'intervention' from the complainant prompted a *voir dire* on the nature of the questions that defence counsel planned to ask about F to ensure relevance and compliance with the statutory restrictions on sexual experience evidence. This

[30] Emphasis added.
[31] Emphasis added.

discussion established that defence counsel would not ask the complainant about the nature of her relationship with F, and then cross-examination subsequently recommenced.

Overall, we saw few instances of judicial disallowance of a question on relevance grounds. Where judges did take this course of action it was typically in relation to questioning on topics that were *extremely* remote from the events that were the basis for the rape charge. For example:

D: *You weren't shopping around for doctors were you?*
C: *No I go to that doctor's all the time seriously.*
D: *Did you ask the doctor to give you a letter to support a compensation claim or anything like that?*
C: *No.*
D: *Have you made a claim for compensation in relation to this--*
TJ: *I disallow that question Mr [defence counsel]. It's not relevant to any fact in issue in the proceedings.*
D: *May it please the Court.*

In some cases, it was only *repeated* questioning on a topic of dubious or marginal relevance that prompted gentle judicial intervention.

We noted in Chapter 7 that complainants are regularly questioned on details that are peripheral at best to the alleged sexual offence. A recurring dimension of this was cross-examination on the theme of 'time', including questions about *when* particular prior events occurred, often with little obvious relevance to matters in issue. In one case, the complainant was subjected to significant questioning about the timing of going to a Cash Converters (pawn shop) with the accused on the day of the alleged rape. The complainant had travelled from inter-state, was unfamiliar with the suburb in which the Cash Converters was located, and gave evidence that she was not wearing a watch. In these circumstances, cross-examination on the timing of the trip to the Cash Converters and return to the house (where the alleged rape occurred) was not only of no obvious relevance to the alleged rape, but was also underpinned by an assumption that these were questions that *could* be answered precisely when, in fact, given the context, they could only be answered with guestimates. Nonetheless, the trial judge tolerated this line of questioning for some time before finally intervening. Defence counsel was eventually persuaded to move on to matters more directly relevant to the events of the alleged rape.

In another trial, the judge intervened after a prosecution objection to steer defence counsel towards putting the heart of the accused's case to the complainant (ie that she had consented to the sexual activity) only after having granted defence counsel wide latitude to ask questions about a pet dog that were of no obvious connection to the facts in issue:

TJ: Your cross-examination . . . is drifting into the territory that is pro - would entitle me to close it down.
D: Of course, your Honour.
TJ: The questions of what the puppy was doing is neither here nor there.
D: May it please, your Honour.
TJ: There's a great deal of detail has been gone over with this witness, it's getting close to the time when you should put your client's case to her whether--
D: I'm about to do that your Honour.
TJ: --and we can leave the puppy wherever it was.
D: May it please.

These are both examples of where the trial judge did not intervene firmly to disallow a line of (arguably irrelevant questioning) but instead gave counsel a 'wind up' signal, and encouragement to return to a relevant topic. Overall, our transcript analysis of trials in Victoria and NSW suggests that the calculations that are at the heart of evidence rules on relevance are routinely made in ways that leave very wide parameters for questioning on a broad range of topics. In the trials we analysed, prosecution objections to questions on subjects remote from the alleged acts of sexual violence were rare. Judicial interventions to disallow such questions were rarer still.

Such practices are not simply a problem of volume of evidence, or length of trial, or preponderance of 'distracting' information for juries to receive and absorb. Complainants bear the brunt of the latitude extended to the cross-examiner. There is a strong relationship between broad legal parameters for relevance and credibility, and the prevalence of rape myths and stereotypes in trials—with adverse implications for both process justice and outcome justice.

Alongside the rules on relevance, the breadth of the cross-examination exception to the credibility rule also facilitated intense and potentially distressing questioning. A number of complainants in the trials we analysed had to endure being questioned about sensitive aspects of personal history. We saw relatively few instances of prosecution objection to such questions, and ever fewer occasions where the line of questioning was ruled out of order. Being asked invasive and potentially humiliating questions about matters such as substance use and addiction, mental illness, criminal convictions, and having had their children placed in out-of-home care, is likely to be especially distressing for many complainants, and a contributor to retraumatization.

In the following example, the complainant was under scrutiny from the very beginning of cross-examination:

Q: Can you see me madam?
A: Yes I can.
Q: 2017 wasn't a good year for you was it?

A: *No, it wasn't.*
Q: *Your son . . . was taken off you by the Department of Family and Community Services on [day/month] 2017, is that correct?*
A: *That's--*
Q: *Because you were considered by the department of being incapable of looking after him, is that right?*

On this occasion, the prosecution did object, and defence counsel declined to press the specific question, but the possible effect was to immediately cast the complainant, in the eyes of some jurors, as of 'suspect' character. The very next question asked by defence counsel was as follows:

Q: *You see, in 2017 you had a serious drug addiction to cannabis, didn't you?*
A: *I wouldn't say a serious drug addiction.*

In another trial, the complainant was questioned about her mental health status:

D: *Had your borderline personality disorder or whatever else or however you think and behave caused you trouble with past relationships?*
P: *Objection, relevance your Honour.*
TJ: *I will allow it.*

Our analysis of these dimensions of Victorian and NSW rape trials suggests that evidence which is underpinned by rape myths (and other stereotypes, including those related to substance use and mental illness) is still regarded as comfortably satisfying the evidence law tests pertaining to credibility. That questioning on these topics is rarely a matter of debate and judicial adjudication speaks to the cultural embeddedness of problematic markers of 'real rape' and the 'genuine victim' (and their inverse), and the *unreformed* nature of the governing evidence laws. The terms of the contest and the evidentiary parameters are understood and enacted by the key legal actors in the trial—judge, prosecutor, defence counsel, and jury. Sections 55–56 and 102–103 of the Evidence Act do nothing to interrupt this dynamic; in fact, they facilitate it.

Trial to trial variation and the wrong sort of judicial intervention

A conventional wisdom about the judicial function in the adversarial system is that there can be no pre-determined 'correct' level of judicial intervention: much will depend on the conduct of others, including counsel and witnesses. Traditionally, judges have been regarded as having a degree of autonomy over their preferred 'judicial style'—including when and how to intervene—from a spectrum of legitimate options.[32] Later we offer a critical appraisal of the implications of this mentality, as applied to rape trials—in terms of both process justice and outcome justice. Here, we simply record that our analysis of more than 100 trials across two Australian states revealed considerable variability in terms of how judges managed the evidence phase of the trial. This was true of judicial interruptions to disallow improper questions (as well as questions that called for speculation on the part of the witness and questions that contained a submission from counsel) and, to a lesser extent, trial judge interventions on the relevance of evidence, and the admissibility of evidence going to the credibility of the witness being cross-examined. This judge-to-judge (or trial-to-trial) variation echoes the findings of comparable research on rape trials undertaken in other common law jurisdictions.[33]

While this variability is likely to be a feature of criminal trials generally, rather than being unique to rape trials, we would argue that the implications are acute in rape trials, where the impact of the trial process on the complainant is an important consideration—and a major driver of 50 years of rape law reform. Claims to significant system-wide transformation and modernization—even if in relatively narrow process justice terms alone—can't really be sustained if the experience of the complainant in any given trial is materially affected by the personal style or preferences of the trial judge when it comes to interventions. This observation extends to prosecutors, who play a key role in deciding when to object to lines of defence questioning during cross-examination. Judges and prosecutors are pivotal players in whether the full potential of progressive statutory reforms is realized in practice.

Finally, while we have focused here on the implications of trial judge passivity during cross-examination—and have effectively argued for *more* intervention—we also observed forms of active judicial intervention that have the potential to make things worse. Specifically, they can *amplify* and implicitly endorse the rape myths that underpin lines of cross-examination questioning. In one case in which the complainant was cross-examined as to why she had not resisted, defence counsel went on to ask questions designed to introduce evidence of the complainant's physical strength. At the time of the alleged offence, she was doing strength training at the gym:

> Q: *You weighed at that stage about 70 kg?*
> A: *Yep.*
> Q: *And [the accused] was pretty skinny?*

[32] Murray Gleeson, 'The Role of a Judge in a Criminal Trial' (LAWASIA Conference, Hong Kong, 6 June 2007) 6.

[33] Eg Elaine Craig, *Putting Trials on Trial: Sexual Assault and the Failure of the Legal Profession* (McGill-Queen's UP 2018) 177–80; McDonald (n 19) 121, 342, 385; Olivia Smith, *Rape Trials in England and Wales: Observing Justice and Rethinking Rape Myths* (Palgrave Macmillan 2018) 60–62.

A: *Yep.*
Q: *And he weighed about 65 kilos, would you agree with that?*
A: *Yep.*
Q: *And so again, I put it to you, if you had used all your strength to push him off on the night of [date], you could've done so?*
A: *If I wasn't in a state of shock, then yes.*
Q: *So you say the only thing from preventing you from pushing him off was your shock?*
A: *Yeah, I was in shock and trying to process what was going on, and I was scared.*

At the time, the line of questioning directed at the complainant's weight and strength attracted no objection from the prosecutor, but the defence returned to the topic later in cross-examination, aided by a photograph of the complainant at the gym (retrieved from her Instagram account) which depicted her lifting a large barbell:

D: *So I suggest to you that the young woman depicted in that photograph is not someone who would've chosen, as you say you did, not to use all your strength to resist [the accused] when he was allegedly raping you . . . ?*
P: *I object to that question, Your Honour.*
TJ: *Yes.*
P: *It's sort of speculative and it's really a comment.*
D: *I'll withdraw the question, Your Honour, nothing further.*

To this point, the exchange could have represented an instance of defence counsel asking an improper (or otherwise inappropriate) question, the prosecutor objecting, and the defence conceding that the question should not have been put. The inference that rape victim-survivors are expected to resist, if they are strong enough, would at least have been dampened. Unfortunately, the sequence did not entirely end there. The trial judge asked a question of the complainant which risked enlivening that very implication and expectation:

TJ: *Ms[complainant], do you know how much weight is on that bar?*
C: *Um, 90 kilos.*

In another case, a self-initiated judicial intervention seemed only to underscore (and potentially validate) a line of questioning during cross-examination that appeared designed to infer consent based on prior 'suggestive' behaviour. The complainant and the accused were work colleagues who had been out drinking and socializing. The accused lived some distance away, and as it was late, the complainant offered the accused a place to sleep on a sofa at her home. The sofa was located in the same lounge room where the complainant would be sleeping on a different sofa (she having chosen to sleep in the lounge room, so as not to disturb her housemate sleeping upstairs). The Crown case was that the accused left his sofa, made his way to where the complainant was sleeping and raped her:

> Q: *You chose to stay in the lounge room with [the accused]?*
> A: *Yes.*
> Q: *You undressed in the lounge room?*
> A: *Yes.*
> Q: *You were standing next to one of the couches when you undressed?*
> A: *Yes.*
> Q: *By undressing, I'm referring to taking your top off?*
> A: *Yes.*
> Q: *Taking your pants off?*
> A: *Yes.*
> Q: *And remaining in your underpants?*
> A: *Yes?*
> Q: *And a bra?*
> A: *Yes.*
> Q: *[The accused] was sitting on the couch you'd made up for him?*
> A: *Yes.*
> Q: *While you were undressing?*
> A: *Yes.*

Following some further questions from defence counsel about exactly where she and the accused were located in the lounge room during these events, the judge intervened:

> TJ: *Ms [complainant], do you remember which way you [were] facing as you got undressed?*
> C: *No.*
> TJ: *Yes.*

We can't know what motivated the trial judge to ask this additional question, but this example serves as a further reminder about the range of approaches adopted by different trial judges, and that not all interventions are desirable or appropriate. In this case, there is a risk that the jury was left with the impression that the complainant had actively undressed 'in front of' the accused, evoking one of the oldest rape myths of all: seduction.

4. Jury Directions

Hunter and colleagues have described judicial directions and warnings to juries as 'fundamentally directed at insulating a robust jury verdict from certain frailties of lay decision-making'.[34] As the Victorian Law Reform Commission (VLRC) has pointed out: 'Historically, jury warnings in sexual offence cases existed solely to protect accused persons against unfair convictions.'[35] However, in the context of rape trials, one of the 'frailties' about which concern has long been expressed is that jurors may be influenced in their deliberations by rape myths and stereotypes that form part of their personal worldviews, values, and attitudes. This has resulted in jury directions being adapted for different fairness purposes: fairness to the complainant and the broader community on whose behalf prosecutions are pursued.

In earlier chapters, we have shown that it would be a mistake to entirely blame juries for the entry of rape myths into the courtroom, given that rape myths are often engaged by the prosecution in framing the Crown case (Chapter 6), and regularly engaged by the defence, including during cross-examination of the complainant (Chapter 7). Nonetheless, jury directions warrant our attention. Not only do jury directions have a long history as part of the architecture of progressive rape law reform, they have also enjoyed a surge in popularity in Australia in recent years.[36] The ALRC recently concluded that 'jury directions can be an effective, simple, and cost-efficient way to correct myths and misconceptions and educate jurors about trauma responses to sexual violence'.[37]

At the time of our Victorian and NSW transcript studies, two rape myth-correcting jurisdictions were in operation—relating to 'delay' in complaint and differences in the complainant's account.[38] Section 294(2) of the Criminal Procedure Act 1986 (NSW) provides for a jury direction that 'delay in making a complaint in respect of a sexual offence is a common occurrence' and 'there may be good reasons why a person may not complain, or may delay in complaining, about a sexual offence'. The equivalent Victorian direction in s 52(4) of the Jury Directions Act 2015 (Vic) is drafted in wider and stronger terms:

[34] Hunter and others (n 2) 618.
[35] VLRC, *Sexual Offences* (Final Report, 2004) xxxvi.
[36] Jury directions for sexual offence trials have also been legislated in some other common law jurisdictions: eg, Evidence Act 2006 (NZ), ss 126A–127 (as amended by the Sexual Violence Legislation Act 2021 (NZ); Criminal Procedure (Scotland) Act 1995, ss 288DA–288DB, as amended by the Abusive Behaviour and Sexual Harm (Scotland) Act 2016. A number of jurisdictions offer guidance and (optional) specimen directions on a range of rape myth topics. For England and Wales, see Martin Picton and others (eds), *The Crown Court Compendium Part 1: Jury and Trial Management and Summing Up* (Judicial College, United Kingdom 2024) para 20-1. For Canada, see National Committee on Jury Instructions, *Model Jury Instructions*, Part D.7, Offence 271: Sexual Assault (National Judicial Institute 2019). See also Judicial Institute for Scotland, *e-Jury Manual* (2024) 12.1–12.15; Te Kura Kaiwhakawā: The Institute of Judicial Studies (NZ), *Responding to Misconceptions about Sexual Offending: Example Directions for Judges and Lawyers* (2023).
[37] ALRC, *Safe, Informed, Supported* (n 15) 253.
[38] See Chapter 3 at p. 68.

> In giving a direction under this section, the trial judge must inform the jury that experience shows that—
> (a) people may react differently to sexual offences and there is no typical, proper or normal response to a sexual offence; and
> (b) some people may complain immediately to the first person they see, while others may not complain for some time and others may never make a complaint; and
> (c) delay in making a complaint in respect of a sexual offence is a common occurrence; and
> (d) there may be good reasons why a person may not complain, or may delay in complaining, about a sexual offence.

In addition, s 52(2) mandates that a direction must be given 'as soon as is practicable' when the judge assesses that delay evidence has been adduced. This is significant in a context where, although there is still debate about the impact of directions on jury deliberations and trial outcomes,[39] the literature does suggest that, in order to *maximize* the potential benefits of corrective jury directions, they should be actively deployed, not only during the traditional end of trial summing up, but at the time the relevant evidence is given during the trial.[40]

The differences in account direction addresses the misconception that a 'truthful' victim-survivor will describe events in exactly the same way each time they provide an account:

> (2) . . . the Judge may direct the jury—
> (a) that experience shows—
> (i) people may not remember all the details of a sexual offence or may not describe a sexual offence in the same way each time, and
> (ii) trauma may affect people differently, including affecting how they recall events, and
> (iii) it is common for there to be differences in accounts of a sexual offence, and
> (iv) both truthful and untruthful accounts of a sexual offence may contain differences, and

[39] For a recent overview, see Fiona Leverick and others, 'Rape Myths and Jury Decision Making: An Evidence Review' (University of Glasgow 2025) 36–45; and references below at n 40.

[40] See Julia Quilter, Luke McNamara, and Melissa Porter, 'New Jury Directions for Sexual Offence Trials in NSW: The Importance of Timing' (2022) 46 Criminal Law Journal 138; Rachel Cush and Jane Goodman-Delahunty, 'The Influence of Limiting Instructions on Processing and Judgments of Emotionally Evocative Evidence' (2006) 13 Psychiatry, Psychology and Law 110; Emma Henderson and Kirsty Duncanson, 'A Little Judicial Direction: Can the Use of Jury Directions Challenge Traditional Consent Narratives in Rape Trials?' (2016) 39 University of New South Wales Law Journal 750, 778.

(b) that it is up to the jury to decide whether or not any differences in the complainant's account are important in assessing the complainant's truthfulness and reliability.[41]

In addition, legislation in both jurisdictions prohibits the traditional corroboration warning.[42]

Since our transcript studies were completed, the number of educative directions designed specifically for sexual offence trials has been increased in both Victoria and NSW, and in other Australian jurisdictions.[43] While we can't speak to the operation of these newer directions—that cover a larger number of rape myths about consent and victim-survivor behaviour—our findings offer important insights into statutory jury directions as a *mode of statutory influence*. Of course, we could not discern from trial transcripts what affect directions had on juries in those trials where they were given. However, we did glean insights about how statutory jury directions operate in trials, including what conditions and practices are necessary to maximize their potential benefits, and whether they have the capacity to contribute to the larger rape trial transformation project that is the subject of this book.

As we explained in Chapter 4, we encountered significant gaps in our transcript datasets when it came the trial judge's directions, especially in Victoria.[44] However, the Victorian transcripts to which we did have access offered good insights into the use of 'mid-trial' directions, as well as whether the prosecution requested that one or both of the directions be included in the end of evidence judge's charge to the jury. In NSW, we had a stronger foundation for assessing the use of jury directions throughout the trial: we had transcripts of the trial judge's summing up and directions in 69 of 75 trials.

Our findings

In Chapter 7, we noted the frequency with which the rape myth-based expectations of 'immediate' complaint and 'consistency' in accounts were engaged during cross-examination of the complainant. Although our assessment is that either a 'delay' or 'differences' account was required in each of these trials, this did not always occur. In NSW, where the near completeness of our transcripts dataset enabled us to undertake this calculation, the delay direction was given in only 38% of trials. The differences in account direction was given in 34% of the trials for which it was available (having come into operation in late 2018). Sometimes the failure to

[41] Criminal Procedure Act 1986 (NSW), s 293A; see also Jury Directions Act 2015 (Vic), s 54D;

[42] Evidence Act 2008 (Vic), s 64(4); Criminal Procedure Act 1986 (NSW) s 294AA. See Chapter 3 at p. 67.

[43] See Chapter 3 at pp. 69–71.

[44] See Chapter 4 at p. 88.

do so was an active decision; that is, after submissions from counsel, the trial judge decided that the direction was not warranted. On other occasions, it appeared that the option was not even canvassed, and this may have been attributable to the prosecution's failure to request the direction.

Overall, across both jurisdictions, we were struck by the variability of judicial practice when it came to the use of jury directions. At one end of the spectrum, we observed trials that we would characterize as 'best practice' approaches. These included:

- judges who were proactive about jury directions from the beginning of the trial;
- prosecutors who raised the need for a direction at the first opportunity;
- judges who were responsive to such submissions, or self-initiated and gave a 'mid-trial' direction at the time the direction was engaged during the complainant's evidence;
- defence counsel who acknowledged and conceded that a line of questioning they had pursued during cross-examination of the complainant required that the direction be given; and
- judges who incorporated the direction into their end of trial summing up (or 'charge') to the jury in a manner that integrated the direction with the evidence in the trial –which assists the jury to understand the part of the evidence to which the direction related.[45]

The following extract offers an excellent example of a timely mid-trial direction. In this trial, the judge interrupted cross-examination as soon as they realized defence counsel's line of questioning involved suggesting that the complainant's conduct departed from the 'real rape' expectation of immediate complaint, because the first person she (promptly) contacted shortly after the alleged rape was a work colleague with whom she had been out drinking, rather than her own mother or a staff member at the hotel:

D: *So the first person you contact, can I suggest, is your boss?*
C: *Yes.*
D: *You don't contact your mum the minute you walk out the door, do you?*
C: *No.*
D: *You don't contact anybody at the lobby area and ask for help?*
C: *No.*
TJ: *Are you raising that as a delay, Mr [defence counsel], are you?*

[45] See Jonathan Clough and others, 'The Judge as Cartographer and Guide: The Role of Fact-Based Directions in Improving Juror Comprehension (2018) 42 Criminal Law Journal 278; VLRC, *Improving the Justice System Response to Sexual Offences* (Report, 2021) 446.

D: I'm sorry?
TJ: You're raising that as a delay, are you?
D: No, Your Honour. I'm raising it...
TJ: Why are you raising it?
D: Your Honour, I'm raising it as—sorry. It's her delay in contacting her mother because I'm saying...
TJ: A delay in complaining?
D: Yes.
TJ: Really?...

Defence counsel attempted to argue that the line of questioning being pursued—highlighting the fact that the first person to whom the complainant complained (minutes after the alleged rape) was her work colleague, rather than her mother or staff at the hotel reception—did not involve a suggestion of delay in complaint. The judge disagreed:

TJ: Yes, all right. Well, I'll give a s 52 direction. I believe that, inescapably, the provision is now invoked, and the transcript will disclose my reasons for doing so in the circumstances...
I have no doubt that it has been triggered. I don't think it's a big issue, it's almost unavoidable in some respects, and none of it shuts Mr [defence counsel] out from pursuing the line of cross-examination that he wishes to, but I'm now at a point where, having seen the way the matter has unfolded, I have to give this direction as soon as is practicable, which is now. Bring in the jury, please.
D: Your Honour, can I just—I'm not at all quibbling with Your Honour's ruling, but just so there's no misunderstanding my position. We say there is very little or no delay in making a complaint.
TJ: I agree.
D: And we say, Your Honour, that to give this direction now is misleading and confusing to the forensic point that's being made.
TJ: Bring in the jury, please.

The judge went on to give a s 52 delay in complaint direction.

At the other end of the spectrum, we observed trials which, on our assessment, were not conducted in accordance with the expectations of the legislation, including:

- a judge who appeared unaware of the existence of the difference in account direction;
- prosecutors who failed to request a direction even though it had been engaged by questioning of the complainant during cross-examination;
- judges who declined to give a direction properly requested by the prosecution;

- defence counsel who mischaracterized the legal parameters of the direction to (successfully) oppose a prosecution request that it be given; and
- judges who included the statutory direction in a longish sequence of multiple directions, without any reference to the evidence to which it might relate.

In some instances, the delay direction was simply added to the end of an (old) common law direction with which it is fundamentally in tension (ie the complaint evidence direction). For example:

> *... if the complainant has not acted in a way you would have expected someone to act after being assaulted as she described, then that may indicate that the allegation is false but bear it in mind when considering this issue that there may be good reasons why the complainant did not raise the allegation immediately following the alleged assault and that a failure to do so does not mean that the allegation must be false.*

20 years ago, Boniface drew attention to the incongruity and the risk of 'unnecessary complexity which could give rise to jury confusion:

> Take, for example, the directions concerning a delay in complaint. On the one hand, juries are told that there may be good reason for the delay and delay does not necessarily mean that the allegation is false. On the other hand, juries are also told that they can take the delay into account when determining whether to believe the complainant. The two directions together can be nonsensical. If there is a good reason for a complainant to delay in complaining, such as trauma or threat, how does her or his delay relate to the complainant's credibility?[46]

It is sobering for us to be saying exactly the same thing 20 years later.

This paradox was not only evident in how the delay direction was used in the trials we analysed. We also observed it in relation to the difference in account direction. In NSW trials, we observed instances of paradoxical directions here too—'hybrid' directions that invited the jury to engage the (old) common sense that inconsistency might be indicative of fabrication with the 'reformed' wisdom that it might not be. For example:

> *You should certainly have regard to the possible variations and differences which counsel have pointed out to you. They may possibly cause you to have doubt about*

[46] Dorne Boniface, 'The Common Sense of Jurors v the Wisdom of the Law: Judicial Directions and Warnings in Sexual Assault Trials' (2005) 28 UNSW Law Journal 261, 268. We note that the suggested direction in the *Criminal Trial Courts Bench Book* (on which the direction we quoted above was based) has been amended and improved: see Judicial Commission of NSW, *Criminal Trial Courts Bench Book* (2023) [5-055].

their honesty or reliability as a witness. However, I should give you this warning. It is the experience of the courts that people may not necessarily remember all the details of sexual offences, the same way each time they recount the events. They may not describe a sexual episode the same way each time. If a sexual offence occurs, it may have a traumatic effect, which may affect people differently, including how they recall the events.

***

A difference, gap or inconsistency in a complainant's account may be relevant to the complainant's truthfulness or reliability. And, a witness may not remember all the details of a sexual offence or may not describe a sexual offence in the same way each time. Trauma may affect people differently including affecting how they recall events. Both truthful and untruthful accounts of a sexual offence may contain differences. It is incumbent that you decide whether or not any differences in the complainant's account are important in assessing the complainant's truthfulness and reliability.

Recognizing the limits of the jury direction model

How to account for the regularity with which we saw these incongruent directions being given in contemporary rape trials? Was it a case of law-maker error? Surely, if the aim of progressive jury directions is to reorient jury thinking away from rape myths, the legislature should have abolished the antiquated complaint direction that embraced the very rape myth which the delay direction seems designed to correct—that there is a 'correct' way for a person to respond to being the victim of sexual violence? This line of thinking took us back to the NSW parliamentary records from 1981—when Australia's first 'rape myth correcting' statutory direction was enacted. The exercise was revealing.

In explaining the new delay direction that would be introduced by the Crimes (Sexual Assault) Amendment Bill 1981, the Attorney General, Frank Walker, noted the unfairness caused to complainants by the traditional expectation of immediate complaint—and the associated common law rule of evidence (the 'recent complaint rule') that permitted evidence from a person to whom a prompt complaint had been made as an exception to the hearsay rule. The Attorney explained that the Government had considered outright prohibition of evidence that engaged the expectation of recent complaint:

> Great concern has been expressed over recent years that the recent complaint rule in sexual assault cases results in a wrong and artificial emphasis upon what the victim did as distinct from what the accused did. The Women's Advisory

> Council recommended that the recent complaint exception in sexual cases be simply abolished, and that correspondingly *the complainant witness be not open to cross-examination about delayed complaint, or failure to complain.*[47]

However, rather than act on this recommendation—which would have effected a dramatic change in the nature of evidence in rape trials, and a large step away from one of the most prominent rape myths—the Government decided to 'achieve a solution to the problem by different means'.[48] The alternative (a compromise) was to leave the recent complaint rule (and, with it, the opportunity to cross-examine complainants about 'delay'), and to create a requirement that:

> where a witness is questioned as to the absence of or delay in complaint, the judge shall give a warning to the jury to the effect that absence of complaint or delay in complaining does not necessarily indicate that the allegation that the offence was committed is false; and, second, inform the jury that there may be good reasons why a victim of a sexual assault may hesitate in making, or may refrain from making, a complaint about the assault.[49]

Why was a compromise said to be required? Because the Government was persuaded about the existence of:

> . . . a small minority of cases where failure to complain really may indicate fabrication and false witness. To prohibit completely cross-examination as to late complaint or failure to complain could properly be said by critics as likely to lead to injustice in some few but finite number of cases. To avoid this possibility, cross-examination as to failure to complain must be allowed. It is felt that this formula will protect both the complainant witness and the accused. *The prosecution may still give evidence of recent complaint, if one has been made. The accused may still cross-examine as to its delay or absence*, but, in the latter case, the jury will be told clearly not to dismiss a prosecution automatically because *of* late complaint. In my view, that is a very fair result.[50]

That the 1981 introduction of a delay jury direction in NSW did not displace the old common law presumption that a 'delayed' complaint may be indicative of lying and fabrication, and that juries should be directed accordingly, has been confirmed by the High Court of Australia.[51] As we noted in Chapter 6, this is part of the

[47] New South Wales, *Parliamentary Debates*, Legislative Assembly, 18 March 1981, 4772 (Frank Walker, Attorney-General) (emphasis added).
[48] ibid 4772.
[49] ibid 4771–72.
[50] ibid 4772–73 (emphasis added).
[51] See, eg, *M v R* [1994] HCA 63 [21]–[22] (Gaudron J).

explanation for why prosecutors continue to incorporate evidence from complaint witnesses as a prominent part of the Crown case.

What is the significance of this part of the history of the jury direction model as a mechanism of rape law reform?

This account helps to render explicable something we observed in our transcript studies in both NSW and Victoria—the availability of 'corrective' jury directions (on delay and differences in account) appeared to exert very little influence on the propensity of defence counsel to adduce evidence of 'delay' or 'inconsistency' (or the corresponding reliance by prosecutors on evidence of immediate complaint and consistent accounts). At first, this surprised us, because it seemed at odds with the normative values of progressive rape law reform, of which these directions are a part. But we should not have been surprised. Indeed, the practices we observed spoke to something which is often under-appreciated about statutory jury directions as an instrument of progressive rape law reform. Jury directions do not operate to exclude evidence that engages a rape myth with which a direction is concerned. On the contrary, the availability of the jury direction is predicated on the rape myth being legitimately introduced into the courtroom via admissible evidence. Otherwise, there would be nothing to correct or 'neutralize'.

We are also reminded that, contrary to the popular narrative that tends to blame juries for carrying rape myths into the courtroom, the jury directions model involves a recognition that it will be the conduct of lawyers—through the questions they ask and the evidence they seek to adduce—that incorporates rape myths into the evidence on which the jury must ultimately adjudicate.

Finally, the story we have told here highlights the relationship between the accused's right to a fair trial and the parameters of what is possible in terms of progressive rape law reform. An overarching constraint on reform measures is the powerful view that to *prohibit* evidence underpinned by rape myths (such as evidence of a 'delayed' complaint) would be to imperil the right of the accused to a fair trial. On this account, a fair trial is one in which the defence has the opportunity to engage rape myths if they so choose.

Our analysis casts in a new light the recent enthusiasm in Australia for a long list of rape myth correcting statutory jury directions.[52] This development may be less about pushing the boundaries of progressive rape law reform, and more about accepting the compromised conditions under which the rape law reform project has always been conducted. Statutory jury directions—however 'enlightened' they appear—are a mode of statutory influence that fits comfortably in this constrained environment.[53]

[52] See, eg, ALRC, *Safe, Informed, Supported* (n 15) 253.

[53] We note that the ALRC states that its recommendations (which include a 'Model Jury Directions Bill addressing myths and misconceptions in sexual violence trials') 'do not question or interfere with' any aspect of the accused's right to a fair trial (ibid 76). The ALRC also emphasized that it is important for 'the criminal justice system to support complainants as much as possible without limiting the accused person's fair trial rights' (ibid 76).

It is common-place to talk about rape myths being 'rejected' or discredited by progressive law reforms. This *may* be happening at the level of social, political, and educational discourse, but it overstates how the laws governing rape trials are being reformed. At a minimum it is important that the influence exerted by jury directions is not misunderstood. Even if maximally deployed, they will not transform rape trials into rape myth free zones. They are not designed to do so.

We note that almost 50 years after it was recommended in the 1977 report of the Royal Commission on Human Relationships,[54] and 40+ years after it was proposed by the NSW Women's Advisory Council,[55] the option of prohibiting complaint evidence was recently considered by the ALRC. In a 2024 issues paper released for consultation, the Commission asked:

> Should complaint evidence be admissible at all?
>
> Does it perpetuate myths about responsive behaviour to sexual violence trauma (by expecting complainants of sexual violence to complain at some stage and placing weight on what was said)?[56]

In our own submission in response, we answered the first question in the negative.[57] We pointed out that scientific knowledge of sexual violence trauma has discredited the idea that a 'genuine' victim complains immediately, and submitted that complaint evidence should be regarded as no longer having a place in contemporary sexual offences trials. We emphasized that the ban must apply to both sides: 'If rape myth inspired trial architecture is to be regarded as unacceptable for the defence case, it must also be for the prosecution'.[58]

In its final report, the ALRC declined to make any reform recommendations on this topic, stating that it 'was not able to address the complexity of this topic in the time it had'.[59] The Commission did, however, as noted above, enthusiastically embrace jury directions as a mechanism for countering myths and misconceptions in rape trials.[60]

5. Corroboration Warning—Abolished?

As we explained in Chapter 3, one of the first targets of rape law reform in the 1970s and 1980s was the common law rule that required the trial judge to warn the

[54] See Chapter 3 at p. 45.
[55] Above n 47.
[56] ALRC, *Justice Responses to Sexual Violence* (Issues Paper No 49, 2024) 18, Q29.
[57] Julia Quilter and Luke McNamara, Submission to the ALRC, *Justice Responses to Sexual Violence* (14 October 2024).
[58] ibid.
[59] ALRC, *Safe, Informed, Supported* (n 15) 595.
[60] ibid 253.

jury about the danger of convicting the accused if the complainant's evidence was 'uncorroborated'. If the continued prevalence of the immediate complaint expectation in rape trials is a story of under-ambitious statutory reform, the story of the contemporary vestiges of the corroboration expectation includes a greater dose of resistance by some lawyers and judges.

The first steps towards abolition of the mandatory corroboration warning occurred very early in the progressive reform era. The Crimes (Sexual Offences) Act 1980 (Vic) and the Crimes (Sexual Assault) Amendment Act 1981 (NSW) removed the *requirement*, but did not prevent the judge from giving a warning in a specific trial. What developed was a practice of giving a version of the corroboration warning: that in a case where the Crown case is based on 'only one witness asserting the commission of the crime' their evidence 'must be scrutinised with great care'.[61] Over time the legislation was strengthened into a near-complete ban.[62] And yet, in NSW at least, the 'single witness' direction persisted, prompting the NSWCCA in *Ewen* to point out that s 294AA prohibits a corroboration warning and this ban 'cannot be avoided by switching from one linguistic formula ("dangerous to convict") to another ("scrutinise the evidence with great care")'.[63]

Nonetheless, in a quarter of the 71 trials in our NSW study that were conducted after *Ewen*, a form of 'single witness' direction was requested by the defence and given by the trial judge. For example:

> *Where a prosecution case seeks to establish the guilt of an accused person with evidence that* ***depends largely or exclusively on the reliability of a single witness*** *it is important that you be told that you should exercise caution in evaluating that evidence. You* ***must exercise caution*** *before you find the accused guilty on that evidence because the prosecution case largely depends on you accepting the reliability of the evidence of the complainant.*[64]

Again, we observed considerable variability. In some trials, the judge strongly rebuffed the defence request for a 'single witness' direction. In one trial, the defence offered up a draft of what was referred to as a 'limited *Murray* direction'. The judge responded that the requested direction '*does not find favour with me*'. It was regarded as '*just a different form of words for what Parliament's prohibited*'. In another trial, the judge responded to the requested single witness direction as follows:

[61] *R v Murray* (1987) 11 NSWLR 12, 19.

[62] Criminal Procedure Act 1986 (NSW), s 294AA, as amended by the Crimes Amendment (Consent – Sexual Assault Offences) Act 2007 (NSW); Evidence Act 2008 (Vic), s 164(4), as amended by the Jury Directions Act 2015 (Vic).

[63] *Ewen* [2015] NSWCCA 117 [140]–[141] (Simpson J).

[64] Emphasis added.

> *Doesn't that, in effect, wipe out the relevance of Ewen, because a single key witness direction - you'd end up, if that's the case, in every case where the complainant's evidence has some contradictions and the like in it, whether it's prescribed sexual offences or not, the judge would have to give a Murray direction?*

These examples offer a further troubling illustration of something we observed across both the Victorian and NSW studies, and commented on earlier: trial-to-trial (or judge-to-judge) variability. We do not think these differences can be explained away on the basis that all cases are unique and turn on their facts and evidence. What *is* revealed is that legislative changes (including progressive rape law reforms) can be differentially operationalized. One victim-survivor in one trial may enjoy the full benefit of reformed rape laws (however limited these might be). Another victim-survivor, in the next trial, may not. That sort of material inconsistency does not align well with the narrative of (incremental) progressive improvement through statutory reform, and of the guarantees of better process justice and outcome justice embedded in that narrative.

Our findings that show lingering traces of the common law corroboration warning in NSW, despite strong legislative efforts to consign it to history, also prompt us to temper our thesis that *prohibition* is the mode of statutory influence most likely to yield real change. It is clear that this outcome is not guaranteed.

6. Conclusion

We are conscious that we have offered what might be regarded as a largely negative assessment of how trial judges did (and didn't) influence how the rape trials we analysed were conducted, particularly during cross-examination of the complainant. But it would be a mistake to regard judges as the primary target of our critique. We don't resile from what we have found about trial-to-trial (and judge-to-judge) variation. The level of variability we observed is an undesirable feature of criminal justice administration and an impediment to the reliable availability of trauma-informed practice, and to achieving the maximum possible benefits of the reforms that have been made to substantive, procedural, and evidentiary rape laws. The courts play a part, including via appellate decisions which continue to endorse the special status afforded to complaint evidence and distress evidence.[65] However, ultimately, the failures and limits to which we have drawn attention are not primarily the fault of judges.

It is *legislators* who have remade the architecture of rape laws in a way that leaves largely untouched the core of the adversarial trial: where rape myths are permitted

[65] *M v R* [1994] HCA 63; *R v Churchill* [2025] HCA 11. See Chapter 6 at pp. 134–136.

and complainants remain fair game for character-based interrogation. The regime that governs 'improper questions' is directed at managing *how* questions are asked, rather than restricting the content of questions. The scope offered by the capacious legal concept of relevance and the cross-examination exception to the credibility rule continue to facilitate this. Absent an appellate court reinterpretation or legislative rewrite, there is little a trial judge can do to reduce this scope, but it is worth noting that changes to the scope of what is 'proper' and 'relevant' (including to credibility) could materially affect the contents of complainant cross-examination—with benefits for victim-survivor experience (process justice) and, potentially, for trial results (outcome justice). We consider this possibility further in Chapter 10.

Our overall assessment of the value of statutory jury directions must be tempered by the fact that the Australian legislative landscape has changed since our transcript analysis studies were completed. There are now many more directions, covering more rape myth topics.[66] Generally, there is firmer statutory guidance that directions can (and should) be given during the evidence phase of the trial, as well as during the end of trial summing up. For example, in relation to five new consent directions added to the Criminal Procedure Act 1986 (NSW) in 2021,[67] s 292(4) provides that the judge may: '(a) give a consent direction at any time during a trial, and (b) give the same consent direction on more than 1 occasion during a trial.'

We certainly hope trial judges use jury directions more actively and consistently across the course of the trial, including during cross-examination of the complainant—and that prosecutors routinely invite judges to do so whenever rape myths are engaged. In addition to assisting jurors to process the evidence, the chance for complainants to hear the messages that statutory jury directions contain, while they are in the witness box, is likely to be appreciated by complainants, and may play a small part in them feeling less scrutinized and harshly judged (as they so often are during cross-examination).

It is important to recognize the inherent limitations of the jury direction as a vehicle for judicial influence over rape trials and an instrument of rape trial modernization. As we noted in Chapter 2, whether rape myths are of a nature that they can be 'corrected' is a topic of debate,[68] as is whether jury directions are effective,[69] and

[66] See Chapter 3 at p. 69.

[67] Crimes Legislation Amendment (Sexual Consent Reforms) Act 2021 (NSW).

[68] See also Julia Cooper, 'Judges as Myth-Busters: A Re-Examination of Jury Directions in Rape Trials' (2022) 31 Griffith Law Review 485.

[69] Louise Ellison and Vanessa E Munro, 'Better the Devil You Know? 'Real Rape' Stereotypes and the Relevance of the Previous Relationship in (Mock) Juror Deliberations' (2013) 17 The International Journal of Evidence & Proof 299; Greg Byrne and Chris Maxwell, 'Putting Jurors First: Legislative Simplification of Jury Directions' (2019) 43 Criminal Law Journal 180; Yazhi Pang, Kari Davies, and Yong Liu, 'Changes in Certitude, Adherence, and Attitude: Immediate Effects of Rape Myth Intervention on Jurors in a Mock Trial' (2022) 19 International Journal of Environmental Research and Public Health; Harrison D H Lee and others, 'The Effects of Victim Testimony Order and Judicial

whether they adequately respect the boundary between the role of the judge and the functions of the jury.[70] Our argument here is juxtaposed against the discursive tendency in law reform commentary to characterize jury directions as a powerful antidote to rape myths. The plain truth is that jury directions don't remotely prohibit rape myth-themed lines of questioning or evidence.

As explained in Chapter 5, the only rape myths that have attracted the prohibition model of statutory intervention are those that relate to the complainant's 'sexual reputation' and, in a more conditional way, those that relate to past sexual experience and activity. Australian law-makers have *considered* the option of prohibiting other rape myth-based evidence, such as evidence of immediate/delayed complaint but—with the exception of South Australia way back in 1976[71]—have declined to do so. Instead, legislators have preferred the much more modest tool that is the educative jury direction. Rather than pursue *exclusion*, the jury direction model of reform is predicated on the *inclusion* of rape myths in the evidence of rape trials (otherwise there would be nothing to 'neutralize').[72] Their aspirations are modest: they offer the jury an alternative way of thinking about the evidence in question without necessarily supplanting the 'traditional' interpretation preferred by the party that has led the rape myth-engaging evidence. This is not always the defence. As we explained in Chapter 6, the prosecution sometimes engages rape myths to advance the Crown case.

More positively, it is appropriate to acknowledge that the proliferation of jury directions in recent years in Australia does create new opportunities to temper the influence of rape myths in trials. Much will depend on whether and how prosecutors and trial judges take up the new obligations set by the legislature. Our findings on the patchy uptake of older directions in the trials we analysed, and some continued resistance to the prohibition on corroboration warnings, suggests that the transition may not be immediate or comprehensive. However, victims of sexual violence are entitled to expect that the jury directions made available by the legislature are used widely and frequently and become a routine part of how trials are conducted—so that there is at least the opportunity for the relentless influence of rape myths on trials to be diluted.

Education on Juror Decision-Making in Trials for Rape' (2024) 30 Psychology, Crime & Law 509; and other studies discussed in Leverick and others (n 39).

[70] John Willis and Marilyn McMahon, 'Educating Juries or Telling Them What to Think? Credibility, Delay in Complaint, Judicial Directions and the Role of Juries' (2017) 41 Criminal Law Journal 27.
[71] Evidence Act Amendment Act 1976 (SA).
[72] See Chapter 3 at p. 71.

10
Conclusion

1. Responsibility for the Status Quo

Just two years on from the commencement of the progressive rape law reform era in Australia in 1976, O'Connor wrote: 'A summary of the moves to reform the law of rape in Australia presents a picture of great activity with few constructive results.'[1] One of the things O'Connor lamented was a lack of national harmonization. This problem continued to plague law reform efforts for decades, but in recent years, states and territories have begun to move in the direction of a more or less common architecture of 'modernized' rape laws, and the Australian Law Reform Commission (ALRC) has recently called for further moves in the direction of a national uniform standard.[2]

But what of O'Connor's substantive claim: that a 'spate of legislation'[3] was not necessarily producing the intended outcomes? How does that claim resonate now, decades into the rape law reform project? The evidence presented in this book suggests that if it was an apt characterization of the state of the rape reform programme in the late 1970s, nearly 50 years later, it is even more so. In the five decades since, the volume of new legislation has grown massively; and yet, (mostly female) complainants continue to be subjected to intense suspicion, scrutiny, and judgement, and (mostly male) defendants continue to have their criminal responsibility assessed in trials where they have the benefit of the same gendered rape myths and stereotypes that have traditionally hampered justice for victim-survivors of sexual violence. The hold that rape myths continue to have on rape trials means that victim-survivors are too often denied the process justice and outcome justice to which they are entitled—and which the narrative of progressive reform promises.

It is certainly true that much *has* changed about how rape trials are conducted, and those improvements should be recognized and applauded. The special measures for complainants we discussed in Chapter 5 have made practical

[1] Deidre O'Connor, 'Rape Law Reform—The Australian Experience—Part 2' (1978) 2 Criminal Law Journal 115, 128.
[2] ALRC, *Safe, Informed, Supported: Justice Responses to Sexual Violence* (ALRC Report 143, 2025) 82–84. See also Guzyal Hill and Jonathan Crowe, 'Harmonising Sexual Consent Law in Australia: Goals, Risks and Challenges' (2023) 49 Monash University Law Review 1, 4–5.
[3] O'Connor (n 1) 128.

Reforming Rape Trials. Julia Quilter and Luke McNamara, Oxford University Press.
 DOI: 10.1093/9780198948155.003.0010

improvements to what is involved in giving evidence in a sexual offence trial, which is likely to materially improve the complainant's experience.

But things haven't changed as much as they should have. There is a gulf between the narrative of incremental progressive law reform that has brought us closer to a modern transformed rape trial—and the reality of what happens every day in courtrooms where rape charges are being prosecuted. The contemporary rape trial aims to make a fair assessment of the accused person's criminal responsibility *and* to avoid unnecessary distress and retraumatization for the prosecution's main witness: the complainant. The research findings presented in this book cast serious doubt on whether these goals are being achieved. The veneer of sensitivity to victim-survivor traumatization is genuine, but thin. The substance of *what* complainants are questioned about—as distinct from *how* they are asked—is largely unchanged. The intensity of scrutiny and judgement has barely dissipated, even if it is conducted in a more polite manner. Rape myths are everywhere, and while in the witness box, the complainant can expect, to a lesser or greater extent, to be measured against the antiquated expectations of how a 'genuine' victim of sexual violence would behave.

Why has there been so much statutory reform and yet so little *practical* change?

There is little point in simplistic or reductive 'blame' attribution, but we do see value in reflecting on what we have learned about the roles played by prosecutors, defence lawyers, and trial judges, as well as appellate courts, governments, and legislators. In this concluding chapter, we comment on each of these stakeholder groups in terms of their contribution to what has *not* changed about rape trials, including the continued circulation of rape myths in trials. We don't consider the contribution of juries because the data sources and research methods we employed in the project offer no basis for insights or even speculation into jury deliberation and decision-making. This remains a significant gap in the research literature—one that must be addressed in future research on the operation of the raft of statutory jury directions that is now a prominent part of the architecture of 'reformed' rape laws in Australia.

Before we turn to consider the responsibility of justice system stakeholders, we think it is appropriate to engage in some introspection about the role of researchers, scholars, and change advocates. We recognize that this large and diverse group has contributed to the aspiration-achievement gap, in at least two ways. First, some of us have perhaps too readily adopted and communicated the meta-narrative of progressive reform over time, without necessarily considering whether this characterization is fully warranted. To some extent, this has been a matter of conscious strategy—working to *compel* generations of law-makers to keep moving in the direction of their admired predecessors and in due recognition of the efforts of the feminist activists who catalyzed the enduring movement for victim-survivor justice. Second, there has sometimes been a tendency to advocate for the importance and necessity of a discrete law reform initiative (eg the adoption of an 'affirmative consent' model) without due acknowledgment of its significance (relative to the myriad flaws in the system), and the difference between grounding positive messages for wider community education, and achieving material changes to how rape charges are prosecuted and tried. And, of course, all the while that progressive law reform proponents have continued to make the case for statutory change (both piecemeal and large scale), a long line of feminist scholars has questioned the wisdom (or even possibility) of real change through law—and some have abandoned that prospect altogether.

* * *

Examination-in-chief is typically not the most difficult part of the experience of criminal justice system participation for victim-survivors. However, as we explained in chapter 6, prosecutors play a part in the continuation of old patterns in rape trials, with potential implications for the complainant's experience. This is true both in general terms—the design of the Crown case—and with specific reference to the questions complainants are asked during examination-in-chief. We observed that it was common for prosecutors to adduce evidence that highlighted how well the complainant's actions aligned within the archetype of the 'genuine' rape victim (resistance, distress, immediate complaint), or which provided a context-specific explanation for why *this* complainant did not act in accordance with one or more such expectations.

When we have shared these findings with prosecutors, we have been reminded that prosecutors have an overriding duty to ensure a fair trial, and a responsibility to adduce all relevant evidence.[4] We acknowledge that this places prosecutors in something of a bind. So long as evidence suggestive of, say, immediate/delayed complaint, or consistent/inconsistent accounts, is considered to be *relevant*, a prosecutor is likely to feel obliged to adduce that evidence. So long as the defence is allowed to take a 'long bow' approach to relying on the complainant's pre-event behaviour (including, eg, their observed intoxication) as indicative of 'flirtation' or 'disinhibition'—as a basis for inferring that they subsequently consented to sexual activity—the prosecution will be responsible for introducing the evidence (such as CCTV footage from a bar or pub) on which the defence often relies to make such claims. As much as we would encourage prosecutors to more actively frame the Crown case around what reformed legislation posits as the central issue—was there 'free and voluntary agreement' to the sexual activity—and to object a little more strenuously to improper questions, and questions designed to adduce evidence of dubious relevance, our empirical findings, and our analysis of the overall shape of rape laws, show that there are limits. Put simply, it is not within the power

[4] Office of the Director of Public Prosecutions New South Wales (ODPP), 'Prosecution Guidelines' (ODPP NSW 2021) [2.2]–[2.3]; Director of Public Prosecutions Victoria, 'Policy of the Director of Public Prosecutions for Victoria' (DPP Victoria 2023) [21].

of prosecutors alone to radically reimagine the rape trial. Indeed, there is much that confounds ambition of this sort.

* * *

When former High Court of Australia Justice, Virginia Bell, observed recently that, compared to the 1970s when she was a solicitor, reforms have made it 'less harrowing' to be a complainant in a rape trial, she was undoubtedly correct.[5] At the same time, the worst part of the experience remains cross-examination, and few of the improvements that have been made have done much to change the *substance* of that part of the trial. With the exception of questions about sexual reputation (which are prohibited) and sexual experience (which are restricted) defence counsel are as free as they ever were to cross-examine complainants in ways that attack their honesty and credibility, and engage a plethora of rape myths to this end. In Chapter 7, we demonstrated that this is not just a theoretical possibility, but something that occurs on a regular basis in contemporary rape trials.

Our findings about prosecution and defence practice in the trials we analysed challenges the common tendency that juries are to blame for bringing rape myths (and 'real rape' expectations) into the courtroom—through the 'back door' so to speak. Our findings show that whatever baggage jurors are bringing to the role, lawyers are regularly introducing rape myths—through the front door. Both sides regularly build their cases around the presence/absence of 'real rape' attributes, and in so doing, they further entrench the problematic myths and stereotypes that statutory reform has purportedly been designed to write out of rape trials.

Some defence lawyers (and prosecutors) are likely to be affronted by the suggestion that they are regularly engaging rape myths in contemporary rape trials. Our finding may be seen as carrying the implication that they are knowingly or maliciously perpetuating falsehoods, or deliberately acting in a way that is out of step with prevailing social values. Putting to one side the small number of egregious defence cross-examination questions that we observed, that is *not* what we are suggesting. Rape myths are often introduced into trials in more indirect ways. Many of the practices we observed are likely to have been learned as good advocacy methods in rape trials. For example, a prosecutor may well have learned that it (still) makes for a strong Crown case if there is solid evidence that the complainant reported the rape immediately after the event. If this evidence is available, it will be highlighted as often as possible. Conversely, if there is evidence that the complainant's report was 'delayed', defence counsel will very likely regard it as necessary, in their client's interest, to draw attention to the evidence on the topic.

Either way, the expectation of prompt complaint is very much engaged, and the associated rape myth that a 'true' rape victim will complain immediately is in

[5] Virginia Bell, 'Keynote Opening Speech' (Enhancing Safe Practice: A National Justice Forum on Sexual Assault, New South Wales, 2 August 2024).

active circulation during the trial. The trial practices of lawyers are certainly part of the problem (and we address later the influence of the legal profession collectively in law reform processes), but it is fair and appropriate to acknowledge the legal environment in which they operate. And this is where the limited ambition and courage of legislators must be brought into focus. They have generally taken a 'softly' approach to reducing the influence of rape myths in trials, and have done nothing to rein in a capacious concept of *relevant* evidence. This latter aspect of Australian evidence rules, which has barely been touched by rape law reforms, is a key contributor to a cross-examination experience that is often distressing, traumatizing, and in our view, unfair to the complainant.

***

Much of what we have said about the factors that diminish the responsibility of prosecution and defence lawyers for the continued circulation of rape myths in trials—and the adverse implications for the complainant's experience—applies also to trial judges. As we explained in Chapter 9, the main tools that judges have been offered by the legislature are the powers to disallow 'improper' questions and give corrective jury directions (along with the role of adjudicating applications to admit sexual history evidence, discussed in Chapter 5). These mechanisms of statutory influence are not designed to exclude the majority of rape myth-engaging questions, and so judges can't be blamed for the continuation of this deeply embedded feature of rape trials. However, where some criticism *is* due is in relation to the trial-to-trial inconsistency we observed, especially when assessed from the point of view of meeting the complainant's legitimate expectations, and consistency with the promise of progressive rape law reforms.

We recognize that the adversarial system, the commitment to judicial independence, and the drafting of relevant legislative provisions, allow for a range of possible models of intervention—from sparing to more frequent. However, we observed that protections that should be *guaranteed* for all complainants (including closed court arrangements and support persons) were not universally experienced in all of the trials we analysed. Granted that some reform measures require the exercise of judgement—and this is often a reflection of the legislature's preference for guidance and discretion, rather than mandate or prohibition—we were nonetheless surprised that corrective jury directions that were available at the time of our transcript studies (on 'delay' and differences in the complainant's account) were under-utilized. As discussed in Chapter 9, in a number of trials where, on our assessment, a direction was triggered by the evidence, it was not given (noting that in some instances, the prosecutor's failure to request the direction contributed to the trial judge's omission). This finding is concerning, given that, in recent years, the number of sexual offence trial-specific statutory jury directions, and the number of Australian jurisdictions to have adopted them, has grown significantly.

Although some judges took a more rigorous approach to patrolling the boundaries of 'relevance', we are less critical of the many who did not, given the terms of s 55 of the Evidence Act and the breadth embraced by appellate decisions. It was apparent that even if judicial practice in this respect was in conformity with legislation and judicial authority, the breadth of topics traversed in cross-examination would still be a source of consternation and distress for some complainants. Later in this chapter we discuss the implications for practical reform of the prevailing approach to what counts as relevant evidence in rape trials.

***

We have argued in this book that the continued circulation of rape myths in contemporary trials should come as no surprise. It is directly attributable to the statutory reforms that have (and have not) been made by legislators. But before we turn to elaborate on this position and its implications, it is appropriate to acknowledge that in common law countries like Australia, parliamentarians are not the only lawmakers. Appellate courts play an important role, not only in the narrow sense of being custodians of those fields governed by the common law, but as arbiters of the significant number of appeals that arise from sexual offence trials, and authoritative interpreters of legislation—which is important in highly codified areas of the law such as the criminal law of rape, as well as evidence rules of general application.

The work of appellate courts was not the primary focus of our research for this book, which was primarily oriented to what is happening in trials. However, a number of observations arise in the context of our reflections on where responsibility lies for the observed gap between reform promise and trial practice. The overarching reflection is that appellate courts are somewhat hard to place in relation to the trajectory of progressive rape law reform over time. They have both advanced positions that align strongly with that trajectory, and taken positions that have limited the scope of statutory reforms. We offer four more specific reflections about the role of appellate courts in relation to the rape trial reform agenda, focusing mainly on the NSW Court of Criminal Appeal (NSWCCA) and Victorian Court of Appeal (VCA), these being the highest appellate courts in the jurisdictions where most of our empirical work has been undertaken.

First, as we explained in Chapter 3, appellate decisions (of the 'unprogressive' kind) have sometimes served to illuminate areas in need of statutory reform,[6] or have narrowly interpreted reformed laws in a manner that catalyzed further statutory refinement.[7] At other times, courts have sometimes been 'out in front' of the legislation when it comes to dimensions of the progressive reform story. An example of progressive reform leadership occurred in the 1990s when the NSW Parliament was disinclined to depart from a purely subjective fault element, and the NSWCCA expanded the concept of recklessness to effectively include a reasonableness standard.[8] The Court also embraced the positive concept of consent

[6] See, eg, *Mobilio* [1991] 1 VR 339, discussed in Chapter 3.

[7] See, eg, *Lazarus* [2017] NSWCCA 279, discussed in Chapter 3.

[8] *Kitchener* (1993) 29 NSWLR 696; *Tolmie* (1995) 37 NSWLR 660.

as 'free and voluntary agreement' well before the NSW Parliament moved to do so.[9]

Second, although not all recent appellate decisions reflect an 'enlightened' take on the sort of rape myths and stereotypes that have traditionally impeded justice for victims of sexual violence,[10] we have observed an encouraging pattern of scepticism towards some rape myths. For example, in *Harper* the NSWCCA cautioned against 'imposing rigid stereotypical expectations upon complainants in sexual assault matters as to how they *should* behave'.[11] Justice N Adams observed:

> This court has repeatedly observed, in the context of a ground of appeal asserting that a guilty verdict(s) in a sexual assault trial is unreasonable, that it is not helpful to invite this court to make any assumptions as to how a victim of sexual assault might behave in given circumstances. . . .
>
> It seems necessary to observe yet again that the criminal law has moved on from a time when sexual assault trials were overlaid with antiquated stereotypes about how a victim is supposed to behave. The court is not assisted by reliance upon such arguments in a ground contending that a sexual assault conviction is unreasonable.[12]

In *Dwyer*, the VCA made a similar point in relation to defence attempts to use text messages sent by the complainant in the aftermath of the alleged rape to question the veracity of her account. Recognizing that 'there is no typical, proper or normal response' to a non-consensual sexual act, and that 'people who do not consent to a sexual act may not protest or physically resist',[13] the Court found the 'complainant's near contemporaneous statements [via text message] that she thought she had been taken advantage of but not raped to be of little moment in the assessment of her evidence'.[14]

There are also positive signs that appellate courts are beginning to push back against the 'common knowledge' claims that are often advanced in rape trials—such as about the relevance of intoxication to reliability and credibility, and how memory works—and challenge the making of assertions not supported by scientific evidence.[15] These decisions provide evidence that at least some appellate court

[9] *R v Clark* (unreported, NSWCCA, 17 April 1998).
[10] See, eg, *Bloomfield v R* [2025] VSCA 98, discussed in Chapter 5 at p. 115. See also *Hubbard v R* [2020] VSCA 303 and *Frew v R* [2022] NSWCCA 165.
[11] *Harper v R* [2022] NSWCCA 211 [118] (Button J).
[12] ibid [184], [192].
[13] Jury Directions Act 2015 (Vic), s 47E.
[14] *Dwyer v The King* [2023] VSCA 85 [66].
[15] *Keogh v The Queen* [2018] VSCA 145 [93]; *Roberts v The Queen* [2012] VSCA 313 [52]; *AWK* [2024] TASCCA 5 [276]–[280].

judges, some of the time, are embracing the messages and values that underpin the progressive rape law reform agenda.

Our third reflection is that it is less clear that appellate court pronouncements are having a flow-through effect on how future first instance trials are conducted. To the extent that theories of appellate review posit that decisions exert prospective influence on the conduct of future trials, our findings suggest that it may be necessary to re-evaluate the accuracy of this account. Strictly speaking, an appellate court is only adjudicating on the matter before it. Save for those relatively rare instances where an appellate decision produces an authoritative (and binding) interpretation of an aspect of rape law's statutory architecture—noting that this can sometimes yield *contractions* of progressive reforms[16]—sentiments or values expressed during the court's disposal of an appeal do not automatically exert a direct or binding influence on the conduct of future trials. In some appellate decisions, judges have used strong language in an attempt to persuade counsel and judges to comply with an aspect of reformed rape laws where there has been resistance to change. For example in 2015, the NSWCCA issued a strong ruling (*Ewen*) that the continued use of a version of the prohibited corroboration warning was at odds with the legislative prohibition on the traditional corroboration warning.[17] Despite this, as we explained in Chapter 9, we found that this admonishment did not prevent some judges in some subsequent trials from giving a 'single witness' direction of a sort that Simpson J emphasized was impermissible by virtue of s 294AA of the Criminal Procedure Act 1986 (NSW). Later in this chapter we consider another dimension of the appellate court/trial court disconnect—related to expert scientific knowledge, which appears to us to be more visible in appellate matters than it is in trials.

Our fourth and final reflection on the part played by appellate courts in explaining the status quo of contemporary rape trials related to the courts' role as custodians of the rules governing evidence admissibility. Appellate courts have some capacity to influence the parameters of evidence rules—even in an Australian context where most jurisdictions, including NSW and Victoria, have adopted a largely codified set of rules.[18] Appellate courts maintain a very broad general conception of relevance (discussed in Chapter 9) and their continuing endorsement of the special status afforded to complaint evidence and evidence of distress has material effects. As we noted in Chapter 6, even though we think that the prosecution's reliance on such evidence serves to entrench rape myths about how a 'true' victim behaves in the aftermath of a rape, it is important to acknowledge the part that

[16] See, eg, *Lazarus* (n 7).

[17] *Ewen* [2015] NSWCCA 117 [140]–[141] (Simpson J). See also *R v Burton* [2013] NSWCCA 335, discussed in Chapter 5 at p. 114.

[18] See generally Stephen Odgers, *Uniform Evidence Law* (20th edn, Thomson Reuters Australia 2025).

appellate courts (and legislation[19]) play in this practice by continuing to validate (and incentivize) the introduction of such evidence.[20]

* * *

In Chapter 2, we discussed the literature that has tended to characterize the persistence of trial-specific impediments to victim-survivor justice as a case of flawed implementation—where laudable and promising progressive statutory reforms have failed to translate into enlightened practice. Our analysis of the architecture of reformed rape laws in Australia, and its operation in trials in Victoria and NSW, ultimately supports a different conclusion, on which we reflect further later. However, while they do not account for the unreformed core of the rape trial, our findings do suggest that institutional inadequacies, and the actions (and failures) of human actors in some trials, contribute to the shortfall between aspiration and reality.

Examples include the failure of prosecutors to take greater advantage of the option of complainants giving evidence in narrative form (discussed in Chapter 6), and the failure of trial judges to give corrective jury directions in all trials where they were engaged by evidence in the trial (discussed in Chapter 9). However, we conclude that, even if every statutory reform introduced since the 1970s had been operating exactly and fully as intended in the trials we examined, complainants would still have been questioned on the same topics (including embarrassing and judgmental questions about their past substance use or mental illness), they would still have been accused of lying, and rape myths would have been the foundation for many aspects of both examination-in-chief and cross-examination.

The regularity with which we observed questions underpinned by (scientifically discredited) expectations of resistance and prompt complaint—and other unfair and unrealistic expectations, such as distress and consistency of accounts—is a sobering reminder about the allure of rape myths—at both ends of the bar table. But it also speaks to the modesty of statutory reforms, which have never attempted to exclude these myths from trials.

This means that attempts to understand the *failure* of the Australian rape trial transformation project to date must return to the actions (and inactions) of elected governments and legislatures. The Australian jurisdictions that have led the progressive reform movement, and those that have actively followed the trajectory more recently, have not yet made a concerted attempt to change the core of what makes trials retraumatizing and unfair for complainants. With the exception of stereotypes based on sexual 'reputation' or past sexual experience, questions that trade in (frequently gendered) rape myths are as welcome under modern rape

[19] See Evidence Act 1995 (NSW), s 66(2); Evidence Act 2008 (Vic), s 66(2).

[20] *Papakosmas v The Queen* (1999) 196 CLR 297; *IMM v R* (2016) 257 CLR 300; *R v Churchill* [2025] HCA 11.

laws as they ever were. As long as questions are asked in an acceptable *form*, the 'improper questions' regime that operates in Australian jurisdictions[21] appears seriously underpowered as a tool for achieving process and outcome justice for complainants. Jury directions have been warmly embraced by multiple Australian jurisdictions in recent years, but their corrective function is predicated on admission in trials of the very rape myth-based evidence that they address. Even if maximally deployed—not something that can be taken for granted—the most that we can expect is that evidence that relies on rape myths will be 'balanced' by a statutory direction in which the trial judge gently advises the jury that there is more than one way to characterize the significance of the complainant's 'delay', 'inconsistency', failure to resist, pre-existing relationship with the accused, consumption of alcohol, etc.

Rhetorically, there has been a quantum leap forward in the values and attitudes articulated in the many pages of statute books devoted to customized arrangements for sexual offence trials. However, as we explained in Chapter 3, only a minority of reformed provisions employ a strong mode of statutory influence that *mandates* a substantive change to how rape trials are conducted, such as a *prohibition* on sexual reputation evidence or an *entitlement* for the complainant to give evidence remotely via CCTV if they so choose. Of course, the courtroom is not the only 'stage' where rape laws operate, and participants in a trial are not the only audience. Statutory reforms, in theory at least, speak to a much wider audience and aspire to influence behaviours in a positive way so that instances of sexual violence are prevented. For example, in 2021, the following objective statement was added to the part of the Crimes Act 1900 (NSW) that deals with consent and knowledge:

> An objective of this Subdivision is to recognise the following—
> (a) every person has a right to choose whether or not to participate in a sexual activity,
> (b) consent to a sexual activity is not to be presumed,
> (c) consensual sexual activity involves ongoing and mutual communication, decision-making and free and voluntary agreement between the persons participating in the sexual activity.[22]

Such a provision qualifies as a powerful or promising education touchstone, and is arguably important to the communicative or expressive function of the criminal law. But it does not necessarily exert any beneficial impact on the conduct of a given trial. Whether it is actively engaged as an aid in interpreting (reformed)

[21] Evidence Act 1995 (NSW), s 41; Evidence Act 2008 (Vic), s 41. For other states and territories, see ALRC (n 2) 354–66.

[22] Crimes Act 1900 (NSW), s 61HF, as amended by the Crimes Legislation Amendment (Sexual Consent Reforms) Act 2021 (NSW). See also Crimes Act 1958 (Vic), s 37A.

substantive provisions on the meaning of non-consent and knowledge of non-consent remains to be seen.[23]

We recognize that the bills introduced and enacted by legislatures are influenced by a range of factors, including the parameter of recommendations from law reform bodies, and the lobbying of stakeholders, including those that push for further reform and those that resist. For example, when the bill that ultimately became the Crimes Legislation Amendment (Sexual Consent Reforms) Act 2021 (NSW) was introduced, the NSW Bar Association warned that amendments to embrace the concepts of communicative and affirmative consent 'could result in significant injustice'.[24] A year later, the Victorian Criminal Bar Association stated that the equivalent Victorian reforms[25] could lead to 'unintended and unfair consequences'.[26] In the event, these particular interventions did not dissuade the NSW and Victorian legislatures from enacting the bills in question. More generally, both directly and indirectly (through submissions to, and consultations with, law reform bodies and responsible ministers), some lawyers and legal professional bodies in Australia have been voices of constraint when it comes to further reform proposals oriented towards enhanced justice for victim-survivors. Understandably, their contributions have focused on the implications of proposed changes for the rights of the accused.

This brings us to the final point we want to make before turning to the question of whether there is a case for the continued pursuit of change through statutory reform: how is the relationship between the rights of the accused and the continued presence of rape myths (and complainant retraumatization) in rape trials to be understood? The ALRC recently concluded that '[t]he justice system is failing to meet the twin goals of access to justice and accountability: it is not supporting those who have experienced sexual violence to engage with the justice system, or holding those who use sexual violence to account'.[27] Our research aligns with this assessment, which we would apply directly to the part of the justice system response which is the rape trial. Our empirical findings and our wider analysis of the architecture of Australian rape laws as it has developed over the past 50 years,

[23] In the VCA decision of *Bloomfield* (n 10), the comparable 'guiding principles' in s 336 of the Criminal Procedure Act 2009 (Vic) were cited in both the majority and minority judgments, in reaching opposed interpretations of Victoria's rape shield laws: see [29], [138], and discussion in Chapter 5 at p. 116.

[24] New South Wales Bar Association, 'Consent Proposals Could Result in Significant Injustice' (Media Release, 25 May 2021). Not all members of the NSW Bar supported this position, see Michaela Whitbourn, 'Top Silks Break Ranks to Back NSW Plan to Overhaul Sexual Consent Laws' *The Sydney Morning Herald* (2 June 2021) <https://www.smh.com.au/national/nsw/top-silks-break-ranks-to-back-nsw-plan-to-overhaul-sexual-consent-laws-20210601-p57x4u.html> accessed 11 July 2025.

[25] Justice Legislation Amendment (Sexual Offences and Other Matters) Act 2022 (Vic).

[26] David Hallowes, 'Drunken Sex, Misread Signals Could End Up in Court, Defence Lawyers Warn' *The Age* (11 August 2022) <https://www.theage.com.au/national/victoria/drunken-sex-misread-signals-could-end-up-in-court-defence-lawyers-warn-20220808-p5b81h.html> accessed 11 July 2025.

[27] ALRC (n 2) 106.

lead us to consider an unresolved (because rarely spoken) barrier: is the prevailing concept of the rights of the accused so enmeshed with access to rape myths as a defence strategy, that statutory reforms which would assertively *oust* rape myths from the criminal trial are beyond contemplation?

Our own position is that this tangle can and should be undone. That is, a trial that adjudicates a person's criminal responsibility for rape can be fair in all the ways that matter, even if reliance on rape myths and stereotypes is prohibited. The Supreme Court of Canada has strongly endorsed this position. In *Kruk*, the Court observed:

> While the accused's constitutional rights must remain at the forefront of any criminal trial, this Court has also acknowledged that measures can be taken to avoid reliance on myths and stereotypes without compromising those rights. Myths and stereotypes in fact undermine a fair trial — meaning a trial that is fair not only to the accused, but to the complainant and the public.[28]

Australian law-makers (like their Canadian counterparts) have already taken the step of legislating to prevent, or heavily restrict, the entry of promiscuity-based rape myths into trials—via the rules that govern sexual 'reputation' evidence, and evidence of sexual experience and activity. What if evidence on other purportedly 'relevant' topics—such as evidence related to the presence (or absence) of resistance, immediate complaint, distress, or consistency in accounts—was presumptively inadmissible? How much closer might such an approach take us towards realizing the goal of a rape trial without rape myths?

Perhaps the more pertinent question is whether enthusiasm can be cultivated for a concerted attempt to prohibit (or seriously restrict) rape myth-inspired lines of questioning—as the next frontier in rape law reform. If the answer is *no*, it may be time to accept that the rape law reform programme of 50 years has reached its conclusion, with, reminiscent of Deirdre O'Connor's lament just a few years into the reform project, *only relatively modest gains to show for considerable efforts.*

If the answer is *yes*, a number of further reform options warrant consideration.

2. What Else Can Be Done?

Perhaps unsurprisingly, the ALRC has recently encouraged continuation of the statutory reform programme that is now 50 years old. The Commission has made 57 wide-ranging recommendations to this end.[29] Some of these include versions of initiatives that apply to the trial phase of the criminal justice process and which

[28] *R v Kruk* 2024 SCC 7 [43]. See also *R v JJ* 2022 SCC 28 [1]–[2].
[29] ALRC (n 2) 15–44.

have emerged (or are emerging) across the common law world, including the routine pre-recording of the complainant's evidence, and the wider availability of independent legal representation for complainants.[30] These are important new frontiers for the evolving gold standard of reformed rape trials that is discernible across a number of common law jurisdictions. We support their pursuit, as well as rigorous evaluations of their operation.[31] We noted, that even if implemented, they are unlikely to materially alter the trial conditions and practices revealed by our research, including the considerable space that exists for rape myths to circulate and find purchase.

In the final part of this chapter and book, we outline four change options that could have a material effect on the visibility and impact of rape myths in criminal trials—with tangible benefits for the complainant's experience and the accurate and ethical assessment of the accused's responsibility. That is, our suggestions aim to improve the delivery of both process justice and outcome justice for victim-survivors of sexual violence.

1. Existing special measures should be available and adhered to in each and every trial. This means that counsel and trial judges must be fully familiar with all of the requirements of running a rape trial, including closed court arrangements and prohibitions on public identification of complainants; that complainants always have access to appropriate remote location facilities which are set up for the complainant, including with relevant exhibits or documents and their preferred support person (if they so choose), and that courtroom technology works as required. Even without formally embracing a specialist sexual violence court model—something Australian jurisdictions have not yet embraced for adult complainants[32]—it should be possible to guarantee and assure complainants ahead of time that these arrangements will be in place. This would address one aspect of the trial-to-trial variability we observed in the rape trials we analysed. The good practices that we observed in many trials should be occurring in every trial. They must be *routine*, and never dependent on amenable counsel or a favourable ruling from the trial judge, or good fortune (eg in relation to the operation of courtroom technology). Each criminal trial is, of course, a unique event, and deserves to be treated as such. However, some procedural aspects of rape trials occur with such regularity and/or are of such significance for the complainant that they

[30] See ibid 123–31 and ch 9. See also Fair Agenda and Sexual Assault Services Victoria, 'Improving the Court Experience: A Model for Pre-Recording Testimony in Sexual Assault Cases' (Report, November 2024).

[31] See, eg, Vanessa E Munro and others, '"It's the Judicial Equivalent of Robbing Peter to Pay Paul"—The Implementation Gap in Section 28 Youth Justice and Criminal Evidence Act 1999' (2025) 29 The International Journal of Evidence & Proof 117; Mary Iliadis, Olivia Smith, and Jonathan Doak, 'Independent Separate Legal Representation for Rape Complainants in Adversarial Systems: Lessons from Northern Ireland' (2021) 48 Journal of Law and Society 250.

[32] See Amanda-Jane George and others, 'Specialist Approaches to Managing Sexual Assault Proceedings: An Integrative Review' (Australian Institute of Judicial Administration and Commonwealth Attorney-General's Department 2023).

warrant reliable arrangements to guarantee best practice for minimizing the risk of retraumatization.

2. Ground rules hearings (GRHs) have become well-established in Australia in the context of trials where the complainant is a child or has a cognitive impairment.[33] In Victoria, GRHs were introduced for all sexual offence trials from mid-2023, including those that involve adult complainants.[34] The ALRC has recently recommended that all Australian jurisdictions follow suite, by making GRHs an option in all sexual offence trials.[35] We consider this a valuable development, but are cautious in expectations, given that, to date, GRHs have mainly focused on matters such as the form and duration of questioning, rather than the content of proposed lines of questioning. How GRHs take shape over the next few years will be instructive. If a deep transformation of the rape trial is to be pursued, including the exclusion or major dilution of rape myths, we advocate for a robust GRH exercise, including scrutiny of proposed cross-examination questions for relevance and reliance on rape myths. GRHs may also be valuable in framing the Crown case—on matters such as whether routine forms of evidence like DNA and other medical evidence are strictly necessary, or whether they might be avoided through 'agreements as to facts'[36]). A robust GRH will also allow trial judges to be on advance notice about the need to give, *at the time* the relevant evidence is adduced, one or more of the many sexual offence trial-specific jury directions available. Jury directions may have their limitations, but their fullest possible potential should be realized in every trial where questions or submissions engage the rape myths that they are designed to correct.

3. The definition of *relevant* evidence requires attention. If the next (admittedly radical) phase of rape law reform involves setting our sights on excluding rape-myth evidence from the courtroom—rather than simply balancing or neutralizing them with a jury direction—the carte blanche that is currently offered to defence counsel by Australian evidence law on relevance must be addressed. Many questions that we observed during our analyses of Victorian and NSW trial transcripts *relied* on a rape myth for their asserted relevance. We recognize that it may be perceived as a bold move to characterize a topic as *irrelevant* where it is connected to an attitude known to be in circulation in the broader community in relation to sex and consent. The myth that a 'delayed' report is more likely to be a false complainant is a good example. However, the experience of many jurisdictions with rape shield laws to prohibit questions about sexual experience evidence shows that lines of relevance/irrelevance *can* be redrawn. A rape myth-evoking topic which

[33] See ALRC (n 2) 296–97.

[34] Criminal Procedure Act 2009 (Vic), s 389B(3)(b), as amended by the Justice Legislation Amendment (Sexual Offences and Other Matters) Act 2022 (Vic).

[35] ALRC (n 2) rec 32, 296–301.

[36] Evidence Act 1995 (Vic), s 191.

was once considered as highly relevant—a woman's sexual history—is now considered presumptively irrelevant and excluded. We suggest that more rape myth-evoking topics should be similarly re-categorized as irrelevant, and questions about them treated as inadmissible.

To put our position at its highest: if the case for the 'relevance' of evidence that the defence seeks to adduce during cross-examination is underpinned by a myth or misconception, we submit that the evidence is, by definition, irrelevant, and the proposed question(s) should be disallowed. If a rape myth is ipso facto a misconception, how could it be said to '*rationally* affect . . . the assessment of the probability of the existence of a fact in issue . . .'?[37]

We note that Canadian law and practice has moved in this direction, starting with the 1983 abrogation of the 'doctrine of recent complainant',[38] and subsequently through a body of appellate decisions that seek to create a 'prohibition against myths and stereotypes that undermine the credibility of sexual assault'.[39] In *Kruk*, the Supreme Court of Canada emphasized that 'relying on myths and stereotypes to discredit sexual assault complainants amounts to an error of law, as opposed to being an ordinary factual finding reviewable for palpable and overriding error'.[40] The Court observed:

> The legislative and jurisprudential treatment of these issues reflects a collective understanding that courts should strive to eradicate myths and stereotypes from their decisions because they threaten the rights of complainants and undermine the truth-seeking function of trials. . . .
>
> This Court has repeatedly held that 'myths and stereotypes have no place in a rational and just system of law, as they jeopardize the courts' truth-finding function'. A trial is a truth-seeking process, and reliance on myths and stereotypes distorts the truth.[41]

Australia's Uniform Evidence Act similarly requires that rationality be the touchstone for assessing the relevance of evidence. Myths and misconceptions do not meet this standard.

[37] Evidence Act 1995 (NSW), s 55; Evidence Act 2008 (Vic), s 55 (emphasis added).
[38] Criminal Code (RSC 1985, c C-46), ss 274–275.
[39] *Kruk* (n 28) [31].
[40] ibid [44]. See also *R v Ewanchuk* [1999] 1 SCR 330; *R v Mills* [1999] 3 SCR 668; *R v AG* [2000] 1 SCR 439; *JJ* (n 28); *R v Kinamore* 2025 SCC 19.
[41] *Kruk* (n 28) [42]–[43], quoting *AG* (n 40) [2]. Research suggests that the prohibition has not operated as evenly or consistently as this strong judicial language might suggest, see Elaine Craig, *Putting Trials on Trial: Sexual Assault and the Failure of the Legal Profession* (McGill-Queen's UP 2018); Lisa Dufraimont, 'Myth, Inference and Evidence in Sexual Assault Trials' (2019) 44 Queen's Law Journal 316; Lisa Dufraimont, 'Current Complications in the Law of Myths and Stereotypes' (2021) 99 Canadian Bar Review 536; Elaine Craig and Isis Hatte, 'Rape Myths Endure in Judicial Decisions' (*Policy Options*, 10 March 2023) <https://policyoptions.irpp.org/magazines/march-2023/judges-and-rape-myths/>.

If a reformed approach to relevance was considered untenable, an invigorated approach to 'improper' questions could be an alternative path to a similar end. It may be regarded as stretching the acceptable parameters of the improper questions regimes that operate in Australia, but arguably, the subset of disallowable questions described by the phrase 'has no basis other than a stereotype' offers Australian courts a legislative 'hook' for crafting a mechanism of prohibition—if this provision was interpreted as including stereotypes of the rape myth variety.[42]

If either of these approaches to rape myth removal was in play, GRHs could become a powerful mechanism for pre-trial vetting of proposed lines of questioning. We recognize that this challenges conventional approaches to defence disclosure obligations, but advance rulings on the (ir)relevance (or improper nature) of proposed questions would be beneficial for all parties (*and* the complainant).

The breadth of the cross-examination exception to the credibility rule also facilitates broad-ranging cross-examination of complainants about aspects of their present or past life, such as substance use, mental illness, or removal of children from their care. In addition to their dubious relationship to the issues in dispute in the trial, such questions are likely to be embarrassing, shaming, and distressing to have to answer. The spectre of character assassination of this sort sits very uncomfortably in contemporary courtrooms which purport to be striving for trauma-informed best practice.[43]

We are sanguine about the prospects of a judicially engineered change to the scope of the relevance, improper question, and credibility rules in Australian evidence laws. If enhanced relevance or improper question standards are to be introduced, they are more likely to be the result of legislative reform, although we are not optimistic about a political appetite for such a change developing any time soon, noting that this topic was not addressed by the ALRC in its recent report.[44] If relevance reform *was* raised for consideration, it would likely attract criticism from the defence bar on the basis of a threat posed to the accused's right to a fair trial—although, as noted earlier, it would not be the first progressive rape law reform proposal to be challenged on this basis. In addition, the evidence does suggest that where consequential reforms are introduced, over such objections, defence strategy in rape trials adapts to the new legal environment. The introduction of laws that restrict questions about sexual experience effected a radical shake-up of traditional defence practice. While they still have their critics, these days rape

[42] See Evidence Act 1995 (Vic), s 41(3)(d); Evidence Act 1995 (NSW), s 41(1)(d). Our doubts about the likelihood of such an interpretation being adopted is partly explained by the full terms of the relevant provision, which suggests a narrower conception of stereotype: 'has no basis other than a stereotype (for example, a stereotype based on the witness's sex, race, culture, ethnicity, age or mental, intellectual or physical disability).'

[43] See ALRC (n 2) 80–82; and Chapter 5 at p. 94.

[44] ALRC (n 2). See also Law Commission (UK), *Evidence in Sexual Offences Prosecutions: A Final Report* (Law Com No 420, 2025) rec 62, 400-05.

shield laws are a routine part of the trial landscape, and defence counsel are adept at working with these rules (including testing their limits from time to time).[45]

Despite all the circumstances that dampen our optimism, we nonetheless think the reform options we have canvassed here are worth recording, if only to challenge the assertion that statutory reform has 'maxed out' and nothing further is possible. Of the three pillars of rape law architecture outlined in Chapter 3—substantive, procedural, and evidentiary—it is *evidence* rules that have mostly evaded reform. In Chapter 1, we used numbers to convey the sheer volume of statutory reform: 99 statutes enacted to amend the three primary statutes affecting rape trials in NSW. Here, a further level of detail is illuminating: 39% of these Acts amended the *Crimes Act*; 55% amended the *Criminal Procedure Act*; and only 6% amended the *Evidence Act*. Granted, this is a superficial measure, but it does symbolize the blind spot in the Australian rape law reform project revealed by our research. The mission to modernize Australian rape law will remain unfinished until law-makers confront the fact that *evidence rules* are more heavily implicated in the denial of justice to victim-survivors than substantive definitions of consent or procedural arrangements for the conduct of trials.

4. Our research suggests that rape trials continue to rely heavily on lay 'common sense', 'common knowledge', and 'the experience of the law'. This is a problem for realizing progressive reform because lay understandings frequently encompass the rape myths that also permeate trials, with adverse results for complainants. As things stand, the common focus of the jury's decision-making in rape trials is not a technical legal assessment of the offence elements, but a socio-cultural judgement—with the complainant as the person who is being judged. The problem is compounded when juries are actively encouraged to call on what they 'already know' in making this assessment. This is powerfully illustrated by our analysis in Chapter 8 of how evidence of the complainant's intoxication features in rape trials.

We noted earlier that there are positive signs of appellate court judgments displaying greater cognizance of what is known in the scientific literature about matters such as trauma, memory, and alcohol and other drug (AOD) effects—but this stands in contrast to what we observed in first instance trials. We argue for a more comprehensive and consistent modernization of the *knowledges* that inform criminal court adjudication—at all levels.

Trials that remain largely closed off to expert scientific knowledge cannot deliver on the legitimate expectations of victim-survivors for process justice and outcome justice. Much is known about matters such as the range of responses to sexual violence, the effects of trauma, how memory works, the effects of AOD consumption on cognition and recall—to name just some of the topics that regularly arise for consideration in rape trials. The jury should have the benefit of this scientific knowledge as a matter of course in all rape trials. It is insufficient for such knowledge to make its way into the courtroom only through the attenuated mechanism

[45] See, eg, *Bloomfield* (n 10); *Jackmain (a pseudonym) v R* [2020] NSWCCA 150.

of words contained in a statute that might form part of a judge's explanation of the elements of the offence to the jury (eg that 'a person who does not offer physical or verbal resistance to a sexual activity is not, by reason only of that fact, to be taken to consent to the sexual activity'[46]), or a judge's direction to the jury (eg 'trauma may affect different people differently, including by affecting how they recall events').[47]

The need for expert guidance is even greater for topics where jurors are effectively told (by defence counsel and sometimes judges) what they are considered to already know—where the proffered common knowledge is scientifically inaccurate or partial in a way that serves the interests of the accused, but not the complainant or the broader community on whose behalf the prosecution is taken. Our findings (in Chapter 8) about the epistemically impoverished environment in which jurors are asked to assess the magnitude, and evaluate the significance, of the complainant's intoxication at the time of the alleged rape illustrate this point. Defence counsel should not be permitted complete freedom to assert as fact, claims such as:

- drinking large quantities of alcohol causes women to become sexually disinhibited (asserted to bolster the contention that the complainant consented); or
- AOD consumption results in impaired memory (asserted to found an attack on the reliability of the complainant's account of events); or
- an intoxicated person who could perform certain motor functions can be assumed to have the cognitive capacity to consent to sexual activity.

None of these assertions align with the current state of scientific knowledge about AOD effects.[48] We suggest that prosecutors and trial judges have a responsibility to intervene where the defence attempts to ask questions or make submissions that are underpinned by such assumptions. Our position finds support in a recent statement from the Tasmanian CCA about the danger of defence counsel submitting on topics for which expert knowledge is available—in this instance, memory:

> Counsel should expect the Court to be conscious that memory is a field of expertise and specialised knowledge, to be alert to the risk or reality of counsel propounding erroneous beliefs about memory, and to be aware that there was no expert opinion before the jury to support defence contentions made about memory. This observation, of course, applies with equal force to the State and contentions it may make if it is suggested that matters of specialist knowledge are matters upon which the jury or the Court on appeal may speculate.[49]

[46] Crimes Act 1900 (NSW), s 61HI(4). See also Criminal Procedure Act 1986 (NSW), s 292C.
[47] Jury Directions Act 2015 (Vic), s 54D(2)(c)(ii).
[48] See Chapter 8 at p. 194.
[49] *AWK* (n 15) [276]–[280] (Wood J), [318]–[319] (Martin AJ agreeing).

Victim-survivors of sexual violence are poorly served by the traditional (and ongoing) preference for 'common knowledge' over expert knowledge in rape trials. We think improved 'scientific literacy' is essential,[50] and this may well be facilitated by the measures recently recommended by the ALRC, including: the establishment of a national panel of expert witnesses (on a range of 'myths and misconception' topics raised by sexual offences) to which prosecution and defence lawyers would have access; and the preparation of AV recorded materials that could be admitted as evidence in trials as part of the Crown case.[51] It may also be facilitated by better usage of 'agreements as to facts'[52] as was done in relation to 'counterintuitive evidence' in *Lehrmann v Network Ten*[53] (albeit in the civil law context), and has also been referred to by the High Court of Australia as a possibility.[54] We note also that the NSW Director of Public Prosecutions recently announced the establishment of two working groups: one to consider 'the use of expert evidence at trial to address the impact of intoxication on memory and behaviour' and another 'to consider evidence-based research on the impact of trauma upon memory recall, consistency of accounts, and demeanour'.[55]

* * *

Our Chapter 1 starting point for this book's examination of the impact of law reform on rape trials in Australia was the ambition expressed by the Premier of NSW in 1981 about what would be achieved by the major reform bill that was enacted that year—some 45 years ago. While Premier Wran was describing a single bill, he could have been describing the totality of the progressive rape law reform project, over decades, and across the country. The stated ambition was to achieve four goals:

1. 'encourage rape victims to report offences to the authorities';
2. 'serve an educative function in further changing community attitudes to sexual assault';
3. 'protect the victims of rape from victimization under the legal process'; and
4. 'facilitate the administration of justice and the conviction of guilty offenders' while 'preserv[ing] the rights of the accused'[56]

Demonstrable advances have been made via statutory reform in relation to goals one and two. The evidence compiled in this book suggests that achievements

[50] See Chapter 8 at pp. 177–178.
[51] ALRC (n 2) rec 24, 257–64.
[52] Evidence Act 1995 (NSW), s 191; Evidence Act 2008 (Vic) s 191; ALRC (n 2) 251.
[53] *Lehrmann v Network Ten Pty Ltd (Trial Judgment)* [2024] FCA 369.
[54] *BQ v R* [2024] HCA 29 [58].
[55] ODPP, 'Sexual Assault Review Report' (ODPP NSW February 2025) 51.
[56] New South Wales, *Parliamentary Debates*, Legislative Assembly, 18 March 1981, 4758 (Neville Wran, Premier); see Chapter 1 at pp. 1–2.

against goals three and four have been much more modest. There is more to be done. And a necessary starting point is recognition that victim-survivors will continue to be let down until law-makers confront and correct the heart of what makes rape trials such hostile environments for complainants, and so poorly calibrated to the task of holding perpetrators accountable.

* * *

In closing, we return to that part of our research which has yielded such important insights about what is happening in contemporary rape trials: the transcripts. The words we found there express much more powerfully than we ever could what remains so unsatisfactory about how sexual violence is understood and how complainants are questioned and challenged in trials. Even in the highly constrained environment of the courtroom, some complainants in the trials we analysed managed to express their own take on the traumatization of being raped, and the retraumatization of trial cross-examination:

D: *... What I'm suggesting to you, just to be clear ... is this: that the reason you remained in bed, in the same bed as [the accused] for the remainder of the evening was because he hadn't raped you.... [W]hat do you say to that suggestion?*

C: *That, that context is completely wrong. Um, I'll set it for you. I was absolutely scared, panicked. Someone had just broken the trust in the worst way possible you can, and I needed to protect myself so nothing worse happened to me or more happened to me. So I stayed in my bed and curled up into a ball because what are you going to [do], fight, flight or freeze? You're going to run away, you're going to stay there and hope you don't provoke someone else who's already tried to put physical force into you, or are you going to force them away yourself? ... I mean maybe if he hadn't raped me I wouldn't have been this scared of him. So I would have been able to get my car keys, wherever they were, and get out of there but he's gone past that and he's raped me. So, of course, I'm thinking, 'Oh God, what's he gonna do next?'*

* * *

D: *You see, Ms [complainant] what I'm saying to you is that when you woke up you ... realised that you had sex. You hadn't remembered that before you reached down and felt your underwear?*

C: *I recall ... That's why I went and checked my underwear. That's what led me to check ... my underwear. And it wasn't sex 'cause he raped me. So can you ... rephrase that from me having sex with someone ... when I didn't give him consent. Can I have a break please?*

Victim-survivors of sexual violence who seek out redress in the criminal justice system do deserve a 'break'. They deserve a courtroom where rape myths are not welcome.

Index

For the benefit of digital users, indexed terms that span two pages (e.g., 52–53) may, on occasion, appear on only one of those pages.